Effects of German Industrialization on Turkish-German Military-Strategic Relations (1815-1929)

Atakan Büyükdağ

Effects of German Industrialization on Turkish-German Military-Strategic Relations (1815-1929)

PETER LANG

Lausanne - Berlin - Bruxelles - Chennai - New York - Oxford

Library of Congress Cataloging-in-Publication Data
A CIP catalog record for this book has been applied for at the Library of Congress.

Bibliographic Information published by the Deutsche Nationalbibliothek
The Deutsche Nationalbibliothek lists this publication in the Deutsche Nationalbibliografie; detailed bibliographic data is available online at http://dnb.d-nb.de.

ISBN 978-3-631-89132-2 (Print)
E-ISBN 978-3-631-90028-4 (E-PDF)
E-ISBN 978-3-631-90029-1 (EPUB)
DOI 10.3726/b21050

Published by:
Peter Lang GmbH, Berlin, Deutschland

info@peterlang.com - www.peterlang.com

Contents

List of Tables

Foreword

When the German Industrial Revolution is mentioned, some unanswered questions like "when?", "how?", "by whom?" comes to mind. There are some powerful reasons for this, such as the fact that German Industrialization did not take place in a single main location or with a single driving force. Moreover Germany had not completed its political or economic unity at the time of German Industrialization. For this reason, it is not possible to study German Industrialization with a single topic or in a spesific period of time. In the periods of German Industrialization, it is possible to talk about neither a geographical unity nor a political unity. These reasons make the German Industrialization unique and for the same reason the number of studies on German Industrialization is extremely limited.

The main objective of this study is to understand how Germany overcame the obtacles to industrialization, to understand how Germany succeeded in industrialization and how German Industrialization affected Turkish-German military-strategic relations. The other objective of this study is to emphesize the fact that general opinions or studies on German Industrialization are not satisfactory.

Although German Industrialization is generally tried to be explained by data, it is a subject open to interpretation indeed. For this reason, a deep literature study was conducted to create this work. German, English and Turkish sources are used for this study. State Archives Ottoman Archives (BOA), State Archives Republican Archives (BCA), Akten zur deutschen auswärtigen Politik (ADAP), The National Archives and Records Administration (NARA) were very hepful particularly for the second half of the study.

It is not possible to ignore the fact that science is a phenomenon that progresses by putting it on. I would like to express my sincere thanks to every researcher, historian, economic historian and writer who directly or indirectly supported the subjects in this study with their research. Of course, this study will not be enough to eliminate all the academic deficiencies in German Industrialization subject. All the topics and subtitles in this study are subjects that need to be studied on their own. Moreover, one of the main objectives of this study is to enlighten the path of researchers who want to do deeper researches on these titles or subtitles.

I would like to express my sincere thanks to the advisor of this doctoral thesis Prof. Dr. Ali Satan who did not spare his support to me. By biggest thanks is for my family, my wife and my daughter who never spare their unwavering support even though i stole from their time during this long journey.

Abstract

The industrialization of a nation that lived on vast lands and lacked political unity or even a common monetary system is undoubtedly a remarkable fact.

The first traces of industrialization in the German states, which were deprived of a strong central authority and common economy, are encountered starting from the begging of the 19th century. However, the industriaization had not erased the traces of the past, or changed the fact that Germany had needs. Germany was not welcomed in the world politics. The industrialized Germany started to seek for economic, political and strategic remedies to maintain its existence and to guarantee its future. In such a period of time, Germany started a strategic relationship with Ottoman Empire which was also in need of a European ally that would not gaze upon her lands. This relationship which started with Ottoman Empire and continued with the Republic of Turkey is related with German Industrialization in the background, indeed. Economic and political causes had military consequences.

One of the main objectives of this study is to reveal that the both existent studies and general opinions about German Industrialization are not sufficient and to reveal the details that make German Industrialization unique. The other main objective of this work is to examine the German-Turkish relationship on the industrial and political perspective not on the axis of colonialism or pragmatism as it is generally done.

Keywords: german industry, turkish-german relations, reforms, german banking models, arms trade

Introduction

1.1. The Uniqueness of German Industrialization

One of the unique features of German Industrialization is that it did not happen in a systematic way. The German Industrial Revolution did not happen on a specific date or in a short period of time, but spread over a long period of time and over a wide geography. German Industrialization has traces in every corner of the scattered German geography.

Some of the driving forces playing an active role in German Industrialization are important developments such as resource management, communication revolution, demographic revolution, transportation revolution, agricultural revolution, structural and financial innovations, public regulations, scientific and technological initiatives, which are tried to be examined in detail in this study. The disorganization of these driving forces makes the German Industrial Revolution a multi-piece puzzle. The German Industrial Revolution is the result of developments that took place in different locations and at different times. In order to understand an industrialization of this nature, it is necessary to examine the developments in each time period in itself, if necessary also regionaly. When speaking of the German Industrial Revolution, it is important to keep in mind that conditions in the East Elbe were not the same as in Saxony or in the Ruhr at any time in the 19th century. While the traces of German Industrialization can be found in some parts of the states such as Prussia and Saxony since the end of the 18th century, it is not possible to talk about a similar industrialization in the East Elbe or Württemberg at the same time. The enlarged Prussia in 1871 had 60 % of the population in the empire and 64 % of the imperial lands.[1] There are quite a lot differences between examining the developments in the 19th century Germany in the perspective of Prussia and in the perspective of Baden or Dresden.

In 1789, when the French Revolution took place, there were 314 independent political regions in Germany, and each region in this vast geography was differentiated from each other not only politically but also economically.[2] This differentiation enabled the regions to have different development rates and

1 Timothy W. Guinnane, "Delegated Monitors, Large and Small: The Development of Germany's Banking System, 1800–1914", *Center Discussion Paper,* no. 835 (2001), 6.

2 Arthur B. Gunlicks, *The Länder and German Federalism* (Manchester: Manchester University Press, 2003), 17.

different orientations. While talking about 19th century Germany, it is quite variable in which year and between which borders Germany would be evaluated. Modern studies examine German territory within its borders in 1871, but it is often overlooked that Alsace-Lorraine, rich in coal and iron, which had a huge impact on industrialization, was not a German territory before this date. The lands owned by the German Empire in 1871 was the same neither with the lands in Holy Roman Empire, nor with the lands in the German Confederation, nor with the lands in the North German Confederation.[3]

When the German Industrial Revolution took place cannot be expressed with an exact date. It is generally accepted that the "take-off"[4] period of German Industrialization, in Rostow's words, took place around the 1850s. However, in the mentioned period, there was neither a central administration nor a coordinated power governing a single German country with certain geographical borders.

The transition from an agrarian economy to a manufacturing economy, as a result of the lack of a central authority and dispersed order, had already begun in some parts of Germany; therefore, the pace of industrialization varied from region to region, from state to state. When examining German Industrialization, it is not possible to give an exact date for German Industrialization by focusing on a single region. Despite these impasses, there was a factor that kept all this mess in harmony with an invisible thread, which was the "organizational revolution" that made the German Industrial Revolution fast, effective and surprising. As a result of Germany's organizational revolution in the 19th century, production technologies and the speed of transformation into a market economy developed simultaneously in tremendous harmony. While production increased on the one hand, consumption also supported this production and this mobility spread throughout the geography with the transportation revolution. This is a phenomenon that attracts the attention of many researchers. Both economists and economic historians have examined the growth problem in industrial economies. In particular, Hoffman's and Rostow's views on this subject are interesting. Hoffman argues that the industrialization process always follows the

3 Knut Borchardt, *The Fontana Economic History of Europe – The Industrial Revolution in Germany 1700–1914*, trans. George Hammersley, ed. Carlo M. Cippola (Great Britain: London and Glasgow Collins' Clear-Type Press, 1972), 7.

4 W.W. Rostow, "The Stages of Economic Growth", *The Economic History Review*, vol. 12, no. 1 (1959), 4.

same model and claims that the economy passes through four basic stages in the industrialization process.[5]

According to Hoffman, the first phase of industrialization is characterized by a very high amount of final product. This final product can be a textile product such as cotton or a food industry product such as flour or sugar. In this phase, the amount of heavy industry products such as pig iron and machinery is slightly less. At this stage, the ratio of consumer goods to capital goods[6] is 5 to 1. In the second phase of industrialization, the final products produced in the textile and food industry are still the predominant part but pig iron products and engineering products are increasing rapidly. At this stage, the ratio of consumer goods to capital goods is 2.5 to 1. In the third phase of industrialization, consumer goods such as textiles and capital goods such as engineering products are almost equal, but capital goods have a greater tendency to increase. At this stage, the ratio of consumer goods to capital goods is 1 to 1. In the fourth phase of industrialization, the amount of capital goods exceeds consumer goods.[7]

Hoffman argues that the first industry to develop in the industrialization process is the consumer goods industry.[8] He also argues that as industrialization takes place, the ratio of added value from consumer goods to capital goods decreases, and over time, capital goods grow at a faster rate than consumer goods.[9] While Hoffmann's theory is like this, Rostow's economic growth theory is divided into five phases.[10]

---

5 William Otto Henderson, *The Industrial Revolution on the Continent – Germany, France, Russia 1800–1914* (London: Frank Cass & Co. Ltd, 1967), 4.

6 In Hoffmann's work, industries are divided into consumer goods and capital goods. If at least 75 % of the output is sold to the consumer, these are consumer goods, If at least 75 % of it contributes to capital formation, these are capital goods. With this criterion, Hoffman positions the products of industries such as tobacco, textile, food, beverage, clothing, furniture and leather within the consumer goods industry. He positions the chemical, machinery, transportation equipment, engineering and metalworking industries within the capital goods industry. See M. Armando Lago, "The Hoffmann Industrial Growth Development Path: An International Comparison", *Weltwirtschaftliches Archiv*, Bd. 103, (1969), 41.

7 B. Seshadri, *Industrialisation and Regional Development* (New Delhi: Concept Publishing Company, 1991), 60

8 Lago, "The Hoffmann Industrial Growth Development Path: An International Comparison", 41.

9 Seshadri, *Industrialisation and Regional Development*, 60.

10 Henderson, *The Industrial Revolution on the Continent*, 4.

According to Rostow, the first phase is the traditional society phase. In this phase, economy is dependent on agriculture. Trade rate is very low. Society does not have a vision for technology and global markets. Society has no expectation of economic well-being, neither for themselves nor for future generations. The second phase is the phase in which the prerequisites for take-off happen. In this phase, the economic, technical, social and political conditions of the first phase, lasting a century or more, are gradually established and only after this formation complete, transition from a superior agricultural economy to a superior production economy can be made. During this stage, society begins to produce and use technology gradually. Agricultural production increases, people begin to earn money. A tax system and a state authority is established, educational institutions become widespread. Society abandons the regional perspective and begins to look at the country as a whole, even looking abroad becomes a fact. The third phase is the take-off phase. In this phase, an intense and automatic growth takes place in a short period of 20–30 years. The share of the investment rate in the national income increases from 5 % to more than 10 % and vital advances are made in production techniques. Industrialization begins to appear. Workers and institutions begin to adapt to new industrial sectors. The entrepreneurial class is born. The social and economic structure changes radically. The fourth phase is the phase of progress towards maturity. In this phase, self-sufficiency occurs. In this phase, which takes a long time, the economy reaches maturity to grow on its own. The ratio of investments and savings is large enough to automate economic growth. New leading sectors develop, the number of agricultural and rural populations decreases, the country's foreign trade structure changes radically. The living standards of the society improve, the use of technology increases, the national economy grows and diversifies. In the fifth stage, there is the period of high mass consumption. In this phase, economy fully adapts to the capitalist system. Mass production and mass consumption take place. The society has a surplus of money to spend, and the new leading sectors are born that make the society make mass consumption.[11]

According to Rostow, the phase called "take-off" is vital. Rostow claims that this phase took place in Britain between 1783 and 1802, in France and Belgium between 1830 and 1860, and in Germany after 1850 (no end date).[12] Of course,

11 W. W. Rostow, "The Stages of Economic Growth", *The Economic History Review*, vol. 12, no. 1 (1959), 1–16.

12 Henderson, *The Industrial Revolution on the Continent*, 4.

it should be noted that Rostow's economic growth model is one of the most criticized models.

While economists such as Schumpeter, Colin Clark, and Kuznets argue that industrial growth is a normal process under the influence of economic fluctuations and is not stimulated by a sudden burst of extraordinary expansion, Rostow necessarily looks for an extraordinary impetus in the "take-off" phase. For example, according to Rostow, the take-off in German Industrialization became possible with the driving force of the railways. Kuznets, on the other hand, attributes the German industry's overtaking of British industry in some areas to the fast-growing industries in Britain. According to Kuznets, rapidly booming industries end up with a rapid decline and in the longer run are surpassed by their steadily growing competitors.[13] The case of Britain is an example for Kuznets' theory.

It is possible to emphasize once again the originality of the German Industrial Revolution by considering various economic growth theories. Moreover, what makes the German Industrial Revolution different is that it does not have a texture that fully integrates with these generalizations. Germany could not advance towards its goal in a systematic way by placing it on its investments. Its cultivated lands were devastated, its population decreased, and it could not create capital accumulation due to the wars that continued for centuries. The gains gained were lost in a moment in the war environment. For example, in the first phases mentioned by Rostow, even in the agriculture-oriented period, when he predicted that the society was not yet technically developed, Germans made significant contributions to knowledge and technology, however there was no investment environment provided to evaluate them. The Magdeburg experiments of the 17th century are just a small example of this.[14]

---

13 Patrice L. R. Higonnet et al., *Favorites of Fortune: Technology, Growth, and Economic Development Since the Industrial Revolution* (Cambridge: Harvard University Press, 1991), 409.

14 After the Thirty Years' War (1618–1648), it was German engineer Max Eyth's efficient use of the steam slingshot who saved people from slavery who were trying to survive by day and night picking cotton or spinning yarnGerman engineers had always been on a quest. Even Otto von Guericke, who was originally the mayor of Magdeburg, prepared the inscriptions of the Magdeburg experiments and with the famous hemispheres experiment, he tried to prove the power of nothingness, the existence of vacuum, which operated all machines and constituted the first step of the Industrial Revolution. By these efforts Guericke built the foundation of the engine. After the Thirty Years' War, many behind-the-scenes developments took place both in Germany and in different geographies by Germans. For example, Heinrich Goebel,

When the Germans showed signs of industrialization or engaged in technological inventions, there was always an external threat or political turmoil that drove them back. In this way, German Industrialization was permanently pushed out of systemic developments. For this reason, seeking the answer of the German Industrial Revolution in formulated schemes may not yield satisfactory results. It would be a more correct approach to examine each detail in itself and induce it. The characteristically different nature of the German Industrial Revolution is one of the main reasons why its breaking points are open to debate.

German Industrialization faced different obstacles from other industrialized countries. Until the 19th century, Germany's lack of an administrative-centered economic union was one of the biggest obstacles to its industrialization. The commercial traffic that should have occurred in Germany's internal market had been slowed down by numerous customs barriers, currency differences and commercial monopolies, and in many cases the monopoly had been the public administration itself. In particular, the border kingdoms often preferred to trade with their non-German neighbors through more convenient routes, rather than turning to the German internal market by crossing the German mountains and rivers, and paying several customs duties. In such an environment, the concept of "domestic market" could not carry either a moral or a holistic value. On the one hand, wars and on the other hand, the fact that the people only earn enough to live, due to the absolutist policies of the princes, prevented the formation of the capital accumulation necessary for industrialization. This situation created a decrease in the purchasing power of the population in general, and the consequent low consumption was the main reason for the traders to move away from the domestic market.[15]

---

a German lens sculptor who immigrated from Hanover to the United States, made a charcoal-wire light bulb while Edison was still selling newspapers. The foundations of the steam engine were also laid by Denis Papin in Germany. Both the first steam engine built in history and the first steam horse power calculated in history were made by Denis Papin in Germany. It can be said that free thought in Germany had struggled since the early period and technical developments had been supported by discoveries that could affect the world. The German education system, in particular, allowed the dissemination of existing discoveries and the advancement of science by transferring it from generation to generation. The fact that these early technical developments created the basis for rapid development when the time came is a unique point that sheds light on one of the mysteries behind German Industrialization. See Walter Kiaulehn, *Demir Melekler* (Istanbul: Remzi Kitabevi, 1993), 98–115.

15 Borchardt, *The Industrial Revolution in Germany 1700–1914*, 15.

It is possible to attribute the reason for the absolutist policies to the lack of political unity of Germany. The lack of a centralized structure allowed the principalities to rule society on their terms. Even in the 18th century, this fragmented and dispersed order continued, and in an environment where there was no political unity, neither a central administrative structure, nor the concept of nation, nor a domestic market trend could be achieved. Administrative elements in the Holy Roman Empire consisted of the judiciary named Reichskammergericht in Wetzlar (Supreme Court), the Eternal Congress in Regensburg, the Reichshofkammer in Vienna, and the emperor himself in Vienna.[16] The effect of these were at a level between mediocre and nonexistent.

Adding to all these negativities, the tragic wars supported by the regional powers who wanted to take advantage of Germany's political turmoil, the effect of the ongoing obstacles became devastating. In the 1630s, when the Thirty Years' War was raging, the urban population of Brandenburg, whose capital was Berlin, fell abruptly from 113,500 to 34,000, and its rural population fell from 300,000 to 75,000. Almost a third of the population lost their lives or were forced to migrate and cultivated lands were burned and destroyed. While they were about to recover after the war, Sweden, the prominent military power of Northern Europe in the 1670s, occupied Brandenburg again with the French. However the Elector of Brandenburg Frederick William, known as the Great Elector, was able to defeat them this time by maneuvering better, but still the war had a great impact on the public.[17] The people were systematically fragmented both as a population and psychologically. The war did not only happen among the soldiers, but most of the time the people were directly targeted. For the people in German lands, war meant forced migration, poverty, rulelessness and death. What happened in the Thirty Years' War created a deep fear of invasion on the people.[18]

---

16 Richard Tilly – Tony Pierenkemper, *The German Economy During the Nineteenth Century* (Oxford: Berghahn Books, 2004), 4.

17 Neil MacGregor, *Germany-Memories of a Nation* (Great Britain: Penguin Books, 2016), 11.

18 Many Western historians do not want to talk about the extent of the violence experienced in the Thirty Years' War, and some even say that what is told is urban legend. However, when we go into detail from the result, it is obvious that it would not be possible to lose so many lives without a massacre. Official reports from the period clearly mention people being beaten to death, people whose homes were burned while they were inside, women raped, and private property vandalized for no reason. People living on the outskirts of Plaue, a few kilometers east of Brandenburg, reported that the invading royal forces advancing into Saxony beat many elderly people to death on New Year's Eve in 1639. They also reported that the invading royal forces shot people

The wars in which both rich and poor were brutally murdered, escape was prohibited and misery prevailed, pushed the Germans to support militarizm. The impact of these wars did not diminish over the centuries. What Germany lived through at that time resulted in the people who needed to participate in production to be wasted in wars, and moreover, this turmoil provided a stable continuity.

By the 18th century, the German geography was not at peace, but in turmoil again. Political division had made the wars that broke out in the German geography in the 18th century a habit rather than an exception. The possibility of war on German soil was always felt, and this hindered the growth of interregional economic independence. Due to the protection psychology created by the wars, the expenditures on the military increased, and both the economy and raw materials started to be used primarily for the military.[19] Between 1740 and 1786, 70 %–80 %, some years even up to 90 %, of public expenditures in Prussia were made for the military, and the number of soldiers in the army was increased

---

to death, raped many women and girls, hanged the children, burned the people alive and stripped the people naked to freeze to death in the freezing cold. The stories of Peter Thiele, the customs officer and the inspector of the town of Beelitz near Potsdam, are also chilling. Peter Thiele achived to survive in Brandenburg. According to Thiele, the royal army, passing through his town in 1637, inserted a half-finger-long wooden stick into the genitals of the town's banker Jürgen Weber to find out where the he kept his money. According to Thiele, the "Schwedentrunk" (Swedish Drink) torture, named by those who survived the Thirty Years' War, although invented by the Swedes, was later used by many armies during the Thirty Years' War. According to the survivors' accounts, the invaders mixed a mixture of feces, soil, urine, and boiling water with a piece of wood and strangled them to the throats of the villagers who did not pay them what they thought was sufficient. They would pour this torture mixture down their throats until they got what they wanted or until the villager passed out. Many people died because of this torture. Another citizen, Krüger Möller, was captured by royal soldiers and left to be burned on the fire with his hands and feet tied. When he told where he kept his money, then he was released. After the royal soldiers took 100 thalers and left, another group of royal soldiers, who learned this became angry, because someone else in their own army had taken the money. They put Möller on the fire again, they burned him alive until his face was burned to ashes and his soul came out of his body. See: Christopher Clark, *Iron Kingdom – The Rise and Downfall of Prussia 1600–1947* (London: Penguin Books, 2007), 32–34.

19 According to what is stated in the Sefâretnâme of Ahmed Resmi Efendi, the ambassador sent to Vienna, the militarist trend in Prussia in the relevant period made Vienna very uneasy. See Ahmed Resmi Efendi, *Ahmed Resmi Efendi'nin Viyana ve Berlin Sefaretnameleri* (Istanbul: Tercüman 1001 Eser, 1980), 33.

regularly by new recruitment plans. As a result of these developments, the Prussian army became the largest army in Europe in terms of soldier/population ratio, however, this result was achieved as a result of considerable financial sacrifices. Under Frederick the Great, officers were not even allowed to marry because they had no money to pay their widows in the event of death.[20]

In the 19th century, the situation was not so different. This time, a Napoleon hurricane emerged that engulfed Europe, and this hurricane completely changed the order of the German states. Napoleon attracted the attention of the German states not only with his military successes but also with the successful reforms he carried out in France, therefore he encouraged the German states to voluntarily join the French Empire directly or indirectly. This situation showed its effect quite clearly. The fact that Napoleon followed an expansionist policy and promised reforms to the places under his rule turned the fragmented structure in Germany into a complete political turmoil. For example, while Prussia confronted Napoleon, its close neighbor Saxony preferred to stand next to Napoleon. Likewise, many German states in the west of the Rhine entrusted themselves to Napoleon's protection and reforms, establishing the Rhine Confederation instead of being incorporated into the Holy Roman Empire. There were even volunteers from the Rhine region who joined Napoleon's army.[21] The establishment of the Rheinbund (Rhine Confederation) by 16 German states,[22] including important names such as Bavaria, Württemberg, Hesse-Darmstadt, erased the Holy Roman Germanic Empire, which had been ineffective for a long time, from the stage of history in every respect on 6 August 1806.

While the tragic wars in previous centuries were effective with their military and social consequences, Napoleon's influence in the commercial field was at least at a level that could compete with the effects in the military and social fields. Napoleon's commercial system was one of the biggest obstacles in front of both the German states that were not affiliated with the Rhine Confederation and the domestic producers who were trying to grow.[23] King of Prussia Friedrich

20 Geoffrey Parker, *Askeri Devrim – Batı'nın Yükselişinde Askeri Yenilikler 1500–1800*, trans. Tuncay Zorlu (Istanbul: Küre Yayınları, 2018), 279.

21 Michael Rowe. "France, Prussia, or Germany? The Napoleonic Wars and Shifting Allegiances in the Rhineland", *Central European History*, vol. 39, no. 4 (2006), 619.

22 Katherine Aaslestad – Karen Hagemann. "1806 And Its Aftermath: Revisiting the Period of the Napoleonic Wars in German Central European Historiography", *Central European History*, vol. 39, no. 4 (2006), 549.

23 In the province of Roer in the First French Empire, 20 % of the population started to work in non-agricultural fields due to the Napoleonic system, and 1200–1300 businesses were established in the non-agricultural field. The first 46 companies

William sent an ultimatum to France demanding its withdrawal from Germany and declared war on France in September 1806.[24] The French army had been fighting for a long time. Moreover, Napoleon was enlarging his army day by day, both because of his preparation for a great war that might occur against Britain and his enthusiasm to expand the borders of French Empire in Europe. On the contrary the Prussian army had been waiting for reform for a long time and it was unprepared. Thus, the French army defeated the Prussian army at the Battle of Jena on October 14, 1806. After the war, Prussia was forced to sign the Treaty of Tilsit in 1807. On the occasion of this peace, Prussia had to give all its lands in the west of the Elbe and some eastern regions to France, and agreed to limit its army to 40,000 soldiers. Moreover, Prussia was punished with a compensation payment and forced to provide human and financial aid for Napoleon's future campaigns.[25]

Since the Treaty of Tilsit did not produce sustainable results, this defeat forced Prussia to make a series of reforms. Prussia launched a rapid reform programme, and started it from the army with the help of pioneering leaders such as Scharnhorst ve Gneisenau.[26] Serfdom was abolished in 1807, peasants were liberated (Bauernbefreiung), provincial authorities were appointed to the cities to govern themselves (Stadteordung), trade regulations were made (Handels und Gewerbegestzgebung), and all these were integrated with the renewed tax system.[27] Innate status groups were removed, nobles could do middle-class jobs, and liberated peasants became eligible to buy their lands. As can be expected, particularly this reform accelerated the economy in the long run by increasing the capitalist activity in the geography. The education system, which had been developing since the 18th century, was further developed with technical

---

employed 17,000 people on their own. The arrival of the mechanized loom in Roer as early as 1812 also sheds light on the breakthrough in the field of mechanization. See Rowe. "France, Prussia, or Germany? The Napoleonic Wars and Shifting Allegiances in the Rhineland", 630.

24 Gunlicks, *The Länder and German Federalism*, 18.

25 John Breuilly, *Avusturya, Prusya ve Almanya'nın Oluşumu 1806–1871* (İstanbul: İletişim Yayınları, 2020), 40. and Mary Fulbrook, *Almanya'nın Kısa Tarihi*, trans. Sabri Gürses (İstanbul: Boğaziçi Üniversitesi Yayınevi, 2017), 103.

26 Reforms in the military field were carried out not only in equipment and tactics, but also operationally and strategically. Conscription was introduced in 1813 and a militia force called *Landwehr* was established. However, two years later, flexibility was made in this regulation.. See Fulbrook, *Almanya'nın Kısa Tarihi*, 105.

27 Tilly – Pierenkemper, *The German Economy During the Nineteenth Century*, 23.

education and higher education, and the spread of this advanced education throughout Prussia enabled the transformation of the existing workforce into an educated workforce on behalf of industrializing Germany in the long run.

Napoleon was afraid of revolts in Europe and had an opinion that Russia was triggering the revolts. He saw waging war on Russia as a solution in order to prevent revolts. So, he invaded Russia in 1812, and it was the first step which ended a unique period. Thinking that Napoleon was successful in his offensive operations, he entered Russia and even occupied Moscow. However, the resistance of the Russian Emperor Alexander I to make a treaty, the French army's inability to withstand the cold Russian climate and the French army's supply problems ended up with the loss of power for Frenchs. This situation gave the coalition, which was waiting to end Napoleon's domination in Europe, the opportunity it was looking for. While invading Russia, Napoleon had amassed an army of over 600,000 soldiers, made up of French military and allied support, but in December he returned with 93,000 troops at best.[28]

The first significant blow to Napoleon came from the coalition forces of Austria, Prussia, Sweden and Russia, which did not allow him to regain power. The coalition amassed 320,000 allied troops and they defeated the French army of 185,000 troops in Leipzig.[29] As a result of this defeat, the Napoleonic states in northern Germany and the Rhine Confederation were dissolved. The last of this series of wars, called the Wars of Independence, was the war of the sixth coalition of Austria, Prussia, Russia, the United Kingdom, Portugal, Sweden, Spain and several German states, which started on March 3, 1813 and ended with the Treaty of Paris on May 30, 1814. After the invasion of Russia, Napoleon was gradually pushed to his former borders so much that the Russians had entered Paris before the Treaty of Paris was signed. As a result of the decision of the coalition, which feared that Napoleon would gather his army again and threaten Europe more furiously, Napoleon was exiled to the island of Elbe.[30]

---

28 Geoffrey Parker, *Cambridge Savaş Tarihi,* trans. Füsun Tayanç – Tunç Tayanç (İstanbul: Türkiye İş Bankası Kültür Yayınları), 226.

29 Encyclopaedia Britannica, "Battle of Leipzig", https://www.britannica.com/event/Battle-of-Leipzig, Accessed: 18 July 2020.

30 The Napoleonic wars, which started on May 18, 1803 and continued until November 20, 1815, caused significant damage to the German economy during and after this twelve and a half years. The plunder of the invaders left huge national, provincial and municipal debts as a legacy, and only a small part of the German geography was spared from the large amount of French compensation that was required to be paid. As expected, the result of such destruction was economic disorder. Some German principalities, including Prussia, deliberately followed a policy of deflation

A congress was held in Vienna between October 1814 and June 1815 to answer the question of under what conditions the lands that Napoleon annexed to the French Empire would be redistributed. Prussia's main goal at the congress was the establishment of a centralized structure that could dominate the small German states. Prussia was also ready to share the leadership position of the German states between Austria and itself in this structure to be established.[31] Austria, on the other hand, was after a fractional structure consisting of completely independent German states. As a result of the decisions taken at the Congress of Vienna, the political structure in the German geography was the way Austria wanted. Austria integrated itself instead of the French Empire into a structure similar to the Rhine Confederation, on the condition of accepting revolutions such as the abolition of serfdom brought by Napoleon. This structure was the German Confederation (Deutscher Bund). German Confederation was decided to be established as a result of the Congress of Vienna. As a result of the German Confederation, the administrative structure of Germany was shaped among 39 member states of the Confederation.[32]

Land distribution decisions taken at the Congress of Vienna were also a factor that played a major role in German Industrialization. Prussia initially attempted to reclaim its lands in 1805. However, the Russian Empire, which dreamed of an independent Kingdom of Poland, opposed it. Prussia had to give East Frisia, which it had held since 1744, to the Kingdom of Hanover. Since the Russians repelled Napoleon, the demands of the Russians were great. Having to agree to this, Prussia wanted the whole of Saxony, however Austria and Britain, thinking that Prussia would become very powerful with the whole of Saxony, gave Prussia a part corresponding to two-fifths of Saxony.[33] In response to Prussia's remaining

---

in order to stabilize the value of their currencies. Of course, such a depression period did not have a positive effect on the economy or industrialization. Even a city like Berlin witnessed the disappearance of existing enterprises, and the city's population decreased significantly compared to 1801. See Claphamm, *The Economic Development of France and Germany 1815–1914*, 87.

31 Henry A. Kissinger, "The Congress of Vienna: A Reappraisal", *World Politics*, vol. 8, no. 2 (1956), 269–270.

32 Wolfgang Keller – Carol H. Shiue, "Endogenous Formation of Free Trade Agreements: Evidence from the Zollverein's Impact on Market Integration", *The Journal of Economic History*, vol. 74, no. 4 (2014), 1171.

33 The Electorate of Saxony, which had managed to own quite large lands in the past, paid the price of standing by Napoleon by losing 60 % of its territory and 40 % of its population. While the population of the Electorate of Saxony was 2,117,512 in 1814, the population of the Kingdom of Saxony, whose new borders were determined after

demands, Prussia was given places in the Swedish-dominated part of West Pomerania and the useless Rhineland, which had no direct land connection with Prussia.[34] Prussia, in its opinion, ceded to the Russian Empire the 3 million Polish peasants who had not yet been liberated in the east, and replaced them with the less populated German peasants under the influence of French liberalism or Roman Catholicism.[35] At first, this did not seem like a victory for the Prussians. However, both Austria, the western states, and Prussia would later learn that these areas harbored the most important underground resources in pre-1871 German Industrialization, that beneath what was known as a distant farmland were some of Europe's largest coal deposits. As a matter of fact, the Rhine region would make a difference in the Prussian economy with the high level of education of its people, the convenience of its geography in transportation and the entrepreneurial tendency of its educated people. There would be such an active trade on the Rhine that by 1845, half of the railways in Germany would be in the Rhine state alone.[36]

As a result of the Congress of Vienna, Prussia both obtained the Rhine region, which would be one of the leading regions of German Industrialization, gave up Slavic lands and instead acquired more German lands. In other words, Prussia oriented further west. Austria, on the other hand, showed a general expansion trend with gains like Italy as a result of the effort to appoint the Habsburg monarchy as Europe's arbiter. This preference of Austria resulted in Prussia taking control of more German lands than Austria for the first time in its history, and also by this way Prussia gained a great advantage in the future competition with Austria for the leadership of German states. In addition to all these gains, an additional population of 1,870,908 people was granted to Prussia, which reached an open border length of 7,000 km with the Congress of Vienna in 1816.[37] This additional population would reach approximately 2,5 million by 1838.[38]

---

the Congress of Vienna, was 1,226,583 as of 1814. One of the main reasons for these losses was that Saxony provided animals, food and military aid to the Napoleonic army, and sent two-thirds of its entire army to Russia. See Ulrich Pfister, "Agricultural development during early industrialization in alow-wage economy: Saxony, c. 1790–1830", *Ehes Workıng Papers In Economıc Hıstory*, no. 39 (2013), 3–4.

34 Clark, *Iron Kingdom*, 389–390.

35 A.J.P Taylor, *The Course of German History – A survey of the development of German history since 1815* (London: Routledge, 2001), 45.

36 Steinberg, *Bismarck*, 35.

37 Hans Rosenberg, "The Struggle for a German-Austrian Customs Union (1815–1931)", *The Slavonic and East European Review*, vol. 14, no. 41 (1936), 333.

38 Steinberg, *Bismarck*, 34.

All these gains did not immediately improve the economy of either Prussia or other German states. The German economy was not very well in the period after the Napoleonic Wars. While the German ports were reopened upon the collapse of the land trade system, the lifting of Napoleon's continental embargo had a completely different negative result. With the lifting of the embargo, textile and hardware products imported from Britain at great speed and in stocked volumes prevented the sales of German industrialists and German merchants in the domestic market. The depression in industry and commerce reached its peak in 1817, and the simultaneous decline in harvest led to severe famine. The rising prices due to the decreasing agricultural production during the war crashed to the bottom with the productive harvest periods after the war, the income from farming fell, and the economic crisis due to agriculture affected the entire country's economy.[39] In Germany, neither the people nor the states could accumulate capital.

Many other political factors that developed in the aftermath of the war also continued to hamper Germany's economic growth.[40] As a result of the Napoleonic Wars, Germany was divided into 39 different states. The enforcement powers of the German Confederation (Bund), which was far from being a central authority, were very limited. Considering the economic events, each state considered itself entitled to make independent decisions in its own way. Each state tried to control its own customs duties, use its own currency, determine its own commercial and political orientations, and host its own subsidiaries in agriculture, mining, production and banking within their own systems.

Another reason why the economy could not recover quickly was that the German states could not get used to either Napoleon or the absence of Napoleon. The German states, which were included in Napoleon's commercial system, could not suddenly adapt to the changes after the Napoleonic era. After Napoleon, both economic opportunities and monetary assets changed hands, and the importance of the traditionalist and absolutist attitude decreased. Most German

39 Borchardt, *The Industrial Revolution in Germany 1700–1914*, 23.

40 Revolutionaries like Engels also accept this situation. In his work titled *Revolution und Konterrevolution in Deutschland*, which he wrote in 1851, Engels attributes the large number of small shopkeepers in Germany to the obstacles placed in front of capitalists and industrialists in Germany. Moreover, he associates the backwardness of the German working class with the immaturity of the German bourgeoisie compared to England and France, and uses the phrase "Such a servant to such a master". See Friedrich Engels, *Almanya'da Devrim ve Karşı Devrim*, trans. Kenan Somer (Ankara: Sol Yayınları, 1992), 15–17.

states or small German principalities that were not in Napoleon's commercial system collapsed under the wind of the French armies during the Napoleonic era. This descent to the bottom necessitated a new beginning and the inefficiency of the old order was exposed. When the old ones were destroyed, the traditional political system was shaken and a pressure for modernization began to be built. It became obvious that modernization was needed in every field from economy to military, from agriculture to industry. At this point, most German states did not go unanswered, and by the 1840s, a commercial mobilization was created by increasing the means of transportation, but this led to an uncontrolled commercial boom. Every entrepreneur invested disproportionately in the hope of making a fortune in a short time, and a bubble economy emerged due to a supply above the demand. As a result of the economic fluctuations created by the investment in risky stocks and the increase in the stock prices, bankruptcies started as of 1843. When the financial crisis that followed, combined with the famine in Europe in the same years, the bankruptcies were followed by starvation.[41] In the 1840s, Germany was dominated by a significant amount of social unrest. The Silesian weavers' revolt in 1844 was an example of large-scale community revolt. Thousands of weavers and spinners died of starvation and typhoid fever in the 1840s. There were many strikes and riots in the towns, showing that local workers and factory workers were just as unsatisfied as peasants, artisans, and smallholders.[42]

The lack of harvest and the commercial crisis in Europe since 1845 caused bankruptcies, unemployment and even deaths from starvation. In 1847 and 1848, high cost of living and unemployment combined, created serious social disorder and turmoil across Europe. In 1848, events got out of control and the period that would go down in history as the Revolutions of 1848 began. The February 1848 revolution in France showed its effects with revolts throughout Germany in March and April. When the riots seemed to be unending, many German states stopped reacting and enacted constitutional reforms.

The priority demands on the German side of the revolution were as follows; the establishment of a much stronger central government than the federation, the establishment of a German people's House of Representatives, the promulgation of the constitution that the King had bitterly opposed for many years, the army's oath of allegiance to the constitution, the elimination of political restrictions based on

41 Steinberg, *Bismarck*, 96.
42 Henderson, *The Industrial Revolution on the Continent*, 24.

religious beliefs, a regulation for fair distribution of tax obligations.[43] The liberal middle class, mostly composed of professionals and businessmen, demanded constitutional reforms and liberal reforms such as the creation of parliamentary institutions, trial by courts, freedom of press, freedom of speech, freedom of assembly. On the other hand, the working class, peasants and craftsmen class had other complaints and demands. For example, the rural proletariat complained of long working hours, low wages and poor housing conditions. In the 1840s, the poor grain harvest and the potato famine increased food prices and reduced the earnings of farmers and peasants. The agricultural economy in southwestern Germany hit the bottom. The traditional farming system collapsed due to the separation of communal areas, the reduction of forests and trees. Small peasant landowners were beginning to lose their grazing rights and food resources that were passed down from generation to generation. Meanwhile, the serfs in the great estates in the east of the Elbe were also quite restless. The freedom promised to them in 1811 had still not fully realized. In Prussia, from the promulgation of the serf emancipation law to 1848, only 240,000 peasants had been freed from manorial duties and obligations.[44] For this reason, although the Revolutions of 1848 are known as a movement of intellectuals,[45] it could be said that they had the support of rural leaders who were waiting to get a share from the new order that would follow. Carl Fraas, the director of the Bavarian Agricultural Association, said that two-thirds of the population lived on agriculture and for this reason, in a newly established German state, agriculturalists should have had more rights than industrialists and citizens. He even went further and suggested the establishment of an agricultural state. Taking all these into consideration it could be said that the people dealing with agriculture had strong expectations from the Revolutions of 1848.[46]

The Revolutions of 1848 had important consequences. First of all, the Frankfurt Parliament, one of the most important messages given by the German states in the name of political unity, convened on May 18, 1848 at 15:00 in Frankfurt am Main.[47] A monarchy-based constitution was adopted in 1849

43 Hans Fenske (ed.), *Quellen zur Deutschen Revolution 1848–49* (Darmstadt: Wissenschaftliche Buchgesellschaft, 1996), 48–49.

44 Henderson, *The Industrial Revolution on the Continent*, 23–24.

45 Felix E. Hirsch, "Frankfurt, 1848 and 1948: The Problems of German Liberty and Unity", *Current History*, vol. 14, no. 81 (1948), 284.

46 Finlay, *Science, practice and politics: German agricultural experiment stations in the nineteenth century*, 73–74.

47 Hirsch, "Frankfurt, 1848 and 1948: The Problems of German Liberty and Unity", 284.

in the Frankfurt Parliament, where representatives from all over Austria and Germany discussed many economic and social problems. This constitution, known as the 1849 Frankfurt Constitution, although it supported the monarchy, also contained democratic elements. For example, it was decided that the lower house of the Frankfurt Parliament would be elected by adult male votes. The emperor's sanctions on the parliamentary will were curtailed. It was decided that the Reichstag would consist of two assemblies (Staatenhaus and Volkshaus), and for a Reichstag decision to be valid, both assemblies had to agree with it.[48] Although this constitution was never fully implemented, the efforts of the Frankfurt Parliament and its Economic Committee had not been entirely in vain. Some of the reforms proposed by the Frankfurt Parliament were implemented and put into effect by some German states at a later date.[49]

One of the most important consequences of the Revolutions of 1848 was emmigration. Workers had tended to immigrate to America, especially since 1815, due to better working conditions and promises of cheap land, but the numbers of emigration gained high momentum during the Revolutions of 1848. Although there is no proven data, it is estimated that 2,500,000 Germans emigrated between 1815 and 1870. The disorder that followed the Napoleonic Wars caused 200,000 southwestern Germans to immigrate to the United States. In the 1820s the wave of emigration waned and only 8500 emigrated. But this number increased again in the 1830s, and in the 1830s 167,000 people emigrated. In 1830 alone, 30,000 people emigrated. Most of these immigrants headed to America. When the bad harvest and industrialization crisis were added to this wave of emigration, and the Revolution of 1848 took place, 470,000 people emigrated from German lands in the 1840s. The years of 1851–60 were the year of the most intense wave of emigration with 1,000,000 people. Emigration of people working in sectors affected by the commercial crisis of 1857 had been an important factor in this wave of emigration. But while it was influential, it was not the main factor, as industrialization and economic recovery had become widespread in Germany after the 1850s. The reason for these emigrations was not to survive, to feed any more, but to work in better conditions. For the same

48 Huber, E.R. (ed.), *Dokumente zur deutschen Verfassungsgeschichte, 1 Cilt: 1803–1850* (Stuttgart: Kohlhammer, 1978), 323–324.

49 Henderson, *The Industrial Revolution on the Continent*, 25.

reasons, more than 800,000 Germans immigrated to various geographies in the 1860s.[50]

The political calmness after the Revolutions of 1848 created the necessary environment for the emergence of the "take-off" period of German Industrialization. As of the 1850s, the beginning of industrialization began to be witnessed in Germany. There are many different views on how German Industrialization took place. One of the objectives of this study is to try to find answers to how German Industrialization took place by taking these views into account.

As mentioned earlier, German Industrialization faced many obstacles, but it also had some important advantages. For Germany, for example, it was an advantage to have the industrialized Britain ahead of it. Since 1780, Britain had begun to create concrete precedents that Germany needed for industrialization.[51]

---

50 Similarly, 96 % of the emigrations from Germany between 1871 and 1896 were made to America. See Marie Von Eschen, "The Commercial Expansion of Germany 1871–1914" *Social Science*, vol. 2, no. 3 (1927), 227.

51 England, as the first country to industrialize, carried out this process without being indebted to its technological or scientific capacity. In the relevant period, Germany's education system was far superior to England, which did not even have a primary education system until the 19th century. Similarly, France was well ahead of England in terms of humanities at that time. In order to emphasize the importance of the mechanization of French industry, the term Industrial Revolution was first used in France as *révolution industrielle* (Karl Marx also used this expression for the Industrial Revolution in Das Kapital). Similarly, Germany was also notorious in certain industries such as paper and knives in the early period. However, neither Germany nor France were the first country to industrialize.. Its geographical location and good ports allowed England to develop its fishing industry and develop overseas trade. Raw materials and tropical food-rich colonies in India, North America, and the West Indies fueled Britain's maritime and overseas trade. Adding to all these, the period of peace that emerged on British soil after 1745 was added, an autonomous period was born in which a Britain, freed from both internal turmoil and foreign invasion, could freely focus on its internal development. Britain had resources of coal and iron ore located close to the ports, had the wool and linen needed for the textile industry, and could produce the hides needed for the leather industry. In short, it had the necessary raw materials and conditions for its industrialization. In particular, the importance of cotton as a driving force was great. Thanks to the cotton industry, England was able to leave the whole world dependent on it, and thanks to the cotton industry, it became the supplier of the entire European continent as an island stateThe cotton industry therefore had an extraordinary contribution to capital accumulation. In fact, the fact that colonialism and slave trade went hand in hand had a great impact on the formation of capital accumulation. African slaves were bought in exchange for cotton

The developments in Britain set a precedent for a traditionalist political structure like Germany, and set an example of where industrialization could take a country to. Traders, civil servants, ministers or manufacturers in trade with Britain

goods brought from India. When supply was restricted in India, purchased slaves were taken to plantations in the Antilles. In this way, cotton raw materials were supplied to England, and in this way, Lancashire mills could periodically become the new supplier of both exports and the local market. This is a prime example of a double earnings cycle. Between 1750 and 1769, British cotton exports increased more than tenfold with this cyclical and stable supply and took off in the following years. While the amount of raw cotton entering England in 1785 was 11 million pounds, this number increased to 588 million pounds in 1850. Similarly, exports increased from 40 million yards to 2025 million yards during the same period. By 1833 the cotton industry had become a locomotive industry, now employing 1,5 million people, epitomizing the shift of the working class from agriculture to industry. The fact that already wealthy landowners, merchants and early producers had the capacity to finance new industrial enterprises with their own capital was an advantage that Germany at the time did not have. The fact that giant banks such as "The Bank of England", which took on the task of spreading a new industrial economy financially, met the capital needs of banks and commodity exchanges in other countries and transferred the surplus money to those who needed money, accelerated the industrial initiatives. Long-existing craftsmen and craft guilds ensured that the need for craftsmen for new factories could be easily met, and the skilled segment provided workforce for quick ventures. Discoveries in the metal and mining industries provided increased means of transport (toll highways, railways, and canals) necessary to accelerate trade. Innovations in the machinery industry and agricultural changes blended with technology contributed to the growth and development of industrial enterprises. Railways should also be mentioned here. The period of railroad production, which took place between 1830 and 1850, was an important driving force in the industrialization of Britain. 300 tons of iron were required for the construction of each mile of pure rail, and as a result, iron production in Britain increased from 680,000 tons to 2,250,000 tons in 20 years. Likewise, coal production increased from 15 million tons to 49 million tons. This is an important indicator of the need-based development of mining and mineral processing. Britain reached such a capacity in railroad production that in 1848 even one-third of the capital used in French railways belonged to the British. It was now possible for British investors to finance heavy industry investments with the money they earned from the cotton industry. England's first capital accumulation and then its progress by putting industrialization in an unhindered cycle made England the first industrialized country. See: Rondo Cameron,. "A New View of European Industrialization." *The Economic History Review*, vol. 38, no. 1 (1985), 3. and See Eric Hobsbawm, *Devrim Çağı 1789–1848*, trans. Bahadır Sina Şener (Ankara: Dost Kitabevi, 2016), 38–47 and Henderson, *The Industrial Revolution on the Continent*, 5.

observed the developments in Britain and they saw that sectors they had not encountered before were emerging and that these new or renewed sectors made entrepreneurs wealthy. It was evident that the new industrial economy linked to coal, iron, machinery, steam turbines and factories made Britain both wealthy and powerful.

Another advantage of Germany in the industrialization process was its slow start in industrialization from the end of the 19th century. Thanks to its slow industrialization, German society did not invest a large amount of capital in old technologies. While the process of transforming the machines in the factories and workshops in Britain into new technology was quite painful due to the reluctance of the private sector to make new investments, Germany gained a competitive technology advantage by making its first investment in the most up-to-date machinery. Another advantage of late industrialization was salaries. While the welfare level of the developed society and the wages of the workers increased gradually and reached high levels in Britain, Germany provided a great advantage against Britain in production costs by employing the workers who had just met with the industry from their starting wages. It is also possible to say that while the German manufacturers industrialized, they benefited from the materials that the industrialized countries supplied quickly. Considering that German cotton weavers imported 62 % of their yarn in 1849, it can be predicted that in a scenario where Britain was not industrialized, Germany would surely have experienced shortages or lack of supply in the yarn it would import. British capital goods played an important role in the creation of German industry. From 1835 onwards, the first German railways extensively used British engines, wagons and railways. This was possible by the existence of British industry that could process iron and steel. It is obvious that in the absence of a railway, it would not be easy to talk about Germany's raw material supply and product export.[52] On the other hand, it is a fact that these advantages alone would not be sufficient for German Industrialization. Another essential need for German Industrialization, such as technical knowledge, labor, access to raw materials, was capital. In order for the capital to be transferred to the industry, the rich people who had accumulated capital had to invest their savings in industry, which was the case in Britain. To achieve that, savers had to be directed to the industry and encouraged to put their money at risk. In Britain, this was relatively easy. Britain, which had commercial relations with both its colonies and international markets before industrialization, had obtained the necessary capital by transferring

52 Borchardt, *The Industrial Revolution in Germany 1700–1914*, 12.

the money of land owners with rental income, merchants trading in local and international markets and entrepreneurs who had made profitable investments to the industry.[53] With a few exceptions in Germany, no one wanted to invest their limited capital in an adventure they didn't know about. Whatever was gained from agriculture that year, the people were prepared to gain the same following year, the last thing to incentive for the people who had been suffering prolonged economic decline was the possibility of losing existing limited wealth. Therefore, unlike Britain, Germany had to adopt an alternative industrialization model in which state intervention was intense. This is an important factor that makes German Industrialization unique.

German Industrialization is also unique because it began to take place before Germany completed its political union. The proclamation of the German Empire also had important effects on industrialization. One of the most important of these effects was land gains. If these gains are not mentioned, it will be insufficient to explain the reason for the sudden increases in raw material production and exports.

The first of three important wars on the way to German Empire was between the German Confederation and Denmark. King of Denmark Frederik VII died on November 5, 1862, leaving no heirs behind. The new Danish King IX. Christian signed a constitutional text that included Schleswig on Danish territory on November 18. This signature turned into a crisis. It turned into a war when Denmark did not take a step back against the ultimatums.[54] In the war between the Bund and Denmark, Prussia actually annexed Schleswig and determined its geographical expansion in the direction of Holstein and Lauenburg.[55] The cause

53 There was already a wealthy elite in Britain before the Industrial Revolution, and it was easy for this group, who made relatively easy money, to shift their capital to industry. The effect of trade with the colonies is very important.. The target markets where the raw material came from and the final product was sold were the mainstay of the British wealthy. Therefore, easy-earned money enabled the capital accumulation in Britain to occur quickly and more importantly, in a sustainable way. See E.J. Hobsbawm, *Sanayi ve İmparatorluk*, trans. Abdullah Ersoy (Ankara: Dost Kitabevi Yayınları, 2013), 54.

54 At an international congress held in London in 1852, Austria and Prussia agreed in principle that they would preserve the integrity of the Kingdom of Denmark, while Denmark would never try to incorporate the duchies. The ultimatums given to Denmark were related with its obligations from the agreement in 1852. See Steinberg, *Bismarck*, 258, 266.

55 Wolfgang Neugebauer (ed.), *Handbuch der preußischen Geschichte. Band 2: Das 19. Jahrhundert und große Themen der Geschichte Preußens* (Berlin: Verlag De Gruyter, 1992), 340.; Breuilly, *Avusturya, Prusya ve Almanya'nın Oluşumu 1806–1871*, 248–249.

of the second war was the first war. The result of the first war was that Prussia annexed Schleswig, and Austria had its occupying army in Holstein, hundreds of kilometers from its borders. The inability of Prussia and Austria to determine exactly how they would make the land share brought Austria and Prussia face to face in 1865. In order to reduce this tension and eliminate the possibility of war, Bismarck hosted the Austrian ambassador Gustav von Blome in the hot springs in Bad Gastein in the Austrian Alps, where he often visited.[56] The 14 August 1865 Agreement, which was signed here and called the Gastein Agreement, could not bring a permanent peace to the situation. Shortly afterwards both sides began to make war preparations, but Austria was not quite prepared for Prussia.

Although the Austrian army seemed larger on paper, some dynamics had changed the balance over time. First of all, the reduction of Austria's army due to military savings made the Prussian army approach the Austrian army in size. On the other hand, Prussia had the support of the Italian army. As a result of the three-month treaty signed with Italy, which entered into force on April 8, 1866, Prussia had an advantage of adding Italy's 233,000-strong army. With the support of Italian army Prussia closed the gap and also had a significant advantage in numbers.[57] Apart from all these, the Prussian army was equipped with more modern equipment than the Austrian army. Austria, on the other hand, had the military support of Saxony, Bavaria, Württemberg and Hannover. As a result of the war, Prussia defeated Austria at the Battle of Königgrätz on 3 July 1866 and the preliminary peace treaty was signed in Nikolsburg by Austria and Prussia on 26 July 1866. Under the treaty, Austria agreed to withdraw completely from the union of German states, and also accepted a federation to be established by the northern German states under Prussian leadership. Also, Austria accepted to transfer its rights over the Duchy of Schleswig and Holstein coming from the Vienna treaty of 30 October 1864 to the King of Prussia. Moreover Austria accepted to recognize the territorial changes to take place in northern Germany and to pay 40 million Taler war reparations to Prussia.[58] In addition, Austria

56 Neugebauer (ed.), *Handbuch der preußischen Geschichte. Band 2: Das 19. Jahrhundert und große Themen der Geschichte Preußens*, 340.

57 Although this number is unrealistic according to many authorities, the presence of Italy forced Austria to send 100,000 soldiers to the south. See. Breuilly, *Avusturya, Prusya ve Almanya'nın Oluşumu 1806–1871*, 131.

58 According to the treaty of October 30, 1864, 15,000,000 thalers were to be deducted for the war indemnity that Austria was entitled to receive from the duchies of Schleswig and Holstein, and 5,000,000 thalers for the expenses of the Prussian army in the occupied Austrian territory. See Breuilly, *Avusturya, Prusya ve Almanya'nın Oluşumu 1806–1871*, 244–245.

committed to accept that the relations between the German states in the south and the member states of the North German Federation be freely decided by treaties.[59] Undoubtedly, the war reparations Prussia received from Austria not only eased Prussia's financial situation, but also increased Prussia's investment capability.

The war with Austria was a critical factor that would pave the way for Prussia to become an effective power in the future. For example, on September 23, 1866, Hanover was annexed by Prussia and became a province of Prussia.[60] Austria, on the other hand, was only a spectator to this situation. Moreover, in 1867, a North German Confederation was established independent from Austria.[61]

The third important war was the war between Prussia and France. Bismarck differentiated his constructive stance only for France, because he believed that if the French threat was not completely eliminated, the French would soon regroup and stand against Prussia. The attitude of the French towards the Germans had not been very merciful. The conflict that Bismarck expected to occur with France happened in Spain. In September 1868, Queen Isabella II was overthrown by a memorandum of generals, leaving the crown vacant. Under the leadership of the President of the Council of Generals, field marshal Juan Prim, it was decided to propose the throne of Spain to Leopold von Hohenzolern. However, he did not take kindly to the proposal because the government did not have solid foundations and could be overthrown with a similar memorandum. On the other hand Bismarck insisted on accepting this offer. Probably, he predicted that this acceptance would bring Prussia and France face to face, and he wanted to benefit from the chaos that would arise. As a result of Bismarck's persuasion of the king and the Spanish council's persuasion of Leopold von Hohenzollern, Leopold sent a letter on 19 June, stating that he accepted the offer.[62] France showed its reaction to this situation by declaring war on 19 July 1870. As a result of this war, marked by the strategic achievements of the Chief of the General Staff Moltke, Prussia waged a series of wars up to the bombardment of Paris and came out victorious.

This war, which united all German states against France, was also important in terms of awakening the spirit of nationalism. Kaiser was offered to be an

59 Steinberg, *Bismarck*, 310.

60 Steinberg, *Bismarck*, 321.

61 The North German Confederation had a parliament, a "Reichstag" and a superstructure "Bundesrat" in which states were represented. The 58-member Bundesrat was dominated by Prussia with 17 seats and 14 votes sufficient for a veto. See James, "Monetary and Fiscal Unification in Nineteenth Century Germany", 5.

62 Steinberg, *Bismarck*, 343

emperor,[63] and the date of the ceremony for the proclamation of the new Reich was chosen as January 18, 1871.[64] The place for the ceremony was chosen as the "Hall of Mirrors" in the Palace of Versailles due to the continued occupation of France. At the ceremony, in which Kaiser attended by wearing all his medals, Bismarck's address to the German people and the sermon of Father Rogge were read, the ceremony was held and the German Empire was declared.

After the Paris bombardment, France had no choice but to surrender. On January 28, 1871, the surrender treaty was signed. In the following month, peace terms were negotiated with France, and as a result, a preliminary peace agreement was signed on February 26, 1871, again at the Palace of Versailles, in which the compensation amount to be paid by France was determined as 5 billion francs.[65] This money was quite a large amount under the conditions of that period.

Disraeli, in his speech in the House of Commons, interpreted the Franco-Prussian war in these words:

> *This war represents the German revolution, a greater political event than the French revolution of last century. I don't say a greater, or as great a social event. What its social consequences may be are in the future. Not a single principle in the management of our foreign affairs, accepted by all statesmen for guidance up to six months ago, any longer exists. There is not a diplomatic tradition which has not been swept away. You have a new world, new influences at work, new and unknown objects and dangers with which to cope, at present involved in that obscurity incident to novelty in such affairs. We used to have discussions in this House about the balance of power. Lord Palmerston, eminently a practical man, trimmed the ship of State and shaped its policy with a view to preserve an equilibrium in Europe. [. . .] But what has really come to pass? The balance of power has been entirely destroyed, and the country which suffers most, and feels the effects of this great change most, is England.*[66]

This war, which resulted in the establishment of the German Empire, was a political event even greater than the French Revolution, according to Disraeli. In

63 Steinberg, *Bismarck*, 367.

64 January 18 is also the date of the glorious ceremony in which Frederick III, Elector of Brandenburg, received the title of King Frederick I of Prussia in 1701. See Hans A. Frambach, "Great Nations at Peril – Rise and fall of Prussia", *Great Nations at Peril*, ed. Jürgen Backhaus (Switzerland: Springer International Publishing, 2015), 24.

65 Steinberg, *Bismarck*, 373.

66 John C.G. Röhl, *From Bismarck to Hitler* (Londra: Longman Publishing Group, 1970), 23.

accordance with the subject of this study, it will be tried to focus on the economic importance of the German Revolution rather than its political importance.

It is an undeniable fact that the establishment of the German Empire created an important environment of trust for the investors. The economic welfare level of Germany increased in a short time. The unification of Schleswig and Holstein gave Germany the ports of Kiel, Altona and Fiensburg. It became possible to connect the North Sea and the Baltic Sea with a channel flowing from the German land. This canal called the Kiel Canal was built and put into service between 1887 and 1895.

The lands of Alsace and Lorraine, which were annexed as a result of the war with France, were a very important economic gain. Thanks to these gains, Germany had the largest iron ore reserves in Western Europe, and it also incorporated the already existing iron processing factories, engineering firms and textile factories in the region. The iron ore production of Lorraine increased from 684,000 tons to 1,859,000 tons between 1872 and 1882. Moreover, significant potash reserves were discovered in Wittelsheim in Alsace in 1904.[67]

In the diplomatic framework, the difference between before and after the German Empire is quite clear. Leaving behind diplomatic traditions had a very positive effect on social life and investors. Between 1870 and 1873, the capital of joint stock companies in Germany doubled in just three years. While the investment rate was 8.7 % in the 1850s, it increased to 17.2 % in 1874.[68] It is also seen that large investments were made in this period and investor earned money as long as there was demand. Although this situation seemed attractive to investors in the first years, an uncontrolled supply explosion was experienced as a result of the enthusiasm of all the investors who saw the profitability. In particular, the compensation of 5 billion gold francs, which France was obliged to pay at that time, dragged Germany into an abundance of liquidity and encouraged people to make risky investments in an unrealistic bubble market with easy gained money. As a result of the supply being much higher than the demand, both profitability and investments began to decrease by 1880. Moreover, as a result of the deflating of this bubble in a short time and the inability of investors to pay their loans and cover their existing inflated expenses, citizens who want to get rich in an easy way or who want to grow very quickly were dragged into a financial crisis. The first modern global crisis began with the collapse of the Vienna Stock Exchange on May 9, 1873.[69] The financial fire in Austria was fueled by the investment of

67 Henderson, *The Industrial Revolution on the Continent*, 45.

68 Borchardt, *The Fontana Economic History of Europe*, 47.

69 Steinberg, *Bismarck*, 397.

banks and the crisis reached global dimensions. Germany was affected by the crisis, and the London Stock Exchange and the Paris Stock Exchange followed the Vienna Stock Exchange. So much so that even the famous banking company of Philadelphia, Jay Cooke and Company, went bankrupt.[70] Although the effects of this situation were experienced until 1895, some important financial policies managed to balance the crisis. Before 1896, the investment rate rose above 17 % again, but this was a healthy economic rise as this rise was not formed in a short time, but over time.[71] This positive economic stability continued until the First World War.

German Industrialization was a long and multi-part process. It is obvious that it did not happen only by copying the technology in Britain or by the acquisition of raw material-rich regions after the Treaty of Vienna. Each type of bank, cartels, infrastructure investments, striking education models, economic policies, resource management, making the right investment at the right time and the state interventions contributed separately to German Industrialization. To understand German Industrialization, each of these concepts must be evaluated in its own right. As Gerschenkron puts it, if the coal mines were not processed, the railways could not be built, if the ports and cities were not connected, the railways would have no effect.[72]

It is quite an expected phenomenon that a radical development such as the German Industrial Revolution created both political and economic developments. Particularly considering the developments in the world at the beginning of the 20th century, this fact becomes more clear. At the beginning of the 20th century, the Balkans was in complete disarray and regularly saw new border changes. Austria-Hungary was in an effort to keep the nations within it under control, to try to prevent the Russians from being neighbors to it in the Balkans, and to establish a balance in its deteriorating relations with Serbia. The industrialization of Russia and its alliance with France began to pose a complete threat to the Germany. Germany, which was late in the colonization race, had to cling to the Austrian alliance inherited only from Bismarck against the threat of Britain, France and Russia. In such an environment, Germany's economic penetration and military support to the Ottoman Empire undoubtedly responded

---

70 Steinberg, *Bismarck*, 397.

71 Borchardt, *The Fontana Economic History of Europe*, 47–48.

72 Alexander Gerschenkron, *Economic Backwardness in Historical Perspective – A Book of Essays* (Cambridge, Massachussets: The Belknap Press of Harvard University Press, 1962), 9.

to the needs of Germans as well as the Ottomans. The Ottoman Empire, which still maintained its political authority even though it suffered from economic depression as an empire, became a target market for industrialized Germany and a highly populated and geographically critical ally for isolated Germany.

1.2. Global Literature on German Industrialization and Turkish-German Relations

The German Industrial Revolution is a topic with global potential in that it has not been studied much. When the books and articles in foreign languages are examined, it is striking that the number of historians doing research on the German Industrial Revolution is quite limited. There is hardly a study that deals with the concept of the German Industrial Revolution as a whole. Existing detailed studies focus on specific stages of the German Industrial Revolution. Since these studies are generally handled by economists or economic historians, they are far from conveying the semantic result required by historiography. The results that these empirical studies aim and reach are usually quantitative conclusions; however, some studies contributed greatly to the literature.

Although the importance of state intervention in German Industrialization is a generally accepted phenomenon, authors such as Frank B. Tipton[73] have interpretive and empirical studies questioning the effect of state intervention on industrialization. Although most of these studies generally focus on one or a few sectors, clustered on selected data and focused on short-term effects, they draw attention in terms of presenting concrete data. Sibylle Lehmann-Hasemeyer and Fabian Wahl's study,[74] by analyzing saving banks in more than 900 Prussian cities, sheds light on the active role played by government-established or at least government-supported saving banks in German Industrialization. This study is noteworthy as it focuses on the positive effects of state intervention on German Industrialization.

73 Frank B. Tipton, "Government Policy and Economic Development in Germany and Japan: A Skeptical Reevaluation", *The Journal of Economic History*, vol. 41, no. 1 (1981).

74 Sibylle H Lehmann Hasemeyer – Fabian Wahl, "Savings banks and the industrial revolution in Prussia: Supporting regional development with public financial institutions", *Hohenheim Discussion Papers in Business, Economics and Social Sciences*, no. 18 (2017).

There are important researches about Zollverein.[75] Perhaps the most important of these is the three-volume *Vorgeschichte und Begründung des deutschen Zollvereins 1815–1834*,[76] which contains many documents. Many different researchers have prepared many different publications on the light of this work. Particularly William Otto Henderson's book and articles[77] on Zollverein are important studies that are frequently cited. Among the studies on Zollverein, there are those who make shallow inferences by linking German Industrialization only to the effect of Zollverein, and those who focus only on the working principles of Zollverein. However, almost all of these studies are far from interpreting the real impact of Zollverein as a transportation revolution factor in the German Industrial Revolution.

One of the main actors in German Industrialization is undoubtedly Bismarck. What makes Bismarck stand out is that he followed a chess-like policy throughout his political life and acted by thinking about his next moves; therefore as well as his political achievements, Bismarck's economic policies on the road to German Industrialization, which some historians praised and some criticized, are also noteworthy. Steinberg's biography of Bismarck[78] is one of the most comprehensive Bismarck biographies ever written, and it is also remarkable in that it contains numerical information about the period.

The impressive works of prominent authors such as Alexander Gerschenkron[79] and Hans Rosenberg[80] on the oppressive role of heavy industry investors and large landowners on tariffs is invaluable for understanding the development of the 1879 tariffs. The study of Helmut Bölme,[81] which examines the concrete effects

---

75 It is one of the most important free trade agreements of the 19th century, which came into operation in 1834. A customs union was established between the member countries of Zollverein and customs barriers preventing trade between member countries were overcome. See Keller – Shiue, "Endogenous Formation of Free Trade Agreements: Evidence from the Zollverein's Impact on Market Integration", *The Journal of Economic History*, 1168.

76 Wilfried von Eisenhart Rothe; Anton Ritthaler; Hermann Oncken, *Vorgeschichte und Begründung des deutschen Zollvereins, 1815 – 1834* (Berlin: R. Hobbing, 1934).

77 William Otto Henderson, *Zollverein* (New York: Routledge, 2018).

78 Jonathan Steinberg, *Bismarck,* trans. Hakan Abacı (İstanbul: Türkiye İş Bankası Kültür Yayınları, 2015).

79 Alexander Gerschenkron, *Bread and Democracy in Germany* (Berkeley: University of California Press, 1943).

80 Hans Rosenberg, *Grosse Depression und Bismarckzeit: Wirtschaftsablauf: Gesellschaft und Politik in Mitteleuropa* (Berlin: Walter de Gruyter & Co., 1967).

81 Helmut Böhme. "Big-Business Pressure Groups and Bismarck's Turn to Protectionism, 1873–79." *The Historical Journal*, vol. 10, no. 2 (1967).

of pressure groups on tariffs and Bismarck, is also noteworthy, however, it does not give us an adequate answer about the effect of tariffs on industrialization.

In the German Industrial Revolution, the effects of big banks comes first among the issues that economists attach importance to, but historians generally inadequate to examine this topic. Alexander Gerschenkron's famous articles written between 1951 and 1961 expressed the effects of big banks on German Industrialization. With the approach that Gerschenkron sheds light on, some important articles on the effects of great banks have also appeared in the literature.[82] Empirical approaches of Hugh Neuburger and Houston H. Stokes[83] is an example. Based on the numerical sources Otto Jeidels[84] brought to the literature in 1905, there are also those who argue that German banking focused on German Industrialization in the second half of the 19th century and prevented the growth of small businesses, ignored agricultural investments, did not provide liquidity to the construction industry, and did not give lifeline to small businesses.[85] Writers of this view often argue that the big banks hurt the German economy.[86] Economist Timothy Guinnane has carried out an important study stating that *Sparkaassen* and *Privatbanken* type banking models also played an important role in universal banking.[87] Thomas Hellmann and Marco da Rin's studies on the effect of banking on industrialization are noteworthy.[88]

82 In particular, "Economic Backwardness in Historical Perspective" and "Reflections on the Concept of "Prerequisites" of Modern Industrialization" are the articles that bring this question to the fore.

83 Neuburger, Hugh – Houston H. Stokes. "German Banks and German Growth, 1883–1913: An Empirical View." *The Journal of Economic History*, vol. 34, no. 3 (1974).

84 Otto Jeidels, as a banker who witnessed the development of German banking in the sector at that time, is still cited in the literature. See Otto Jields, *Das Verhältnis der deutschen Großbanken zur Industrie* (Munchen: Duncker&Humblot, 1905).

85 Richard H. Tilly "Banking Institutions in Historical and Comparative Perspective: Germany, Great Britain and the United States in the Nineteenth and Early Twentieth Century", *Journal of Institutional and Theoretical Economics (JITE) /* Zeitschrift Für Die Gesamte Staatswissenschaft, vol. 145, no. 1 (1989), 190–191.

86 General support for sectors other than heavy industry could be provided by the spread of deposit banks and credit banks, which could only be realized towards the end of the 19th century. See Tilly "Banking Institutions in Historical and Comparative Perspective", 191.

87 Guinnane, "Delegated Monitors, Large and Small: The Development of Germany's Banking System, 1800–1914", 43.

88 Marco Da Rin – Thomas Hellmann, "Banks as Catalysts for Industrialization", *William Davidson Working Paper*, no. 44 (October 2001),

With valuable economic theoretical modeling based on the industrialization of Italy, Belgium and Germany, they have shown that industrialization progresses more slowly by a significant margin in scenarios without great banks.[89]

The only case in which opposing views meet in the literature is that great banks contributed to industrialization in the second half of the 19th century. Nevertheless, it can be argued that the existing studies are theoretically satisfactory, but insufficient in illuminating the concrete effects of banks. Apart from authors such as Guianne, Burhop,[90] Hasemeyer, and Wahl, there are not many authors who examine the effects of banks on bank types. Much of the literature has focused on the general effects of universal banks on German Industrialization, where the Kreditbanken model has often been taken into account. Within the scope of this study, the roles of different bank types in German Industrialization have been tried to be discussed independently from each other with data.

The role of banks has always been questioned. There has been a regular voice against the banks in the society, but no one has been able to do without a bank. In 1911, Jacob Riesser, director of the Darmstadter Bank, published a major study[91] showing the role of banks in industrialization and the economy against existing criticism. In the same period, the Marxist revolutionary Rudolf Hilferding, with his work called Finanzkapital, emphasized that banks have a great sanction power on the economy and attracted a lot of attention.[92] This process has been going on since then, but it is a fact that the existence of German Industrialization would be

89 Authors such as Richard H. Tilly, who focused on the 19th century German economy, argue that with the spread and branching of the German mixed banking model that combines commercial and industrial banking, banking could meet the short-term needs of businesses, and therefore German banking was a very important driving force in the German economy. Other industries linked to industry also benefited from banking. For example, in 1896, all 39 joint stock companies in the electricity sector were established with bank financing. See Henderson, *The Industrial Revolution on the Continent*, 64. Similarly, companies such as BASF, AGFA, Degussa, Hoechst and Bayer in the innovative chemical sector, which made a difference in German Industrialization, were also significantly supported by bank financing. German banks, which offered the universal banking school, played an important role in the formation of the chemical industry. See Da Rin – Hellmann; "Banks as Catalysts for Industrialization", 8.

90 Carsten Burhop, "Did banks cause the German industrialization?", *Explorations in Economic History*, Elsevier, vol. 43/1 (2006), 39–63.

91 Jacob Riesser, *The German Great Banks and Their Concentration in connection with The Economic Development of Germany* (Washington: Government Printing Office, 1911)

92 Tilly – Pierenkemper, *The German Economy During the Nineteenth Century*, 114.

questioned in a scenario where there was no banking. It is a controversial issue from where the necessary capital for industrialization would be met in a country that does not have sufficient capital accumulation.

It would be a mistake not to examine agriculture when studying German Industrialization. Just like the fact that employment in the industry shifts from agriculture, it is also a fact that agricultural products can be industrial raw materials, especially in the field of textiles. Therefore, it would be a more accurate approach to examine the industrialization stages in parallel with agriculture. Unfortunately, very few studies have been done on the role of agriculture in German Industrialization. In particular, Nikolaus Wolf[93] has important works in this field. However, it is obvious that these studies will not be sufficient to understand the role of agriculture in German Industrialization, both because the objectives of these studies are to reach a rational conclusion in the presence of empirical methods and because they only focus on a certain phenomenon in a certain period.

Another overlooked, but very important subject when examining German Industrialization is education. There are pioneering studies on education in Germany, but none of them directly target the impact of education on industrialization. Although Thomas Nipperdey's work,[94] which sheds light on the importance of education, does not focus on education in Germany, it has pioneering anecdotes on education. Johan Östling's work[95] focused on Humboldt is a valuable work that sheds light on Humboldt and education reform semantically and conveys Humboldt, his purpose and what he did. However, since it is far from concrete data in general and does not focus on the effect of education on industrialization, it may be insufficient to meet the answers sought in quantitative terms. The study of Fritz K. Ringer,[96] on the other hand, is interesting in that it conveys who receives quality education in Germany, shares

93 Nikolaus Wolf, "Agricultural Productivity Across Prussia During the Industrial Revolution: A Thünen Perspective", *Ehes Workıng Papers In Economıc Hıstory*, no. 13 (January 2012); Michael Kopsidis – Nikolaus Wolf, "Agricultural Productivity Across Prussia During the Industrial Revolution: A Thünen Perspective", *The Journal of Economic History*, vol. 72, no. 3 (2012).

94 Thomas Nipperdey, *Deutsche Geschichte 1800–1866: Bürgerwelt und starker Staat* (Münih: C.H.Beck, 1983)

95 Johan Östling, *Humboldt and the Modern German University – An Intellectual History*, trans. Lena Olsson (Lund: Lund University Press, 2018).

96 Fritz K. Ringer, "Higher Education in Germany in the Nineteenth Century", *Journal of Contemporary History*, vol. 2, no. 3 (1967).

the rates of educational level transitions from primary education to university, and more importantly, emphasizes the importance of education in the formation of social class differences, which is not mentioned much.

Two important works that focus on German Industrialization in general attract attention. One of them is *The Fontana Economic History of Europe – The Industrial Revolution in Germany 1700–1914*[97] by Knut Borchardt. In this work, Borchardt focuses directly on the German Industrial Revolution and provides the reader with a general summary of about 80 pages. In general, the work may be sufficient to give an idea to the reader. However, it is both lacking in modern information as of the date of its preparation, and it is incomplete in terms of not mentioning banks, education, leading sectors, Bismarck's period policies, agricultural reforms, the effects of population on industrialization and even Zollverein.

The second notable work is William Otto Henderson's *The Industrial Revolution on the Continent,*[98] in which he examines the industrialization processes in Germany, France and Russia. In this work, Henderson allocated a limited area of about 50 pages to German Industrialization and gave the weight of the work to French Industrialization. Since he had a dominance of 19th century Germany and he had made extensive researches on the Zollverein, it is possible for a reader to find valuable information in these 50 pages. However, as in Borchardt, there are deficiencies in Henderson's work on issues such as education, innovation, agricultural developments, the roles of banks, and the effect of immigration on industrialization. The common feature of both works is that they were not written in recent times, so they were not fed by current researches, and they basically discussed the German Industrial Revolution from the perspective of Zollverein and the railways. This causes the reader to look at the German Industrial Revolution only from a limited perspective. For this reason, when the German Industrial Revolution is mentioned almost all of the studies conducted around the same period of time have railway-based answers.

One of the most productive economic historians working on the 19th century German economy is undoubtedly Richard Tilly. Richard Tilly has many articles on German economy, however his book *The German Economy during*

---

97 Knut Borchardt, *The Fontana Economic History of Europe – The Industrial Revolution in Germany 1700–1914,* ed. Carlo M. Cippola, trans. George Hammersley (London and Glasgow: Collins Clear-Type Press, 1972).

98 William Otto Henderson, *The Industrial Revolution on the Continent – Germany, France, Russia 1800–1914* (London: Frank Cass & Co. Ltd, 1967).

the Nineteenth Century,[99] written with Toni Pierenkemper, differs from other sources since it examines the distribution of labor and monetary reforms in 19th century Germany. However, altough it is an economic history book, the information it gives about the role of banks in German Industrialization may be found insufficient.

One of the most referanced works on how Germany industrialized and captured Britain is Thorstein Veblen's *Imperial Germany and the Industrial Revolution*.[100] According to Veblen, German Industrialization was not the result of any economic, cultural or technical development, Germany received the mechanical innovation required for industrialization directly from Britain and created industrial efficiency by using its population like a slave in a feudal structure. Prussia's militarism made this feudal power central, and as a result of the unification in 1871, the entire population was able to contribute to industrialization in a feudal structure. According to Veblen, while the cultural consequences of the Industrial Revolution forced Britain to deal with democracy and individual rights, it is an important advantage of Germany that it put the cultural consequences of the German Industrial Revolution out of action with a strong central authority. Thus, Germany increased its productivity by exploiting the workforce. Veblen's view is a highly controversial interpretation. While developing countries are aware of the existence of an effective technology and can quickly switch to the production phase by integrating it, the leading country needs to conduct regular research and development for new technologies and allocate significant capital to it. This fact supports Veblen's interpretation, however, for the necessary capital and R&D, the investors of that country must first be willing to invest capital and engineering power, which is difficult to achieve with traders who are afraid to lose their earnings. This requires larger financial structures and a strong capital accumulation. German Industrialization differs from Veblen's view here. It is obvious that the machine alone will not be sufficient if there is no technical staff to process the machine, the supply chain to transform the raw material into the final product, transportation opportunities, capital accumulation and technical knowledge to perform R&D. To describe German Industrialization as an imitation would not be enough to explain how

---

99 Richard Tilly – Tony Pierenkemper, *The German Economy During the Nineteenth Century* (Oxford: Berghahn Books, 2004).

100 Thorstein Veblen, *Imperial Germany and the Industrial Revolution* (London: The Macmilan Company, 1915).

Germany's blast furnaces in the second half of the 19th century were better than British blast furnaces.[101]

German Industrialization is undoubtedly of a capitalist nature.[102] Veblen's generally accepted interpretations and inferences spread by anti-capitalist circles could not go beyond the claims that Germany industrialized by copying Britain's technology, using brute public force and transforming the population into labor force.[103] This inference is insufficient to answer the question of why every country with a population and a central authority did not industrialize in the same period. With this limited view, it cannot be answered why the Ottoman Empire, China or Austria could not industrialize in the same period. Interestingly, Marxist circles also support this view. "*The industrially developed country only shows the less developed a picture of its own future*"[104] this statement written by Karl Marx in the preface to the German first edition of his famous work Das Kapital, also bequeathed to the Marxists the argument that German Industrialization took Britain as an example.[105] Alexander Gerschenkron was one of those who argued that this argument was insufficient. According to Gershenkron, there are areas where Germany followed Britain, but following is not enough for industrialization; each country has internal obstacles that change and need to be overcome, such as the lack of raw material supply, the serfdom of the peasants, the lack of political unification.[106] His article titled "Prerequisites of Modern Industry" is about the necessity of countries that want to industrialize to meet certain prerequisites and overcome certain obstacles. The perspective that Gerschenkron adds to the reader is valuable, because it encourages people who have the fixed view that "Germany industrialized with imitating from Britain" to think a little more deeply. Since Gershenkron's article has a comment-oriented

---

101 Alexander Gerschenkron, *Economic Backwardness in Historical Perspective – A Book of Essays* (Cambridge, Massachussets: The Belknap Press of Harvard University Press, 1962), 10.

102 Jurgen Kocka. "Capitalism and Bureaucracy in German Industrialization before 1914", *The Economic History Review*, vol. 34, no. 3 (1981), 454.

103 Veblen Thorstein, *Imperial Germany and the Industrial Revolution* (London: The Macmilan Company), 1915.

104 Original text: "*Das industriell entwickeltere Land zeigt dem minder entwickelten nur das Bild der eignen Zukunft.*" See Karl Marx, *Das Kapital – Kritik der politischen Oekonomie* (Hamburg: Verlag von Otto Meissner. 1867).

105 Although Marx and Engels' *The German Ideology* is not directly related to German Industrialization, critical texts can be found here as well. See Marx, Karl – Engels, Friedrich, *The German Ideology* (New York: Prometheus Books, 1998), 33–34.

106 Gerschenkron, *Economic Backwardness in Historical Perspective – A Book of Essays*, 8.

structure, it is of course neither specific to Germany, nor does it refer to how the obstacles he mentioned were overcome in Germany.

Turkish-German strategic and military relations at the end of the 19th century and at the beginning of the 20th century is a subject with more accessible documents than German Industrialization. In addition to the Turkish and German archives related to Turkish – German relations in that period, the density of American archival documents is also noticeable. The detailed reports received by the United States through its consulates provide valuable information regarding Turkish-German relations at that time. When the global literature is examined, important studies besides archival documents draw attention. The article by Michael Epkenhans,[107] which looks at military and industrial relations from a German perspective, is very valuable. Gregor Schöllingen's work,[108] which provides an effective perspective on Germany's Middle East policy, has important comments and information about Germany's relations with the Ottoman Empire. The work of Gerhard Grüßhaber[109] regarding Turkish-German military relations has an important perspective and details. M. Larcher's famous work *The Turkish War in the Great War*[110] contains important information as a classic that has been translated into Turkish with the unique contributions of Mehmed Nihad. Considering the period in which it was written, the meaning of the work increases even more. Similarly, the book *What I Saw and Experienced in World War I,*[111] which actually contains the memoirs of Erich Lundendoff from the Hindenburg – Ludendorff duo who were called the heroes of Germany since they inflicted great casualties on the Russians on the Eastern Front in the First World War, gives important details about Turkish-German Relations during the First World War. It should not be forgotten that this work is a memoir, and what is written in this work should not be expected to be an objective war narrative. The important point in these memoirs is the view of a nationalist German general in the German army towards the Turkish army and the possibility of reaching the

---

107 Michael Epkenhans, "Military—Industrial Relations in Imperial Germany, 1870–1914", *War in History*, vol. 10, no. 1 (2003).

108 Gregor Schöllgen, *Imperialismus und Gleichgewicht: Deutschland, England und die orientalische Frage 1871–1914* (Münih: Oldenbourg, 1984).

109 Gerhard Grüßhaber, *The 'German Spirit' in the Ottoman and Turkish Army, 1908–1938* (Oldenbourg: De Gruyter, 2018).

110 M. Larcher, *Büyük Harpte Türk Harbi*, cilt 1-2-3, trans. and ed. Mehmet Nihad (İstanbul: Ötüken Neşriyat, 2018).

111 Erich Ludendorff, *Birinci Dünya Savaşı'nda Gördüklerim ve Yaşadıklarım* (İstanbul: Dün Bugün Yarın Yayınları, 2014).

story of the data in the archive documents. On the other hand, there are many works from many authors on the Baghdad Railway. In these works, some unique information on Turkish – German relations as of the period can be found. Sean McMeekin[112] is one of these authors.

There are some important books written at that time on the basic reasons and future of relations between German Empire and Ottoman Empire. Paul Rohrbach's work *Der Deutsche Gedanke in der Welt*[113] written in 1912, Karl von Winterstetten's work *Berlin-Bagdat Neue Ziele Mitteleuropaischer Politik*[114] published in 1913, Ernst Jäckh's work *Deutschland im Orient nach dem Balkankrieg*[115] published in 1913, are leading examples for these books. These books drew big attention as intellectuel texts a that time.

Paul Rohrbach claims that Germany needed the Turks as an ally, that in a scenario without the Turks, the balance of the world would deteriorate in favor of the British, and that all the problems that the British had about the Baghdad Railway were due to the British policy of establishing a safe area that would connect Egypt and India. Rohrbach states that the risk of Britain attacking Germany could be balanced with the threat of Turks attacking the areas under British protection in the east, and therefore he sees the Turks as an indispensable ally for Germany.[116] Rohrbach states that Germany should not have had a thought and action such as occupying land, and that the Germans should have pursued an economic and cultural influence policy by spreading to the world with their education, thoughts, culture and industry.[117] Considering that he was educated in the Humboldt model in Berlin, the reason for these thoughts can be understood.

---

112 Sean McMeekin, *Berlin – Bağdat Demiryolu*, trans. Azize F. Çakır (İstanbul: Picus Yayınları, 2012).

113 Paul Rohrbach, *Der Deutsche Gedanke in der Welt* (Leipzig: Karl Robert Langewiesche, 1912).

114 This work was published in 1914 as *Avrupa'i Vusta Siyasetinde Yeni Hedefler BERLİN – BAĞDAT*, and later simplified as *Berlin Bağdat – Alman Yayılmacılığı ve Osmanlı Politikaları*. See Karl von Winterstetten, *Berlin Bağdat – Alman Yayılmacılığı ve Osmanlı Politikaları*, ed. Faruk Yılmaz (İstanbul: İz Yayıncılık, 2011).

115 This work was published in Turkish by Yeditepe Yayınları in September 2021 under the name of *Balkan Harbinden Sonra Şarkta Almanya*· See Ernst Jäckh, *Balkan Harbinden Sonra Şarkta Almanya* (İstanbul: Yeditepe Yayınları, 2021).

116 Rohrbach, *Der deutsche Gedanke in der Welt,* 156–160.

117 Rohrbach, *Der deutsche Gedanke in der Welt, 6.*

Similarly, Karl von Winterstetten in his Berlin-Baghdad book, emphasizes that Germany needed the Ottoman Empire as a military power by calculating the corps that the alliances had.[118] While Winterstetten sees the Balkan Union as an action that brought the end of the Ottoman Empire, he harshly criticizes Germany's failure to support the Ottomans. He argues that with the Balkan Union, Germany was surrounded and when a European war broke out, Germany would have to attack all four sides. Moreover, he fiercely argues that the Balkan Union closed Germany's southern gate. If the food lines were closed the nation would starve. Moreover, the argues that the military power was sufficient to a certain extent. Also, Rohrbach argues that the territorial integrity of the Ottoman Empire in the Balkans should have been preserved. Rohrbach refers to the balance that the Ottoman Empire established in the Balkans, and says that even threatening the Ottoman Empire was a valid reason for Germany to declare war. However, Ernst Jäckh differs on this point. Ernst Jäckh, like Rohrbach and Winterstetten, sees the Turkish-German alliance as a long-term commercial and strategic partnership, however he has different opinions about the Balkans. Ernst Jäckh interprets Germany's silence as a strategic success while the Ottoman Empire lost lands in the Balkans. Jäckh argues that the Balkans were an out-of-control burden for the Ottoman Empire. Claiming that these lands exposed the Ottomans to many threats, he argues that the Ottoman Empire's focus on Asian lands was better both in terms of defense and efficiency.[119]

On the subject of colonization, Winterstetten is a fierce defender of the gathering of hundreds of thousands of German citizens, who were not sure where to migrate every year, in Anatolia. However, he imagines this within a large German-Austrian-Turkish Empire with ports like Hamburg and Istanbul and an uninterrupted border from the Elbe to the Euphrates and Tigris.[120] Winterstetten argues that the British put a permanent barrier in front of this project with the Balkan Union. For this reason, he harshly criticizes that the Germans did not support the Ottoman Empire in the Balkan War. Winterstetten sees Berlin-Baghdad as a continuous line of unity.[121] Ernst Jäckh and Rohrbach, on the other hand, do not favor the idea of colonization in Anatolia due to political, cultural and climatic conflicts. Jäckh, on the contrary, argues that the population should

118 Winterstetten, *Berlin-Bağdat*, 43.

119 Jäckh, *Balkan Harbinden Sonra Şarkta Almanya*, 74–75.

120 This view was first mentioned by an Englishman, Sir Hamilton Johnston, and was defended by both Ernst Jäckh and Winterstetten by quoting. See Jäckh, *Balkan Harbinden Sonra Şarkta Almanya*, 19.

121 Winterstetten, *Berlin-Bağdat*, 82–84.

be concentrated in a single geography with definite borders. According to Jäckh, Germany derived its strength from the coexistence of its population, which formed a solid line of defense on its borders. Jäckh argues that this created both a military and economic strength for Germany, and that the provinces in eastern Prussia could be improved agriculturally so that the surplus population could be brought there.[122] According to Jäckh, a dispersed population only does harm to the homeland.[123]

The views of left-wing writers on the reasons for Turkish-German relations are much harsher and one-sided. In Rosa Luxemburg's work *Die Krise der Sozialdemokratie,*[124] which she wrote in 1916 while the First World War was still going on, it is possible to come across opinions on the reasons for Turkish-German relations and claims that the Germans approached the Ottoman Empire with the aim of colonization. The work written by Lothar Rathmann and published in 1962 with the name *Berlin – Bagdad: Die Imperialistische Nahostpolitik Des Kaiserlichen Deutschland,* later translated in Turkish with the name *Alman Emperyalizminin Türkiye'ye Girişi,*[125] has claims that support

---

122 There had been a lot of voice in Germany about colonization. As Kazım Karabekir reported, German Anatolian Committee spokesman Hugo Grate stated that they were in favor of rescuing the Germans in Russia and relocating them to AnatoliaImhoff Pasha, who rose to the rank of lieutenant general in the Ottoman army and later took the title of Pasha, also stated at a conference in Berlin in 1913 that Anatolia could host 60–70 million people, but that there were only 15 million people at the moment and only 3 % of the land was used. He stated that Anatolia was a place suitable for full colonization. See Kazım Karabekir, *Tarih Boyunca Türk-Alman İlişkileri* (İstanbul: Truva Yayınları, 2021), 112. Although various words had been said about colonization, it is a fact that there was neither a demand nor an action regarding colonization. German historians also know that the Ottomans directly rejected the colonization offers. Even the British engineer Sir Wilcock's offer to bring workers from Egypt and India for the irrigation works to be done in Iraq was strongly rejected by the Ottoman Empire. The Ottoman Empire considered that foreigners, who were dependent only on their consulates due to the capitulations in force, were neither subject to the Ottoman courts nor had tax obligations. For this reason, Ottoman Empire predicted that the foreigners living collectively in the Ottoman lands were equivalent to a foreign state established in the Ottoman lands. This fact was also known to the Germans. See Jäckh, *Balkan Harbinden Sonra Şarkta Almanya*, 36.

123 Jäckh, *Balkan Harbinden Sonra Şarkta Almanya*, 25.

124 Rosa Luxemburg, *Die Krise der Sozial Demokratie* (Grafrath: Boer Verlag, 2019).

125 Lothar Rathmann, *Alman Emperyalizminin Türkiye'ye Girişi* (İstanbul: Gözlem Yayınları, 1976).

those of Rosa Luxemburg about the basic causes of Turkish-German relations. Another work defending the colonization argument defended by left-wingers is Stefanos Yerasimos's *Azgelişmişlik Sürecinde Türkiye*.

Stefanos Yerasimos claims that Germany emerged as a new great power during the Ottoman-Russian War. According to Yerasimos, Germany was the first state that aimed to directly exploit and colonize the Ottoman Empire.[126] This is the opinion of other left-wing writers in general. For example, Lothar Rathmann places the responsibility of Germany's relations with Turkey entirely on Germany and claims that Germany developed these relations to establish world domination, and that with this strategic colonial model, it was aimed to go first to Egypt and then to India. According to Rathmann, the Ottoman Empire; In addition to being rich in raw materials such as copper, chrome and oil, it had interesting aspects such as being away from technology, having a large peasant population, and allowing value-added products to be sold with very high profitability. According to Rathmann, Germany also tried to colonize the Ottoman Empire for the sake of these interests. Thus, as Rathmann describes Anatolia as the first target of German imperialism, he interprets the Ottoman Empire as a state riveted to Germany by loans and enslaved to Germany by railroads and arms trade.[127] Lenin, Rosa Luxemburg and Jerussalimski were of similar views. While emphasizing that capital is the main means of exploitation, like Karl Marx, Lenin argues that the Ottoman Empire was exploited by capital.[128] Soviet historian Arkadij S. Jerussalimski similarly claims that Germany's financial aid to the Ottoman Empire was a capital export for the purpose of colonization, and in this way the colonial intentions of the German bourgeoisie were tried to be concealed. According to Jerussalimski, the interests of German capital owners in the Ottoman Empire were also supported by the government, and the Kaiser directly mediated the interests of these capital owners.[129] Rosa Luxemburg also describes the Ottoman Empire as a rotten structure and claims that the Germans built railways and sold weapons with the promise of reviving the Ottoman Empire, that this was colonization, not revival.[130]

126 Stefanos Yerasimos, *Azgelişmişlik Sürecinde Türkiye 2 – Tanzimattan I. Dünya Savaşı'na* (İstanbul: Gözlem Yayınları, 1975), 907.

127 Rathmann, *Alman Emperyalizminin Türkiye'ye Girişi*, 69–71.

128 Rathmann, *Alman Emperyalizminin Türkiye'ye Girişi*, 99.

129 Rathmann, *Alman Emperyalizminin Türkiye'ye Girişi*, 52,61.

130 The original version of Luxemburg's critique is as follows:: *Es war auch eine echtpreußische Idee, daß es lediglich strategischer Eisenbahnen zur raschen Mobilisation und schneidiger Militä-rinstrukteure bedürfe, um eine so morsche Baracke wie den*

Different perspectives from the global perspective, which have been given with various examples above, emphasize the importance of this study more. There are no rational inferences in most of the works that include views on Turkish – German relations. The texts mostly consist of ideas and the claims are not supported by concrete data. This study differs from others in these areas as well. One of the most original aspects of this study is that it aims to provide the reader with the opportunity to make rational inferences.

1.3. Turkish Literature on German Industrialization and Turkish-German Relations

It is very difficult to find information about the stages of German Industrialization in Turkish literature.[131] Moreover, the number of sources studying and researching Germany before the First World War is also quite limited. Here, a work that stands out because of its title is Yunus Kobal's *Birinci Dünya Savaşı Öncesinde Almanya.*[132] Although Yunus Kobal has examined the establishment, administrative structure, basic policies and social structure of the German Empire in general terms in this study, he presented a three-page information under the title "Tarım Devletinden Sanayi Devletine" in the first sub-heading with item A of the second part. Although the Kobal's study does not seek answers to the basic questions of German Industrialization, and does not go beyond the selection of three pages of information with a limited source, it draws attention as one of the few works containing the phrase German Industrialization. However, it would be useful to review some of the information in Kobal's work. Although the article titled "Almanya'da 1850 Sonrası Endüstrileşme Sürecinde Bankaların Rolü"[133] by an economist, Ayda Polat, does not deal with how the German industrialization took place and does not study the banking models in the

türkischen Staat lebensfähig zu machen (It was a perfectly Prussian idea that all that was needed for mobilization was strategic railways, and that all that was needed to bring a rotten structure like the Turkish State to life was daring military instructors.). See Rosa Luxemburg, *Die Krise der Sozial Demokratie* (Grafrath: Boer Verlag, 2019), 48.

131 The reason for using this expression is the possibility that there is a work that may be missed, even though any publications on German Industrialization in the literature searches made could not find.

132 Yunus Kobal, *Birinci Dünya Savaşı Öncesinde Almanya* (Ankara: Gece Kitaplığı Yayınları, 2015) .

133 Ayda Polat, "Almanya'da 1850 Sonrası Endüstrileşme Sürecinde Bankaların Rolü", *Dumlupınar Üniversitesi Sosyal Bilimler Dergisi,* no 51, 148–164 (Jan 2017).

German Banking system separately, it is noteworthy since it refers to the effects of the universal banking model on German Industrialization. İlber Ortaylı's study *Osmanlı İmparatorluğu'nda Alman Nüfuzu*[134] is an important work as it mentions the advantages that German Industrialization brought to Germany and it contains important information in terms of Turkish – German military relations. Murat Belge's book *Militarist Modernleşme – Almanya, Japonya ve Türkiye*[135] is noteworthy in that it contains qualified summary information about Germany and even Prussia before the First World War. Orhan Koloğlu's work *Prusya'dan Enverland'a ve Günümüze – Türk Alman Tarihi*[136] takes the reader to a short historical journey from the pre-German period to the present and contains valuable visuals and important quotations from western newspapers. The fact that Koloğlu's work deals with a general field of study in a fairly large period of time did not allow it to focus on any subject in detail, so it should not be expected to give a detailed answer to any subject. On the other hand, Burak Samih Gülsoy's article "İngiltere ile Almanya Arasındaki Donanma Rekabeti ve Büyük Güç Olma Paradoksu",[137] prepared by giving rational information about the British and German navies, is remarkable in that it draws attention to an important and original issue.

Sefâretnâmes have the feature of mirroring the life of centuries ago, as they convey the period in the first person. In this respect, the Vienna (1757) and Berlin (1763) Sefâretnâmes[138] of Ahmed Resmi Efendi have an important place. Similarly, Sadullah Pasha's letters and telegrams are very valuable in that they shed light on the loneliness of the Ottoman Empire as of the period and reflect the Ottoman Empire's perspectives on Germany and Germany's on the Ottoman Empire. In this respect, Ali Akyıldız's work *Sürgün Sefir Sadullah Paşa*[139] is remarkable both in terms of conveying Sadullah Pasha's writings and

---

134 İlber Ortaylı, *Osmanlı İmparatorluğu'nda Alman Nüfuzu* (İstanbul: İletişim Yayınları, 2004), 23.

135 Murat Belge, *Militarist Modernleşme – Almanya, Japonya ve Türkiye* (İstanbul: İletişim Yayınları, 3. Baskı, 2014).

136 Orhan Koloğlu, *Prusya'dan Enverland'a ve Günümüze Türk-Alman Tarihi* (İstanbul: Tarihçi Yayınevi, 2018).

137 Burak Samih Gülboy, "İngiltere ile Almanya Arasındaki Donanma Rekabeti ve Büyük Güç Olma Paradoksu", *100. Yılında Birinci Dünya Savaşı ve Mirası,* ed. Halil Çetin vd. (Çanakkale: Çanakkale Valiliği, 2015).

138 Ahmed Resmi Efendi, *Ahmed Resmi Efendi'nin Viyana ve Berlin Sefaretnameleri* (İstanbul: Tercüman 1001 Eser, 1980).

139 Ali Akyıldız, *Sürgün Sefir Sadullah Paşa* (İstanbul: Türkiye İş Bankası Kültür Yayınları, 2011).

giving detailed coverage to the dynamics of the period and Sadullah Pasha's life. Memories are also very valuable because they were transferred from the first person at the time they were lived. In this respect, Cemal Pasha's memoirs *Anılarım (1913–1922)*[140] and Talat Pasha's memoirs *Talat Paşa'nın Hatıraları*[141] contain very valuable information as a primary source.

There are important and valuable texts both published and unpublished on the subject of Turkish-German strategic and military relations. It is obvious that Prime Ministry Ottoman Archives is a very large resource. The study of Necla Geyikdağı[142] contains important information in order to understand the financial situation of the Ottoman Empire in that period of time and the processes of the transfer of foreign capital to the Ottoman Empire. Similarly, Rifat Önsoy's work[143] in which he examines Turkish-German economic relations between 1871 and 1914 is a work that has important contributions to the literature and contains valuable data about Turkish-German economic relations as of the period he examined.[144] Some information about the economic situation of the Ottoman Empire can be accessed in Parvus Efendi's[145] works titled *Türkiye'nin Mali Tutsaklığı*[146] and *Cihan Harbine Doğru*

140 Cemal Paşa, *Anılarım (1913–1922)*, ed. Fahri Parin (İstanbul: Paraf Yayınları, 2010).

141 Talat Paşa, *Talat Paşa'nın Hatıraları*, ed. Hüseyin Cahit Yalçın (İstanbul: Cumhuriyet Gazetesi Yayınları, 1998).

142 Necla V. Geyikdağı, *Osmanlı Devleti'nde Yabancı Sermaye 1854–1914* (İstanbul: Hil Yayınları, 2008).

143 Rifat Önsoy, *Türk-Alman İktisadi Münasebetleri (1871–1914)* (İstanbul: Enderun Yayınları, 1982).

144 This work has deficiencies in Turkish-German military relations in that it does not coincide with a period when the Krupp archives were opened.

145 He is a famous socialist, known in Europe as "Alexander Helpland". He was born in Russia, received a doctorate in Germany, then participated in the 1905 Russian Revolution in line with the ideas he defended and was exiled to Siberia. After escaping from exile, he went to Germany and Switzerland, where he joined the socialists. He came to Turkey in 1910 and wrote under the pseudonym Parvus for publications such as Tanin, Bilgi and Türk Yurdu. See Mehmet Eröz, "Parvus'un Türkiye Hakkındaki Yazıları", *İstanbul Üniversitesi İktisat Fakültesi Mecmuası*, c. 43 (1917), 347–348. Parvus Efendi was a socialist who got rich by trading his connections in Turkey. On the other hand, he was a revolutionary who thought and advocated that a socialist revolution that would radically change the order in Russian lands could only be realized with a great world war in Europe. Therefore, his articles about Turkey should be approached with suspicion. In this study, only the economic and rational data of Parvus Efendi's works were used.

146 Parvus Efendi, *Türkiye'nin Mali Tutsaklığı* (İstanbul: May Yayınları, 1977).

Türkiye.[147] Seyfi Kurtbek's book *Harp ve Ekonomi,*[148] published in 1942, is a significant source since it was published during the most heated period of the Second World War. Although the book focuses on the state-level responsibility of states' preparation for war and the economic and subsistence measures to be taken in this regard, there are brief and valuable touches on Germany's economic and subsistence situation before and during the First World War. Kazım Karabekir's views on Turkish-German relations[149] are very valuable due to the period they were written down. Naci Yorulmaz's work,[150] which sheds light on the arms trade between the Ottoman Empire and Germany during the reign of Abdulhamid II, and Fahri Türk's work[151] in the same field are also works that contain important information about the arms trade, especially at the end of the 19th century. Jehuda L. Wallach's study[152] about the military delegations which came to Ottoman army is one of the main sources in this field. Ersoy Zengin's study,[153] which sheds light on the production of national defence industry products before the First World War, is a carefully prepared study with valuable information. Similarly, Fatih Tetik's *Sultanın Silahları – II. Abdülhamid Dönemi Savunma Sanayii ve Silah Teknolojisi*[154] is a remarkable work that has been carefully prepared based on archival documents. Mustafa Gencer's work, *Jöntürk Modernizmi ve Alman Ruhu,*[155] also has very important information on education and cultural transfer. Vahdettin Engin's work *II. Abdülhamid ve Dış Politika,*[156] which contains many important archive documents, is important in terms of gaining a vision about the foreign policy attitude of Abdulhamid II and positioning Germany on the side of "smooth and stable relations". There are

---

147 Parvus Efendi, *Cihan Harbine Doğru Türkiye* (İstanbul: Ayrıntı Yayınları, 2013).

148 Seyfi Kurtbek, *Harp ve Ekonomi* (İstanbul: İnsel Kitabevi, 1942).

149 Kazım Karabekir, *Tarih Boyunca Türk-Alman İlişkileri* (İstanbul: Truva Yayınları, 2021),

150 Naci Yorulmaz, *Arming the Sultan* (New York: I.B. Tauris, 2014).

151 Fahri Türk, *Türkiye ile Almanya Arasındaki Silah Ticareti 1871–1914* (İstanbul: IQ Kültür Sanat Yayıncılık, 2012)

152 Jehuda L. Wallach, *Bir Askeri Yardımın Anatomisi – Türkiye'de Prusya-Alman Askeri Heyetleri 1835–1919*, trans. Em. Tuğgeneral Fahri Çeliker (Ankara: Gnkur. Askeri Tarih ve Stratejik Etüt Bşk. Yayınları, 1985).

153 Ersoy Zengin, *Osmanlı Devleti'nde Harp Sanayii* (İstanbul: Kitabevi Yayınları, 2020).

154 Fatih Tetik, *Sultanın Silahları – II. Abdülhamid Dönemi Savunma Sanayii ve Silah Teknolojisi* (İstanbul: Dergah Yayınları, 2018).

155 Mustafa Gencer, *Jöntürk Modernizmi ve Alman Ruhu – 1908–1918 Dönemi Türk-Alman İlişkileri ve Eğitim* (İstanbul: İletişim Yayınları, 3. Baskı, 2015).

156 Vahdettin Engin, *II. Abdülhamid ve Dış Politika* (İstanbul: Yeditepe Yayınevi, 2017).

opinions and texts open to interpretation in Burhan Oğuz's works on Turkish-German relations.[157] The industrial censuses of 1913 and 1915[158] are also a very important source in order to understand the general situation of the Ottoman industry on the eve of the First World War and in its first years. However it does not contain data about the subjects like war industry and mining; therefore these censuses alone may not be sufficient to make inferences on some issues. *Savaşanların Gözüyle Türk-Alman İttifakı*[159] prepared by Necmettin Alkan and Eyyub Şimşek is a current and valuable study in terms of compiling first-hand views. Similarly, Mustafa Çolak's works *Enver Pasha*[160] and *Talat Pasha*[161] also contain important information about the Turkish-German relations during the First World War and just before. Mustafa Aksakal's *Harb-i Umumi Eşiğinde – Osmanlı Devleti Son Savaşına Nasıl Girdi?*[162] is a work that was prepared using German archive documents and contains up-to-date and valuable information about the Ottoman Empire's entry into the First World War. Ali Sedar Mete's current work *Türk Mavzeri*[163] is a remarkable work since it covers an important deficiency in Turkish literature.

There are also valuable thesis on Turkish-German military, political and economic relations. Halit Arslan's master's thesis titled *Sultan II. Abdülhamid Devri Osmanlı Ordusunda Alman Etkisi*[164] is noteworthy since it refers to the activities of German delegations.[165] Due to its title, Mahmut Özdil's master's thesis *İttihat ve Terraki Dönemi Osmanlı – Almanya Siyasi İlişkileri (1908–1918)*[166]

---

157 Burhan Oğuz, Faşizm, *Alman Kimliği Türkiye ile İlişkiler* (İstanbul: Anadolu Aydınlanma Vakfı, 2008); Burhan Oğuz, *Yüzyıllar Boyunca Alman Gerçeği ve Türkler* (İstanbul: Anadolu Aydınlanma Vakfı, 2007).

158 *Osmanlı Sanayii 1913–1915 Yılları Sanayi İstatistiki*, Tarihi İstatistikler Dizisi vol 4 (ed. A. Gündüz Ökçün), Ankara: TC. Başbakanlık Devlet İstatistik Enstitüsü, 1997.

159 Necmettin Alkan et al. (ed.), *Savaşanların Gözüyle Türk-Alman İttifakı* (İstanbul: Kronik Kitap, 2018).

160 Mustafa Çolak, *Komitenin Kahramanı: Enver Paşa* (İstanbul: Yeditepe Yayınevi, 2019).

161 Mustafa Çolak, *Komitenin Kahramanı: Talat Paşa* (İstanbul: Yeditepe Yayınevi, 2020)

162 Mustafa Aksakal, *Harb-i Umumi Eşiğinde – Osmanlı Devleti Son Savaşına Nasıl Girdi?* (İstanbul: İstanbul Bilgi Üniversitesi Yayınları, 2018).

163 Ali Serdar Mete, *Türk Mavzeri* (İstanbul: Doğu Kütüphanesi, 2022).

164 Halit Arslan, II. *Abdülhamid Devri Osmanlı Ordusunda Alman Etkisi* (Ankara: Gazi Üniversitesi, Sosyal Bilimler Enstitüsü, Yüksek Lisans Tezi, 2012).

165 The thesis is highly dependent on Turkish literature. For this reason, it has stayed away from cross-research and presenting different perspectives to the reader.

166 Mahmut Özdil, *İttihat ve Terraki Dönemi Osmanlı – Almanya Siyasi İlişkileri (1908–1918)* (İstanbul: Yeni Yüzyıl Üniversitesi, Sosyal Bilimler Enstitüsü, Yüksek Lisans Tezi, 2017).

also stands out, however since it is a short text written with approximately 20 sources, all in Turkish, it is far from offering a new perspective on such an important title. Similarly, Bilge Karbi's master's thesis *Alman Kaynaklarına Göre Osmanlı İktisadı'nda Alman Etkisi (1908–1914)*[167] is remarkable since it mostly uses German sources; however, the amount of quantitative data it provides is open to debate. Cevat Şimşek's master's study titled *Almanya İmparatoru II. Wilhelm'in Osmanlı Devlet'ini Ziyaretleri*, which deals with the Ottoman visits of Kaiser Wilhelm II, using the Ottoman archive, also has satisfactory information about these visits.[168] The adequacy of the relevant part of the study in terms of the industry-focused commercial and political results of the visits is open to debate, but considering the fact that the main subject of the study is the visits, it is natural not to expect a text that includes comprehensive and cross-sectional views on the commercial and political results of the visits. Özge Erdölek Kozal's doctoral thesis *Türkiye'de Sanayileşmenin 200 Yıllık Tarihi: Süreklilikler ve Dönüşümler*[169] is also an interesting study that offers conceptual answers to why the Ottoman Empire could not undergo an Industrial Revolution in the axis of capital accumulation. Although Hayati Aktaş's doctoral thesis *Türk-Alman Askeri İlişkileri (1913–1918),*[170] which he completed in 1994, does not examine German Industrialization or the effect of German Industrialization on Turkish-German military relations, it examines in detail the Turkish-German military alliance and military activities before and during the First World War. Similarly, Salih Kış's work, *Osmanlı Ordusunda Alman Ekolü Von der Goltz Paşa (1883–1895),*[171] which was prepared with a detailed archival study, draws attention. Mehmet İhsan Cantermir's doctoral thesis *Osmanlı – Prusya Münasebetleri (1808–1871) (A.Dvn.Dve. D. 073/2 Numaralı Prusya Ahkâm Defteri Işığında)*[172] is noteworthy

---

167 Bilge Karbi, *Alman Kaynaklarına Göre Osmanlı İktisadı'nda Alman Etkisi (1908–1914)* (Ankara: Ankara Üniversitesi, Sosyal Bilimler Enstitüsü, Yüksek Lisans Tezi, 2011).

168 Cevat Şimşek, *Almanya İmparatoru II. Wilhelm'in Osmanlı Devlet'ini Ziyaretleri* (Ankara: Gazi Üniversitesi, Sosyal Bilimler Enstitüsü, Yüksek Lisans Tezi, 2019).

169 Özge Erdölek Kozal, *Türkiye'de Sanayileşmenin 200 Yıllık Tarihi: Süreklilikler ve Dönüşümler* (İzmir: Ege Üniversitesi, Sosyal Bilimler Enstitüsü, Doktora Tezi, 2019).

170 Hayati Aktaş, *Türk-Alman Askeri İlişkileri (1913–1918)* (Konya: Selçuk Üniversitesi, Sosyal Bilimler Enstitüsü, Doktora Tezi, 1994).

171 Salih Kış, *Osmanlı Ordusunda Alman Ekolü Von der Goltz Paşa (1883–1895)* (Konya: Palet Yayınları, 2017).

172 Mehmet İhsan Cantemir, *Osmanlı – Prusya Münasebetleri (1808–1871) (A.Dvn.Dve. D. 073/2 Numaralı Prusya Ahkâm Defteri Işığında)* (Balıkesir: Balıkesir Üniversitesi, Sosyal Bilimler Enstitüsü, Doktora Tezi, 2019).

since it contains some information on the commercial agreements between Prussia and the Ottoman Empire and the commercial relations of the Prussian merchants in the Ottoman Empire on a certain level. The article "Osmanlı-Alman Ticari İlişkilerinin Niteliksel Analizi: 1890 Ticaret Anlaşmasının Öncesi ve Sonrası",[173] written together by Önder Deniz and Hüseyin Vehbi İmamoğlu, is remarkable in that it refers to the Zollverein and contains a meaningful summary about Turkish-German relations, even though it is quite short.

Many important written texts not mentioned here have made important contributions to certain areas covered by the study subject of this study, but the fact that the focus of the relevant studies is not the German Industrialization and/or the military and strategic effects of German Industrialization is another fact that reveals the originality of this study.

173 Since the article uses almost entirely Turkish sources, apart from a few English sources, its adequacy in containing a diversity of views on Turkish-German relations can be discussed. Önder Deniz – Hüseyin Vehbi İmamoğlu, "Osmanlı-Alman Ticari İlişkilerinin Niteliksel Analizi: 1890 Ticaret Anlaşmasının Öncesi ve Sonrası", *International Journal of Social Science*, no. 30 (2014).

Chapter 1 Fundamentals of German Industrialization

1.1. Agrarian Reforms and the Developments in German Agriculture

Until the middle of the 19th century most of the states' main source of livelihood was agriculture, and most of the active working population was agricultural workers. This situation was valid for Germany, too. It is estimated that in 1800, 80 % of the German population was engaged in agriculture.[1] This was actually an advantage for Germany. The development of agriculture paved the way for German Industrialization and agriculture went hand in hand with industrialization.

In the 18th century, the population of Germany increased. Prussia's population, which was 2,240,000 in 1740,[2] reached 10,340,031 in 1816.[3] When the results of the regional concentration triggered in accordance with the mercantilist economic policies were added to this situation, the concentration in the important cities increased even more. Berlin's population alone grew from around 68,000 to over 100,000 in just 14 years, between 1740 and 1754.[4] As a result of population growth, the need for livestock and agriculture increased. The necessity of cultivating German lands with higher caloric and more efficient crops became more apparent with the increase in population. Agrarian reforms, which the French Revolution also affected especially in matters such as land ownership,[5] were born out of a number of needs. The fact that Saxony, deprived of arable land, had the strongest agricultural systems among all German states[6]

1 Borchardt, *The Industrial Revolution in Germany 1700–1914*, 17.

2 George W Kyte, "Frederick the Great and the Development of the Prussian Army", *The Historian*, vol. 5, no. 1, Wiley (1942), 24.

3 Bernard Hebeler, "Statistics of Prussia", *Journal of the Statistical Society of London*, vol. 10, no. 2 (1847), 157.

4 Jürgen Reuleke, "Population Growth and Urbanization in Germany in the 19th Century", *Urbanism Past & Present*, no. 4 (1977), 21–22.

5 Clapham, *The Economic Development of France and Germany 1815–1914*, 29.

6 Pfister, "Agricultural development during early industrialization in alow-wage economy: Saxony, c. 1790–1830", 9.

between 1750 and 1870, and that the first agricultural experiment station was established in Saxony as of 1851[7] was a result of the need.

In the 18th century, the German lands were introduced to clover, lucerne, potatoes, beets, hops and tobacco. With the increase in diversity, the fallow lands decreased, and with the increase in the need, cattle rearing in closed areas in winter environments became widespread, the quality of farm animals increased significantly, swamps and heathlands were reclaimed.[8] The expansion of arable land and increasing productivity throughout the German geography developed agriculture, and the development of agriculture paved the way for economic prosperity. Local production began to become self-sufficient. When the peasant paid the feudal tax and rent, he could have a small amount of cash that he could freely spend with the money he made from the produce he sold.[9] The increase in productivity in agriculture provided relief for the economy. The impact of the transformation of an agrarian economy was, as expected, multifaceted. For this reason, agrarian reforms can be defined as a breaking point with great effects on the events that followed. Some key features of the reforms deserve emphasis. These are emancipation of serfs, redefinition of private property rights, and improvements in cultivation.

Agrarian reforms triggered the restructuring of the rural socioeconomic order. Of course, it is an undeniable fact that these reforms also contained significant risks. In particular, the turmoil that would occur between economic and social classes and various problems that could be experienced in the transition process were inevitable risks. Being ready to face these risks was undoubtedly the prerequisite for realizing these reforms, and these reforms were the preconditions for the transition to a modern industrial society. Such reforms, with both winners and losers, could only be enforced by a strong authority. The first step of this risky reform process in Prussia was taken with the law dated October 9, 1807, Silesia made its step in 1809, Pomerania, Ostmark and Neumark joined the states which legislated the reforms. The reform law of October 9, 1807, which was first implemented in Prussia, paved the way for many important changes. The most important of these changes was the emancipation of serfs. This law removed land ownership from the social class to which it belonged, and

7 Mark Russel Finlay, *Science, practice and politics: German agricultural experiment stations in the nineteenth century* (Iowa: Iowa State University, History of Technology and Science, Doctoral Thesis, 1992), 13.

8 Henderson, *The Industrial Revolution on the Continent*, 8.

9 Borchardt, *The Industrial Revolution in Germany 1700–1914*, 17.

reduced inherited property to the status of individual property, and increased productivity in cultivating the land by paving the way for peasants to own land.[10] The peasantry, which was handed down from generation to generation as a legacy,[11] ceased to be a necessity, and the class label attached to individuals gave way to preference. Individual rights over land and labor probably encouraged more efficient and intensive use of these resources, and peasants began to receive a greater return on their labor. Landowners, who had to hire more workers, started to employ workers with cost awareness. These changes had significant effects on the increase of labor and productivity in agriculture. Between 1816 and 1865, the population in Prussia increased by 59 %, while agricultural productivity increased by 135 %.[12]

The positive aspects of agricultural reforms were not perceived by everyone and the laws were not adopted as they were enacted. The rich also used their influence to put pressure on the government, and debates arose over the principle of full compensation for property rights. The reforms could not be extended until the revolutions of 1848–49. It took until 1832 for other states to take the first steps or similar steps taken by Prussia.[13] With the "Commutation Law", which came into force on March 2, 1850, the peasants were given complete legal emancipation and the same law also ensured the establishment of a land bank that would provide the necessary financing for the peasants to buy their holdings. This development was very important because it put an end to compensations paid to lords. This transformed Prussia from a manor-based rural society into a capitalist-enterprise state where land could be freely bought and sold. The foundations of the capitalist economy were laid in this way and the contribution

10 Peasants were compelled to pay compensation to the landowners for their losses. Villagers were able to pay their compensation in service, money, or something equivalent (for example, the harvest). See Tilly-Pierenkemper, *The German Economy During the Nineteenth Century*, 26.

11 Before the law on the emancipation of serfs, there were hardly any free peasants, especially in eastern Germany. The existing ones migrated to the cities. Peasants could have the exception of freedom only if they belonged to some exceptional class. An example of these classes was the *Cölmer*. Individuals belonging to this class were descendants of peasant farmers who were brought and settled in the region by the Teutonic Knights. See Guy Stanton Ford, "The Prussian Peasantry Before 1807", *The American Historical Review*, vol. 24, no. 3 (1919), 359.

12 Steinberg, *Bismarck*, 95.

13 Finlay, *Science, practice and politics: German agricultural experiment stations in the nineteenth century*, 26.

of agriculture to capital formation, which is an indispensable requirement for industrialization, was paved.[14]

Land reform brought more capitalist systems of production to landowners. In this way, the landowners were able to increase the efficiency of cultivating the land by employing the workers for wages.[15] This could also be interpreted as the nominal emancipation of rural poor agricultural workers, since they were transformed into a modern, landless working class rather than truly liberated.[16]

Looking at the state of agriculture in German lands until the middle of the 19th century, some important details stand out. Between 1816 and 1852, corn was planted on meadows and pastures that were considered unproductive in Prussia, and the cultivated area increased by more than 30 %. The harvest rate increase for hectrare from 1800 to 1848–1852 was %19 for wheat, %19 for of rye, %38 for barley and %60 for oats. The rate of fallow land fell, and the grain cultivated area in Prussia increased from 7.3 million hectares to 12.46 million hectares between 1815 and 1849. However, the increase in soil fertility were not as radical as the increase in cultivated area. The increase in productivity was relatively small until the 1850s.[17] Germany's wheat-led grain exports to Britain was 25,405 tons between 1831 and 1835, it increased to 163,673 tons per year between 1856 and 1860.[18]

One of the most important developments in German agriculture in the middle of the 19th century was the introduction of high-calorie root vegetables into agriculture. At a time when the average German citizen was fed lower than European standards, high-calorie foods added to agriculture provided great advantages in terms of public health, coping with diseases and effective workforce. Root vegetables accounted for 3 % of crops in Prussia in 1800, while

---

14 Tilly – Pierenkemper, *The German Economy During the Nineteenth Century*, 27–28.

15 Finlay, *Science, practice and politics: German agricultural experiment stations in the nineteenth century*, 72.

16 Christoph Dipper, *Die Bauernbefreiuna in Deutschland. 1790–1850* (Stuttgart: Kohlhammer, 1980), 9–23.

17 Productivity in agriculture had increased even more since the middle of the 19th century. Related products had an average increase of 2 % since the 1850s, and achieved an average of 100 % increase in the next 50 years. See Tilly – Pierenkemper, *The German Economy During the Nineteenth Century*, 76–77.

18 Kopsidis – Wolf, "Agricultural Productivity Across Prussia During the Industrial Revolution: A Thünen Perspective", 639.

this proportion increased to 24 % 40 years later.[19] Despite the increase in the population in Germany in the first half of the 19th century, these root vegetables were the factor that enabled the citizens to meet their basic food needs relatively. Root vegetables such as potatoes and sugar beets[20] were also quite effective in balancing the food supply. These root vegetables also filled the supply shortage caused by the harvest fluctuations that Germany faced from time to time, especially in corn. The production of animal products increased faster than vegetables after 1815. An important reason for this was that the period was a war-free period. There was always the potential for animal husbandry in Germany, but previous wars had not allowed this potential to be used.[21]

1.2. The Zollverein and the Unifying Strategies of Prussia

There is a broad misconception that traces of German Industrialization should be sought since the establishment of the German Empire in 1871. The triggers for German Industrialization began to occur before 1871, as the Zollverein was one of the most important.

The fragmented political structure of Germany after the Congress of Vienna not only prevented the formation of an economic union, but also enabled each state to act on behalf of its own economy, out of the consciousness of national benefit. The Hanseatic cities and other coastal states placed more importance on their trade with Britain than their trade with the states in the German Confederation. Baden similarly pointed its expectations towards Switzerland

19 This increase continued at an accelerated pace. By 1913, potatoes occupied 7 % of all agricultural land in Germany. See. Tilly - Pierenkemper, *The German Economy During the Nineteenth Century*, 78.

20 Sugar had become one of Germany's main export articles. In 1907, Germany became the world's largest sugar producer, accounting for 22 % of global production. See Tilly - Pierenkemper, *The German Economy During the Nineteenth Century*, 84.

21 For example, Prussia lost one-third of the animals in its stock during the war. As war became a part of life, livestock also became an industry serving the military, horned cattle were used for transportation and as capital goods. Therefore, until the middle of the century, meat supply could not be better than before 1800 and the amount of meat consumed by an average German citizen was below the European standards of 26 kg at that time. The food crisis of 1855 delayed the recovery in per capita meat consumption. For example, it was only in the 1870s that Saxony reached the level of a "high living standard", which was seen as 26 kg of meat consumption per capita in Europe. See Pfister, "Agricultural development during early industrialization in alow-wage economy: Saxony, c. 1790–1830", 7.

and France. Bremen and Hamburg, on the other hand, did not look forward to being included in any union for their own interests, focusing entirely on their commercial income.[22] There were also obstacles that forced the states to make these choices. Because the necessity of paying numerous customs duties for a product that had to go from one end of Germany to the other was an important factor that kept the border states away from the German domestic market.

In the 19th century, Prussia made several attempts to remove barriers to trade in the German domestic market. The 1818 tariff, pioneered by Maasen,[23] is still a laudable step. This tariff was one of the most important initiatives led by the Prussian government to encourage economic expansion. With the 1818 tariff, with a few exceptions the confusion of customs duties and other taxes were eliminated within the borders of the province and town gates were replaced by a single tariff placed on the state border; moreover, these tariffs were kept at very reasonable levels.[24] During the period of prohibitions and high taxes, Maasen adopted rather moderate tariffs.[25] This reform, also called the 1818 Prussian Customs Union, had important results in terms of unifying Prussia's eastern, central and western lands politically, administratively and economically as well as affecting the trade in Europe. Its financial success was indisputable. The new system, in which the bureaucratic and taxation barriers were removed, accelerated the economic integration to be formed with the east and the more industrialized west by making domestic trade tax-free, facilitated trade and

---

22 Hamburg had been a location that never lost its importance. Imports from Hamburg grew by 5,5 % each year between 1885 and 1913, while exports grew by 5,3 % between 1890 and 1913. In 1913, 42 % of German imports and 38 % of exports passed through Hamburg. On the eve of the First World War, the city's share in world trade was approximately 4,5 %. See Niall Ferguson, *Paper and Iron* (Cambridge: Cambridge University Press, 2002), 33.

23 Karl Georg Maaßen (Generally referred to as Maasen in the literature, here it is also used as Maasen), He was Prussia's chief taxation officer and later finance minister (1830–1834). Maasen had a very active role in the fiscal reform of Prussia. See Hans – Werner Hahn. "Zwischen Deutscher Handelsfreiheit Und Sicherung Landständischer Rechte. Der Liberalismus Und Die Gründung Des Deutschen Zollvereins", *Geschichte Und Gesellschaft. Sonderheft*, vol. 9 (1983), 259.

24 Keller – Carol H. Shiue, "Endogenous Formation of Free Trade Agreements: Evidence from the Zollverein's Impact on Market Integration", 1174.

25 Maasen published a list to make certain raw materials tax-free, levying a 10 % tax on industrial products, and a 20 % to 30 % tax on colonial products such as coffee and sugar. And he imposed a transit fee of 1h. 6d. per cwt on goods crossing Prussian territory. See Henderson, *The Industrial Revolution on the Continent*, 15.

provided much higher net turnover. Moreover, the abolition of customs duty on raw material imports, accelerated industrialization and increased earnings.[26] These successes undoubtedly led to an increased interest in the union.

In a short time, minorities in Prussian territory were also included in the Prussian customs system. The first was Schwarzburg-Sondershausen, whose territory was surrounded by Prussia. Schwarzburg-Sondershausen joined the union in 1819. Other minor states also adopted the Prussian Customs Union between 1822 and 1823. Extreme pressure was required to impose the new customs system on the Duchies of Anhalt-Köthen and Anhalt-Dessau, which smuggled the goods they brought from abroad into Prussia and sell. They accepted to join the union in 1828. In other words it took nearly 10 years for them to adopt the Prussian Customs Union.[27]

The signatory states received a share of the joint revenue based on their population,[28] and they often earned much more than they could have earned on their own. In other words, Prussia started the road to the Customs Union by first making a pilot application in its own geography.

The states in the lands surrounded by Prussia caused a lot of problems to Prussia due to smuggling. Importing foreign goods without customs duty and selling them without paying taxes to Prussian territory or abroad by taking advantage of the deficiencies in customs controls was a source of income for them.[29] Tightening border controls did not become a profitable solution to this problem, because the financial burden of monitoring these borders was much greater than the taxes to be collected. Therefore the Prussian Customs Union Treaty set a precedent. In return for the centralization of control of the foreign trade in Prussian territory, the surrounding states had the chance to negotiate intensely. As a matter of fact, surrounding cities such as Schwarzburg-Rudolstadt (1822), part of Saxony-Weimar (1823), Saxony-Coburg-Gotha (1824), Hessia-Homburg (1829) and Oldenburg (1830) joined the union.[30]

The achievements of the 1818 Prussian Customs Union undoubtedly set an important precedent. However not all foreign encircled states were easily

26 Tilly – Pierenkemper, *The German Economy During the Nineteenth Century*, 32.

27 Henderson, "The German Zollverein and the European Economic Community", *Zeitschrift Für Die Gesamte Staatswissenschaft / Journal of Institutional and Theoretical Economics*, vol. 137, no. 3 (1981), 492.

28 Keller – Carol H. Shiue, "Endogenous Formation of Free Trade Agreements: Evidence from the Zollverein's Impact on Market Integration", 1174.

29 Henderson. "The German Zollverein and the European Economic Community", 492.

30 Tilly – Pierenkemper, *The German Economy During the Nineteenth Century*, 33.

integrated into Prussia's system. Other border states, especially several states in south Germany were less than willing to abandon their autonomy on their customs in exchange for a financial gain. Some states in the south sought to find a solution within themselves.[31] On 19 May 1820, Bavaria, Württemberg, Baden, Hesse-Darmstadt, Nassau, Sachse-Weimar, the Saxon duchies and the Principalities of Reuss agreed that they agreed on the need for a regional customs union in south Germany.[32] This treaty opened the door to negotiations leading to a regional customs union to be made between them, and negotiations started as of the following year. The possibilities of establishing a regional union were discussed in Darmstadt (1820–1823) also in Stuttgart (1825). Although all these negotiations did not result in a large regional agreement and partially came to a standstill in certain periods, they resulted in a treaty signed between Bavaria and Württemberg on January 18, 1828. By this agreement Bavaria and Württemberg accepted the customs union between them. Although this agreement could not operate effectively since it was binding only for two states, it was a very important breaking point due to its theoretical importance and probably it was the most important customs union initiative on the way to Zollverein.

The fact that the states in south Germany sought a different way was because they did not want to accept the leadership of Prussia. As a result of the Congress of Vienna in 1815, not only did Prussia's territory expand, but many important industrial areas in the Rhineland and Westphalia and also the unique resources of the Ruhr region fell into Prussia's hands. Prussia became the ruler of the most important trade routes from north to south (Rhine, Elbe, Oder and Vistula valleys), and from west to east on the northern German line (Köln-Minden and Magdeburg-Berlin-Königsberg).[33] However, although Austria became less Germanized with the acquisitions it gained after the Congress of Vienna, it still had a powerful influence especially on the states in south Germany.[34] The

---

31 William Otto Henderson, *Zollverein* (New York: Routledge, 2018), 16.

32 Royal Historical Society, *British Envoys to Germany 1816–1866*: vol 1, 1816–1829 (London: Cambridge University Press 2000), 157.

33 Henderson, *The Industrial Revolution on the Continent*, 15.

34 Nationalist historians such as Johann Gustav Groysen and Heinrich von Treitschke argued that Prussia was trying to create the Zollverein in order to remove the Austrian influence from the German geography. On the other hand, historians such as A.J.P Taylor, Arnold Price and Martin Kitchen disagreed with this view and argued that Prussia's aim was economic. The view held by these historians is that Zollverein's political conclusions only came out towards the 1850s. See David T. Murphy, "Prussian Aims for the Zollverein, 1828–1833", *The Historian*, Vol. 53, No. 2 (Winter

customs union agreement signed between Bavaria and Württemberg in 1828 was a telltale sign of this.

Prussia did not easily give up on the idea of a great customs union in which it would be the pioneer and only the German states would take part. Thus, less than a month after the agreement between Bavaria and Württemberg (on 14 February 1828), another treaty was signed for the establishment of a regional customs union. This treaty was between Prussia and Hesse-Darmstadt.

Motz, the new finance minister of Prussia at that period, who continued his successful activities on behalf of Prussia, put pressure on Hanover, Brunswick and Hesse-Kassel and asked these states to join the Prussian Customs Union. Prussia sought to unite the economies of its eastern and western parts. Especially Hesse-Kassel stood in the middle of Prussia in a position separating east and west. Over the years, Hesse-Kassel used its unique geographical location to its advantage and refused to join Prussian Customs Union, it even went one step further and established its own customs union, which worked in its own interests. Important states such as Mitteldeutscher Handelsverein, Hanover and later Saxony also joined this union.[35] However, although the names were strong, this union, which lacked infrastructure and administrative power, could not be effective either. It was only after this union that Hesse-Kassel realized that it needed a larger customs union with the economic and administrative power to provide the necessary infrastructure for the union.

The establishment of these two regional unions greatly stimulated other German states. Some German states tried to prevent the spread of these units, which were exempt from tariffs within their borders, but were subject to tariffs at the border gates. They wanted to get free goods transit from the ports of Hamburg and Bremen to major trade centers such as Leipzig and Frankfurt am Main.[36] With these objects in view, Saxony, Hanover, Oldenburg, Brunswick, Hesse-Casel, Nassau, Frankfurt am Main and the Thuringian states formed the Middle German Commercial Union in December 1828.[37] They agreed to be independent from all other customs unions and agreed to expand their highway connections. The treaty of October 1829 extended the life of the union from 1834 to 1840. But the union did not adopt a common tariff. The purpose of the union was

---

1991), 258. Also See Abigail Green, "Representing Germany? The Zollverein at the World Exhibitions, 1851–1862." *The Journal of Modern History*, vol. 75, no. 4 (2003).

35 Tilly – Pierenkemper, *The German Economy During the Nineteenth Century*, 9.

36 Because of the world-famous fairs held in Frankfurt am Main and Leipzig, both were very important commercial centers.

37 Henderson, *The Industrial Revolution on the Continent*, 17.

limited only to achieve the status quo and to prevent the spread of the recently enlarged customs unions in Germany. The mutual jealousies of the members of the Middle German Commercial Union also became the biggest obstacle to the construction of highways that should have been built. At this point, Motz's highway project, which did not lose its motivation despite the alternative unions, was a move that was powerful enough to break the crackling Middle German Commercial Union structure despite the support of the British.[38]

Motz planned to build two highways joining the territories covered by the customs unions of Hesse-Darmstadt and Bavaria-Württemberg and presented it to the member states of the union. The highways proposed by Motz were also planned to pass through the Middle German Commercial Union, and he emphasized that these highways would significantly increase the revenues of the member states since they were also linked to the Prussian Customs Union. In the first place, the promise of "being independent from all other customs unions" when becoming a member of the union prevented the member states from integrating into the Prussian Customs Union. However, commercial concerns soon prevailed, and members led by a few smaller Thuringian states (Saze-Meiningen, Saze-Coburg and Reuss provinces) almost completely left the Middle German Commercial Union. Thus, they gave approval to Prussia to build a highway that would pass through their territory. In 1828, while there were actually three different customs unions in Germany, Prussia's insistence was enough to deteriorate the balance. The border state of Hesse-Darmstadt, which was very important financially, joined the union in 1828. This was an important turning point for the Prussian Customs Union. Other unions were not as disciplined and successful as the Prussian Customs Union. Eventually, the Middle German Commercial Union was dissolved as a result of Motz's plan to build Prussian-controlled highways connecting the southern and northern customs unions. In 1831, Hesse-Kassel finally joined the Prussian Customs Union and an uninterrupted trade route was formed between Prussia's eastern and western provinces. The Saxony and Thuringian states soon followed the path of Hesse-Kassel. Now, there was a reason for Bavaria and Württemberg to join the Prussian Customs Union. They also agreed to join the union in 1833.[39] Most of the states participating in the Prussian Customs Union agreed to be a

---

38 The British gave their support both because some Hanseatic cities were members of the union and because they defended the free trade policy of the union. See Claphamm, *The Economic Development of France and Germany 1815–1914*, 100.

39 Henderson, *The Industrial Revolution on the Continent*, 17.

part of this formation after very hard bargains. However, when the strengthened position of Prussia forced the German states economically, these states had no choice but to be a part of the union.[40]

As a result of the participation of other states, the German Customs Union (Zollverein) was officially established on January 1, 1834. The Zollverein covered an area of 163,000 square miles with its signatory states and contained a population of approximately 23.5 million.[41] Baden, Nassau, Luxemburg and Frankfurt am Main also joined this union in a short time.

Hanover, Brunwick and Oldenburg preferred to establish their own separate union called "Tax Union". Hamburg, Bremen, Lübeck, Schleswig-Holstein, Lauenburg, Mecklenburg-Strelitz and Mecklenburg-Schwein also wanted to maintain their independence.[42] Although the Hanseatic cities' desire to stay outside the Zollverein prevented the Zollverein from having a direct connection with the North Sea, this situation did not become a significant obstacle as originally envisaged.[43] Zollverein paved the way for trade in large volumes in a much larger geography than the Hanseatic cities, which want to trade with anyone they can trade with and want to import cheaper goods from England and put them on the German market.[44]

Zollverein had a very positive impact on the German economy and simultaneously encouraged the industrialization of the country. Before Zollverein came into force in 1834, there were times that some 300 different administrative political borders existed among German states.[45] With Zollverein, the hostile tariffs applied in a large part of Germany and preventing the transfer of raw materials, products, food products disappeared. The increasing competition between the producing regions increased the technical progress and efficiency.

---

40 W. O. Henderson "The Rise of German Industry", *The Economic History Review*, vol. 5, no. 2 (1935), 121.

41 Keller – Shiue, "Endogenous Formation of Free Trade Agreements: Evidence from the Zollverein's Impact on Market Integration", 1174.

42 Henderson, *The Industrial Revolution on the Continent*, 18.

43 Brunswick joined the Zollverein in 1841, Hanover in 1851, Oldenburg in 1852, and Mecklenburg and Luebeck in 1867. For Bremen and Hamburg this decision took a long time. They joined the union in 1888 See. Keller – Shiue, "Endogenous Formation of Free Trade Agreements: Evidence from the Zollverein's Impact on Market Integration", 1175.

44 Claphamm, *The Economic Development of France and Germany 1815–1914*, 100–101.

45 Keller – Carol H. Shiue, "Endogenous Formation of Free Trade Agreements: Evidence from the Zollverein's Impact on Market Integration", 1168.

Prussia was able to get more concessions in trade bargaining agreements than other countries, because thanks to Zollverein it was speaking not only for itself anymore but for the whole union. For example, in 1841 Britain agreed to change the navigation code for the Zollverein trade, declaring all ports between the estuaries on the Elbe and Muse a "natural exit". In 1844, Belgium agreed not to collect transit tax for transit passes on the railway line between Antwerp-Cologne and gave priority to Zollverein in its iron exports to Germany. Zollverein not only affected the Germany but also Europe. One of the most tangible short-term consequences of Zollverein in this respect is the inclusion of Swiss, Belgian and Alsace businesses in the German customs system in order to profit from a larger market.[46]

The Zollverein began operations in 1834 with 18 sovereign states and a population capacity of approximately 23.5 million and majority of the member states were satisfied with the financial and commercial results in the first years of the union.[47] The revenue of customs duties increased from 14,500,000 Taler in 1834 to 27,400,000 Taler in 1845. Prussia had no trouble renewing the Zollverein treaties on the same terms when the original treaties expired in 1842.[48] The continuity of the Zollverein was never guaranteed, as the Zollverein consisted of treaties signed between sovereign states for a limited period of time; however, the increase in the customs revenues of the member states in the 1830s and the significant development of their trade led to the renewal of the Zollverein also in the 1840s.[49]

---

46 Important figures such as Friedrich List advocated the expansion of the Zollverein on a line extending from the mouth of the Rhine to the Polish border and including the Netherlands and Denmark for the completion of the Zollverein. Moreover, they even raised the bar on Zollverein targets by arguing that in order for Zollverein to be a strong trade union, it should have included the Netherlands, Belgium and Switzerland. Prussia, on the other hand, rejected these offers, insisting that the Zollverein should not have crossed the borders of the German Federation. Against the fact that the Habsburg influence in the Federation was also felt in the Zollverein, Prussia did not bend its position. See Henderson, "The German Zollverein and the European Economic Community", 492.

47 Emmanuel N. Roussakis, "The Common Market and the Zollverein: Experiences in Integration", *Recherches Économiques De Louvain / Louvain Economic Review*, vol. 35, no. 3 (1969), 203.

48 Henderson, *The Industrial Revolution on the Continent*, 18.

49 The Zollverein was not a permanent organization. At first the Zollverein agreements lasted only 8 years, but were then renewed over two 12-year periods. Changes to the tariff could be made at periodic Zollverein Congresses or agreement renewal negotiations. In fact, unanimity was required for the decisions taken at the Zollverein

In the 1860s the share of Zollverein in European trade was three times that of Austria. Apart from mass production, with the advantages of both technical education and working discipline, the per capita production within Zollverein also reached much higher amounts than in Austria.

The institutional changes caused by the Zollverein greatly increased the likelihood of a national market for products and services arising within German borders. The fact that entrepreneurs shifted their capital from one location to another in order to open factories in different parts of the German territories with the advantage of the customs union also caused the capital to be mobilized, a kind of capital union was formed. It was also a result of Zollverein that by 1851 the engineering industry in Karlsruhe was founded by businessmen from leading production areas such as the Rhine and the Ruhr.[50]

Together with Zollverein, textile industries in Saxony, beverage production in Bavaria, and manufacturing industries in Silesia were able to come out of their shells and target large markets. The increase in trade volume not only triggered innovative moves in the field of transportation, but also increased the need for coal, which activated the coal industry, one of the catalysts of German Industrialization.[51] In a short time, Zollverein handled not only the products but also the food trade,[52] and with the expanding trade volume, the newly formed industries started to grow. There were two more noteworthy results of Zollverein. First was railway construction. Increasing commercial rivalries with the establishment of Zollverein accelerated the construction of railways. Latter was the impetus it gave to monetary integration. This effect was a vital effect.

In the pre-Zollverein period, when there was no monetary integration, the national market trade, which was already struggling with many other obstacles, was struggling with the barrier of currency differences. In the 1820s, metallic coins accounted for 80 % of the money circulation within the German states. Even the wholesale trade between states was carried out with gold or silver coins, however, the size of the coins and the purity of the silvers or golds were also variable, this situation was causing various problems. Small states such as Nassau, Coburg, Hildburghausen in particular were making a significant

---

Congress. See Henderson, "The German Zollverein and the European Economic Community", 495.

50 James, "Monetary and Fiscal Unification in Nineteenth Century Germany", 3–4.

51 Roussakis, "The Common Market and the Zollverein: Experiences in Integration", 204.

52 Sidney Pollard. "Industrialization and the European Economy", *The Economic History Review*, vol. 26, no. 4 (1973), 643.

amount of income by putting coins with low silver content into circulation,[53] while inflicting losses on other states.

Two of the most important coins in circulation in Germany were taler, prevailing in Prussia and the northern German states, and gulden, prevailing in the southern German states, both of which were silver-based, but their density and weight were not standardized.[54] Even taler differed significantly from state to state.[55] This meant that the trader would first research each state's own gulden or taler value and then negotiate an appropriate gulden-taler exchange rate.

This situation could only change as a result of Zollverein. The member states of the Zollverein began to feel the necessity to standardize the exchange rates of their currencies in order to distribute the customs revenues among the member states. Since customs revenues were the lifeblood of the Zollverein, this issue gained seriousness and two joint monetary system agreements took place in the 1830s. The Munich Coinage Treaty in 1837 bound the most important states of Southern Germany with some important decisions. As a result of the treaty, it was decided that the silver value of the gulden coins would be at least 90 % of the nominal value (seignorage charges would not be more than 10 %). Moreover gulden would be the legal currency between all signatory states, but that the states could continue to circulate low value coins as they wished. A year later, at the Dresden Coinage Convention, it was decided to integrate the Munich Coinage Treaty with all the member states of Zollverein and, in particular, to link the value of taler against its rival gulden. As a result of this opinion, it was decided that both currencies would be linked to silver at a fixed rate, called in "Cologne fine marks". Cologne fine marks would be equal to 233,855 grams of fine silver. This unit was equal to 14 taler and 24.5 gulden. In other words on taler would be equal to 1.75 gulden. And also, a common legal coin was accepted amongst signatory states. This coin would be equal to 2 taler or 3.5 gulden, and this unit would be called "Champagnetaler" since it was worth a bottle of champaigne.[56]

After these developments, which led to the formation of the monetary system, the German trade volume increased, the capital could enter the circulation more easily and positive signals started to be seen in the economy. Thanks to these vital influences of the Zollverein, Germany recovered relatively sooner from the

53 Harold James, "Monetary and Fiscal Unification in Nineteenth Century Germany: What can Kohl Learn from Bismarck?", *Essays in International Finance*, No:202, Deparment of Economics, Princeton: Princeton University (March 1997), 5–6.

54 James, "Monetary and Fiscal Unification in Nineteenth Century Germany", 6.

55 Claphamm, *The Economic Development of France and Germany 1815–1914*, 125.

56 Tilly – Pierenkemper, *The German Economy During the Nineteenth Century*. 35.

effects of the Revolutions of 1848. Briefly, Zollverein expanded the trade volume, had a positive effect on industrialization, and ensured the German economy to show an upward trend.

1.3. State Intervention in German Industrialization: The Case of Prussia

State intervention in German Industrialization is a phenomenon that is still debated among historians today. While there are those who argue that state intervention hindered entrepreneurs, free trade, and thus unrealized potential innovations in 19th century Germany, there are also some who argue that the sectors necessary for industrialization could not have formed spontaneously in Germany at the time without state intervention.

Even in the 18th century some states in Germany[57] were eager to industrialize and were ready to make state intervention and be the leading actor when necessary. This fact can be clearly seen in the case of Prussia. Friedrich II (Frederick the Great) emphasizes the importance of industry in the Political Testament of 1752 with the following words "The power of Prussia is not founded on any instrinsic wealth, but uniquely on the efforts of industry".[58] This expression, which was used in a relatively early period for the concept and effort of industrialization in Germany, supports the view that Prussia was aware of the importance of industrialization from the middle of the 18th century at the latest.

Indeed, some traces of industrialization can be found even in the 17th century in the reign of the "Great Elector"[59] Friedrich Wilhelm. Friedrich became the King of Prussia by crowning himself in Königsberg in 18 January 1701.[60] One of Friedrich's first acts as King was to establish the "Fifth Depatment of the General Directory", the task of which is to manage the "commerce and manufacturing" activities. In detail, this department were responsible to improve the existing factories, to introduce new manufacturing industries and find immigrants as much as possible to work in manufacturing enterprises. For his purpose, Prussian

57 In this study, the term "Germany", used for a period before 1871, represents the German states on the borders of the German Empire, which was proclaimed in 1871.

58 Clark, *Iron Kingdom*, 174.

59 In the Holy Roman Empire, rulers who had the power to elect the Emperor were given the title of "Elector". His nickname, the Great Elector, is a compliment to the military and political skills of Friedrich Wilhelm, which set him apart as of the period.

60 Encyclopedia Britannica, "Frederick I", https://www.britannica.com/biography/Frederick-I-king-of-Prussia. Accessed 2 October 2022.

colonization agencies were opened in Hamburg, Frankfurt/Main, Regensburg, Amsterdam and Geneva. Experts were brought from neighboring states, France, Geneva, regardless of their religion or race. With the "know-how" provided to Prussia, the wool industry was established, silk factories were established and developed, knife and scissors factories were opened, and the hat and leather industry was established. Immigrants were accepted according to their abilities in order to create non-existent sectors within Prussia. Thus, more importance was given to those coming from different sectors.[61] Prussia embraced and hosted qualified people who were driven out of their homes for reasons such as religion wars or financial sufferings. The efficient activities of colonization agencies increased the functionality of this policy. As a result, experts who took place in the industrialization steps in various centers of Europe gathered in Prussia and contributed to the industrialization of Prussia. This flow of information featured Prussia as an economic power.

The administrative role of Prussia was not limited to the opening of colonization agencies. The government gave very important subsidies for the sectors that needed to be established or developed. The silk industry is an example of this. The government protected the areas where mulberry trees grew from the cold, as it benefited silk production. With the royal order issued in 1742, it was reported that the land would be provided by the government to those who would plant mulberry trees. Farmers who planted a 1,000 or more mulberry trees with their own budgets were given government subsidies, and the government subsidized the gardeners' salaries until the investors made a profit. When the mulberry trees were mature enough, the farmers were rewarded with Italian silkworm eggs free of charge. Every silk produced in mulberry cultivation areas was guaranteed to be purchased by the state. Special export subsidies were given to the silk industry and tax exemption was offered. Import of silk was banned in certain regions, and in other regions local production was supported by protective customs tarrifs. All in all 1.6 million talers invested in silk production by the government.[62] The acceleration of the silk industry in the short term with these subsidies is a concrete indication that this policy was quite effective at that time. Another example is porcelain industry. According to the Sefâretnâme written by Ahmed Resmi Effendi in 1763, it was forbidden to even bring porcelain from Saxony, so that the Berliners, who were fond of porcelain, would not take the money out of the city. Instead, the king gave an order to establish a porcelain factory,

61 Clark, *Iron Kingdom*, 175.
62 Clark, *Iron Kingdom*, 175.

brought some craftsmen from Saxony to Prussia, and encouraged the domestic production.[63]

After 1815, an active effort was made by both government and businessmen to revive industry and commerce in Prussia. Motz, Minister of Finance from 1825 to 1830, sold some royal lands, introduced tax reforms, and accelerated road construction. Rother, head of the Overseas Trading Corporation from 1820 to 1848, held control of many nationalized businesses, such as textile mills, flour mills, ironworks, and chemical works, with a total value of 10,500,000 thalers in 1848.[64] The financial relief of factory owners with repayment appropriations and installment reductions,[65] and the help of state loans to overcome occasional cash crises[66] also indicate the industrialization incentives of the government.

As mentioned before, the acceleration of German Industrialization is often associated with railway construction. When looking at the railway constructions, until 1850, 73.3 % of the total railway investment made in the German states excluding Prussia was made by the state. When Prussia was included, about 50 % of the railway investment made in all German states until 1850 was made by the state.[67] One can argue that industrialization through state intervention was more effective than the industrialization that took place with the support of private banks, particularly in the Rhine region, until 1850.[68]

There were those who supported the interventionist policy of the state, and those who argued that it did not create a free market and monopolized it in certain sectors at that time. There were also those who claimed that the state intervention was occasionally an obstacle to the development of technology and related industry. Those were emphasizing the reasons such as the government's

63 Ahmed Resmi Efendi, *Ahmed Resmi Efendi'nin Viyana ve Berlin Sefaretnameleri* (İstanbul: Tercüman 1001 Eser, 1980), 58.

64 Henderson, *The Industrial Revolution on the Continent*, 15.

65 Claphamm, *The Economic Development of France and Germany 1815–1914*, 82.

66 Borchardt, *The Industrial Revolution in Germany 1700–1914*, 31.

67 Compared to Germany, even as late as 1915, public intervention in the Ottoman Empire was quite low. According to the industrial censuses made in 1915 by considering certain groups, only 2 of 264 establishments were in the hands of the government and the Hazine-i Hassa (The ministry responsible for the private income and expenses of the sultan in the Ottoman Empire). In other words, the ratio of industrial establishments under public domination was 8,3 %. See *Osmanlı Sanayii 1913–1915 Yılları Sanayi İstatistiki*, ed. A. Gündüz Ökçün, vol 4 (Ankara: TC. Başbakanlık Devlet İstatistik Enstitüsü, 1997), 15.

68 Jeremy Edwards – Ogilvie Sheilagh. "Universal Banks and German Industrialization: A Reappraisal." *The Economic History Review*, 49/ 3 (1996), 435.

opposition to the use of the telegraph at first since the government was considering the possibility of sending unauthorized political messages, and also the government's tendancy to delay the approval of new inventions that could be used in mining.[69] However, the interventionist policy of the state decreased partially between 1790 and 1840 and the state served as a control mechanism over the sectors in this period, while between 1840 and 1914 the principles of modern economy became more evident and private enterprises were further paved in all areas.[70] Moreover, private enterprises would bypass the public enterprises in a short time and would reduce the need for public enterprises in a short time.

Many historians have been putting forward different views for years on behalf of the industrialization in Prussia. There are those who argue that state intervention was the biggest factor, and that state intervention was an obstacle to greater development. Friedrich List, who also had a decisive influence on Germany's foreign policy, also argues in his book titled "The National System of Political Economy" that the state should direct entrepreneurs in order to carry out activities for the public good.[71] Considering that List was a respected economic theorist who could influence a wide audience, it can be said that state intervention in the private sector also found support in German society.

Industrialization through state intervention has advantages such as creating a new sector, providing opportunities with capacity and providing organizational discipline in a cultural way. For this reason, there are some historians and economists that finds the government interventions right until the last quarter of the 19th century in Germany. In addition, the state was also an actor that provided the necessary capital accumulation for industrialization.[72] Particularly, after the financial crisis in 1880, deficiencies in the response speed of the public bureaucracy and in overcoming operational bottlenecks quickly were noticed, and businesses that embodied public discipline, private sector modernity and internal

---

69 Tipton, "Government Policy and Economic Development in Germany and Japan: A Skeptical Reevaluation",141–142.

70 Clive Trebilcock, *The Industrialisation of the Continental Powers 1780–1914* (London: Routledge, 2014), 26.

71 Zsófia Naszádos, "The Involvement of the State in the German Economy", *Seeking the Best Master*, ed. Miklós Szanyi (Budapest: Central European University Press, 2010), 80.

72 Germany still maintains this feature. For example, the State of Lower Saxony holds close to 15 % of the shares and 20 % of the legal voting rights of Volkswagen, one of the world's largest automotive manufacturers, with legal assurance. See Piketty, *Kapital*, 153.

bureaucracy came to the fore. The factors that accelerated the transformation were that prominent businesses in this period, after 1890, chose their managers from technical university graduates rather than civil servants, and that they went for new models in the organizational structure.[73] Undoubtedly, the expansion of Humboldtian model of education and the increased ability of graduates with technical knowledge to manage and produce solutions to problems had a great impact on the formation of this new generation of administrators. As it can be seen, public intervention was not permanent. It was used when needed, then it changed shape, adapted to the changing situation.

Taking all these into consideration, instead of arguing that public intervention was indispensable or claiming that public intervention was completely wrong, to argue that the private sector benefited from the public bureaucracy in Prussia's industrialization and that industrialization took place with the simultaneous, sometimes successive efforts of the public and private sectors, would be a better approach.

1.4. The Transportation Revolution

The Zollverein was a very important initiative that succeeded in removing many obstacles. Increasing transportation facilities was one of the main factors that increased the efficiency of this initiative. Prussia was able to open the door to the Zollverein by increasing the means of transportation. Highways for Germany were necessary, but a partial solution. In a geography that was not surrounded by seas and was not considered very rugged, the only way to reach every location was the railways.

The interest in railways in the German states did not arise with the Zollverein, it was there before. Joseph von Baader, a Bavarian engineer and medical doctor, first proposed a railway between Nuremberg and Fürth in 1814. This idea was supported by a group of merchants, it was widely discussed both by the Bavarian administration and the parliament during the 1820s, and in 1826 the government assigned an engineer to survey the route.[74] As early as 1825, Fritz Harkot, a Westphalian merchant, presented his railway projects to the skeptical public. In 1828, Motz, also called the founder of the Zollverein, considered a project to build a railway from the Rhine to the Weser to avoid customs duty on

73 Kocka, "Capitalism and Bureaucracy in German Industrialization before 1914", 459–460.

74 David J. S. King, "The Ideology Behind a Business Activity: The Case of the Nuremburg-Fürth Railway" *Business and Economic History*, vol. 20 (1991), 163–164.

the Dutch Rhine. In the early 1830s King Ludwig of Bavaria sent engineers to England, France and Belgium to have research done and reports prepared.[75] The German economist Friedrich List even published his toughts on the benefits of the German railroad network connection all major cities througout Germany, in 1833.[76] However, it took 1835 to build the first public railway.

The first German railway started operating in 1835, on the short distance between Nuremberg and Fürth.[77] Traveling at a distance of 6 km, this train line, which had two tracks and used a steam engine locomotive, had become the symbol of a unique railway construction process.[78] In 1839, a longer line Leipzig-Dresden was opened and by 1841 580 km of railways were built.[79] In the first place, railways were built to meet the demand in passenger transportation and to connect the towns, However, in a short time, it also took an important role in the transportation of critical raw materials such as steel and coal and industrial products. The unique role of railways in industrialization, as an investment tool that both consumes and transports raw materials, showed itself in a short time. The 1840s were years of heavy investment in railroad construction. In Prussia alone, shares and debentures valued at 107 million taler were issued.[80]

The completed railways on the South, North, east and West of Germany, such as Cologne-Aachen (1843), Berlin-Hamburg (1846), Cologne-Minden (1847), Berg-Mark (1849), Munich-Augsburg (1840), Nuremberg-Bamberg (1844), created a potential not only for passenger transport but also for future freight traffic. Eligibility of the land and the low cost of labor were also important factors in rapid progress. By 1850, east, west, north and south had been linked in Germany. The total length of rails laid was then about 6,000 km, of which 2,000 km were state railways. Brunswick, Baden, Bavaria and Saxony were some of the states where the state was the railway investor itself. Until 1850, the German states together made half of their total investments in the railway with 150 million taler.[81]

---

75 Claphamm, *The Economic Development of France and Germany 1815–1914*, 150.

76 Erik Hornung, "Railroads and Growth in Prussia." *Journal of the European Economic Association*, vol. 13, no. 4 (2015), 702.

77 Adam Willis Kirkaldy, *The History and Economics of Transport* (London: Sir I. Pitman&Sons,1920), 134.

78 King, "The Ideology Behind a Business Activity: The Case of the Nuremburg-Fürth Railway", 162.

79 Jean Maillet, *18. Yüzyıldan Bugüne İktisadi Olayların Evrimi* (İstanbul: Remzi Kitabevi, 1983), 49.

80 Borchardt, *The Industrial Revolution in Germany 1700–1914*, 35.

81 Borchardt, *The Industrial Revolution in Germany 1700–1914*, 35.

Although Prussia, which was familiar with creating sectoral development with public intervention, did not show interest in railway construction at the first stage and left the railway construction to the private sector. Prussia considered the strategic importance of the railways more in the following years. Prussia created the Railroad Fund in 1842 and began buying some railroad shares both for giving some assitance to railway companies and for strategic reasons. For example, the shares of the Cologne-Minden line, were bought by the fund. Then Prussia began to construct its own railway lines. In 1847 Prussia constructed its first state railway which ran through the Saar coalfield. The situation was almost the same in southern side. 1840s were the years of nationalized railways also in the southern states.[82]

Despite the fact that each state built railroads according to its own "significant route" preference and timing, and thus was built piecemeal and devoid of the advantages of cooperation, German railroads were one of the fastest built on the continent.[83] In 1850, Germany had 5856 kilometers of railway lines operating. It is noteworthy that the length of the railway operating in France in the same period was only 2,996 kilometers.[84] It is a noteworthy fact that between 1840 and 1880 the open line length of railways increased from 144 km to 18,507 km in Austria – Hungary, from 496 km to 23,089 km in France, from 20 km to 9,290 km in Italy, from 27 km to 22,865 km in Russia, from 469 km to 33,839 km in Germany.[85] Germany was far faster in building railways from those countries.

As early as 1842, railway lines were opened between Leipzig and Magdeburg, between Munich and Augsburg, between Frankfurt am Main and Mainz, between Mannheim and Heidelberg, between Berlin and Anhalt, between Düsseldorf and Elberfeld, between Cologne and Aachen. In the middle of the 19th century, there

82 Henderson, *The Industrial Revolution on the Continent*, 20.

83 Belgium is the country that started laying rail lines in Europe the earliest after the UK, so its initial speed was higher than Germany. Indeed, the fact that it was a bridge connecting England, France, Germany and the Netherlands encouraged Belgium to make this investment. In Belgium, which also produced locomotives, the first line was opened between Brussels and Mechelen in 1835. Moreover, Belgium was the first country to establish a national railway system in Europe, but the length of railway laid by Belgium due to its area was not at a level comparable to Germany, England or Russia. The railway length in Belgium was as follows by years: 854 km in 1850, 1729 km in 1860, 2897 km in 1870. See Technische Universiteit Eindhoven, https://www.atlas-infra.eu/t05/rail/Railway_1850-1870.pdf, Accessed: 13.10.2020 and also See Claphamm, *The Economic Development of France and Germany 1815–1914*, 1141.

84 Henderson, *The Industrial Revolution on the Continent*, 19.

85 Steinberg, *Bismarck*, 96.

were three railway lines, each forming a route from east to west and from north to south of the country. These were;

From West to East;
1) Aachen-Cologne-Minden-Anhalt-Berlin-Wrocław-Krakow
2) Essen-Dresden-Beuthen
3) Mannheim-Munich-Vienna

From North to South;
1) Szczecin-Berlin-Prague
2) Hamburg-Kassel-Munich
3) Cologne-Basel

The main railway hub became Berlin, east of the Elbe. Lines were opened to Anhalt-Köthen in 1841, to Stettin in 1843, to Breslau, Magdeburg and Hamburg in 1846. In this way, the capital Berlin had now access to the industrial areas of the Baltic, North Sea, Silesia and Saxony. Cologne became an important rail hub in the west. The Rhine railway to Aachen opened in 1843, connecting Cologne to the Belgian line to Antwerp. Opened in 1847, the Cologne (Deutz)-Minden railway began serving the Ruhr industrial area.[86]

According to the German economist and sociologist Werner Sombart, German railway network expansion are divided into four phases. The first phase lasted until 1845 and the major cities were connected. The second phase lasted until 1860 and in this phase most of the important cities had an uninterrupted connection through trunk lines. The third phase lasted until 1880 and the full system of standard-gauge railroads and a coarse network were completed. The fourth phase lasted until 1913, the railways were ramificated and reached smaller towns through branch lines.[87]

In the 19th century, Germany not only built a railroad, it saw it as a national affair. Germany purchased its locomotives from Britain, Belgium and the USA in the first years when it started to build railways. However, it began to manufacture its own locomotives in the 1840s. In 1850, Germany's purchase of locomotives from Britain or USA or Belgium was zero.[88] This mercantilism had a great effect on German Industrialization.

86 Henderson, *The Industrial Revolution on the Continent*, 20.
87 Hornung, "Railroads and Growth in Prussia", 703.
88 Rainer Fremdling, "Railroads and German Economic Growth: A Leading Sector Analysis with a Comparison to the United States and Great Britain" *Journal of Economic History* 3 (1977), 588.

By the effect of expanding railway lines, new industrial centers sprung up in easily accessible areas, usually around the Ruhr and Berlin. This was of course due to the cheapness of the transportation cost. Cheap transportation costs depended on the length of the line and the volume of industrial and agricultural traffic on that line at the time. When the conditions were at the desired levels, the cost of transporting in bulk was reduced by 80 % or 85 %. The drop in freight costs, combined with the abolition of taxes, made domestic producers able to compete with British goods, and this encouraged risk-taking businesses to open. On the other hand existing traditional transportation facilities also showed significant improvements between 1830 and 1850. By 1850, 730 km of canals and 1,400 km of rivers were ready for use. This situation led to a significant increase in domestic transportation[89]

Railway transportation, on the other hand, took an important share in freight transportation from maritime transportation. In 1844, the Antwerp-Cologne line carried 115,000 tons of freight in its first year in full operation, and in the same year, freight transportation on the Rhine decreased by 70,000 tons, by 16 %.[90]

The impact of the railways was not only industrial but also social. It is remarkable that the death rate in Germany decreased during this period. One of the main reasons for this decline was railways. With the development of railway transportation, the society was able to access agricultural products faster, more regularly and at more affordable prices. This was a factor that increased the immunity of the society against diseases. In addition, as a side effect of industrialization, the development of medical technology and easier access to water resources necessary for public health had also a high impact.[91]

Increasing transportation opportunities allowed Germany to use its resources with higher capacity. Raw material mobility was ensured, supply could be moved from one point to another, capital was moved, new industries were formed, existing ones spread over a wider geography, and production facilities increased. As food products could be delivered to many points quickly by railways, food shortages ended, welfare increased, and industrialization became easier. Moreover, the ease of transportation created a demand by increasing

89 Borchardt, *The Industrial Revolution in Germany 1700–1914*, 37.

90 Hein A. M. Klemann – Schenk Joep. "Competition in the Rhine Delta: Waterways, Railways and Ports, 1870–1913", *The Economic History Review*, vol. 66, no. 3 (2013), 830.

91 Tilly – Pierenkemper, *The German Economy During the Nineteenth Century*, 91.

consumption. Considering that only in Prussia, the population increased by 59 % between 1816 and 1864, the cultivated lands increased by 24.8 % and the product per acre increased by 135 %,[92] it can be easily said during at that period both population and productivity increased.

Also, highways were of great importance for the delivery of both raw materials to the producers and final products to the consumers. After 1800, more and more attention was paid to the construction of highways. In Berg, a Prussian land, roads were built around the year 1800 to connect the coal mines with the receiver, or at least the river banks. Even the French army encouraged road construction in Germany for its own interests. Prussia, one of the earliest German states in the construction of highways, had doubled the connections of its roads in 15 years. By 1850 Germany had about 50,000 km of stone roads, especially in the west. The stone path length of Saxony alone nearly doubled between 1827 and 1845.[93] This situation increased the passenger transportation rates and the reliability and speed in freight transportation even before railway transportation. Moreover, it caused an increase in production and a positive effect on the economy before the industrialization period.[94]

Sent from England in 1840 to report on the effect of the Prussian Commercial Union, Dr. John Bowring's statements about canals and highways in his report characterize the impact of the transport revolution: "*By directing capital to internal in preferance to external trade*" it had "*already had a great influence in improving the roads, the canals, the means of travelling, the transport of letters - in a word in giving an impulse to inland communications in every sort*".[95]

1.5. Sectors Where Industrialization Started

In Germany, the factory system slowly increased until the middle of the 19th century, and heavy industry, which would gain high importance later on, started to show signs of existence in the 1840s. Between 1820 and 1840 German production of coal and pig iron was not as rapid as British production. The smelters remained small and firewood remained the most important source of energy. Mining was able to increase its production by only 70 % between

---

92 Steinberg, *Bismarck*, 67.

93 The total road length, which was 1255 km in 1827, reached 2527 km in 1845 and reached 2925 km in 1850. See Pfister, "Agricultural development during early industrialization in alow-wage economy: Saxony, c. 1790–1830", 13.

94 Borchardt, *The Industrial Revolution in Germany 1700–1914*, 37.

95 Claphamm, *The Economic Development of France and Germany 1815–1914*, 101–102.

1800 and 1837, but from the 1830s, investments in mining increased with both developing transportation opportunities and new financing resources. Cologne merchants were now investing their earnings from trade in mining. Capital accumulation began to shift towards industrialization. Of course, it took time for these investments to pay off and to realize the organization that mining needed. In 1846, Prussia's coal output was 3,200,000 tons a year, while only London was consuming more than this amount.[96]

The labor required for industrialization was generally met by population growth. Despite the massive immigration to America as a result of the promises of freedom of religion and cheap land, the population grew at an unexpected rate,[97] especially between 1816 and 1830. On the the main reasons of the speed in population growth was the high marriage rate after the Napoleonic wars. Population doubled between 1800 and 1846 in Prussia alone.[98] Particularly the 1850s and 1860s were crucial years in shaping the modern German economy. It was precisely this process that Rostow called "take-off". Beginning in 1850, agriculture experienced a decline, while mining and industry took up more space among the occupations in which the working class worked. Even in the rural areas of Saxony, the ratio of the non-agricultural population to the total population reached 43.6 % in 1870.[99] Of course, it is also noteworthy that some sectors such as commercial banking, insurance and communication developed even faster than industry in this period.[100]

Some factors that laid the foundation of German Industrialization continued to be factors that boosted industrialization in this period as well. Zollverein increased its influence with the participation of Hanover, and the railway construction, which accelerated after 1848, created a great demand for the industry. While between 1851 and 1854 the annual avarage net investment tot the German railways was 88 million marks, it became 425 million marks between 1870 and 1874.[101] As a matter of fact, in the 20-year period between 1850 and 1870, the length of the railway tripled.[102]

96 In the same period, the annual amount of coal output of France was 4,500,000 tons. See Claphamm, *The Economic Development of France and Germany 1815–1914*, 90.

97 Niall Ferguson, *İmparatorluk – Britanya'nın Modern Dünyayı Biçimlendirişi*, trans. Nuretiin Elhüseyni (İstanbul: İş Bankası Yayınları, 2019), 84.

98 Hobsbawm, *Devrim Çağı 1789–1848*, 186.

99 Pfister, "Agricultural development during early industrialization in alow-wage economy: Saxony, c. 1790–1830", 5.

100 Borchardt, *The Fontana Economic History of Europe*, 6.

101 Tilly – Pierenkemper, *The German Economy During the Nineteenth Century*, 62.

102 Fulbrook, *Almanya'nın Kısa Tarihi*, 125.

These factors had such a transformation that Fiedrich Engels, who returned to Prussia a generation after the Revolutions of 1848, stated that, "*Whoever last saw the Prussian Rhineland, Westphalia, the kingdom of Saxony, upper Silesia, Berlin and the seaports in 1849 found them unrecognizable in 1864. Everywhere machines and steam-power had spread. Steamships gradually replaced sail-ships, first in the coastal trade, then in maritime commerce. The railways multiplied in length many times. In the dockyards, collieries, and iron works there prevailed an activity of the kind the ponderous German had previously thought himself incapable.*"[103]

1.5.1. Textile

Local industry continued to expand, largely through textile production, until the middle of the century. Between 1848 and 1870, more than 750,000 people worked full-time in this industry, and thousands weaved on handlooms. In the 19th century, no other economic activity other than farming could provide employment to so many people in Germany.[104] One reason for this was the search for livelihoods in areas with population growth. Especially in a state like Saxony whose lands were not suitable for agriculture, the population almost doubled. It had the highest population density per square kilometer in Germany and therefore focused on developing its economy with light industry sectors such as textile production and textile exports.[105] The importance given to textiles also caused the acceleration of industrialization. As expected, cotton yarn production had become more easily mechanized compared to others and in a short time, cotton yarn production was almost completely transferred to the factories. Therefore, the amount of production increased and a downward trend was realized in prices.[106]

As of the relevant period, the disadvantage in the German textile industry was that linen lost its role to cotton. Bohemian linen, which was sold to great German merchant houses in the second half of the 16th century and soon began to be

---

103 Jonathan Steinberg, *Bismarck – A Life* (New York: Oxford University Press, 2011), 144..

104 Henderson, *The Industrial Revolution on the Continent*, 30.

105 Only the population within the geographical boundaries of the shrunken Kingdom of Saxony after 1815 is mentioned. Within these borders, while the population in 1750 was 1,046,627 and the population density per km^2 was 70, in 1850 the population increased to 1,912,600 and the population density increased to 128 per km^2. See Pfister, "Agricultural development during early industrialization in alow-wage economy: Saxony, c. 1790–1830", 3–4.

106 Borchardt, *The Industrial Revolution in Germany 1700–1914*, 32.

sold to Dutch and English merchants, is an example of the importance and deep-rootedness of linen in Germany.[107] While linen products constituted 40 % of all products produced in Prussia and 60 % of total exports in 1787, the balances changed as of the 19th century. In the 1850s, the consumption of modern cotton clothing reached three times the consumption of linen clothing, and the cotton industry prominently started to take place of linen industry. However cotton and silk were more industrial and more capitalist products than wool or linen. The peasant alone could not be enough for cotton and silk industry, industrialization was needed. Although regions such as the Rhine region in Germany were relatively responsive to the industrialization needed by the cotton and silk industries, the transition from linen to cotton was not easy.[108]

Even in 1861 the number of linen looms worked as a by-employment was not less then 250,000. Spinning of flax by hand was alive till 1882. Linen industry was a failure for Germany. In the 1830s, while England was producing linen yarn in its spinning mills, Germany was still trying to export hand-spun linen yarn.[109] The industrialization of England made German hand-spinners, who could not easily adapt themselves to cotton,[110] become more and more unemployed. As a result, during the Revolutions of 1848 and the harvest famine, thousands of spinners died from starvation-related typhoid. The German linen industry, which had dominated the global market for a while, lost its dominance over time. In the 20th century, Germany came to the situation of importing linen yarn in big amounts from Belgium, Ireland and Austria, and also fine Irish linen.[111]

The beginning of the cotton industry with exotic raw materials was one of the factors that prevented Germany, which had no colony in the relevant period, from making a rapid transition to the cotton industry. Consumption was limited, as was production. It could even be said that before 1850 the Germans did not wear cotton. Between 1846 and 1850, the annual cotton consumption of Britain

107 Arnošt Klíma, "The Role of Rural Domestic Industry in Bohemia in the Eighteenth Century." *The Economic History Review*, vol. 27, no. 1 (1974), 48.

108 Claphamm, *The Economic Development of France and Germany 1815–1914*, 92–93.

109 Claphamm, *The Economic Development of France and Germany 1815–1914*, 290 - 292.

110 Even by 1870, hand spinners still existed, and the famous economists of the time claimed that hand spinning would not die easily. See Guftav von Schmoller, *Zur Gefchichte der deutfchen Kleingewerbe im 19. Jahrhundert. Statiftifche und nationalökonomifche Unterfuchungen* (Halle: Verlag der Buchhandlung des Waifenhaufes, 1870), 467.

111 Claphamm, *The Economic Development of France and Germany 1815–1914*, 290–92.

was 230,000–240,000 tons, France's was 55,000 tons, and Germany's was 15,000–16,000 tons. This situation began to change in the 1850s and 1860s. There was a rapid increase in the cotton consumption of Germany during these dates, and cotton consumption increased to an average of 68,000 tons per year between 1886 and 1870, and to an average of 116,000 tons between 1871 and 1875. The fact that the consumption of Britain increased to 600,000 tons per year in the same period reveals how big an industry the cotton industry was at that time.[112] By the 1860s, the cotton industry surpassed other textile industries in Germany. The German cotton industry had 2,250,000 spindles in 310 mills, 142,000 hand looms and 23,000 power looms. As for the workforce, there were almost 38,000 spinners and 193,000 weavers. In the 1850s, large weaving mills such as Baumwollspinnerei am Stadtbach and Aktienspinnerei Cehmnitz were established in Augsburg. The main production centers were Rhineland (Ekberfeld, Barmen, Crefeld, Rheydt and München-Gladbach), Southern Germany (Augsburg and Göpingen) and Saxony (Erzgebirge and Voigtland regions). In Berlin, finishing processes such as calico printing were carried out.[113]

At this time, the wool industry spread to a wider area of the country compared to cotton. In Saxony, the Thuringian states of Reuss-Gera and Reilss-Greiz, Lausitz, Silesia and the Elberfeld region, Aachen and München-Gladbach on the Belgian border, Hanover, Berlin, Alsace and elsewhere wool production took place. An important reason for this expansion was that the sudden price drop in the 1860s allowed small enterprises to be included in the sector.[114] By 1860 the German woolen industry had over 1 million spinners, 2,600 power looms[115] and 11,800 hand looms. Germany made both wool imports and wool exports during this period. Germany imported wool from Australia, the Cape Colony, Russia, and Austria, while it also exported some high-quality German wool and

112 Claphamm, *The Economic Development of France and Germany 1815–1914*, 295–296.

113 Henderson, *The Industrial Revolution on the Continent*, 32.

114 Claphamm, *The Economic Development of France and Germany 1815–1914*, 293.

115 The number of power looms in 1850 was 1200. The increase in 10 years was remarkable. Because the German peasants' short-term use of woollens, which they used as winter clothes, and the longevity of the product, enabled German woollens to manage with their old production amounts for a certain period of time. With the increase in the need for wool due to the increase in population and economic development, imports also increased. Productivity problems in production in the domestic market began to come to the fore and all of these developments triggered mechanization.

products made from German wool. In 1864, net exports of woolen products exceeded net imports of raw wool by a margin of about 13 million thalers.[116]

The textile industry was the pioneer of the German consumer goods industry, where two-thirds of all industrial workers engaged in even in the 1870s. Textile industry continued its leadership position until the German heavy industry took over in the last quarter of the 19th century.[117]

1.5.2. Mining

In Germany, mechanization had been slow, despite the availability of technical means and a clear demand. In 1840 the most industrialized German state, Saxony, had less than 50 steam engines with a combined power not exceeding 900 horsepower. At the same time, there were 211 steam engines in the Rhine province of Prussia. Eighty-two of them were used only in mining. While the power available in all of Germany was 40,000 horsepower, this amounted to only 6 % of Britain's usable power in the same period. The main distinction here was that Britain had already made great strides towards industrialization, while Germany was just taking its first steps. However towards the middle of the century, things started to change, and Germany gained momentum. The fact that Borsig, operating in the machinery industry and established with 50 employees in 1837, increased the number of its employees to 12,000 within 10 years was an important indicator of this rapid development.[118]

One of the areas where this development was most evident was mining. Towards the middle of the century, technical innovations began to be seen in mining, and the use of coke-fired blast furnaces began to be seen. Although only 32 of the 247 blast furnaces in Prussia in 1849 were powered by coke, they were still able to produce a third of the pig iron in the Saar and Upper Silesia. Pig iron production, which was 46,000 tons in 1810, increased to 529,000 tons in 1850.[119]

An important development was the start of exploitation of the great coalfield in the north of the Ruhr valley in the 1840s. At the *Graf Beust* mine in Essen and the *President* mine in Bochum, the shafts were sunk much deeper than had been attempted in the Ruhr. The production of Germany's main coalfields in

116 Henderson, *The Industrial Revolution on the Continent*, 33.
117 Eiji Ohno, "The Hıstorıcal Stage Of German Capıtalısm—An Analysis Of The Bismarck Regime." *Kyoto University Economic Review*, vol. 40, no. 2 (89), (1970), 25
118 Claphamm, *The Economic Development of France and Germany 1815–1914*, 91.
119 Borchardt, *The Industrial Revolution in Germany 1700–1914*, 38. ve Henderson, *The Industrial Revolution on the Continent - Germany, France, Russia 1800–1914*, 22.

the Ruhr, Saar and Upper Silesia increased from just over 1 million tons in 1820 to about 6 million tons in 1850.[120] Of course, the meeting of the supply with the demand was achieved with the developments in transportation. Railways made a difference in this period. Prussia began to impose a special tariff on coal transport by rail and this set an example. Thus, German coal began to be able to find new markets within the country. By 1850, coal from the Saarland could now be sold to Bavaria, Baden and Württemberg.[121]

The two mining laws of 12 May 1851 were also a driving force in the expansion of coal mining in Prussia, where the largest coal mines were located. The first law abolished the stringent measures imposed on privately owned mines in Prussia. The government controlled the mining industry in a way that had not been applied to any other industry until then. From the operation of the mines to the financing of the quarries, from the sale of coal to salaries, even daily activities, were controlled. With the first law, the government gave a free space to all mine owners and mine operators as in other sectors and allowed mines to be more liberal.[122] With the second law, mining products tax was reduced from 10 % to 5 %. This arrangement was important in terms of ensuring equality. Because the 5 % mining products tax in the western part of the Rhine, where the French mining law of 1810 was still valid, and the eastern part of the Rhine were brought under equal conditions with this law. As a result of this law, a miner could move freely from one part of Prussia to another to find work. The workforce capacity in the Ruhr increased rapidly as agricultural workers from East Germany and Poland migrated to the Rhine and Westphalia. In the 1860s, Prussia alone produced %90 of the pig iron and coal produced within the entire Zollverein. Moreover, at this time Prussia was making alone the two-thirds of iron ore production,[123] and all of steel and tin production.[124]

Although the mining laws of the 1850s liberated private enterprise, the mining industry remained a state-dominated industry. The Prussian government was still the largest mine owner in Germany. Saar mines and some of the important mines in Upper Silesia were state owned and operated by the state. In other

120 Henderson, *The Industrial Revolution on the Continent*, 21–22.

121 Tilly – Pierenkemper, *The German Economy During the Nineteenth Century*, 67.

122 Henderson, *The Industrial Revolution on the Continent*, 33–34.

123 Steinberg, *Bismarck*, 178.

124 The impact of the Ruhr mines on this increase was quite large. Indeed, coal production in the Ruhr had doubled in just five years between 1860 and 1865, and the Ruhr's share of national coal production had risen to 46 %. See Klemann-Joep, "Competition in the Rhine Delta: Waterways, Railways and Ports, 1870–1913", 830.

words the state was the largest miner. It was the development of the banking sector that changed this situation. The effect of this development started to be felt in the Ruhr in the first place. The large mines in the Ruhr were started to be operated by a private group of entrepreneurs who quickly expanded their businesses with the contribution of the burgeoning banking sector. The number of mining firms continued to grow until the 1860s, when the oligarchy was started to show its signs.[125] Sometimes by merging, sometimes with bank credits, the replacement of small mining companies by joint stock companies enabled the operation of larger mines. The banks offered bigger loans to bigger companiesAs the financing of the companies increased, larger mines could be opened. This is why Germany's largest mines were opened in the 1850s and 60s. Only six mines in Upper Silesia was now enough to produce two-thirds of all coal in the region. By 1864, 670 coal mines had been opened in Germany. Between 1860 and 1871, bituminous coal output increased from 12.3 million tons to 29.4 million tons, while lignite output increased from 4.4 million tons to 8.5 million tons. While 1 million tons of coal was imported by Germany in 1855, this number decreased to 750,000 tons in 1864, and small amount of exports could even be seen in this period. Coal from the Ruhr began to be exported to the Netherlands, and coal from the Saar to France. By 1871, Germany had become the second largest coal producer in the world after the United Kingdom. Undoubtedly, the factor that made the real difference was the combination of production increase with transportation efficiency. The expansion of railway lines, the reduction of prices in freight transport, the construction of the Saar Coal Canal, the introduction of powerful steam tugboats on the Rhine ensured that coal was consumed faster and delivered to the demander.[126]

The Iron and Steel sector was also a very important factor for German Industrialization. After 1850, Germany was almost self-sufficient. Germany had reduced its iron imports from Belgium and even started to export to Eastern Europe, Russia, South-West Europe, Austria, Romania and even America, in short, Germany had become an important competitor to Britain In the 1840s, while the Prussian railways grew by 20 %, iron and coal grew by 4 % and 4.5 % respectively. Prussian railways met a large part of their needs by importing due to the intense need for iron in this periodThis demand increased the amount of investment made in iron and steel, and in the 1850s, while the railways grew by 10 %, the iron industry grew by 30 % and the coal industry by 9 %.[127]

---

125 Borchardt, *The Industrial Revolution in Germany 1700–1914*, 59.

126 Henderson, *The Industrial Revolution on the Continent*, 34–35.

127 Tilly – Pierenkemper, *The German Economy During the Nineteenth Century*, 63.

Germany's pig-iron production was 130,000 tons in 1834 when the Zollverein was founded. By 1870, this number increased to 1,400,000 tons with the establishment of blast furnaces. With this amount of production, Germany left both Belgium and France behind. With 838,000 tons in 1850, Germany's iron output was less than half of France's iron output and one-sixth of Britain's in the same year. By 1870 Germany's iron output had risen to 4,300,000 tons. This increase was partially realized by the opening of new mines and partially by increasing the efficiency with new technological methods applied to existing mines. Of course, the inclusion of blast furnaces in the process also had a great impact.[128]

Steel production also increased in the same period. While in 1848, the steel valued at 1,600,000 thalers were produced annually, by 1864 steel valued at 11,900,000 thalers were produced annually. Many sectors using iron and steel also started to rise with this increase in production.[129] Big companies began to shift their direction to locomotive and railway production. Between 1850 and 1875, 8,000 kilometers of railway lines were built. Almost one fourth of the net investments made during this period were allocated only to railways.[130] As of 1866, Austria's coal production was 5.7 million tons, while only Prussia's was 12 million tons. Likewise, while Austria's pig iron production was 460,000 tons, only Prussia's pig iron production was 850,000 tons. The gap between these rates widened further. In 1870 Austria's coal production was 6.3, while Prussia's coal production was over 20 million tons.[131]

---

128 Henderson, *The Industrial Revolution on the Continent*, 36.

129 In this period, companies that used iron and steel together with technology were born by investing in mechanization. In 1861, these engineering firms employed 51.000 workers. The world-famous defense industry brand Krupp is an important example of this. The Krupp company, which presented its first revolver at the London fair in 1851, received its first big order of 120 steel guns from the Russian government in 1859 and took an important step into the global markets. By 1861, Krupp had reached the level of employing 2,000 people. By 1864, that number had risen to 6,000. By 1865 Krupp was now producing 8 million thalers annually. What Krupp presented at the Paris exposition in 1867 were pioneering works. The Krupp's 50-ton steel cannon, which the world had never seen before, received orders from all over the world. Firms like Krupp and railroad builder Borsig owe their existence to iron and steel. See Henderson, *The Industrial Revolution on the Continent*, 36.

130 Borchardt, *The Industrial Revolution in Germany 1700–1914*, 47.

131 Breuilly, *Avusturya, Prusya ve Almanya'nın Oluşumu 1806–1871*, 166- 167.

In this chapter; It has been seen in the light of the data how the population growth, the transportation facilities and the determination of the state towards industrialization laid the foundations of German Industrialization in the light of a unique organizational revolution. Agricultural economy met with railways, revived trade provided capital accumulation, fields such as textile and mining formed the first steps on the road to German Industrialization.

Chapter 2 Industrialization in the German Empire

The German Empire was established in 1871 as a result of Prussia's wars against Denmark, Austria and France in a seven-year period. The German Empire had started its existence with many restructurings. These structures were so strong that they would make Germany feel ready for a possible world war and would be an impetus to search for more. Therefore, it is necessary to examine this post-take-off period both with the effects of the politicians and with the characteristics of the structures. In this part, the economic policies of Bismarck, the cartels that gave Germany a global image in many areas, the effects of the big banks that created these cartels and many other industrial branches, both agricultural and industrial developments, and the absolute contribution of education will be the focus and answers will be sought.

2.1. Bismarck's Effects on German Industrialization

It is a generally accepted fact that Bismarck was one of the most important political figures of the 19th century. Despite having neither public nor parliamentary support behind him, Bismarck rose to the point of determining Germany's fate, he masterfully established the balance policy despite his aggressive foreign policy understanding when necessary, and took his steps in the light of his long-term strategies. These are the elements that made Bismarck unique. The traces of these unique strategies could be found not only in foreign policy but also in domestic reforms.

Bismarck was a leader with a good understanding of agricultural politics due to his descent from a landed family. Also, it didn't take long for him to realize the importance of the industry as a visionary personality. Bismarck's visit to Alfred Krupp in 1864 and his visit to Manchester to see the world's largest machinery factory during his youth,[1] when he had no interest in politics, were indicators of his interest in the development of the industry. Therefore, Bismarck was a statesman who both came from within the traditional economy and understood the importance of the modern economy.[2] Although Bismarck's reforms with

1 Steinberg, *Bismarck*, 69.

2 There were also important statesmen such as Karl H.F. Stein and Karl A.F. Hardenberg, who carried out important economic reforms on the way to German Industrialization in the period before Bismarck era. As a matter of fact, names such as Gottlieb JC

this awareness were innovative, they did not aim to change the existing order completely, but to develop the existing one and put it on a more solid foundation. The most striking of these innovations were exchange rate regulation, nationalization of railways, customs tariffs and insurances.

2.1.1. Regulation of the Currency

One of the most important economic reforms in the German Empire, proclaimed under the leadership of Bismarck, was exchange rate regulation. The taler, gulden, and various other coins were replaced by the mark by the law of 1873. Simultaneously, the gold standard was introduced.

The necessity of making some initiatives in order to facilitate international trade and to determine some monetary standards was a topic that came to the fore from time to time since the 1850s. In the second half of the 19th century some international congresses were held to make implementations about international trade. An international postal congress was convened in Paris in 1863, 1865 and in 15 September 1874 in Bern. On October 9 a "Treaty concerning the Establishment of a General Postal Union" was signed, and it was implemented on 1 July 1875. Thus, General Postal Union came into being. The title was changed to Universal Postal Union (UPU) in 1878, and the treaty was renamed as Universal Postal Convention.[3] Moreover, an international statistics congress was held in Berlin in 1863, European states made another meetings on statistics till the second half of 1870s and tried to converge national standards.[4] The Manhaim-Rhine Shipping agreement was signed in 1868, enabling the standardization of waterway transportation in Europe's domestic routes in many areas. The monetary standard, on the other hand, remained a problem that

---

Kunth, Ludwig FG Bülow, Christian Beuth and Christian Rother, who came to their positions after them, also made industrialization moves under the leadership of the state. Moreover, by transferring these to the private sector, they made efforts to transform industrialization into broad action, to support new ventures by creating organizations and funds. See Timothy Lenoir, "Revolution from above: The Role of the State in Creating the German Research System, 1810–1910", *The American Economic Review*, vol. 88, no. 2 (1998) 22–27.

3 Encyclopædia Britannica, "International postal reform: the Universal Postal Union", Accessed: 03 December 2022. https://www.britannica.com/topic/postal-system/History#ref367093

4 Although statistics congresses did not produce direct concrete results, they had many long-term positive effects. See Nico Randeraad, "The International Statistical Congress (1853–1876): Knowledge Transfers and their Limits", *European History Quarterly*, vol. 41, no. 1 (2011), 59–62.

needed a solution as it was an area that everyone was aware of but was relatively more difficult to solve. Although only Britain and Portugal had set the gold standard in the 1860s, gold as a reliable metal was predicted as the most suitable metal to be accepted by other states. Since gold is a precious metal even in small sizes, Since gold is a precious metal even in small sizes, large purchases would be able to made with portable coins. Germany's acceptance of the gold standard was an important step for the globalization of the gold standard.[5]

The silver standard had not been considered as stable as the gold standard. Most likely, the increased gold supply of Britain from Australia and California in 1870s also had a great impact on this decision. Until then, seven different silver currencies indexed to taler or gulden had been in circulation. In 1871–5 these rates were replaced by a single gold currency, the "gold mark", one of which was equivalent to three silver talers. After the regulation, silver coins also remained in circulation, but were no longer freely minted. Until then, Britain was the only country that had adopted the gold standard among the states with large trade volume. The progress of the German Empire on the path led by Britain was rapid, which helped Germany to trade with the west.[6]

2.1.2. Nationalization of the German Railways

One of Bismarck's greatest ideals was to nationalize all German railways. Railways were one of the most important driving forces of the German economy. Between 1840 and 1860, German railway lines increased from 462 km to 14,030 km. Likewise, rail transport increased from 3.2 to 1675.2 million tons – km. Accordingly, the cost per ton-km for freight decreased from 16.9 to 7.5 pfenning in the same period.[7] As a result of this 4.4 % annually decrease, the transport of capital, raw materials and products from one point to another accelerated and the trade volume increased.

From 1835 to 1849 there had been no state owned railway in Prussia.[8] The main reason for this was financial inability. In 1820, Prussia had entered into an

5 James, "Monetary and Fiscal Unification in Nineteenth Century Germany", 6–8.

6 Borchardt, *The Industrial Revolution in Germany 1700–1914*, 80.

7 Klemann –Joep. "Competition in the Rhine Delta: Waterways, Railways and Ports, 1870–1913", 827.

8 Between 1843 and 1849, the state did not take over the construction of the railroad itself until 1849, although the state assisted some private enterprises by providing a guaranteed return to the buyers of the shares. See Ernest S Bradford. "Prussian Railway Administration", *The Annals of the American Academy of Political and Social Science*, vol. 29 (1907), 310.

obligation not to borrow money without the consent of the nation. In Prussia, which was tired economically after the Napoleonic Wars, the state at that time did not have the budget to build railways without additional financing. Getting the consent of the nation was a possibility. However, it would have been necessary to call a representative assembly into being for that. This was not a thing the crown would have wanted to do at that time. This situation changed as a result of the Revolutions of 1848. A constitution was introduced and a parliament was opened. Thus, as of 1849 state railways were able to be built.[9]

Although the state could not build a railway until 1849 in Prussia, as a result of a law enacted in 1838, it allowed private sector to build railways. In the same year, a railway connecting Berlin and Potsdam was built by private sector. It was owned, financed and operated by private sector.[10] In other words, private sector had started to construct the railways 10 years before the state in Prussia.

During the period from 1850 to 1880, both the public and private sectors were active in the railways. In 1871, the Prussian State was able to catch up with the dominance of the private sector in the railways and almost owned half of the milage in the kingdom. Bismarck believed that the nationalizaton of the railways and forming a single unified railway administration would have great effects. He believed that by this way, railways could provide more economic benefits to the government as their efficiency would increase. They could assist German industries by favorable freight rates on imported raw materials and finished goods for export. Moreover, they could provide great advantages in case of military need.[11] This view was also corresponding with Moltke's view which proven itself during the wars against both Austria and France. In 1871, there were more than 60 independent railway administrations in Germany. In 1875, the length of the railway had reached 27,956 km. 12,062 km of this was owned by various federal states and also operated by themselves, 12,641 km were privately owned and operated by private administrations, and other 3,253 km were privately owned and operated by federal states. Southern German states such as Bavaria, Württemberg and Baden had nationalized most of their railway lines. In Prussia, more than half of the railway lines, 9,183 km, were privately owned at this time. 4,281 km of Prussian railways were nationalized railways,

9 Gustav Cohn, "On the Nationalisation of Railways", *The Economic Journal*, vol. 18, no. 72 (1908), 520–521.

10 Hornung, "Railroads and Growth in Prussia.", 703.

11 Sidney B. Fay, "State Ownership In Germany" *Current History*, vol. 18, no. 103 (1950), 130.

and the other 2,736 km were privately owned railways which were under state administration. The Alsace-Lorraine railways were also state-owned. All this confusion had led to the emergence of more than 1400 different freight tariffs.[12] Moreover, when the average 20 % increase in freight costs after the 1873 crisis was added, businessmen revolted and voices demanding a solution began to rise.

Bismarck first announced that he wanted a national railway system in 1875, but strong protests against this proposal began to rise from the parliaments of Württemberg, Bavaria and Saxony. These states saw Bismarck's proposal as a threat to their independence and they did not want to give more to the central authority than they had already given at the foundation of the German Empire.[13] Bismarck predicted that it was unnecessary to present his proposal to the parliament under these conditions, waited for the right time, and in 1879, taking advantage of the voices rising due to the sudden declines with the railway turnovers, he presented a draft law to the assembly and started the activities of nationalization of the railways in Prussia. Between 1878 and 1891, many private railways were nationalized as a result of negotiations with the companies that owned them.

The first railway built by the state was built and opened for military purposes in 1850, Prussia built 5,350 km of railways until 1880 and nationalized 700 km. From 1880 to 1886, the state nationalized a total of 12,800 km more railway lines and built another 2,000 km of railways. From 1886 to 1905, the state built another 10,000 km of railways and nationalized 3,300 km of railway lines. At the beginning of the 20th century, 90 % of all railways in Prussia were state-owned or nationalized.[14] While large railway networks brought great profits, many of the small German states that opposed Bismarck's proposal started to make losses because their railways could not offer transportation diversity due to their limited line diversity. In the following years, some of these states agreed to combine their railways with the Prussian railways. For example, the Grand Duchy of Hesse agreed to link its railway system on that of Prussia.[15] In 1897, they agreed to nationalize and jointly manage the Ludwig railway.

Considering that 46 % of Prussia's total revenues came from the railways in 1911 it becomes clear how important the nationalized railways were for the state.

12 Henderson, *The Industrial Revolution on the Continent*, 47.
13 Cohn, "On the Nationalisation of Railways", 529.
14 Ernest S. Bradford, "Prussian Railway Administration." *The Annals of the American Academy of Political and Social Science*, vol. 29 (1907), 310–311.
15 Cohn, "On the Nationalisation of Railways", 530.

This rate in 1911 was even higher than the tax revenue, which constituted 44 % of the total revenues in the same year.[16]

Almost all Prussian railways were nationalized in 1914. There were seven railways in Germany, which were under the control of state and operated by states. These were; Prussia, Bavaria, Saxony,[17] Württemberg, Baden, Mecklenburg-Schwerin and Oldenburg. Only a portion of 3,000 km remained privately owned. All state railways were operating and in 1917 they made a profit of 786 million marks. The policy that Bimarck advocated in 1876 was finally realized in 1919.[18] With the Weimar Constitution, all railways were nationalized by the Reich.[19]

2.1.3. Protective Tariff Policy

In the 1870s, Germany was surrounded by high tariff borders. Even Austria-Hungary and Russia were applying high, protective tariff at that time. There were only Britain and some small continental countries which continued to apply free trade policy. On the other hand, Germany was more on the free trade side. Import duties were very affordable and this was pushing traders to import. The domestic manufacturer was not at all happy with a situation. When the commercial crisis started, the voices for higher import duties got louder. Pressure groups were formed to make these voices even louder, especially in heavy industry sectors such as iron and steel. These pressure groups, consisting of important representatives of important companies, were able to raise their demands to the office of the chancellor and to the parliament. Although their definite demands were rejected at the first stage, they were able to implement their demands on some issues by going step by step.[20]

---

16 Fay, "State Ownership In Germany", 129–130.

17 Saxony was also one of the states that gave importance to the nationalization of the railways. Between 1871 and 1907, Saxony purchased 1,255 km railway line from the private sector. See Dan Bogart "Nationalizations and the Development of Transport Systems: Cross-Country Evidence from Railroad Networks, 1860–1912" *The Journal of Economic History*, vol. 69, no. 1 (2009), 211.

18 Henderson, *The Industrial Revolution on the Continent*, 48.

19 The importance given to railways continued to increase. From 1871 to 1892, the length of Germany's railway lines increased by another 17,000 km and grew by 64 %, while the growth rate for domestic sea transport was less than 2 % during the same period. See Klemann-Joep "Competition in the Rhine Delta: Waterways, Railways and Ports, 1870–1913", 833.

20 Böhme, "Big-Business Pressure Groups and Bismarck's Turn to Protectionism, 1873–79", 225–226.

In February 1876, an institution was established under the name *Centralverband Deutscher Industrieller* (CVDI) to advocate a reform in order to increase the import duty and to protect the German industrialists in the domestic market. Through this institution, industrialists began to convey their demands in a more organized, effective and persuasive way. CVDI conducted a campaign called "protect the domestic workforce" to announce tariff demands to the public[21] and expressed its demand regarding the import duty on iron. Some major landowners had also changed their views on fiscal policies. Especially the eastern side of the Elbe was an important exporter of grain and agricultural products. Since they had nothing to import, they were fueling free trade. However, as the transportation revolution had dramatically reduced the shipping costs, the prices of agricultural products dropped significantly.[22] The globalization of the transportation revolution caused German farmers to lose their markets to their British, French and especially American competitors in the countries they had been exporting to. The domestic market had become more important for German farmers, but there were problems in the domestic market as well. The fact that an imported product was now cheaper to bring to Germany and that it could be transported from one location to another within the country much cheaper than in previous years had also caused difficulties in the domestic market competition of German farmers.[23] Under these conditions, landowners and agriculture-based pressure groups such as the *Deutsche Bauernbund*[24] decided to support the industrialists and demand a protectionist policy,[25] despite a few initial doubts.[26]

---

21 Cornelius Torp, "The Coalition of 'Rye and Iron' under the Pressure of Globalization: A Reinterpretation of Germany's Political Economy before 1914", *Central European History*, vol. 43, no. 3 (2010), 405.

22 While the average price of wheat was 225 marks per ton between 1866 and 1875, this price decreased to 196 marks in 1879, 185 marks in 1883, and 157 marks in 1886. See Torp, "The Coalition of 'Rye and Iron' under the Pressure of Globalization: A Reinterpretation of Germany's Political Economy before 1914", 406.

23 Steven B. Webb, "Agricultural Protection in Wilhelminian Germany: Forging an Empire with Pork and Rye", *The Journal of Economic History*, vol. 42, no. 2 (1982), 310.

24 German Farmers Association.

25 Torp, "The Coalition of 'Rye and Iron' under the Pressure of Globalization: A Reinterpretation of Germany's Political Economy before 1914", 405.

26 The doubt here was as much need-oriented as it was political. One of the reasons was that the farmers growing soft wheat, especially in East Germany, needed imported hard wheat and the tariffs would make this import difficult. The German economic historian Karl Hardach argued that the 1879 tariffs did not benefit great

It was an example of Bismarck's political talent that Bismarck brought together the different expectations of landowners and heavy industrialists in protectionist policy on a common plane. Some researchers, such as the German historian Cornelius Torp, argue that in the absence of Bismarck, a common agro-industrial pressure could not occur and the 1879 tariff could not be realized.[27]

In the 1878 general election, more than 200 members supported the return to protectionist tariff in the Reichstag. The new tariff law was read for the third time in July 1879. In fact, this tariff was also relatively moderate. It is still lower than the tariffs of other countries and also tended to retain tax exemption in some segments such as raw cotton, wool, scientific equipment and ships. The new import duties on agriculture were also relatively low, too. However, very import duties were placed on coffee, tea, tobacco, petroleum, and wine-derived alcohol.[28] The protectionist tariff on iron and steel, became quite clear. Depending on the price of the imported iron and steel product, new import duty placed were between 15 % and 25 %. This tariff law, which was supported by steel companies since they protect the domestic market, continued to exist until 1914.[29] This

---

grain producers, especially in the first years. See Karl W. Hardach, *Die Bedeutung wirtschaftlicher Faktören bei der Weidereinführung der Eisen und Getreidezölle in Deustchland 1879* (Berlin: Duncker und Humblot, 1967).

27 Torp "The Coalition of 'Rye and Iron' under the Pressure of Globalization: A Reinterpretation of Germany's Political Economy before 1914", 410.

28 Steven B Webb, "Tariffs, Cartels, Technology, and Growth in the German Steel Industry, 1879 to 1914", *The Journal of Economic History*, vol. 40, no. 2 (1980), 310.

29 From 1890 onwards, Germany began to lose certain markets due the protectionist policies. The McKinley tariff, which entered into force in the United States in 1890, dealt a huge blow to Germany's exports to the United States as the most protective tariff in American history up to that time. Between 1890 and 1894, German exports to the United States fell from 417 million marks to 271 million marks. Russia, on the other hand, had slowed down the import of industrial products since the 1880s. Therefore, between 1880 and 1887, Germany's exports to Russia fell by 50 %. Germany's decisions against Russia's restrictions, such as not allowing Russian loans, worsened relations between the two countries. Thus, Russia banned the import of many products from Germany with the 1891 Mendeleev Tariff, which was more strict than the American McKinley tariffThese developments had significant effects on German exports and economy. In order to find a solution to this situation, Bismarck's successor Caprivi made bilateral agreements with Austria-Hungary, Italy, Switzerland, Belgium in 1891, with Serbia, Romania in 1893–94, and with Russia in 1893, and reduced Germany's customs duty on agricultural products. In return, Caprivi enabled other countries to reduce their customs duties on industrial products imported from Germany. In a way, Caprivi reversed Bismarck's moves to protect agriculture to stimulate industry.

success, which was called the "marriage of iron and rye",[30] were depicting the meeting of agriculture and industry on a common ground. It was clearly one of the pioneers of Bismarck's prominent original policies.

2.1.4. Compulsory Health Insurance

Bismarck's another initiative that raised the German social standards considerably, was the insurance reforms. Working conditions in industrializing Germany were very poor and work-related mortality rates were high. With the compulsory health insurance allowance, the financial conditions of both the employees themselves and their families after a possible death were guaranteed. Moreover, Bismarck's health insurance move became an indirect compensation[31] for the employee and reduced immigration.[32]

It should be noted that Bismarck had a rational mindset. Bismarck's view supported the principle that "It is easier to deal with an old German with a monthly income than with an old German who does not".[33] On the other hand, it would not be wrong to state that Bismarck tried to get the support of the working class, which was the base mass of the Social Democratic Party, while enforcing these laws. With this point of view, Bismarck enacted three important laws regarding the insurances for occupational accident, retirement, illness and disability in the 1880s.

The first of these laws was health insurance, adopted on June 15, 1883. With this law, the world's first national health insurance program became a German law.[34] This insurance covered the income and medical expenses of the worker when the worker fell ill and could not come to work. Every worker with an annual income

---

See Henderson, *The Industrial Revolution on the Continent,* 50. And See Torp, "The Coalition of 'Rye and Iron' under the Pressure of Globalization: A Reinterpretation of Germany's Political Economy before 1914", 412.

30 Paul A. Papayoanou, "Interdependence, Institutions, and the Balance of Power: Britain, Germany, and World War I." *International Security*, vol. 20, no. 4 (1996), 42–76.

31 Indirect compensations are evaluated apart from direct income such as salaries and bonuses. They do not come in the form of cash. They are additinoal benefits that are offered in favor of the employee, generally as a social support.

32 David Khoudour-Castéras, "Welfare State and Labor Mobility: The Impact of Bismarck's Social Legislation on German Emigration before World War I", *The Journal of Economic History*, vol. 68, no. 1 (2008), 211.

33 Ferguson, *Paranın Yükselişi – Dünyanın Finansal Tarihi*, 163.

34 Donald W Light, "Values and Structure in the German Health Care Systems." The Milbank Memorial Fund Quarterly. Health and Society, vol. 63, no. 4 (1985), 616.

of less then 2,000 marks benefited from the insurance. Thanks to this insurance, the hospital expenses of the workers for up to 13 weeks were covered and it was ensured that they could receive 3/4 of their average daily wage during their absence from work. The second law on occupational accidents passed on 6 July 1884. In any work accident that the employee would experience, all responsibility was given to the employer. And the employee would not be asked to prove that this accident was the responsibility of the employer. If an employee had a permanent disability as a result of an accident, the employer would be obliged to regularly pay an amount equal to two-thirds of the employee's annual earnings. If the employee died as a result of a work accident, the employer was obliged to pay compensation to the widow and orphaned children of the employee. This law, which was initially for only industrial workers, was expanded to include agricultural workers in 1886. The third law, adopted on 22 June 1889, was about pension and disability. With this law, the salary of the worker who retired after reaching the age of 70 or was disabled so that he could not continue to work, was partially covered by the government, partially by the employer, and partially by the worker himself. These compulsory insurances were consolidated under the name of the National Insurance Law in 1911 and the pension insurance expanded to cover the salaried employees.[35]

Considering Bismarck's moves in the insurances for working class, it could be said that Bismarck had also some political goals. It is possible that, with these laws Bismarck wanted to make the working class less attached to the trade unions and the Social Democratic Party. He possibly aimed to bring the working class closer to the state, to show that the state is on the side of the working class and to direct the expectations and the loyalty of the working class to the state.[36]

Moreover, considering these laws it could be said that influence of the state was no longer as a founder but as a regulator and developer in the Bismarck era. If the influence of the state on German Industrialization is examined in three phases; the first phase will be the process until 1840. it could be said that in the firt phase the government itself was an entrepreneur and made the sector itself attractive. In the second phase, between 1840 and 1870, the government took a step back and encouraged private investments to enter the sector it had once founded as an entrepreneur. In the thrid phase, after 1870, with the policies of Bismarck, the government assumed the role of a regulator of the settled sector,

35 Khoudour-Castéras, "Welfare State and Labor Mobility: The Impact of Bismarck's Social Legislation on German Emigration before World War I", 218–221.

36 Light, "Values and Structure in the German Health Care Systems.", 616.

protected the sector with tariffs when necessary, increased workers' rights and controlled the sectors with an external hand, not internally.

2.2. Innovative Solutions to the Problem of Capital Accumulation: German Banking Models

German banking models are still influential today. Established in 1870, Deutsche Bank was a leader in the world even as recently as 2012.[37]

The German banks formed a bridge between the saver and the investor to cover the risky, heavy industry investments and railroad financings between 1840 and 1870. In this way, they made the investor use the money of the saver as an intermediary. Since there was no sufficient capital accumulation in Germany in the half of the 19th century, it could be said that most of the investments during the German Industrialization period would not have been possible without the banks. The innovative German banking models that influenced German Industrialization were *Kreditbanken, Notenbanken, Sparkassen, Kreditgenossenschaften and Privatbanken.*[38] However, the banking model with the greatest effect on German Industrialization was *Kreditbanken.*[39]

2.2.1. Kreditbanken

The *Kreditbank* model, which made significant contributions to German Industrialization, was implemented after the Revolutions of 1848. Before 1848, there were no joint stock banks in Germany, and the existing banks were traditional private banks. After the Revolutions of 1848, changes began to occur in the banking sector in Germany. In 1848, Prussia let Schaaffhausen Bank to be established in Cologne, the Darmstadt Bank was established in 1853, the Discount

37 Andrea Fiano, "World's 50 Bıggest Banks 2012 "*Global Finance* (Accessed: 12 December 2020).

38 Although other important banking models such as *Hypothekenbanken* (Mortgage banks) are included in German banking models, they are not mentioned here in detail since they are out of the scope of this study.

39 The exact English equivalent of some banking models in Germany may be misleading. Kreditbank can be translated into English as a credit bank, but it is preferred to use the terms in their native language in this study, since it can directly evoke any 21th century credit bank. The plural form of banking models is used in the sub-headings. Although Kreditbank is a banking model and a type of bank, Kreditbanken is the plural form of Kreditbank. The same is true for the examples of Sparkasse, Sparkassen and Notenbank, Notenbanken.

Company in Berlin and the Berlin Commercial Company were established in 1856, the Deutsche Bank and the Hamburg Discount Bank were established in 1870, In 1872 the Dresden Bank was opened and in 1881 the German National Bank was established.[40] All these developments changed the balance. Until the 1870s, more than a 100 similar institutions and 40 different *Kreditbanken* had been established, but the above-mentioned ones were the most important ones that could make a remarkable amount of profit and provide surplus reserves.[41] These banks both collected deposits like savings banks, coordinated money transfers, and provided long-term loans to the industry like investment banks. Providing the necessary capital for industrialization through long-term investment loans in Germany,[42] where there was no capital accumulation, was possible with *Kreditbank* model, which distinguishes German Industrialization from British Industrialization.

As the successes of *Kreditbanken* increased, their share values also increased, so *Kreditbanken* were able to obtain more capital and give more loans. For this reason, it was an expected development that *Kreditbanken*, which branched out over time, intimidated the private banks that had dominated the sector before 1850.[43] *Kreditbanken* had adopted a banking model that was directly intertwined with the industry, and they tended to manage and direct their heavy industry portfolios as if they were their own companies.[44] At one point, these

---

40 In order, with their original names: A. Schaafhausen (Cologne), Bank für Handel und Industrie (Darmstadt), Discontogesellschaft (Berlin), Berliner Handelsgesellschaft (Berlin), Deutsche Bank (Berlin), Commerz und Disconto Bank (Hamburg), Dresdener Bank, Nationalbank für Deutschland (Berlin). See Hugh Neuberger – Houston H. Stokes, "German Banks and German Growth, 1883–1913: An Empirical View", *The Journal of Economic History*, vol. 34, no. 3 (1974), 711.

41 For example, the average dividend rates in the 1850s and 1860s were 6.7 % for Bank für Handel und Industrie, 7.0 % for Disconto Gesellschaft, 7.2 % for Schaaffhausen Bankverein and 7.3 % for Berliner Handelsgesellschaft. See. Marco Da Rin – Thomas Hellmann, "Banks as Catalysts for Industrialization", *William Davidson Working Paper Number 44* (October 2001), 7–9.

42 Hugh Neuburger, "The Industrial Politics of the Kreditbanken, 1880–1914", *The Business History Review*, vol. 51, no. 2 (1977), 190–191.

43 Neuberger – Stokes, "German Banks and German Growth, 1883–1913: An Empirical View", 712.

44 German Kreditbanks was a successful synthesis of French Credit-Mobilier type and commercial banking. Kreditbanks, apart from Credit-Mobiliers, were directly involved in the vital processes of their industrial portfolios. See Alexander Gerschenkron, *Economic Backwardness in Historical Perspective – A Book of Essays* (Cambridge, Massachussets: The Belknap Press of Harvard University Press, 1962), 13–15.

expectations of *Kreditbanken* were also considered reasonable by companies, it was risky to lend large sums of money with fixed, favorable interest rates and a long-term repayment. In order to minimize the risk, the banks that accepted this risk imposed obligations on companies such as taking loans only from their own banks and accepting the appointment of a representative to the board of directors of the companies. This obligation was also based on the German Company Law, which came into force in 1870 and required every joint stock company to have a supervisory board. Banks appointed their representatives to supervisory boards of companies, where they voted either as direct shareholders or as representatives of the shares in their portfolios.[45] These appointments made significant contributions by providing bilateral information flow. The bank had the opportunity to directly know the managers, short-term and long-term plans and internal dynamics of company. On the other hand, through the bank representative, the company had the opportunity to know the short and long-term expectations in the financial markets, to obtain possible investment instruments that could be offered to the company, and to become a cartel when necessary.

In 1905, the eight great banks mentioned above had 819 directors in industrial companies.[46] Great German banks often directly influenced the business decisions of industrial firms and they had become centers for "business decision making". Representatives of banks sat on the boards of directors, sometimes by buying shares in the company, sometimes simply because they financed the companies. In 1912 Deutsche Bank had seats on the boards of 159 companies and as a bank was represented on company committees that decided on long-term business plans and investment plans.[47]

The branching of banks had increased the movement of money from one location to another, giving an unprecedented speed to trade. The fact that Deutsche Bank, which was founded in 1870, had branches in coastal areas such

45 Great banks had significantly reduced their direct purchases of shares from the 1880s. The biggest factor in this was the financial crisis that took place in the period between 1873 and 1879, which decreased the share values and caused serious losses to the banks. From the 1880s on, the relationship between big banks and joint stock companies was on the model of providing financing with credit. See Jeremy Edwards – Sheilagh Ogilvie, "Universal Banks and German Industrialization: A Reappraisal", *The Economic History Review*, 49/3 (1996), 428–429.

46 Neuberger – Stokes. "German Banks and German Growth, 1883–1913: An Empirical View.", 713.

47 Borchardt, *The Industrial Revolution in Germany 1700–1914*, 77.

as Hamburg and Bremen and overseas such as London, Shanghai and Yokohama towards the end of the 1870s, was an indication that *Kreditbanken* were large-capital corporations with a tendency to globalization.[48] Between 1852 and 1870, the amount of loans given by *Kreditbanken* grew by 19,4 % annually, reaching 492 million marks from 20 million.[49] While the assets of *Kreditbanken* were 0.39 billion marks in 1860, this number rose to 22.04 billion marks in 1913.[50]

Although the impact was great and the literature insists on emphasizing the importance of *Kreditbanken* in the context of the effect of banks on German industrialization, *Kreditbank* was not the only banking model in Germany in the second half of the 19th century. The effective support of other banking models to the process has been underestimated or incomplete in the literature. There were also banking formations such as note issuing banks, private banks, savings banks, mortgage banks, credit cooperatives, and these also had important effects.

2.2.2. Notenbanken

Notenbanken were the banks with banknote issuing authority. Their greatest effect had been to increase the amount of money in circulation. While the volume of banknotes in circulation in Germany at the beginning of the 1850s was 120,000,000 marks, this number increased to 1,352,000,000 marks in 1873 with the activities of *Notenbanken*[51] whose numbers had reached to 33 in the 1870s.[52] In 1875, just before the establishment of the Reichsbank, the uncovered

48 Guinnane, "Delegated Monitors, Large and Small: The Development of Germany's Banking System, 1800–1914", 43.

49 Tilly, "Banking Institutions in Historical and Comparative Perspective: Germany, Great Britain and the United States in the Nineteenth and Early Twentieth Century", 193.

50 Tilly – Pierenkemper, *The German Economy During the Nineteenth Century*, 115.

51 James, "Monetary and Fiscal Unification in Nineteenth Century Germany", 11.

52 Germany's policy of printing money was different from that of the United States and United Kingdom at the time.. Especially in the United States, printing money was carried out in an almost uncontrolled manner throughout the 19th century. Gary Gorton, in his study, states that between 1839 and 1858, about 3000 different banknotes were in circulation in the U.S. While the UK had more restrictions than the US, it was common practice for rural banks to print money in compliance with non-coercive restrictions. In Germany, on the other hand, this process was kept under strict control. In 1851, only nine banks were authorized to issue money in all German territory within 1871. Although this number had increased to twenty-nine in 1859, the number of banks still authorized to issue money in all of Germany was less than the number of authorized banks that existed only in New York in the same year.

circulation of notes were 385,000,000 marks in total. Among the 33 note-issuing banks, the Imperial Bank alone was responsible for 250,000,000 of this sum.[53]

In 1876, with the establishment of the Reichsbank, all banks had to transfer their banknote issuing authorities to the Reichsbank. As the gold standard could be applied with the Reichsbank, credit banks and commercial banks were also able to provide more generous liquidity to emerging companies with the Reichsbank's liberal support policies.[54]

2.2.3. Sparkassen

Sparkassen was a deposit and savings banking model which played a very important role in German Industrialization.

The emergence of deposit banks in Germany dates back to the end of the 18th century, but they became widespread after the Napoleonic wars. These banks enabled citizens and workers to save and convert their money into deposits with a certain interest rate. The saving banks were conservative. They were holding the savings in unrisky investments such as real estate or government bonds. On the other hand, the money deposited in these savings banks, some of which belonged to the state, was secured by both the state and the bank owners, and the depositor was given a guarantee that the money would be paid back in case of any negativity. This made it difficult for banks to distribute money in deposits

---

The financial crisis of 1856/57 was experienced as a result of the uncontrolled and unrestricted printing of money by the banks of some small German states. After this crisis, some big German states, especially Prussia, even banned the use of another German state's currency on their own territory. See Guinnane, "Delegated Monitors, Large and Small: The Development of Germany's Banking System, 1800–1914", 15–16.

53 Before 1875, uncovered notes were generally used for small and fractional payments, while the Bank Act of 1875 was set to certain standards. In accordance with these standards, uncovered notes were protected with an upper limit and the excess was taxed. The right to exceed the limit was determined by a certain percentage of the reserves held by the banks. See *The Reichsbank 1876–1900*, National Monetary Commision (Washington: Washington Post Office, 1910), 76–78 and See "German Bank Act of the 30th January, 1875", *Journal of the Statistical Society of London*, 268. Therefore, the amount of uncovered notes in circulation of a bank could indicate the reserve strength and size of the bank.

54 Tilly "Banking Institutions in Historical and Comparative Perspective: Germany, Great Britain and the United States in the Nineteenth and Early Twentieth Century", 195–196.

as loans in the first place.[55] For example, in 1811, deposit banks in Bavaria did not make any loans without taking a mortgage on real estate. In Prussia, bail was obligatory.[56] This conservative attitude loosened over time as savings banks adapted to the universal banking model. The money in savings was also put into circulation through loans.

The fact that the citizens were forced to save, led to the formation of a significant capital accumulation in Germany. On the eve of the First World War, even in British banks, total deposits were £1.2 billion, while the money in circulation remained around £45.5 million.[57] This high demand for deposit banks was a very important driving force that ensured the circulation of money and the provision of liquidity to those who needed it. Even in 1880, the share of *Sparkassen* among all bank types in terms of total assets was quite high at 20.6 %. Before the First World War, in 1913, it was in the first place among other bank types with the share of 24.8 % in terms of assets.[58] One of the main reasons why *Sparkassen* were preferred was that, as a result of the check law enlarged in 1909, check collections were allowed to be made from *Sparkassen* and that depositors were given the opportunity to withdraw money from different cities.[59] As the demand for *Sparkassen* increased, the number of *Sparkassen* also increased. While there were 234 *Sparkassen* in Prussia and 57 *Sparkassen* in Saxony in 1850, these numbers increased to 1,191 and 175, respectively, in 1880. By 1910, there were 1,171 *Sparkassen* in Prussia, 361 in Saxony, 376 in Bavaria, and 3,072 in all of Germany. The same year total deposits per capita became 266 marks.[60]

As demand grew, so did banks. While the assets of *Sparkassen* were 0.51 billion marks in 1860, this number rose to 22.56 billion marks in 1913.[61] *Sparkassen*

---

55 Nevertheless, there were cases where deposit banks gave loans to large and small businesses and artisans, as well as the cases where deposit banks gave important loans to companies in the transport sector. For detailed examples See Sibylle H Lehmann Hasemeyer – Fabian Wahl, "Savings banks and the industrial revolution in Prussia: Supporting regional development with public financial institutions", 7.

56 Guinnane, "Delegated Monitors, Large and Small: The Development of Germany's Banking System, 1800–1914", 14,18–20.

57 Ferguson, *Paranın Yükselişi – Dünyanın Finansal Tarihi*, 50–51.

58 In the same period, Kreditbanken rates were 10 % and 24.2 %, respectively. See Guinnane, "Delegated Monitors, Large and Small: The Development of Germany's Banking System, 1800–1914", 69 (Table 1).

59 Guinnane, "Delegated Monitors, Large and Small: The Development of Germany's Banking System, 1800–1914", 29.

60 Guinnane, "Delegated Monitors, Large and Small: The Development of Germany's Banking System, 1800–1914", 70.

61 Tilly – Pierenkemper, *The German Economy During the Nineteenth Century*, 115.

were one of the most important tools for German citizens to contribute to capital accumulation.

2.2.4. Kreditgenossenschaften

Kreditgenossenschaft was a kind of credit cooperative. Kreditgenossenschafts were unique institutions in supporting small producers and non-industrial sectors. *Kredit Genossenschaften* carried out the task of giving the money, deposited by citizens, to small companies for commercial purposes as short-term loans, much more actively.

*Kreditgenossenschaft*en were established after the events of 1848 with the aim of supporting those with insufficient financial means. It was a financial support tool that tried to support agriculture, producers and traders, working with a membership system and collecting their assets from members or non-member regional investors. Since *Kreditgenossenschaft*en generally provided regional services, they gave loans to citizens who could not meet the standards of banks. Neighborhood information was the main criteria for them. By this way, *Kreditgenossenschaft*en were the only financel institution that supported non-industrial sectors and small businesses which could not obtain financing from the bank.[62]

2.2.5. Privatbanken

Privatbanken were privately owned banks or bankers. The role of private banks in German Industrialization is not much talked about. However, the private banks, whose numbers are quite high especially in the Rhine region, made significant contributions to German Industrialization by intertwining with the industry, exchanging financing among themselves and facilitating import and export with their inter-country connections.

---

62 It should be noted that *Sparkassen* got stronger by obtaining financing from regional banks such as *Landesbanken* (banks established in small German states) and *Provinzialbanken* (banks established in large states such as Prussia), established by German governments in order to have more liquidity in the future. Similarly, *Kreditgenossenschaften* also did business with state-owned central banks such as *Preussenkasse* or with private central banks such as *Deutsche Genossenschaftsbank von Sörgel, Parrisius und Co*, where they could periodically transfer money surpluses and sometimes made up for shortfalls. See Guinnane, "Delegated Monitors, Large and Small: The Development of Germany's Banking System, 1800–1914", 14, 25–30.

Privatbanken invested quite actively in the coal and iron industries. Darmstadt Bank, for example, supported the Deutsch-Luxemburg Mining and Iron Smelting Company. Schaaffhausen Bank similarly held the majority of the shares of the large mining company Internationale Bohrgesellschaft and operated the sales and accounting offices of the Union of German Wire Manufacturers. It should be noted that these bankers were quite strong at that time; so much so that in 1904 the Commercial Company of Berlin and the finance house of S. Bleichröder successfully resisted the Prussian Treasury's attempt to nationalize the Hibernia Coal Mining Company in the Ruhr, and they triumphed. Carl Fürstenberg, one of the most prominent bankers at that time, described it as the greatest triumph of his career.[63] It should also be mentioned that bankers financed even the railways in the period between the 1840s and 1870s. In the 1830s, the first railway companies were started to be established, and these companies were financed by bankers. Apart from being financiers of companies, these bankers had also become their stakeholders and direct managers.

The situation of bankers began to change with the establishment of great banks. One of the factors that compelled this change was the necessity of large financings for risky projects. In order to provide these financings, the necessity of financier mergers became more evident. These requirements transformed the structure of bankers into the concept of joint stock companies, and bankers were able to provide financing to industrializing sectors in a more institutional manner by combining capital with the necessary universal and mixed banking practices. The rail industry was an example of this.

Private banks were insufficient to provide capital for the intensive investment period between 1871 and 1873 and the intense investment wave in the markets in 1873 could not find sufficient demand. The financial crisis, which reached its zenith with the collapse of the Vienna Stock Exchange on May 8, 1873, depending on the crisis experienced, caused the existing capital of private banks to melt down and changed the banking structure in Germany.[64] While some of these private banks were incorporated and turned into *Kreditbank*, some did not become a corporation, remaining as a regional *Privatbank* providing loans to industry.[65]

---

63 Henderson, *The Industrial Revolution on the Continent*, 63.

64 Helmut Böhme, "Big-Business Pressure Groups and Bismarck's Turn to Protectionism, 1873–79", *The Historical Journal*, vol. 10, no. 2 (1967), 219–220.

65 Kreditbanken were far superior to Privatbanken in terms of capital. While giant *Kreditbanken* such as *The Schaaffhausen Bankverein, the Disconto Gesellschaft, the Bank für Handel und Industrie and the Berliner Handelsgesellschaft* had an average

The value of "mixed banks" assets in Germany also increased from 600 million marks to 17.5 billion marks (nearly one-fifth of the value of the stock of industrial capital) between 1870 and 1913.[66] Moreover, while there were 71 banks in Germany in 1883, this number increased to 94 in 1895 and to 144 in 1907.[67]

Universal banks were an important part of Germany's capital exports. For this reason, after a certain period of time, Germany's need for great banks was not only for industrial or commercial development, but also for politics. Joint-stock company mergers had become an inevitable need for the formation of great banks. One of the most important factors that provided this opportunity was that the North German Confederation passed the law allowing the establishment of joint stock company banks as of June 11, 1870.[68] After this process, the only area of activity of great banks was no longer the local market, they began to be directly involved in investments abroad. As will be discussed in more detail in the following chapters, the financial support of the German banks during the construction of the Baghdad Railway was quite large. German banks played a major role in the establishment of the Anatolian Railway Company (*Chemin de Fer Ottomans d'Anatolie*) in 1889.[69] Similarly, together with Weiner Bank Verein,

---

founding capital of 33 million marks, the average founding capital of *Privatbanken* in the Rhine region was 1 million marks. Moreover, considering that *Kreditbanken* generally used their own capital until 1870, the difference in terms of capital becomes more clear. See Da Rin – Hellmann, "Banks as Catalysts for Industrialization", 7.

66 Richard H. Tilly, "Banking Institutions in Historical and Comparative Perspective: Germany, Great Britain and the United States in the Nineteenth and Early Twentieth Century", *Journal of Institutional and Theoretical Economics (JITE) / Zeitschrift Für Die Gesamte Staatswissenschaft*, vol. 145, no. 1 (1989), 190.

67 Claphamm, *The Economic Development of France and Germany 1815–1914*, 395.

68 James, "Monetary and Fiscal Unification in Nineteenth Century Germany", 5. From this date on, large-capital Kreditbanken, especially in Prussia, started to appear more and the activities of great banks increased, the door to cartelization was opened by paving the way for universal banking. On the other hand, the fact that Prussia made this decision at a relatively late date was undoubtedly because the state was afraid of losing its influence on financial policies due to great banks. See Da Rin – Hellmann, "Banks as Catalysts for Industrialization", 25.

69 The consortium behind Anadolu Railway Company was established under the administration of Deutsche Bank, Würtembergische Vereinsbank and Deutsche Vereinsbank, apart from other small shares. Deutsche Bank's shares had an absolute predominance in this consortium. See Lothar Rathmann, *Alman Emperyalizminin Türkiye'ye Girişi* (İstanbul: Gözlem Yayınları, 1976), 48.

Deutsche Bank bought Baron Hirsch's shares in Rumeli Railways.[70] The nuance here is that industry and banks were intertwined. Banks were roaming the mining sites and investing with technical knowledge and administrative authority.

The only benefit of the mixed banking model, which included both commercial banking activities and savings banking activities, was not limited to meeting the needs of commercial activities. The mixed banking model also benefited the industry. Towards the end of the century, some great banks discovered that long-term capital supply was also possible. This development was one of the main turning points in industrialization. Because the investments that could receive long-term financing did not have to grapple with heavy paybacks before they reached the breakeven point, and they were able to create their business development budgets even in the early period. For this reason, at the end of the century German banks became an intermediary institution that could convert all kinds of savings into capital.

Great banks became dominant in German finance and industry as mergers became more common and merged companies linked up with cartels. The great banks grew bigger and became the controllers of joint stock banks, small private banks and savings banks. Great bank relations networks were established through exchange blocks of shares agreement between banks. In 1908, the major banks other than the Reichsbank and other federal banks were Deutsche Bank, Discount Company, Schaaffhausen Bank, Darmstadt Bank and Commercial Company of Berlin. The largest of these was Deutsche Bank, with reserves of 300 million marks and equity divided into shares. Dozens of other major banks were associated with Deutsche Bank. The entire Deutsche Bank Group had a capital of 588 million marks and reserves of 197 million marks. The total capital and reserves of the 6 big banks and their connections at that time were over 2,500 million marks.[71] It should also be noted that in 1913, Germany's three largest institutions were banks, and even 17 of Germany's 25 largest institutions were banks.[72]

---

70 Deustche Bank and Wiener Bank Verein took over Baron Hirsch's two disputed receivables of 23 and 20 million francs from the Ottoman Empire and his shares in the Rumeli Railways project. 88.000 shares and two receivables were sold to the Eastern Railways Bank, which was established in Zurich on October 1, 1890, for 72.355.509 francs. See Vahdettin Engin, *Rumeli Demiryolları* (İstanbul: Eren Yayıncılık, 1993), 196–197.

71 Henderson, *The Industrial Revolution on the Continent*, 63.

72 Tilly – Pierenkemper, *The German Economy During the Nineteenth Century*, 113.

2.3. Global Representatives of German Industry: Cartels

According to Alfred D. Chandler, one of the main factors in Germany's overtaking of Britain in certain areas was Germany's successful application of managerial capitalism model, while Britain applied the failed personal capitalism model. For sure, this model was realized in the light of the great banks and also under the leadership of the cartels.[73]

Cartelization in Germany was a unique process due to its dependence on external factors. *Kreditbanken* played a major role in this process. According to Gerschenkron, the acceleration of cartelization in German Industrialization cannot be fully explained without considering the intervention of German banks. According to Gerschenkron, it was the banks that caused cartelization. They involved in company managements and did not allow competition to collapse any business in their portfolio. They were determined to drag companies into marriage where necessary.[74] Two hundred and fifty-nine companies merged between 1851 and 1870.[75] Some of these mergers were signed inside the banks.[76]

The rise of mergers in the mid-19th century accelerated the German Industrialization. As the capital increased, the big jobs that the small companies could not get became available with mergers. These big jobs made the companies bigger. While the number of companies with capital over 10 million marks was 74 in 1886, this number increased to 229 in 1909. As large-capital companies took over the big jobs, their increase in market shares became more evident. In 1893, the coal output of 10 large mining companies was 14.3 million tons. This amount corresponded to 36.6 % of the total coal output at that time. Likewise, in 1910, 49 million tons of coal output of the 10 largest companies was equivalent to 59.3 % of all the coal output in the Ruhr.[77] In 1903, it was 24 "mixed Works" (Gemischte Werke) i.e. combined management in the west of Germany that produced 73 % of the pig iron output in the whole country with 10 million tons.[78] These large ratios allowed the cartels to reduce competition in the markets, to

---

73 Carsten Burhop – Lübbers Thorsten, "Cartels, Managerial Incentives, and Productive Efficiency in German Coal Mining, 1881–1913", *The Journal of Economic History*, vol. 69, no. 2 (2009), 500–501.

74 Gerschenkron, *Economic Backwardness in Historical Perspective,* 15–16.

75 Da Rin – Hellmann, "Banks as Catalysts for Industrialization", 7.

76 Hirth, "State, cartels and growth: The German Chemical Industry"

77 Henderson, *The Industrial Revolution on the Continent*, 58.

78 Ohno, "The Hıstorıcal Stage Of German Capıtalısm—An Analysis Of The Bismarck Regime", 22.

reduce risk, to prevent radical price changes, and to make larger investments in stable markets.[79]

Large corporations not only grew, they also tended to cartelize in a way that prevented competition from occurring, because one of the main purposes of the cartels was to prevent price fluctuations as much as possible and keep the prices at a profitable level.[80] It is not possible to disagree with Gerschenkron from one point of view, but it is useful to examine the cartelization, which is of great importance in German Industrialization, a little more deeply.

Cartels were also divided into two as vertical and horizontal structures. In previous times, mergers were only formed by the combination of capital and power of two companies operating in the same sector. In the new cartelization structures, company mergers were formed in such a way that the entire process, from the company supplying the raw material to the company producing the final product, would be in the same body. This situation led to the emergence of trusts in a short time. Cartels became widespread after the financial crisis of 1873, called *Gründerkrise*. Firms that were on the verge of bankruptcy due to the financial crisis merged in order to survive. These mergers paved the way for the emergence of trusts. For this reason, the saying "*Kinder der Not*"[81] in German literature describes cartels.[82]

As descent is a cause, ascent is also a cause. The formation of cartels was also observed in the periods of increased trade, such as 1888–91.[83]

Although there was a backlash against the cartels because the cartels generally sold their products to the domestic market at higher prices and cheaper to the foreign market, this was never at a level to trigger anti-trust riots as in the United States. Since German cartels were unrivaled in the domestic market, they kept the prices at the desired levels in the sectors with protective tariffs. On the other hand, due to the competition they had to offer competitive prices in the foreign market. Undoubtedly, one of the important factors that allowed the growth of the cartels was the tariffs that made imports difficult. At this point

79 Burhop – Thorsten, "Cartels, Managerial Incentives, and Productive Efficiency in German Coal Mining, 1881–1913", 501.

80 Claphamm, *The Economic Development of France and Germany 1815–1914*, 310.

81 The most appropriate translation into English might be "Children of the danger of bankruptcy".

82 Steven B. Webb, "Cartels and Business Cycles in Germany, 1880 to 1914", *Zeitschrift Für Die Gesamte Staatswissenschaft / Journal of Institutional and Theoretical Economics*, vol. 138, no. 2 (1982), 216.

83 Claphamm, *The Economic Development of France and Germany 1815–1914*, 311.

public intervention was evident.[84] It was also another public intervention that the German government did not prevent cartelization in order for the cartels to grow more easily in the foreign markets. Cartels were the ones who brought German industry to international markets. For the government, the fact that a sector was in the hands of a cartel was a factor that facilitated the nationalization of that sector in case of need. On the other hand, the fact that the cartels were able to export in volume during the periods when the domestic market was stagnant also enabled the economy and sectors to come out of the crisis with little damage.[85] In Germany, the number of cartels increased from 4 in 1865 to 8 in 1875, 90 in 1885, 210 in 1890, almost 400 in 1905, and 600 in 1911.[86] In 1907, there was a cartel dominance of 90 % in paper sector, 74 % in mining, 50 % in crude steel, 48 % in cement, 36 % in glass and 23 % in rail transport. For example, only two groups dominated the electricity sector after 1901. These were Siemens and AEG. In the field of chemistry, dyestuffs cartels were formed with the merger of the group companies in 1904 (I.G.).[87] In the field of organic chemistry, more than three-quarters of all product output in the sector was under the domination of cartels, as well.[88]

Although the cartels signed agreements with the aim of guaranteeing profitability, they were ready to cut the production in order to achieve this. For example, large-scale coal producers in the Rhine-Westphalia region decided to cut production by 10 % in order to increase profitability in 1876–1877, and they repeated to take the same decision in the following years when needed. Although incorporating a regional production quota gave the cartels freedom of pricing, it was also seen that the cartels took serious measures not to lose customers to a comptitive non-cartel domestic market player. For example, some cartels offered

---

84 Although many authors argue that tariffs had a deliberate effect on cartelization, some writers such as Robert Liefmann, a German economist who lived in the period, argue that the coinciding of the tariffs of the period with the cartelization period was just a coincidence. See Robert Liefmann, *Kartelle und Trusts und die Weiterbildung der volkswirtschaftlichen Organisation* (Stutgart: Ernst *Heinrich* Moritz, 1922).

85 Webb. "Cartels and Business Cycles in Germany, 1880 to 1914", *Zeitschrift Für Die Gesamte Staatswissenschaft / Journal of Institutional and Theoretical Economics*, 209.

86 Hirth, "State, cartels and growth: The German Chemical Industry"; Henderson, *The Industrial Revolution on the Continent*, 60.

87 Borchardt, *The Industrial Revolution in Germany 1700–1914*, 66.

88 Webb, "Cartels and Business Cycles in Germany, 1880 to 1914", 208.

discounts of 4 % to 5 % if their customers purchased all their products from them for a year.[89]

Cartels were Germany's gateway to foreign markets. In some way, they were the reasons of the emergence of unions.

2.4. The Importance of Education in German Industrialization

The 19th century was a century of industrial and economic growth for Germany, as well as a century in which educational and scientific activities were significantly triggered.[90] Two factors in this period were the main factors that distinguished Germany from other countries. These were the integration of research into the education system and the introduction of general education to all German citizens.

Until most of the 18th century, education in Germany could not bridge the gap between the state and the citizen because it was under the intense influence of the church for a long time.[91] The lessons were encyclopedic, education was sometimes anti-state[92] and did not contribute to the development of the society, especially the worker. This reality is a generally accepted fact that has been mentioned by many historians from Christopher Clark to Thomas Nipperdey. This situation changed decisively in the 19th century. In the 19th century, education in Germany realized an awakening from its slumber a century ago to become a leader in Europe, and even set a precedent for many overseas countries. One of them was the United States. The pioneers of the education reform that took place in the second half of the 19th century in the USA (such as Daniel Coit Gilman at Johns Hopkins University, Charles William Eliot at Harvard, William Rainey Harper at the University of Chicago, Henry Tappan at the University of Michigan) were either educted in Germany or modeled after German universitiesWhen John Hopkins University opened in 1876, almost the entire faculty consisted of people educated in Germany.[93]

---

89 Webb, "Tariffs, Cartels, Technology, and Growth in the German Steel Industry, 1879 to 1914", 312.

90 Ulrich Schmoch, "Germany: The role of Universities in the Learning Economy" *Universites in Transition*, ed. Bo Göransson-Claes Brundenius (Ottawa: Springer, 2011), 261.

91 Thomas Nipperdey, *Deutsche Geschichte 1800–1866: Bürgerwelt und starker Staat* (Munich: C.H.Beck, 1983), 56.

92 Clark, *Iron Kindom*, 331.

93 Louis Menand et al. (ed.), "General Introudtion" *The Rise of the Research University: A Sourcebook* (Chicago: The University of Chicago Press, 2017), 1–2.

Even as early as 1899, the fact that technical universities in Germany offered doctoral education and thus qualified as academic institutes[94] is an indication of the diversity in education levels in 19th century Germany and the separation of further education from general education in Germany.

Traces of educational reform in Germany could be found in Prussia at the end of the 18th century. In Prussia, innovations such as holding professors responsible not only for teaching but also for devoting themselves to research, ending the courses with a seminar, and developing environments where the academics and students could ve involved in the research were present from the end of the 18th century.[95] In this period, the influence of the state on education was also felt. Compulsory education began in some parts of Germany in the 18th century. Technical education was promoted by state-established colleges and academies.[96] With these education channels, knowledge was transferred from generation to generation, from person to person, from land to land. Germany aimed to create a widespread and permanent qualified workforce in this way. This was an educational revolution that took place at a time when education in Europe and even Britain was generally quite bad. Its effects on industrialization would be felt even more in the future.

The first traces of the reformist period, in which research was formalized as a part of education, could be found at the University of Berlin, which was founded in the early 19th century on the basis of the Humboldt concept.[97] These traces

---

94 Schmoch, "The Evolving Role of Universities in Economic Development", 266.

95 The university structure in Germany was greatly changed by the Napoleonic Wars. In 1789, while there were 35 universities in Germany (German geography within the borders of 1871), 16 universities remained after the Napoleonic wars, and the rest were closed due to war and occupation or were forcibly closed. Halle University, the pioneer of the four universities (Halle, Göttingen, Jena, Leipzig) where half of the students in these 35 universities were enrolled, also remained within the borders of the Kingdom of Westphalia founded by Napoleon. Therefore, the founding of the University of Berlin was not a coincidence, but a necessity that was largely confirmed by the political developments at the beginning of the 19th century. See Johan Östling, *Humboldt and the Modern German University – An Intellectual History*, trans. Lena Olsson (Lund: Lund University Press, 2018), 26.

96 The College of Carolina Wilhelmina, founded in Brunswick in 1745, the college of commerce established in Hamburg in 1767, the mining academies established in Clausthal and Freiberg in 1765, and the Royal Academy of Sciences in Berlin were examples of these. See Henderson, *The Industrial Revolution on the Continent*, 8.

97 Prasada Reddy, "The Evolving Role of Universities in Economic Development: The Case of University-Industry Linkages" *Universites in Transition,* ed.Bo Göransson-Claes Brundenius (Ottawa: Springer, 2011), 27.

were also the first traces across the European continent. For this reason, the roots of the modern university concept in Europe are associated with the educational institution that was established in the capital of Prussia in Berlin in 1809, opened in 1810 and referred to as the "University of Berlin"[98] in the literature.

While the University of Berlin started its education life with 262 students in 1810,[99] it enrolled more than 1750 students in 1840[100] and became a leader in the field of education and research in that period.[101] Previously inactive disciplines such as medicine and veterinary medicine came to life and set an example for other German universities.[102]

The primary difference of the University of Berlin undoubtedly lies in the fact that it had intellectually filled and independent academics such as Fichte, Hegel,

---

98 While doing research on the University of Berlin, the names *Humboldt University of Berlin*, *Freidrich Wilhem University* or *Universität unter den Linden* can be encountered in different sources. Üçü de Berlin Üniversitesi'nin isimleridir. The official name of the University of Berlin was *Friedrich Wilhelms Universität*, or Friderich Wilhelm University, from its establishment until its closure in 1949 due to the separation of East and West Germany. It was named after Friedrich Wilhelm III, who was the King of Prussia at the time it was founded. In the relevant period, it was also unofficially called *Universität unter den Linden*, since the main building of the university was located on the street of Unter der Linden. After the East-West split in 1949, the university was named after the educational reformer, linguist and philosopher Wilhelm von Humboldt and his brother Alexander von Humboldt. Humboldt contributed greatly to the founding of the University of Berlin, and is even widely regarded as the original founder of the University of Berlin. The university was renamed Humboldt Universität zu Berlin in memory of Humbdolt. See Encyclopædia Britannica, "Humboldt University of Berlin", Accessed: 05 December 2020. https://www.britannica.com/topic/Humboldt-University-of-Berlin.

99 Östling, *Humboldt and the Modern German University*, 34.

100 Encyclopædia Britannica, "Humboldt University of Berlin", Accessed: 05 December 2020 https://www.britannica.com/topic/Humboldt-University-of-Berlin.

101 The number of students enrolled in universities across Germany in 1885 was approximately 27.000 (in 1900 this number would rise to approximately 34.000). See Ringer, "Higher Education in Germany in the Nineteenth Century", 132–136.

102 For example, the educational model of the University of Bonn, opened in 1818 targeting the population of the Rhine region, was directly modeled after the University of Berlin. The University of Bonn soon became the most successful university in science and medicine after the University of Berlin. See Thomas Neville Bonner, *Becoming A Physician: Medical Education in Britain, France, Germany, and the United States, 1750–1945* (New York: Oxford Unıversıty Press, 1995), 161–162.

Schleiermacher, Carl Ritter, August Boeckh and Christoph Wilhelm Hufeland,[103] and for sure the reformist views advocated by Wilhelm von Humboldt.[104] Humboldt, then Prussian minister of education, argued that every individual in society had the right to receive a general and basic academic education.[105] Humboldt argued that craftsmen or professionals could take the technical information about their profession on top of this general education, that their research subjects should have been independent of government intervention, and that in this way, the group of employees with general education could be more open to technical development in their profession. According to Humboldt, with this educational programme professionals or craftsmen could switch to another profession whenever they want.[106]

---

103 Östling, *Humboldt and the Modern German University*, 35.

104 Humboldt, who was in Stein's reform cabinet, was appointed to head of the Prussian Department of Education in 1808. Humboldt sent a letter to Frederick Wilhelm III in the summer of 1809, saying that a university should be established in Berlin and emhasized the necessity of what is called the Humboldt-style education system today. The king approved this request in August 1809. See Östling, *Humboldt and the Modern German University*, 34.

105 Günther, Karl H., "Profiles of educators: Wilhelm von Humboldt (1767–1835)", *Prospects 18* (1988), 130–133.

106 Professor Robert J. Zimmer, president of the University of Chicago in 2009, stated that the concept of modern university was born in Humboldt's university, the University of Berlin, even though it was founded 600 years after Bologna, Paris, Cambridge and Oxford. According to Zimmer, Humboldt had three main visions. The first was that education aimed not at teaching a profession directly, but at teaching each individual to think. Second, research had to be at the center of education. As a result of blending research with education, students would be taught how to think. Third, universities should not serve the state and should be independent. Zimmer also stated that those who did not have a vision for research and independence before, gave harsh responses to Humboldt model education, but despite the loud voices, this efficient education model spread throughout Germany in a short time and in Europe in the long run. See Louis Menand (ed.) et al. *The Rise of the Research University: A Sourcebook* (Chicago: University of Chicago Press, 2017), 5. While liberal historians such as Rudolf Haym and Friedrich Meineeke consider Humboldt's ideas on the independence of education consistent and compatible with Prussia's policies, especially with Stein's policies mentioned in the "The Transportation Revolution" section, revisionist historians such as Siegfried Kähler and Leonard Krieger finds Humboldt's ideas on the independence of education inconsistent. In particular, David Sorkin, in his article on Humbdolt's "Bildung" theory, refers to an important part of the works that contain opposing views. See David Sorkin, "Wilhelm Von Humboldt: The Theory and Practice of Self-Formation (Bildung)

The fact that the education model pioneered by Humboldt was implemented first at the University of Berlin and then throughout Germany enabled individuals to conduct research on independent subjects, and this privilege was very effective in terms of the technical and intellectual development of the working population. However, it would not be right to limit all this success to Humboldt. The steps of Prussia under the leadership of visionary and reformist statesmen such as Stein and Kunth had a great impact on the integration of education with industry. Prussia's effort to abandon traditional methods in the industry and to be intertwined with university research in order to integrate industrialization with R&D and advance on a technological basis was an important driving force in the contribution of education to industrialization.[107]

Today, Humboldt's proposal of "independence from the state in research" is perceived as Humboldt's advocacy of the complete independence from the state in education. This is partly true and partly false. Humboldt advocated independence in research, but along with Stein, as a statesman, he also opposed giving full control of the university to academics. Humboldt noted in 1810 that university academics' jealousy, envy, prejudice, and desire to manage things made them unreliable; Indeed, the state's desire for control over the administration of universities, especially when it comes to academic appointments, continued throughout the 19th century. Faculties were obliged to nominate three candidates for vacant academic positions, the ministry usually chose one of these three, but when necessary, the ministers were able to appoint people who were not

---

1791–1810", *Journal of the History of Ideas*, vol. 44, no. 1 (1983), 55–73. Humboldt's view of independence is seen in his important work, *The Limits of State Action*. Humboldt accepts that the state must have a power to provide internal and external security, but he opposes an authoritarian power that will prevent the independence of internal elements. The consistency of this situation shown itself more in the second half of the 19th century, when the withdrawal of state intervention from industry and economy accelerated. Humboldt's coherence was also an important phenomenon that enabled university scholars to be active in exchanging information with the government, and it demonstrates the behind-the-scenes importance of universities in actions taken by public intervention. The fact that Humboldt himself was a diplomat supports the fact that his liberal view could be compatible with state intervention. Therefore, it would be more rational to consider that Humboldt's view of the independence of the university is consistent among these views.

107 Lenoir, "Revolution from above: The Role of the State in Creating the German Research System, 1810–1910." 22.

on the proposal list or even rejected by the faculty.[108] Between 1817 and 1900, at least 322 academics were placed against or outside the recommendations of the faculties.[109] The dependency of the universities to state was to be expected. Because universities were dependent on the state, both financially and partially administratively. University expenses and academician salaries were the responsibility of the state. Moreover, German universities were directly subordinate to the ministry of education. Even in 1871, 91 % of the University of Berlin's income came from the state.[110] The idea that state intervention was only aimed at raising the education level of the society could also be defended by the Ministry of Education's refusal to establish a central publishing house to print schoolbooks. The state did not want to limit private sector initiatives and rejected the offer. Moreover, a binding curriculum and lesson schedule were not established for both primary schools and teachers. Administrations in educational institutions acted with independent decisions, except for extreme contradictions.[111]

It was one of the driving forces behind the scientific independence of the education model in Germany in the 19th century that the state encouraged independence in research matters, ensured that the needs of the industry became the subject of research, and allowed academics to focus on research by giving additional rights and higher salaries. In the 19th century, academics in Germany started to come to the fore with their studies and articles they wrote. Society was also improving. The spread of general education to the general population also contributed significantly to the increase in the productivity of the workforce. This was the general difference of the German education model. The schools such as Cambridge and Oxford in England at the same time were very expensive

---

108 Lenore O'Boyle, "Learning for Its Own Sake: The German University as Nineteenth-Century Model", *Comparative Studies in Society and History*, vol. 25, no. 1 (1983), 11–12.

109 Fritz K Ringer, "Higher Education in Germany in the Nineteenth Century", *Journal of Contemporary History*, vol. 2, no. 3 (1967), 125.

110 This rate was above the average, as the University of Berlin was a university of special interest to the state as a model university. In 1871, the average state-funded income of all German universities was 71 %. See G. W. Roderick – M. D. Stephens. "Scientific Education in England and Germany in the Second Half of the Nineteenth Century." *The Irish Journal of Education / Iris Eireannach an Oideachais*, vol. 16, no. 1 (1982), 71–72.

111 Nipperdey "Mass Education and Modernization: The Case of Germany 1780–1850: The Prothero Lecture", 163.

institutions that served wealthy families whose purpose was to have their sons enter parliament or to become high-ranking statesmen. It was rare at that time that a graduate from Oxford or Cambridge entered a competitive business life rather than politics.[112] In Germany, however, this situation was different and unique. The son of a poor family, who came from any corner of Germany, had the right to receive general education, and the son of a rich family had the opportunity to become an engineer or entrepreneur by getting technical education.

The fact that taking an academic position at the university became a full-time job due to salary increases enabled many academics to leave their secondary jobs and concentrate on their academic life.[113] This development was also a factor that increased competition and efficiency. As early as the 19th century, one of the first questions asked of a professor in Germany was what he published.[114] While research at the academic level come to the fore, with the help of the state the general education spread through Germany. *Volksschulen*, which was the state primary education institution where basic education was given for eight years and where citizens who could not afford to have their children educated in private institutions, sent their children, were very effective in terms of basic education spread throughout Germany. In 1885 when the population was 47 million, 7.5 million children were registered to *Volksschulen* in Germany. Although the quality of education in Volksschulen was not enough to carry the student to higher institutions such as the *Gymnasium,*[115] it was very effective in teaching every child to read and write and providing general education to the society at that time in Germany.[116] In 1850, the ratio of literate people to the population was 52 % in England, 61 % in France, while this rate was 85 % in Prussia.[117] Although there was a deep difference between the people who received a high quality education and those who received basic education from the social class, and although the high quality jobs were continued to be run by the owners' well

---

112 O'Boyle. "Learning for Its Own Sake", 14.

113 O'Boyle. "Learning for Its Own Sake", 6.

114 Robert R. Locke, "Business Education in Germany: Past Systems and Current Practice", *The Business History Review*, vol. 59, no. 2 (1985), 233.

115 Ringer, "Higher Education in Germany in the Nineteenth Century", 132–133.

116 The effect of the strictly supervised compulsory education law, which obliged all children between the ages of 6 and 14 in Prussia to go to school, was also great. See Richard Breitman, "Education and Class Cleavage in Late 19th Century Germany", *International Labor and Working-Class History*, no. 12 (1977), 19.

117 Steinberg, *Bismarck*, 178.

educated sons,[118] the basic education spread throughout the society was also a reason for the increase in productivity.[119]

The creation of an educated worker group by basic education and the increase in productivity thanks to this group of workers was one of the driving forces behind the increase in agricultural and industrial productivity in Germany and the overcoming of the obstacles on the way to the German Industrial Revolution. It is a clear indication of this situation that the percentage increase in the agricultural productivity of each male agricultural worker on the basis of final product between 1840 and 1900 was 21 % in France and 45 % in United Kingdom, while it was 190 % in Germany.[120] In the 1840s, the industrial production per capita within the Zollverein was 8.1 guilders and the craft production was 15.2 guilders, these rates were 3.6 and 4.0 respectively in the neighboring Austria-Hungary. Even this data is another indication of the high productivity of workers and craftsmen at that period in Germany.[121] The increase in these data from the beginning of the 19th century was a result of the effect of general education on production.

Apart from basic education, vocational education's gaining an academic dimension was one of the direct effects of education on German Industrialization. In Prussia and some other German states, the opening of state owned industrial and technical schools began in the 1820s. Due to the government's desire to invest in industry, entry to industrial and technical schools was not difficult in the first years, and many scholarship opportunities were offered. However, in the following years, entry to these schools became more and more difficult. The importance given to mathematics and science was increased significantly, students were given the opportunity to specialize in certain fields, faculties became more independent, entry restrictions were increased. While it had been enough to be a primary school graduate in the 1830s, in the 1870s, the requirement to graduate from the *Gymnasium* or a similar secondary school was imposed for application. Scholarships were reduced, wages increased. Along with all these developments,

---

118 Ringer, "Higher Education in Germany in the Nineteenth Century", 137–138.

119 The level of education in the general population showed regional variations. It should be noted that the education level of the society in states such as Bavaria, where an agriculture-based economy was still very important even at the end of the 19th century, and the education level of the citizens in Prussia were different. See Rondo Cameron, "A New View of European Industrialization", *The Economic History Review*, vol. 38, no. 1 (1985), 13.

120 Trebilcock, *The Industrialisation of the Continental Powers 1780–1914*, 434.

121 Breuilly, *Avusturya, Prusya ve Almanya'nın Oluşumu 1806–1871*, 165.

the names of the schools were changed to industrial institute, industrial academy and finally in 1879 it was named as technical university.[122] Increasing the barriers to entry enabled people with the capacity to receive modern and higher quality education. The higher capacity students meant the higher level of education. Particularly after the 1870s, technical universities were able to provide qualified personnel to private enterprises competing in global markets. For this reason, in the last quarter of the 19th century, construction offices of large machinery companies were established, and chemical companies increased the number of laboratories and their capacities.[123]

The importance of integrating science with education in Germany becomes even more apparent when the fact that scientific research was not an essential part of education in France and Britain until after World War I was taken into consideration.[124] Victor Cousin, who reformed French primary schools as a minister of education, and Horace Mann, who founded the public school system in America, were just two of the experts who examined the development of the German education system to modernize education in their own countries.[125] Similarly, Calvin Stowe, one of the most inspiring names in the spread of public education in America, noted in 1836 that "Prussia does more for the education of the whole people than any government on the earth".[126]

While the development of education was carried out by the state in general, support was also received from the new, educated generation. The push by institutions such as the *Verein Deutscher Ingenieure (VDI),* founded in 1856 by graduates of the Berlin Academy of Industry, to provide higher technical education and more theoretical foundation education to understand the mission and vision of engineering helped to advance technical education.[127] The development of technical education undoubtedly led to the formation of a well-educated white-collar group in Germany, and engineers, who had been known

---

122 Technische Hochschule. See Kocka, "Capitalism and Bureaucracy in German Industrialization before 1914", 462–463.

123 Kocka, "Capitalism and Bureaucracy in German Industrialization before 1914", 463.

124 Robert R. Locke, "Business Education in Germany: Past Systems and Current Practice", *The Business History Review*, vol. 59, no. 2 (1985), 233.

125 Thomas Nipperdey, "Mass Education and Modernization: The Case of Germany 1780–1850: The Prothero Lecture", *Transactions of the Royal Historical Society*, vol. 27 (1977), 156.

126 Karl A. Schleunes, "Enlightenment, Reform, Reaction: The Schooling Revolution in Prussia", *Central European History*, vol. 12, no. 4 (1979), 317.

127 Kocka, "Capitalism and Bureaucracy in German Industrialization before 1914", 464.

as a military unit that builds roads, bridges and machinery before 1850, gained status as civilian individuals after 1850.[128]

The effect of technical education on industrialization was also seen in the field of chemistry. The fact that industrial products that were not in Britain, the first industrialized country, were discovered by German chemists and created a new industrial market for Germany, was met with astonishment and uneasiness, especially from the perspective of Britain.[129] Germany was the first country to establish a mutual and symbiotic working environment between public resources and academics, particularly in the institutes of technology (technische hochschulen).[130] The rapid spread of applied technical education in German universities and the positive effects of German Institutes of Technology also increased the number of academics capable of innovation and R&D in Germany. The fact that German scientists could easily implement their discoveries was of great importance in the spread of the German chemical industry in this period. Even in 1850 foreigners praised the standards of German technical schools. Under the vision and practice of educated people, experiments were carried out using university laboratories.[131]

The importance of education could easily be seen in Britain's struggle with the chemical industry. In that period, there was also a significant amount of entrepreneurs in the UK who wanted to invest in the production of innovative chemical products. There was capital, there was idea, there was infrastructure, but there were no trained personnel to run the businesses. Entrepreneurs in Britain needed people educated in Germany even in this regard. Even as late as 1910, the number of university students studying science and technology in Britain

---

128 Kocka, "Capitalism and Bureaucracy in German Industrialization before 1914", 463–464.

129 The following statements in the report of a deputy sent from Manchester to Prussia to analyze the education system in Germany in 1896 are important for us to understand the German education reform from the perspective of British. "It is not difficult to trace the influence of schools and the education system behind the development of German Industrialization. It is time to give our young people the educational advantages enjoyed by their competitors abroad." See Roderick – Stephens, "Scientific Education in England and Germany in the Second Half of the Nineteenth Century", 73.

130 Jeffrey A. Johnson, "The academic-industrial symbiosis in German chemical research,1905–1939", *The German Chemical Industry in the 20.th Century*, Chemist and Chemistry Series vol.18, ed. John E. Lesch (Dordrecht: Springer-Science+ Business Media, B.V, 2000), 15.

131 Borchardt, *The Industrial Revolution in Germany 1700–1914*, 64.

was around 3,000, while this number was around 25,000 in Germany at the same date.[132] The main reason for Germany's ability to have qualified personnel in the chemical industry was undoubtedly technical education. Chemistry was a field where theory and experiment, research and practice went hand in hand in technical education, and this model of education carried out in German technical universities sharply separated Germany from the rest of Europe. As early as 1826, the chemistry laboratory Justus von Lieblig established in Giessen had become a world-renowned and international experimental school.[133] Even James Muspratt, who is called the father of the British heavy chemical industry, sent his four sons to Giessen to study chemistry.[134] Similarly, Germany's dominance in the global market with its dye products was achieved thanks to the chemists in large-capital chemical companies benefiting from academics that specialized in inorganic chemistry. These chemists were a bridge between capital-owning companies and academia.[135]

Unlike Britain, universities were not the only institutions providing technical education in Germany. In the 19th century, the German advanced education system was created by universities, technical colleges and advanced technology institutes. Highly educated scientists and technologists were graduated from these educational institutions.[136] Established between 1840 and 1890, *technische*

132 Even successful British chemical companies such as Crosfields' of Warrington started out with people who were educated in Germany at first. After English technical schools became widespread locally and technical personnel in the field of chemistry could be trained in England, England started to replace German employees with English. See Roderick – Stephens, "Scientific Education in England and Germany in the Second Half of the Nineteenth Century", 69.

133 Roderick – Stephens, "Scientific Education in England and Germany in the Second Half of the Nineteenth Century", 72.

134 Similarly, Sir Edward Frankland, who would later become Professor at Owens College in Manchester, Sir Lyon Playfair, who would later become Professor of Chemistry at Edinburgh University, Sir William Ramsay, who would later become Professor at University College London, and Sir Thomas Edward Thorpe, who would become a Professor at Yorkshire College Leeds, were among some of the British educated in Germany. In that time, about two-thirds of the work in the field of chemistry all over the world came from Germany. See Roderick – Stephens. "Scientific Education in England and Germany in the Second Half of the Nineteenth Century", 77.

135 Meyer-Thurow, "The Industrialization of Invention: A Case Study from the German Chemical Industry", 365.

136 Roderick – Stephens, "Scientific Education in England and Germany in the Second Half of the Nineteenth Century", 76.

hochschulen (technical universities) provided education focused on areas directly related to industry such as shipbuilding, agriculture, mining. In 1900 there were more than 13,000 students enrolled in these schools, nearly all of whom were graduated as skilled workers. Students already had to study at the Gymnasium for a tough nine years to be able to enroll in this school, and they had to go through tough exams in order to enroll. In 1903 there were about 4,000 students enrolled in *Königlische Technische Hochschule* in Berlin alone. The number of academic staff was 402 and the number of professors was 89. Thirteen of these professors were in the chemistry department.[137] The distribution of students enrolled in the *Königlische Technische Hochschule* in Berlin according to the field of study is as in the table below.

Table 2.1. Distribution of Students Enrolled in Königlische Technische Hochschule in 1903 by Departments

Department	Number of Students Enrolled
Architecture	739
Civil Engineering	689
Mechanical Engineering	1,499
Electrical Engineering	321
Naval Architecture	259
Marine Engineering	123
Chemistry	181
Metallurgy	180

Source: Data from G. W. Roderick – M. D. Stephens. "Scientific Education in England and Germany in the Second Half of the Nineteenth Century." *The Irish Journal of Education / Iris Eireannach an Oideachais*, vol. 16, no. 1, (1982), 75.

Germany not only made its society ready for industrialization, but also imposed additional obligations on education to make its individuals a part of industrialization. For example, towards the end of the 19th century, school attendance was made compulsory for the 14–18 age group. Employers were obliged to send their employees to these schools, otherwise they were obliged to pay fines.[138]

137 Roderick – Stephens, "Scientific Education in England and Germany in the Second Half of the Nineteenth Century", 75.

138 Roderick – Stephens, "Scientific Education in England and Germany in the Second Half of the Nineteenth Century", 75–76.

The education of the skilled worker in Germany was both theoretical and practical. At that time, the rookie stage in Britain was formed after graduation, while a person who graduated in Germany did his rookie during his education and was qualified when he graduated. For example, the state had an aim of producing a corps of state-trained engineers. After graduating from the Gymnasium, and spending a year doing an internship at the state construction office, a student could enter the state-owned construction school *Königliche Bauacademic* in Berlin. After the two years of science, engineering and architecture study here, if the student entered the state exam, he could work for the following three years in the filed, making practice. After these three years, he could receive an advanced education for two years, and after this education he could enter a further state examination. If he passed the exam and graduated from here, he was ready to work for state eight years after graduating from school.[139]

Sent from Britain to Germany in 1840 to report on the effects of Zollverein, Dr. Bowring also stated that as early as 1840, the designs in the German textile industry, the metalworking of the masters in the metallurgical industry, and the chemistry knowledge of even the villagers were better than those in Britain. This was, of course, the result of intellectual capacity and technical education transferring knowledge from generation to generation, from person to person. The difference in Britain was that the work done was based on a system-oriented mass production model, not a people-oriented one.[140]

Established at the beginning of the 19th century, German universities were applying an education model based on a four-faculty structure. These faculties were; law, medicine, theology, and philosophy. Along with Humboldt, education in these four faculties was advanced on the basis of research, but the faculty of philosophy had an originality. Science education was integrated and promoted as part of the philosophy faculty. Between 1820 and 1900, the number of students increased five times, and the number of students in the philosophy faculty increased ten times.[141]

German historian Jürgen Kocka attributes one of the factors behind German Industrialization to the fact that the German bureaucratic structure was implenented in the education in German schools, which were also run by civil

139 Roderick – Stephens, "Scientific Education in England and Germany in the Second Half of the Nineteenth Century", 79.

140 Claphamm, *The Economic Development of France and Germany 1815–1914*, 102–103.

141 Roderick – Stephens, "Scientific Education in England and Germany in the Second Half of the Nineteenth Century", 71.

servants. He claims that the fact that the graduate in Germany continued his working life in the field of education was effective in German Industrialization. This was different from Britain and America. Although this view fundamentally diverges from the Humboldt-style education model, it is a fact that the view advocated by Kocka was correct until the 1850s. However, the German companies that entered global competition as a result of industrialization in the second half of the 19th century needed a new generation of managers who graduated from the Humboldt-style education model. For this reason, it can be argued that there was no single truth in the education models of that period, and the truths changed according to the variable conditions.

The progress of German research universities with industrialization, the fact that universities carried out research in line with the needs of the industry,[142] made education one of the main elements of German Industrialization.

2.5. German Agriculture on the Eve of the Industrial Economy

From the second half of the 19th century to the end of the 19th century, the contribution of German agriculture to the economy gradually decreased, because the main goal of German agriculture was to provide enough food for the growing population.[143] It is a fact that basic needs increase productivity. The impact of the agricultural reforms became evident as a result of these needs. Between 1840 and 1880, agricultural productivity increased by almost 100 %.[144]

The main reason for the increase in agricultural productivity was education. Established in Hildesheim in 1858, the full-time agricultural school under certain departments of the universities was an important step towards educating the peasants in fertilizer farming. Until the 20th century, the number of these schools reached 28. "Winter Schools" was a different example of innovation. "Winter Schools", which were established before the German Empire, were educational institutions in Northern and Eastern Germany, where agricultural students and those engaged in agriculture could go and receive education at the time when peasents could not make agriculture due to the petrified snow.

142 Lenoir, "Revolution from above: The Role of the State in Creating the German Research System, 1810–1910", 22.

143 Wolf, "Agricultural Productivity Across Prussia During the Industrial", 640. Revolution: A Thünen Perspective", *Ehes Workıng Papers In Economıc Hıstory*, no. 13 (January 2012), 21.

144 Lynn Abrams, *Bismarck and the German Empire 1871 – 1918* (New York: Routledge, 2006), 18.

While there were 10 of these schools in 1870, the number of these schools increased to 240 in 1906. Education was so intertwined with agriculture that after the efficiency of winter schools was observed, even continuation schools providing agricultural education were established, where the primary school-age sons of the villagers and agricultural workers could attend after the schools. Between 1900 and 1910 there were 2,000 continuation schools actively providing education.[145] Undoubtedly, these data are an indication that education was used as a tool to ensure productivity in agriculture.

On the other hand, German industry also made significant contributions to agriculture. One of them was the application of the artificial fertilization model. One of the factors that brought Germany ahead of England in agriculture was these commercial fertilizers.[146] Thanks to phosphate discovered near Stassfurt in 1860, Germany became an international monopoly on phosphate fertilizer and the artificial fertilizer model was integrated with Germany. The emergence of phosphate as a byproduct of iron smelting after 1886, led by Gilchrist Thomas, also provided additional resources. For the necessary nitrate, farmers continued to rely on organic fertilizer as a byproduct of coke ovens and Chilean saltpeter. This development in the field of fertilization increased agricultural productivity. Another contribution of the German Industrialization to agriculture was in the mechanization of agriculture. The mechanization of agriculture had advanced markedly in Germany in the 1900s. The mechanization of threshing and the increased cultivation of root crops triggered increased irregularity in the need for rural workers. As a result, most of the fixed workers left, especially in the east, large estates were separated from the feudal system. Exceptionally peasant-owned farms became dominant in central and western Germany. Reapers, seeders, and advanced plow drivers began to be found frequently even on medium-sized farms. From 1882 to 1907, the number of threshers increased by 385 %, seeders increased by 450 %, and reapers by 1500 %. Until 1860, almost all new tools and equipment had been imported from Britain and America, the nascent German agricultural machinery industry began to provide these resources from the last quarter of the century.[147] As a result of these developments the agricultural productivity increase by final product per male agricultural worker in Germany

145 Claphamm, *The Economic Development of France and Germany 1815–1914*, 216.

146 Folke Dovring, "Eighteenth-Century Changes in Eropean Agriculture: A Comment." *Agricultural History*, vol. 43, no. 1 (1969), 184–185.

147 Borchardt, *The Industrial Revolution in Germany 1700–1914*, 55.

was %190 between 1840 and 1900. This rate was %45 for Austria, %30 for Russia, %50 for Italy, %45 for U.K. and %21 for France for the same period of time.[148]

Livestock products expanded faster than crops both before and after 1850. With the prices rising regularly, pork production also increased rapidly. From 1883–84 to 1911–13, pork production increased by 3 % annually, while beef and milk production increased by 1.7 %.[149] As the price of wool fell, there was a decline in wool production after 1860. In 1850, Germany provided 10 % of the international wool production, but after the 1850s, as overseas countries made cheap exports to Europe, Germany could not compete. Potatoes became more important than other food crops. Potatoes were not only poor people's food, they were also used as pig fodder. Potato yield increased five times from mid-century to 1910. In 1910, Germany was able to produce one-third of the potato produced in the world. Sugar production due to local sugar beet production expanded even faster than potatoes. Between 1890 and 1900 sugar accounted for 6 % of all export value. With this ratio, sugar left behind areas such as coal, iron and machinery exports.[150]

Until the 1870s, German farmers had made good profits due to rising prices, but then cheap imports from overseas to Europe reversed the trend. In particular, the completion of the first transcontinental railroad in the USA in 1869 enabled first American and then cheap Canadian goods to gain a share from the European market. American sales of wheat, flour and meat products increased sixfold in that period.[151] This resulted in a decrease in agricultural product prices in Germany, and prices re-approached their values in the beginning of 1870 only in 1914.

Germany introduced protective tariffs on grain after 1879, but this did not prevent German prices from falling on the global market, but guaranteed a higher price for the local market. Import duties on grain, which were moderate at first for cereals, had been increased in 1885, increased again in 1887, and in this way, 30 % customs duty on the product price became levied. Between 1891 and 1906, Caprivi's commercial policies slightly reduced the protectionist tariffs. The protective tariffs slowed the contraction of agriculture and their turnover, but also delayed possible structural changes and the associated rise in the amount of

148 Trebilcock, *The Industrialisation of the Continental Powers 1780–1914*, 434.

149 Steven B Webb,"Agricultural Protection in Wilhelminian Germany: Forging an Empire with Pork and Rye", *The Journal of Economic History*, vol. 42, no. 2 (1982), 317.

150 Borchardt, *The Industrial Revolution in Germany 1700–1914*, 57.

151 Steinberg, *Bismarck*, 397.

produce. Even this degree of protection for agriculture could not guarantee that the necessary production would be made to feed the population in a possible force majeure situation. In 1910 40 % of all wheat and 15 % of all grain had to be imported.

In 1913, Germany was 95 % self-sufficient in calorie foods and vegetables, but it could only meet 57 % of its animal food needs. Germany was deficient in important nutrients such as carbohydrates, fats and protein.[152]

Germany's developing industry and economic situation also drove many people who were engaged in agriculture away from agriculture. Both wages and working conditions in agriculture had moved away from the those in the industrializing cities in a negative way day by day. This situation is also seen in the tax payments in Prussia in 1901. While the town population paid an income tax of 8,61 marks per capita in Prussia in 1901, this amount was 2,16 marks per capita for the rural population.[153] Moreover, industrializing cities offered some other attractions such as better living conditions, education and professional training.[154] That's why there was a shortage of workers at harvest time, especially in the East Elbe, where incomes were relatively low. In East Elbe, workers were often supplied by Italy, Austria-Hungary, Ukraine and Russian Poland (also known as the Congress Kingdom of Poland).[155] By 1913, Germany was home to 1 million seasonal migrant workers.[156]

While, in 1871 the ratio of agricultural workforce to total active population was %45, this ratio decreased to %36 in 1895.[157] It is obvious from the rates that Germany left its way of being an agricultural country relatively early in 1895, and that it made this separation much faster than the other leading European countries except U.K.[158]

---

152 Borchardt, *The Industrial Revolution in Germany 1700–1914*, 57.

153 Walther Lotz, "The Commercial Policy of Germany." *Journal of Political Economy*, vol. 15, no. 5 (1907), 258–259.

154 Karl Brandt, "The German Back-to-the-Land Movement." *The Journal of Land & Public Utility Economics*, vol. 11, no. 2 (1935), 123–125.

155 Just before 1914, more than half of the seasonal workers who came to Germany from Austria-Hungary, Russia and Italy came as agricultural workers. See Steve Hochstadt, "Migration and Industrialization in Germany, 1815–1977", *Social Science History*, vol. 5, no. 4 (1981), 457.

156 Tilly – Pierenkemper, *The German Economy During the Nineteenth Century*, 98.

157 Trebilcock, *The Industrialisation of the Continental Powers 1780–1914*, 435.

158 While this rate was %9 for U.K. in 1901, it was %43 for France and %59 for Italy in the same year. For Russia this rate was %86 even in 1910. See Trebilcock, *The Industrialisation of the Continental Powers 1780–1914*, 435.

2.6. German Industrialization and its Effects between 1871 and 1913

Between 1860 and 1880, the average industrial growth in the UK was 2.4 %, while in Germany it was 2.7 %. Between 1880 and 1900, these rates were 1.7 % and 5.3 %, respectively. In 1893, the German steel industry surpassed the British steel industry, and in 1913, the British chemical industry supplied 11 % of the world's chemical products, while Germany supplied 24 %.[159] At the same year, Germany was producing two-thirds of the steel production in Europe, 20 % more than the total electricity produced by Britain, France and Italy, and more coal than all the other countries in the continent combined. In terms of exports, while it had been ahead of France with 10 % in 1890, in 1911 this ratio became %60. Between 1870 and 1913, Germany's GDP per capita grew faster than any other European country.[160] Only in the period from the 1880s to the First World War, Germany's net national product increased by 159 % and its industrial production by 202 %.[161]

Between 1871 and 1913, Germany became a global economy. In the last five years before the begenning of the First World War, Germany's export share in world markets had increased to 15,8 %, while its import share had increased to 19,2 %. At that time, Germany was a major importer of food, raw materials and semi-finished products, as well as a major exporter of products.[162] Value-added products had a positive impact on the economy.

This period, between the proclamation of the German Empire and the First World War, was the transition period of Germany from the agricultural state to the industrial state. Even in 1871, 49 % of the German population was working in agriculture, while in 1907 this rate dropped to 35.2 %, and the ratio of those working in industry increased from 31 % to about 42 % in the same period.[163] The developments in this period, where the workers in the industry surpassed

159 Roderick – Stephens. "Scientific Education in England and Germany in the Second Half of the Nineteenth Century", 80.

160 Hirth, "State, cartels and growth: The German Chemical Industry".

161 Burhop – Lübbers, "Cartels, Managerial Incentives, and Productive Efficiency in German Coal Mining, 1881–1913", 503.

162 Torp, "The Coalition of 'Rye and Iron'" under the Pressure of Globalization: A Reinterpretation of Germany's Political Economy before 1914, 424.

163 H.J. Braun, *The German Economy in the Twentieth Century* (London: Routledge, 1990), 19; Abrams, *Bismarck and the German Empire 1871 – 1918*, 17.

those in agriculture and the productivity increased significantly in the same period, sheds light on some of the reasons behind the First World War.

2.6.1. Population and Emigration

In Germany, the population was still increasing after 1871. The population, which was 35,128,000 in 1849,[164] reached 64,926,000 in 1910, and since most of this population growth occurred within cities, the total population of cities with a population of 100,000 or more in 1890 reached 11.4 % of the entire population.[165] Population growth was a necessary factor for industrialization. It had increased both consumption and workforce. For example; Hamburg, which had a population of 265,000 in 1875, reached 1 million in 1910. Also, Berlin was home to 826,000 people in 1871, its population reached to 2 million people in 1910.[166] In Germany, as elsewhere, population tended to shift to where the money was.

There were some important reasons in the population increase in Germany in those years. Overseas immigration due to political disorder before and after the Revolutions of 1848 had turned into internal immigration as of 1870. This means that the population moved within the German geography and did not decrease in total. The reason of the German internal migration at that time was the economic welfare. With the industrial revolution Germans migrated to German industrial cities not abroad, because the income in those cities were far better then where they had come from. The more economic welfare, the less emigration. An exception to the positive trend after the 1860s was the 1880s. Economic crisis in 1873 was a reason, Bismarck's antisocialist laws, which came into force in 1877–78, was another reason, the rearing up of the American economy at the same time was another one. In conlusion, more than 1 million Germans left the German Empire in 1880s. All these three reasons were related to economic welfare.[167] On the other hand, the effects of Bismarck's providing social rights to

---

164 Based on population within the German Empire.

165 Claphamm, *The Economic Development of France and Germany 1815–1914*, 279.

166 Abrams, *Bismarck and the German Empire 1871 – 1918*, 19.

167 Two important events in the 1860s and 1870s prevented emigration. The American Civil War between 1861 and 1865 was a factor affecting emigration, mostly to the United States. Similarly, the fact that the Franco-Prussian War of 1870 temporarily stopped transatlantic voyages, although it did not prevent the emigration that spread throughout the 1870s, it did create an obstacle to the potential emigrations in 1870. See Khoudour-Castéras, "Welfare State and Labor Mobility: The Impact of Bismarck's Social Legislation on German Emigration before World War I", 213.

workers in the 1880s and the updating of the industrial and agricultural tariffs in the 1890s had positive effects on emigration in the 1890s. Again, as the level of economic welfare increased, people migrated less.

Until the 1860s, Germany was one of the world's main sources of labor, along with Ireland, which was facing famine, and Britain, which had many colonies.[168] The characteristic feature of Germany's tendency to emigrate in the process until the First World War is that these emigrations started to decrease rapidly, with certain exceptions, after the 1860s.

The population growth rate in Germany in the 1850s was 0.8 % per annum, reached 1.1 % in the 1900s and increased to 1.4 % before the First World War. In these rates, the increase in births and the immigration flow also had effects. The excess of births remained stable until the 1870s because birth and death rates did not change much. Alongside the high number of births from 1872, the drop in the death rate is also notable, as the death rate had dropped as far as 1.5 % by 1913. The birth rate, on the other hand, maintained its average value since 1830 for the next 30 years, only falling to 2.7 % between 1900 and 1913. Birth surplus, which was 0.9 % until 1870, increased to 1.5 % until 1900 and decreased to 1.2 % until 1913. Simultaneously, the average man's life expectancy had increased from just 36 years in 1870 to 45 years by 1913.[169] Immigration into Germany, had started to play an important role in the population of Germany. From 1893 onwards, migrants from Russia, Poland, Austria-Hungary and Italy came to Germany. Around 1910, there were an average of 880,000 migrant workers in Germany. This additional population made a significant contribution to the workforce, with a significant positive impact on the seasonal agricultural jobs that existed, particularly in the eastern parts of the country.

The fact that Germany turned the migration trend towards itself after 1880 was a unique characteristic of German emigration as of the period. In the 1890s, while the countries of Southern and Eastern Europe were at their peak in emigration,

---

168 Between 1871 and 1914, 90.6 % of those who emigrated from Germany emigrated to the U.S. More than 5 million Germans emigrated to the U.S. between 1850 and 1914. In the same period, the number of Italians emigrated to the U.S. was 4 million, the number of people emigrated from Austria-Hungary to the U.S was 4 million, the number of Irish emigrated to the U.S was 3.5 million, the number of British emigrated to the U.S was 3.5 million, and the number of the Russians emigrated to the U.S was 3,2 million. See Khoudour-Castéras, "Welfare State and Labor Mobility: The Impact of Bismarck's Social Legislation on German Emigration before World War I", 213.

169 Borchardt, *The Industrial Revolution in Germany 1700–1914*, 50.

Germany had succeeded in reducing its emigration rates considerably. While in Germany, between 1865 and 1884 annual average emigration rate was 2.47 for 1,000 people (this emigration rate represents 1 person migrating annually for every 1,000 people in the population), this rate decreased to 1.01 between 1885 and 1913. This difference in the rates represents –59 % change. In the same time period, this change was –7 % for U.K., 31 % for France, 244 % for Italy, 430 % for Austria and 945 % for Hungary.[170]

2.6.2. Labour Force

According to Alexander Gerschenkron A, creating an industrial workforce is the most difficult and long process of industrialization.[171] Germany is one of the countries with experiences that support this view of Gerschenkron.

The labor force required for industrialization in Germany was provided in two ways. The first of these was the transfer of agricultural workforce to industry after the 1850s. The second was population growth. This population increase was achieved both by the positive trend in birth and death rates and by immigration. Improvement in the working conditions and increasing economic wellness were inviting for the migrants. Thus, Germany received more and more immigrants each year.

In 1891, working on Sunday was prohibited in industrial sectors and limited to five hours in trade-related sectors. Employers were obliged to provide minimum cleaning conditions in the places where employers worked. Working hours for youth and women were restricted. In 1903, employing child labor was strictly prohibited. Some cities, such as Cologne, offered local unemployment support to their unemployed residents.[172] All of these improvements was a factor in pushing workers to work in Germany.[173]

Working hours regulations were also another factor that triggered immigration. Getting more productivity with fewer working hours in Germany

---

170 Khoudour-Castéras. "Welfare State and Labor Mobility: The Impact of Bismarck's Social Legislation on German Emigration before World War I." 215.

171 Gerschenkron, *Economic Backwardness in Historical Perspective – A Book of Essays*, 9.

172 Khoudour-Castéras, "Welfare State and Labor Mobility: The Impact of Bismarck's Social Legislation on German Emigration before World War I", 221.

173 In Germany, the government intervened in child labor relatively early. It was an effective measure that in 1839 the Prussian government banned children under the age of 14 from working and stipulated compulsory education for children to prevent violating this prohibition. See Tilly – Pierenkemper, *The German Economy During the Nineteenth Century*, 110.

was another factor that increased the well-being of industrial workers. The decrease in working hours, which was 80–85 hours a week until the 1850s, to 40–50 hours a week before the First World War, and despite this, the increase in productivity was an indication that both industrialization and investments to increase productivity were successful.[174]

Another important point here was the decrease in the daily wage worker and the increase in the salaried worker. While the ratio of salaried employees to daily wage workers was 11 to 1 in 1865, this ratio was 7 to 1 in 1890 and 3.5 to 1 in 1912.[175] This data can be directly related to the speed of industrialization.

The increase in welfare in the workforce was one of the leading factors that created the workforce. The average annual salary of a coal miner in the Ruhr rose from 863 marks in 1888 to 1,755 marks in 1913. The annual salary of a worker in Upper Silesia increased from 516 marks to 1,053 marks in the same period. Reserves in German savings banks increased from 6,800 million marks in 1895 to 17,800 million marks in 1911. In Prussia, on the other hand, the amount in savings banks increased more than 10 times between 1870 and 1910, from 20 marks per capita to 276 marks.[176] All of these are clearly signs of increased well-being, which was one of the most important motivations behind the creation of the workforce in Germany.

2.6.3. Shipbuilding Industry

Another important heavy industry area during the German Industrialization was the shipbuilding area that showed itself at the beginning of the 20th century.

---

174 Tilly – Pierenkemper, *The German Economy During the Nineteenth Century*, 110.

175 Jurgen Kocka, "Capitalism and Bureaucracy in German Industrialization before 1914", 459.

176 Henderson, *The Industrial Revolution on the Continent*, 74. Although the increase was valid everywhere, the level of welfare was not the same everywhere. According to the calculations made by the Central Statistics Office in 1913, the per capita income was expressed in marks by regions as follows: 1313 marks in Hamburg, 1254 marks in Berlin, 962 marks in Brandenburg, 899 marks in the Prussian provinces of Hessen-Nassau, 897 marks in Rhein province, 832 marks in the Kingdom of Saxony, 763 marks in Prussia's Schleswig-Holstein, 735 marks in Westphalia, 710 marks in Baden, 697 marks in Hannover, 672 marks in Württemberg, 629 marks in Bavaria, 603 marks in Silesia, 576 marks in Pomerania, 486 marks in East Prussia, 480 marks in West Prussia, 465 marks in Posen. See Borchardt, *The Industrial Revolution in Germany 1700–1914*, 67.

It was not until as late as 1886 that Germany could compete with Britain in the production of modern iron and steel ships. Germany's merchant ships amounted to 1.2 million tons at that time, of which 470,000 tons were steamships. Most of these ships had been built abroad. After 25 years, the situation completely changed. Large shipyards such as Blohm & Voss (Hamburg), Rickmers (Bremen), Vulkan (Stettin) were established. Just before the First World War, German shipyards were producing 400,000 tons per year and delivering army orders. In 1913, Germany's merchant ships were 4.4 million tons in total, of which a quarter were less than five years old. German ships were in a position to compete with Britain in both merchant ships and passenger ships.[177]

Steamship tonnage increased from less than 100,000 tons in 1871 to 216,000 tons in 1880, to 724,000 tons in 1890, to 1,348 thousand tons in 1900, and to 2,397,000 tons in 1910. The annual production capacity between 1910 and 1913 was around 400,000 tons.[178] Compared to 20 years ago, most of them were produced in German shipyards in Sttetin, Danzig, Kiel, Hamburg and Elbing instead of being imported. The state-subsidized shipbuilding program led to the development of commercial shipping alongside the empire's own colonial activities.[179]

Until the First World War, Germany's exports in the shipbuilding sector also reached an important level. In this period, since the export of Germany's naval technologies that would provide technological advantage in a possible war, such as diesel-powered warships, was often prevented by the navy, there was a significant restriction on the export of modern navy elements, especially since the beginning of the 20th century.[180] While in 1898, 36,97 % of the warships built in private German shipyards were exported, in 1909 this rate decreased to 0.75 %.[181]

---

177 Henderson, *The Industrial Revolution on the Continent*, 69.

178 Claphamm, *The Economic Development of France and Germany 1815–1914*, 286.

179 The attitude of the states and the importance they gave to waterways were also decisive. Prussia, for example, was well aware of the importance of waterways. In the 1890s, all Rhine states spent between 6 and 8 million marks annually on the Rhine River in total, while Prussia spent 35 million marks annually on the improvement of its waterways. See Klemann-Joep, "Competition in the Rhine Delta: Waterways, Railways and Ports, 1870–1913", 832.

180 Michael Epkenhans, "Military—Industrial Relations in Imperial Germany, 1870–1914", *War in History*, vol. 10, no. 1 (2003), 14.

181 Epkenhans. "Military—Industrial Relations in Imperial Germany, 1870–1914.", 24.

Considering that 40 % of the ships produced in private shipyards between 1881 and 1896 were exported, the value of the ships produced between 1895 and 1898 alone amounted to 100 million marks,[182] the restrictive effect of the navy on shipbuilding exports can become much more evident.

The period when the German navy made aggressive development plans is the post-Bismarck period. Because, while Bismarck was pursuing a policy that adopted to make Germany an economic and political power within its borders, Kaiser Wilhelm II's vision was to carry German influence across the continent. This could only be achieved by the navy at the end of the 19th century. Therefore, the Navy Cabinet was established in 1889, Alfred von Tirpitz was appointed to the Ministry of the Navy in 1897, and navy building programs began to be established under the leadership of Tirptiz.[183]

In his first memorandum presented in 1897, Tirptiz proposed to enlarge the German navy by 30 % until 1905 and to retire old warships and have new ones built. On July 14, 1898, the naval development program led by Tirpitz was accepted by the Reichstag. However, the British navy's development program was progressing much faster and the gap between the British navy and the German navy was rapidly widening. Thereupon, a new construction program was presented to the Reichstag in 1900 and a new plan was adopted, with no spending limit, aiming to increase the navy to 38 warships, 20 heavy cruisers and 38 light cruisers. Also in this plan, the construction of a transoceanic fleet of 3 heavy and 10 light cruisers was approved.[184]

Germany's competition with Britain quickly moved the German navy forward. Tirpitz continued its naval development plans with new plans in 1906, 1908 and 1911. Between 1906 and 1914, France produced 4, Russia 4, USA 8, Japan 8 dreadnoughts and battlecruisers, while Germany produced 17 dreadnoughts and 7 battlecruisers between 1908 and 1914. The only country to surpass Germany was United Kingdom which built 29 dreadnoughts and 9 battlecruisers between 1906 and 1914.[185]

---

182 Epkenhans, "Military—Industrial Relations in Imperial Germany, 1870–1914", 16.

183 Burak Samih Gülboy, "İngiltere ile Almanya Arasındaki Donanma Rekabeti ve Büyük Güç Olma Paradoksu", *100. Yılında Birinci Dünya Savaşı ve Mirası*, ed. Halil Çetin et al. (Çanakkale: Çanakkale Valiliği, 2015), 1/66–67.

184 Gülboy, "İngiltere ile Almanya Arasındaki Donanma Rekabeti ve Büyük Güç Olma Paradoksu",70–73.

185 Gülboy, "İngiltere ile Almanya Arasındaki Donanma Rekabeti ve Büyük Güç Olma Paradoksu",83–84.

2.6.4. Chemistry

One of the most important sectors that made a breakthrough and made a difference during the German Industrialization was chemistry. As a new industry, chemistry revealed a potential market, created a direct target market for Germany and dominated global markets.[186] This sector, which was under the dominance of Britain until the 1860s, faced German competition from the 1860s, and by 1913, it came under Germany's global dominance, particularly in organic chemistry products such as dye. The fact that Germany was the producer of 85 % of all dyestuff output in the global market had not only put Germany in a leadership position, but had also thrown Britain out of the competition.[187] In particular, there are those who interpret the production of dye products as Germany's greatest industrial success.[188] As it can be seen from the table below, Germany had created a market that did not exist yet with its innovative dyestuff products and made itself the main source of supply by creating an additional demand for it.

Until the First World War, three-quarters of the world's synthetic dyes were produced in Germany. While Germany's dyestuff products export were 44 million marks in 1878 and 60 million marks in 1883,[189] it approached 195 million marks in 1913. Although chemical industry employed 30,000 people in the mid-19th

---

186 This innovative structure in German Industrialization continued during and after the First World War. Until the First World War, German industry had advanced under the leadership of the coal, iron and steel industries. However, with the First World War, the weights on the scales began to change. Machine-building, electro-technical and chemical industries started to lead by providing more employment and increasing their share in exports faster. While giants such as MAN, Borsig-Werke and DEMAG emerged in the machinery industry, companies such as Siemens and AEG in the electrical industry began to make their weight felt more. See Gerald D Feldman – Ulrich Nocken, "Trade Associations and Economic Power: Interest Group Development in the German Iron and Steel and Machine Building Industries, 1900–1933", *The Business History Review*, vol. 49, no. 4 (1975), 415–416.

187 Lion Hirth, "State, cartels and growth: The German Chemical Industry", *Grin* (Accessed: 09.12.2020).

188 David S. Landes, *The Unbound Prometheus* (Cambridge: Cambridge University Press, 1969), 276.

189 One of the reasons for the increase over the years was the increase in demand. While the trade volume of dye products in the world was 70 million marks in 1878, it became 92 million marks in 1883. See Georg Meyer-Thurow, "The Industrialization of Invention: A Case Study from the German Chemical Industry", *Isis*, vol. 73, no. 3 (1982), 365.

century and lagged behind the British and French, it started to gain momentum in the 1860s and employed 270,000 people by 1911–13. Aniline dyes, with a share of 15 % in the total turnover, pharmaceutical products and fertilizers were the vehicles that made Germany chemical industry famous in the global markets. As early as 1900, Germany alone supplied 90 % of the world's aniline dyes.[190] Undoubtedly, German education had a great impact on this success of Germany. While aniline was used for dyeing silk in general, in 1868 two German scientists synthesized alizarin dyes to dye cotton products. Alzarin emerged as a new technology and dominated the market. This inovation was an outcome of the German education.[191]

Instead of targeting global markets such as textile, which had been already captured by the UK, Germany created loyal and sustainable global markets with its innovative industrial products in the fields of heavy industry and chemistry. Companies such as Bayer, which had been establishing contractual contacts with academics in order to be intertwined with academic studies since 1880s and had employed full-time chemists in its own laboratories and conducted corporate R&D since 1890s and became popular with "Aspirin" after 1900, or companies such as AGFA and Höchst, which reached large commercial volumes in this field, came to the fore and assumed the leading role in these innovative fields.[192]

When the number of chemists in Bayer's research laboratories taken into consideration Germany's development in the field of chemistry can be clearly seen. Bayer, had a steady increase in the number of research chemists, whose main task was to make innovation, and chemists. While the number of chemists working in Bayer's research laboratories was 99 in 1897, this number increased to 138 in 1902, 171 in 1906 and 262 in 1912.[193] Even the data in the field of chemistry alone can support the argument that German Industrialization was not an industrialization that only followed the developments in Britain. It was a unique achievement of German Industrialization that it created innovative

---

190 Borchardt, *The Industrial Revolution in Germany 1700–1914*, 63.

191 Meyer-Thurow, "The Industrialization of Invention: A Case Study from the German Chemical Industry", 364.

192 Since the 1880s, Bayer had been establishing contractual contacts with academics in order to be intertwined with academic studies, and since the 1890s, it employed full-time chemists in its laboratories and conducted corporate R&D. See Meyer-Thurow, "The Industrialization of Invention: A Case Study from the German Chemical Industry", 368–369.

193 Meyer-Thurow, "The Industrialization of Invention: A Case Study from the German Chemical Industry." 371.

products and created a demand that did not exist in the global markets which had been dominated by an industrialized power like Britain.

2.6.5. Textile

Textile was a sector that existed in every process of German Industrialization and of which influence decreased over the years.

Between 1871 and 1913, the silk industry was especially prominent in the textile industry, as the silk industry was an industry that was directly affected by industrialization. The contribution of the silk industry to exports, which was only 16 million marks in 1887, was more than 200 million marks in 1913. Behind the scenes of this success were technological weaving looms. In 1890 there were 5,400 power looms weaving silk and velvet, while there were 25,000 handlooms. By 1909, the number of handlooms had decreased to 2,700 and the number of power looms had increased to 9,900. German silk producers were now able to compete with their French competitors in the global market.[194] Between 1900 and 1913, exports of French silk products varied from 10,000,000 francs to 16,000,000 francs, while Germany's annual exports of silk products varied between 7,000,000 francs and 10,000,000 francs in the same year. Germany was followed by Switzerland in the third place, while Britain was quite behind in the silk industry. The silk industry was an industry that advanced mainly through handlooms until the 1890s. The fact that there were only 5,400 power looms in 1890 compared to 22,500 handlooms in Krefeld is an indication of this.[195]

Although textile did not grow much in terms of employment in this period, it grew in terms of efficiency and value-added products. The technology, workforce and knowledge that came with the annexation of Alsace undoubtedly had an impact on this development. By 1895 the number of large enterprises in the cotton industry had grown to 304. The employment provided by these 304 large enterprises was 69,441 in the same year. In the same year, German cotton consumption reached 250,000 tons.[196] In 1913, the share of textile products, excluding ready-made clothing, in exports was 12.7 %.[197]

---

194 Henderson, *The Industrial Revolution on the Continent*, 70.

195 Claphamm, *The Economic Development of France and Germany 1815–1914*, 298–299.

196 Claphamm, *The Economic Development of France and Germany 1815–1914*, 297.

197 Naci Yorulmaz, *Arming the Sultan* (New York: I.B. Tauris, 2014), 88.

2.6.6. Mining

Most fundamental steps in Germany's industrialization were taken by mining. The period of 1871–1913 was a period in which the efficiency of mining increased significantly.

Although the production amount of many mines had increased tremendously in the 1850s, it was only in the 1860s that their productivity increased. For example, coal production in Dortmund increased more than 50 times from 1787 to 1867.[198] However, productivity remained stagnant until the 1860s.[199] This enables us to conclude that the increase in production was achieved with more resources and more workers. This situation was not only specific to coal mining. Pig iron production, for example, followed a similar trend. Between 1837 and 1902, the productivity per worker in pig iron industry increased more than 10 times in Germany.[200] The increase in productivity, combined with the increase in the number of workers and the increase in resources such as the mines in Alsace and Lorriane, provided a unique environment for the acceleration of German industry.

The acquisition of Alsace and Lorriane was a very important development in itself for German Industrialization. Together with these gains, technology, workforce and underground wealth came. There was even an important French section who thought that they could never be friends with Germany again just because of Lorraine.[201] The mine-rich Lorraine was a wealth that France never accepted to lose. So much so that Lorraine alone supplied one-third of Germany's need for highly phosphorous ores. Some of these mines were smelted with Ruhr coke. French capital also played an important role in the development of zinc deposits in Stolberg in West Germany and in Upper Silesia. At that time, Upper Silesia alone provided half of the world's zinc, but after 1880 this branch of the economy began to stagnate. The production of hard coal grew at an annual average of 5.3 % between 1815 and 1913. Growth accelerated further between 1850 and 1873 when deep mining activated the Ruhr area. The Ruhr area expanded slightly to the north until 1913, the mines began to get deeper and the workforce increased.[202]

198 Jurgen Kuczynski, "Productivity and Exploitation under German Capitalism." Science & Society, vol. 9, no. 1 (1945), 60.

199 Kuczynski, "Productivity and Exploitation under German Capitalism." 59.

200 Kuczynski, "Productivity and Exploitation under German Capitalism.", 64.

201 Christopher Clark, *Uyurgezerler*, trans. Cem Demirkan (İstanbul: Pegasus Yayınları, 2017), 129.

202 Borchardt, *The Industrial Revolution in Germany 1700–1914*, 58.

2.6.6.1. Coal

Coal was a necessary and indispensable mineral in many areas from the production stage of the metal to the processing stage, from transportation to chemistry, from mining to heating. Therefore, it became one of the lifebloods of German industry. In Germany, coal was mainly mined from three regions; the Ruhr to the west, the Saar to the southwest and Silesia to the east. The most important of these resources were the Ruhr mines, which alone provided 48 % of German coal production in 1880 and 58 % in 1913.[203] In 1913, German coal production caught the same as Britain's coal production. Coal production, which was 60 million annually in 1887, increased to 190 million by 1913. Likewise, lignite production, which was 16 million in 1887, increased to 87 million in 1913. Net coal exports rose to 20 million tons, and the number of workers in coal mines rose from 120,000 in the 1860s to half a million in 1913.[204]

Germany lagged behind only Great Britain in Europe in that period. Germany was well ahead of France and Belgium, the other major coal producers, in coal production since 1871. Germany's major coal deposits were located in the Ruhr,[205] the Saar, and Upper Silesia, but among these three locations the Ruhr held the clear lead. In 1913, 114 million coals were mined from the Ruhr. This amount was half of all German coal output that year. In the same year, 44 million coal was produced in Upper Silesia and 13 million in Saar.[206]

2.6.6.2. Iron – Steel

Along with coal, Germany's other two lifebloods were iron and steel. Keynes's statement that "Germany existed with 'iron and coal' rather than 'iron and

---

203 Although there had been a significant increase in coal production, consumption had similarly increased due to industrialization and the developing means of transport. Therefore, Germany continued to use imported coal, which was imported from the United Kingdom until the beginning of the 20th century and was taken into the imperial borders from the Hamburg port. See Burhop – Lübbers, "Cartels, Managerial Incentives, and Productive Efficiency in German Coal Mining, 1881–1913", 503.

204 Henderson, *The Industrial Revolution on the Continent,* 66.

205 Until the 20th century, the Westphalia coal mine in the Ruhr alone produced almost half of all coal output. Coal mines in Silesia were mines whose value was appreciated later. For this reason, the deep descent operation could be performed late. In 1913, the coal output in Silesia alone was 43,000,000 tons. See Claphamm, *The Economic Development of France and Germany 1815–1914*, 282.

206 Henderson, *The Industrial Revolution on the Continent,* 67.

blood'" is quite significant in this context.[207] Steel output in Germany increased tenfold from 1880 to 1900 and far outstripped British production.[208] Between 1879 and 1913, Germany's steel output grew by 10.4 % and pig iron at 6.3 % per year, compared to 6 % and 1.5 %, respectively, in Britain over the same period.[209] The cost of steelmaking had fallen to 10 % of its level in the 1860s, and by 1913 Germany had melted almost twice as much pig iron as Britain. One of the breaking points was the annexation of Lorraine. Before the annexation in 1871, the iron and steel industries were located in locations where German iron and steel reserves were located. These were mostly Siegerland, Upper Silesia, Luxemburg and the regions of LahnDill and Ilsede-Peine. In the 1860s total production reached 2 million tons. Iron ore production of Silesia showed a downward trend while that of West Germany showed a growth trend. However, the annexation of Lorraine in 1871 suddenly changed the situation. In 1872, 684,000 tons were produced in Lorraine alone. This ore was phosphoric, but with the discovery of Gilchrist Thomas, iron production in Lorraine increased more. German iron ore production, which was 6.7 million tons in 1887, exceeded 28 million in 1913.[210]

The Saar region, Upper Silesia, and especially the Ruhr and Lorraine became new centers of iron mining and smelting.[211] Immediately after the Franco-Prussian war, the iron trade gained a high momentum and a large number of new iron companies were established. In 1875, German pig iron output increased to 2 million tons. In 1913 that number rose to 19.3 million.[212] As of that date, Germany had become the first pig iron producer in Europe and the second largest pig iron producer in the world after the USA.[213] Iron products accounted for 15.8 % of Germany's exports in 1913. Between 1879 and 1913, the

---

207 John Maynard Keynes, *The Economic Consequences of the Peace* (San Diego: Harcourt, Brace and Howe, 1920), 75.

208 Dietmar Petzina, *Die deutsche Wirtschaft in der Zwischenkriegszeit* (Stuttgart: Steiner, 1977), 5–7.

209 Webb, "Tariffs, Cartels, Technology, and Growth in the German Steel Industry, 1879 to 1914", 326.

210 Even this amount was not enough for the iron need of industrializing Germany. In 1913, Germany's net iron import was 11,4 million tons. These countries were usually Spain and Sweden. See Henderson, *The Industrial Revolution on the Continent*, 67.

211 Borchardt, *The Industrial Revolution in Germany 1700–1914*, 57.

212 Yorulmaz, *Arming the Sultan*, 88.

213 In 1913, Germany's iron output was 19,3 million tons, while the USA's was 30,4 million tons and Britain's was 10,5 million tons. See Önsoy, *Türk-Alman İktisadi Münasebetleri (1871–1914)*, 47.

annual rate of increase in Germany's exports of iron and steel products was at a significant level of 5.8 %.[214]

Even in 1870 the pioneering British enterprises were much larger than their biggest German competitors, this changed from 1900. For example, German products in the steel industry dwarfed British products by an average of 300 %.[215]

In every industry there is a link between increasing manufacturing space and equipment and the amount of power required to bring it to life. The Germans carried out these organizations quite successfully. Even in 1882, there were 1,127,003 employed people working in mining and steelworking in Prussia.[216]

With its organizational success, the creation of the workforce, the integration of technology with the industry and the increase in efficiency, Germany achieved a unique success in the industrialization competition it entered later. With the successful use of the Alsace – Lorraine gains, the German industry started to catch up with its competitors and then to get ahead of them over the years. The steel production of Germany grew by %1335 between 1886 and 1910. This rate was only %154.1 for Great Britain, %692.9 for France and 871.2 for Russia.[217] All these economic developments worried both Britain and France.

On the way to the First World War, it was inevitable that German Industrialization would be perceived as a threat. This inevitability ultimately became one of the reasons for the political polarization at the beginning of the 20th century, resulting in the transfer of economic and political developments to the battlefields.

---

214 Webb, "Tariffs, Cartels, Technology, and Growth in the German Steel Industry, 1879 to 1914", 326.

215 Borchardt, *The Industrial Revolution in Germany 1700–1914*, 61.

216 Michael Kopsidis; Daniel W. Bromley "The French Revolution and German industrialization: The new institutional economics rewrites history", *Discussion Paper*, No. 149 (2014), 41.

217 Yorulmaz, *Arming the Sultan*, 50.

Chapter 3 Ottoman-German Military and Strategic Relations after German Industrialization (1871–1914)

3.1. Industrialized Germany's Search for a Target Market

From the second half of the 19th century, industrialized Germany had two main problems that it focused on. The first of these was to provide the necessary living space for its growing population, and the second was to find the target markets necessary for the sustainability of its industrialization. The first need led to the colonization policy, and the second to the economic influence policy. The real question was to which states these policies could be applied.

Germany realized that colonization in Africa was costly and inefficient for itself and moved away from this policy in a short time. The deficit in the colonial budget in 1913 costed German taxpayers more than 1,000 million marks. Of the German colonies, only Samoa and Togoland were able to pay off the financial investment made, while the others caused losses. Neither the raw materials nor the amount of imports in these lands played an important role in the German economy. In 1913, Germany's colonial trade accounted for almost 0,5 % of its entire trade.[1] In all these periods, the German population living in the colonies did not exceed tens of thousands, and most of them were not permanent people but civil servants. Therefore, Germany turned its direction to the states that still maintained their political existence, but did not have the technology to process their raw materials. However, it was obvious that conventional policies of influence would not work, as they were states that still retained their political presence. This situation led to the emergence of a new influence policy peculiar to Germany.

Germany's policy of influence by providing financing and establishing the cycle of selling industrial products and purchasing raw materials was a German-specific policy of influence that showed concrete examples especially in the late 19th century and early 20th century. Germany approached the four big states,

---

1 The situation did not change on the eve of the First World War. Due to the fact that Germany did not have colonies, the foreign active trade that Germany had before the First World War was equivalent to half of France and a quarter of Britain. See Thomas Piketty, *Yirmi Birinci Yüzyılda Kapital*, trans. Hande Koçak (İstanbul: Türkiye İş Bankası Kültür Yayınları, 2nd Ed., 2015), 150.

which it considered to be in the target market category, with this unique policy of influence.

One of these countries was the Russian Empire. Although the Russian Empire had been occupying an important place in the cycle of supplying raw materials to Germany and purchasing value-added final products until the third quarter of the 19th century, it became more and more independent both with the infrastructure investments it made from the second half of the 19th century and with the local applications brought by modern technology. So much so that Russian coal production, which was 21,8 million poods[2] between 1860 and 1864, increased to 1840, 2 million poods in 1910–1913.[3] With the realization of its own production, Russia was no longer a target market for Germany.

Another country on Germany's radar was China. Throughout history, China had been the target of many great states due to its wide geography and dense population. Germany also participated in this race and insisted on obtaining its share in the Far East. In particular, von Bülow's speech at the Riechstag on December 6, 1897 is quite remarkable for analyzing Germany's Weltpolitik and its expectations over China. Von Bülow described Germany's expectations in his speech entitled "Der Platz an der Sonne" (Place in the Sun) as follows.

> *Dr. Schoenlank seemed to fear that we want to throw ourselves into adventures in East Asia. Have no fear, gentlemen! The Reich Chancellor is not the man, and his staff are not the people, to look for any useless business. We also don't feel the need to stick our fingers in every pot. However, we are of the opinion that it is not advisable to exclude Germany from the outset from the competition with other nations in lands with a promising future. The times when the German left the earth to one of his neighbors, reserved the sea for the other, and reserved the sky for himself, where pure doctrine reigns supreme are over. We regard it as one of our most important tasks to foster and cultivate the interests of our shipping, our trade and our industry, especially in East Asia.*
>
> *The dispatch of our cruiser division to Kiaotschau Bay and the occupation of this bay took place on the one hand to obtain full atonement for the murder of German and Catholic missionaries and on the other hand to obtain greater security than before against the recurrence of such occurrences. Negotiations are afoot in both directions, and in the nature of diplomatic negotiations and business this compels me to weigh my words very carefully. However this much I can say: we have only benevolent and friendly intentions toward China…*
>
> *…In a word: We do not want to put anyone into the shade, but we demand a place for ourselves in the sun.*

---

2 Pud is a Russian unit of weight. One pud is approximately 16,3 kg.

3 M.E. Falkus, *Rusya'nın Endüstrileşmesi 1700–1914*, trans. Alaeddin Şenel (Ankara: V Yayınları, 1986), 69.

In East Asia, as in West India, we shall endeavor to protect our rights and our interests, true to the traditions of German policy, without unnecessary harshness, but without weakness, either.[4]

Germany had successes such as obtaining a naval base in China in 1898.[5] However, Germany soon realized that a limited naval power would not be enough to dominate China against Britain, France and the developing Japan. As a result, it lost control of its East Asian policy.

Another target country for Germany was Iran. Iran was a more rational target for Germany, as Iran also welcomed Germany with an inviting attitude. Both the administration and the people of Iran, which they had been exploiting for the interests of Britain and Russia for years, saw Germany as a savior. Moreover, the Shah even told the Germans that he would allow German colonizer groups to settle in Iran if Germans organized the administrative organs and ministries in Iran.[6] However, Germany was too late for Iran. Britain, which received the oil concession, divided Iran with Russia in the north and south, and took absolute measures to prevent Germany from having a say here until the First World War broke out. Germany could not get what it wanted from Iran either.

Only one possibility remained in this category for Germany, The Ottoman Empire.

Particularly in the last century, unlike other countries, the Ottoman Empire was a state that had been subject to permanent retreat due to both internal and external threats. The ethnic uprisings and the wars of the great powers with the Ottoman Empire caused the male population to be devastated in wars for years. This situation created financial difficulties for the Ottoman Empire and paved the way for borrowings up to capitulations. Incessant capitulations also ensured the undermining of domestic production, and the possibility of industrialization of the Ottoman Empire, which was already incapable of processing industrial raw materials and was already consuming its missing capital in wars, was prevented. The Ottoman Empire, unlike the standard European countries, could not industrialize even if it wanted to. This result indicated that the wish of the European states, which had interests in the Ottoman Empire, had come true. The traces of this aim are also be seen in the writings of British Foreign Secretary

4 Michael Fröhlich, *Imperialismus. Deustsche Kolonial und Weltpolitik 1880–1914* (Munich: Deutscher Taschenbuch Verlag, 1994), 301.
5 Henderson, *The Industrial Revolution on the Continent*, 52.
6 İlber Ortaylı, *Osmanlı İmparatorluğu'nda Alman Nüfuzu* (İstanbul: İletişim Yayınları, 2004), 23.

Lord Palmerston, who stated in his letter to Lord Ponsoby in 1883 that Turkish industry must have been prevented in particular.[7]

In the Ottoman Empire, some industrial reforms started in the 19th century. Factories to serve the defense industry were established, In order to ensure the continuity of production here, engineering schools such as Mekteb-i Mühendislikhane-i Bahri-i Hümayun, Topçu Mektebi, Mekteb-i Mühendislikhane-i Berri Hümayun, Mekteb-i Mühendislikhane-i Sultani were opened, a weaving factory was opened, a fez factory (Feshane) was opened, leather and shoe factories were modernized, and steam power was used to increase the efficiency of the cannon and bullet factories in Tophanc. But these moves did not go any further. Low tariffs imposed by force due to capitulations prevented further domestic industrialization moves. As a result of the 1820 Customs Tariff, 3 % customs duty was charged for the goods exported by United Kingdom to the Ottoman Empire, while a 60 % tax was charged in the UK for the goods exported by the Ottoman Empire.[8] With the 1838 trade treaty, known as the Treaty of Balta Liman, the control was completely taken over by the British. The Ottoman Empire was forced into free trade provisions, and the collapse caused by irreversible capitulations continued to undermine local industry day by day.

Although the Ottoman Empire was in a period of weakening due to the inevitable consequences of its inability to industrialize, it was still quite strong both militarily and in terms of population. Unlike other countries, the Ottoman Empire ruled considerable lands in Asia, Europe and Africa, had not even needed to form an alliance for centuries, protected its borders with natural barriers such as the Sahara Desert and the Indian Ocean, and was still a very powerful empire with rich resources in three continents.[9]

The Ottoman Empire was worn out by threats from inside and outside. The Sublime Porte and the Sultan, who saw the destructive attitude of global powers such as Britain, France and Russia against Ottoman Empire and were aware of the possible consequences, did not take kindly to concessions given to foreign countries and tried to keep the colonial countries away. Therefore it was inevitable for a country that wanted to influence the Ottoman Empire to develop a new policy of influence. It was Germany that did it.

---

7 Necla V. Geyikdağ, *Osmanlı Devleti'nde Yabancı Sermaye 1854–1914* (İstanbul: Hil Yayın, 2008), 34.

8 Geyikdağı, *Osmanlı Devleti'nde Yabancı Sermaye 1854–1914*, 45–46, 52.

9 Feroze A.K. Yasamee, *Abdülhamid'in Dış Politikası*, trans. Yusuf Selman İnanç (İstanbul: Kronik Kitap, 1996), 20.

The statements made by Paul Rohrbach in his book *Die Bagdadbahn*, one of the classic works of pancermenism, are the main idea of Germany's attitude towards the Ottomans; "It's not worth spending a penny for a weak Ottoman Empire, but we'd give anything for a strong Ottoman Empire."[10]

3.2. Political Reasons for Turkish-German Rapprochement

The growth in foreign trade volume as a result of transportation and industrial development in Germany created a significant capital abundance with the effect of effective banking models. Financial instruments were an inviting attraction for states grappling with economic problems. Therefore, surplus capital turned into an effective political tool in this period, particularly in the late 19th century when alliances changed radically. Germany, which had a capital surplus, directed its capital transfer towards the Ottoman Empire towards the end of the 19th century, and the Ottoman Empire reacted positively to this approach.

The Turkish-German rapprochement also had a political basis. It was Britain that invaded Cyprus in 1878. It was Britain that occupied Egypt in 1882. It was Britain that supported the unification of Wallachia and Moldavia as Romania. It was Britain that forced the Ottoman Empire to withdraw from Serbia. It was Britain that caused Crete to gain autonomy. And it was Britain that who took Cyprus from Ottoman Empire with diplomatic games. It was France that invaded Tunisia in 1881. It was France that set its sights on Syria and Lebanon. It was Russia that occupied Eastern Rumelia. It was Russia that tended to interfere in the internal affairs of the Ottoman Empire permanently through the Orthodox living in the Ottoman Empire. It was Russia that wanted the Ottoman Empire to be federated by autonomously administering their own regions of the nations within the Ottoman Empire. It was Russia that came to the threshold of Istanbul in the 93 War. It was Russia that took Kars, Ardahan, Doğu Beyazıt and Erzurum. It was Russia that created the project of a giant Bulgarian Principality, whose government and army would be subordinate to the Russian Empire, through the Treaty of San Stefano signed after the war. It was Russia that demanded the granting of larger territories to Romania, Montenegro and Serbia and the recognition of their independence. It was Russia that tried to expel the Ottoman Empire from the Balkans. It was Russia that declared itself the protector of the Slavic nations in the Balkans. It was Russia that posed a constant threat to

10 Sean McMeekin, *Berlin – Bağdat Demiryolu*, trans. Azize F. Çakır (İstanbul: Picus Yayınları, 1st Ed., 2012), 67.

the borders of the Ottoman Empire. Italy's eyes were on Libya. It was Austria-Hungary that claimed it had guarded the eastern border of Europe for centuries against the Ottoman Empire and therefore wanted the Ottoman Empire's lands in the Balkans. It was Austria-Hungary that followed its ambitions on Bosnia-Herzegovina and wanted Bosnia-Herzegovina even in wars that it was not involved in. It was Austria-Hungary that signed a secret treaty with the British on Bosnia-Herzegovina. It was Austria-Hungary that did not allow the Ottoman soldiers to pass through the Dalmatian coast, It was Austria-Hungary that did not attempt to control the Serbs in the 93 war, but instead forced the Ottoman Empire to protect the Serbian border, and therefore kept the military power that the Ottoman Empire would use against the Russians on the Serbian border.[11] The only global power in Europe that did not have an eye on the Ottoman lands seemed to be Germany.[12]

The Ottoman Empire was both a target market and a strong potential ally for Germany. Germany both considered the huge benefit of the uninterrupted transportation line that could be established with the German-Austrian-Ottoman alliance, and thought that the Ottoman Empire could be a potential barrier against a possible Russian aggression. Neither Austria nor Germany forgot the threat posed to them by the Ottoman defeat in the 93 War.

Germany's relations with the Ottoman Empire were friendly, unlike Britain and France. Germany never used the harsh and dominating language of Britain, on the contrary, it respected the decisions of the Ottoman Empire and the Sultan and supported it in many places. For example, while Britain was constantly threatening to impose sanctions on minority rights, Germany gave advice on Turkification of minorities and not making concessions to minorities and supported Sultan Abdulhamid's methods and political choices.[13]

---

11 Yasamee, *Abdülhamid'in Dış Politikası*, 87–90.

12 The statements of the Berlin ambassador Sadullah Pasha also support this inference. In his letter to Safvet Pasha on December 17, 1877, he stated that Europe was no longer the Europe of 1855, and that there was no great power to protect the Ottoman Empire unconditionally. Sadullah Pasha stated that Germany was the effective precautionary power of Europe at that time, and emphasized that Austria was also subject to Germany's instruction and direction. According to Sadullah Pasha, Italy, on the other hand, was under Germany's command, just like a settlement within Germany's own borders. France, on the other hand, was still unable to recover after the defeat in 1870, and it had no way of having a say in eastern affairs while it did not even have a permanent government. See Ali Akyıldız, *Sürgün Sefir Sadullah Paşa* (İstanbul: Türkiye İş Bankası Yayınları, 2011), 295.

13 Yorulmaz, *Arming the Sultan*, 4.

In the United Kingdom, Benjamin Disraeli, who was known for his more moderate policy, was dismissed as a result of the elections held in April 1880, and William Ewart Gladstone, who openly made anti-Turkish propaganda, took office as a result of the elections held in April 1880.[14] This was a sign that Turkish-British relations would get worse. Gladstone, who claimed that the Turks were an enemy of civilization and gained an audience with the propaganda of the Bulgarian agitation,[15] began to put pressure on Sultan Abdulhamid through the minorities in the Ottoman Empire as soon as he took office. Moreover, he continued to fuel the sparks of nationalism in the Balkans. He put pressure on the determination of the borders of Greece and Montenegro and the implementation of the reform package to be realized for the Armenians, in accordance with the Treaty of Berlin, which was unenforceable according to many statesmen.[16] Simultaneously, as a result of his pressure on European states, he enabled European states to give notes to the Ottoman Empire in 1880. As a result of the pressures of Gladstone, the European states even sent their navies to the Ulcinj region in order to intimidate the Ottoman Empire. Although the Ottoman Empire answered the note and created a reform plan, the Turkish hostility that fueled Gladstone's domestic policy did not subside and continued to provoke minorities against the Ottoman Empire during his time in power.[17]

By the end of the 19th century, it was quite natural that the Ottoman Empire was in search of a friend in Europe, as in that period, states were forming policies not only with their own forces but also with their political alliances.[18] Being alone in such an environment meant being powerless. Germany's tendency to protect the geographical and political existence of the Ottoman Empire in general and Germany's supportive attitude to the actions of the Ottoman Empire in domestic politics was quite welcoming for the Ottoman Empire. This policy of Germany began made itself more evident in the reign of Kaiser Wilhelm II, who took foreign policy under his own administration after Bismarck. Bismarck's importance to the League of the Three Emperors[19] had a great role in the German-Turkish

14 W. N. Medlicott, "The Gladstone Government and the Cyprus Convention, 1880–85", *The Journal of Modern History*, vol. 12, no. 2 (1940), 186.

15 Taha Niyazi Karaca, *Büyük Oyun – İngiltere Başbakanı Gladstone'un Osmanlı'yı Yıkma Planı* (İstanbul: Timaş Yayınları, 2018), 173.

16 Yasamee, *Abdülhamid'in Dış Politikası*, 110 – 111.

17 Karaca, *Büyük Oyun*, 245–246.

18 Vahdettin Engin, *II. Abdülhamid ve Dış Politika* (İstanbul: Yeditepe Yayınevi, 2017), 10.

19 It is the alliance signed at the level of emperors between the Austro-Hungarian Empire, the Russian Empire and the German Empire as a result of Bismarck's diplomatic efforts. See H. Brooke McDonald – Richard Rosecrance, "Alliance and

relations during the Bismarck era.[20] Germany also needed alliances and it was in a very insecure geography. Austria had lost power against the Balkan Union and began to damage the friendly approach of the Germans towards the East with its threatening attitudes in the Balkans.[21] Romania had moved away from Austria and the side that the Romanian forces would hold in a possible Russian war was no longer on the side of Germany, but on the side of Russia. In addition to all these, all the corps of Austria, which would be an alliance of Germany during a possible war, consisted of 17 units. It was clear that Germany would not be able to obtain many additional forces from the Austrian alliance in a possible war. Considering that France and Russia had 60 corps at the same time, it became obvious how much Germany needed to ally with the Ottoman Empire and to improve the military power of the Ottoman Empire.[22]

It was also unknown how much of Austria's military power would fight alongside the Germans in the event of a possible war, since there were multiple nations in Austria. The uncertainty of the attitude of the Slavs in Austria in a possible German-Russian war was a phenomenon that made the Germans think. In the event of the collapse of Austria, the turmoil, which would be caused by the freedom struggle of many small nations that would have broken away from Austria could also have closed Germany's doors to Asia. Therefore, Austria was an indispensable but partially problematic and inadequate alliance for Germany. The regular turmoil created by the Austro-Hungarian bilateral administration, the unwillingness of the Hungarian side to give money and soldiers to Austria, which was in charge of the army, made it difficult to create a military budget and blocked the way for army reforms for a long time. Therefore, even in 1912, Austria's military expenditure was only 2,6 % of the net national income. This ratio was considerably below that of Russia, France and Germany in the same period.[23] It became clear that Germany needed other alliances, both in the

Structural Balance in the International System: A Reinterpretation." *The Journal of Conflict Resolution*, vol. 29, no. 1 (1985), 59–60.

20 During the existence of the League of the Three Emperors, Bismarck's attitude towards the Ottoman Empire was cautious. Berlin ambassador Sadullah Pasha also mentioned this attitude of Bismarck in his writings. According to Sadullah Pasha, during the Russo-Turkish War (1877–1878), when the Ottoman Empire began to retreat, both the ambassadors of other countries and Bismarck turned their backs on Sadullah Bey at the invitations. See Akyıldız, *Sürgün Sefir Sadullah Paşa*, 73.

21 Hartmut Lehmann – Silke Lehmann, *Das Nationalitätenproblem in Österreich: 1848 – 1918* (Göttingen: Vandenhoeck & Ruprecht, 1973), 93.

22 Karl von Winterstetten, *Berlin-Bağdat* (İstanbul: İz Yayınclık, 2011), 43.

23 Clark, *Uyurgezerler*, 210.

political and geographical arena. In line with this goal, it was inevitable that the German orbit would return to the Ottoman Empire.

While all this political basis provided realistic reasons for Turkish-German rapprochement, political relations developed day by day since the end of the 20th century, as a result of the leaders' mutual good relations. The German Emperor made his first visit to the Ottoman lands in 1889, one year after his accession to the throne, and this visit provided a great impetus to mutual commercial relations. Kaiser Wilhelm's second visit to the Ottoman lands in 1898 further strengthened the relations. Many mutual gestures were offered during this visit. While the Kaiser was visiting Jerusalem, the Sultan sent a cavalry regiment by land to meet him in Jerusalem.[24] Sultan Abdulhamid presented the German Emperor Kaiser Wilhelm II with the land called "Dormitio" in Jerusalem, which is considered sacred in the Christian religion. While France saw itself as the patron of all Catholics in Palestine, the protection of German Catholics was given to the Kaiser.[25] In his famous speech delivered by the German Emperor in Damascus,[26] he spoke sincerely and praising Sultan Abdulhamid and made references to Ottoman-German relations. The Germans built a hospital in Jerusalem and the Ottoman Empire provided support to facilitate these activities.[27] These were some of the mutual gestures that solidified the foundations of German-Ottoman political cooperation. These relations continued in a very positive way during the Committee of Union and Progress period. Although the German economic influence was interrupted between 1908 and 1909, it continued rapidly from 1909 onwards.

---

24 BOA, Y.PRK.MM, 1 – 89, H-05-01-1316.

25 II. Abdulhamid defended this situation with the following words: *Although the French claim that they have been the patrons of Christians and Christian organizations since the time of Francis, they should know that a strong nation like the Germans will not accept the patronage of another nation.* See Engin, *II. Abdülhamid ve Dış Politika*, 38–39.

26 "...Let three hundred million Muslims living scattered on earth and wholeheartedly devoted to their caliphs rest assured that the German Emperor will always be their friend..." See Fahri Türk, *Türkiye ile Almanya Arasındaki Silah Ticareti 1871–1914* (İstanbul: IQ Kültür Sanat Yayıncılık, 2012), 130.

27 BOA, İ.MBH, 2 – 19, H-28-04-1328.

3.3. Economic Reasons for Turkish-German Rapprochement

Capital abundance in Europe began to manifest itself with industrialization. Therefore, it was not easy for the Ottoman Empire to borrow money during the periods when the major countries in Europe had not been yet industrialized.

The Ottoman Empire had tried to borrow many times since the 17th century, but could not find the positive answer it was looking for most of the time.[28] This attitude had changed as the industrializing countries developed the foresight of acquiring economic and political concessions in return for the loan. Thus, Ottoman Empire was able to get its first debt from Britain through the Crimean War. The financial difficulties behind the adventure of borrowing from Europe, which started with the Crimean War, had reached the point of financial bankruptcy with the famine and Bosnia-Herzegovina uprising in 1875. According to some sources, the Ottoman foreign debt reached more than 75 % of its annual income at that time.[29] The financial bankruptcy of the Ottoman Empire, which had become an inevitable reality, was announced to the world public opinion by the government of Grand Vizier Mahmud Nedim Pasha.[30] In 1876, while the Ottoman Empire had a total foreign debt of 200 million pounds, with an annual payment of 12.5 million pounds, in 1874 the state's revenues were 22 million pounds. In other words, while the annual income covered 11 % of the foreign debt.[31]

While the Ottoman economy was bankrupt, the financial crisis reached its zenith with the outbreak of the Russo-Turkish War (1877–1878). As a result of this war, the Ottoman Empire lost two-thirds of its territory and one-fifth of its population, and was obliged to pay war indemnity to Russia.[32] The loss of these lands, where agriculture and trade were developed, caused a serious loss of incomeThe inability to pay the debts due to the impact of these losses created an interest swamp and the Ottoman Empire, which declared that it had

---

28 Geyikdağı, *Osmanlı Devleti'nde Yabancı Sermaye 1854–1914*, 64.

29 According to A. Heidborn, although the revenue was 25,000,000 in the 1874/75 budget of the Ottoman Empire, the real income was 17,000,000 Ottoman liras. The foreign debt was 13,000,000 Ottoman liras. See Parvus Efendi, *Türkiye'nin Mali Tutsaklığı* (İstanbul: May Yayınları, 1977), 33.

30 Engin, *II. Abdülhamid ve Dış Politika*, 18.

31 Emine Kıray, *Osmanlı'da Ekonomik Yapı ve Dış Borçlar* (İstanbul: İletişim Yayınlar, 2015), 148.

32 It was decided that the Ottoman Empire would pay 300,000 pounds sterling every year for a hundred years as war reparations to Russia. See Kıray, *Osmanlı'da Ekonomik Yapı ve Dış Borçlar*, 32–33.

stopped paying cash debts since 1876, had to allow its finances to be placed under the control of European lending states as of 1881. The Ottoman Public Debt Administration (Düyun-u Umumiye), which was established with the treaty signed on 20 December 1881 and known as the Decree of Muharram, was authorized to seize both the foreign and domestic revenues of the Ottoman Empire. Düyun-u Umimiye, which was managed by the representatives of Britain, France, Germany, Italy, Austria-Hungary and the Ottoman Bank, reduced the total debt of the Ottoman Empire from 212.5 million pounds to 128.6 million pounds. It extended maturities and reduced annual debt payments from £13.6m to £2.7m. However, it further fueled the existing economic depression of the Ottoman Empire, as it increased the income items it seized day by day. Although the share left to the Düyun-ı Umumiye was 20 % of the revenues of the Ottoman Empire, this rate increased to 30–35 % in a short time.[33]

The interesting aspect of the process is that the fact that an economic crisis started in the world in 1873 and that not only the Ottoman Empire but also many other countries could not pay their debts, is generally ignored. During this period, Egypt, Tunisia, Spain, and many Latin American countries were unable to pay their debts.. Italy limited debt interest payments, Greece decided not to pay debt for a long time.[34] While there was no intervention in these countries, the establishment of an external control mechanism such as Duyun-u Umimiye was deemed appropriate in the Ottoman Empire. Salt and tobacco monopolies, stamp taxes, fish and alcohol taxes, silk tithe in many places, the annual tax paid by the Eastern Rumelia province were left to the Düyun-u Umumiye.[35]

Düyün-u Umumiye seized a significant part of the main income of the Ottoman Empire and did not allow the Ottoman Empire to have the financial cycle it needed to maintain its stagnant economy, let alone invest. It established a large organization with more than 5,000 employees in more than 20 cities of the Ottoman Empire in order to collect the taxes effectively and to increase exports in the areas left to it. In short, to collect its receivables more easily.[36] This situation gave the European states the opportunity to impose whatever sanctions they wanted on the Ottoman Empire. Now, the Ottoman Empire could not control its revenues and could not manage relatively.

33 Kıray, *Osmanlı'da Ekonomik Yapı ve Dış Borçlar*, 34–35.

34 Geyikdağı, *Osmanlı Devleti'nde Yabancı Sermaye 1854–1914*, 76.

35 Şevket Pamuk, *Osmanlı Ekonomisinde Bağımlılık ve Büyüme, 1820–1913* (İstanbul: Türkiye İş Bankası Kültür Yayınları, 2020), 62.

36 Pamuk, *Osmanlı Ekonomisinde Bağımlılık ve Büyüme, 1820–1913*, 62–63.

Düyün-u Umumiye did not claim the Ottoman receivables that it was the protector of as a result of the Treaty of Berlin. According to the Treaty of Berlin, it was decided that the Balkan states would also participate in some of the debts that the Ottomans had to pay, but after this decision, no money was paid by them on time.[37] The Balkan states did not pay these moneys for a long time, and the European states did not impose any sanctions for the collection of these payments. On the contrary, these states were also preserved. For example; Bulgaria did not pay the tax it was obliged to pay, and Russia strongly protected it. The Cyprus island was occupied by Britain. The excess of the Cyprus island revenues that had to be paid to the Ottoman Empire was retained by Britain as a security deposit of the borrowing of 1855. The Eastern Rumelian tax, which was determined as 265,000 Ottoman liras for each year, was arbitrarily reduced to 180,000 liras, then to 152,000 liras, and then to 114,020 liras by the Eastern Rumelian National Assembly, and nobody supported the protests of the Ottoman Empire.[38]

In such a period, the constructive attitude of Germany brought the Ottoman Empire and Germany closer in economic terms, and distanced the Ottoman Empire from France, which was the main source of support financing, and Britain, with which it had high commercial relations. One of the first positive steps was the "Friendship, Trade and Maritime Treaty" signed between Germany and the Ottoman Empire on August 26, 1890. This treaty was the harbinger of the situation of separation from the policy of Bismarck, who did not want to be included in the oriental politics by saying Balkans were not worth the healthy bones of a single Pomeranian grenadier,[39] and the predominance of economic

---

37 For example, the payment of Bulgaria was not made until the Istanbul Protocol, when Bulgaria gained its independence in 1909. See Abidin Temizer, "The Independence Process of Bulgaria and the First Ambassador of the Ottoman Empire to Sofia, Mustafa Asım Bey" *Belleten*, vol. 85, no. 304 (2021), 1085. Similarly, there was a war indemnity that Greece was obliged to pay upon its defeat in 1897, but there is no information about the payment. See Pamuk, *Osmanlı Ekonomisinde Bağımlılık ve Büyüme, 1820–1913*, 189.

38 Parvus Efendi, *Cihan Harbine Doğru Türkiye*, 72.

39 This quote of Bismarck, which is often quoted, is associated with Bismarck's perspective on the Ottoman Empire; However, only commenting on this quote may lead to wrong conclusions. Bismarck was a politician who followed the developments in the Ottoman Empire day by day. When Bismarck hosted Ali Efendi, the publisher and writer of the Basiret newspaper, in Berlin in 1871, he said to him, "The love between the Turkish and German nations is so old that it will never be broken." In addition, Bismarck told Ali Efendi that he had all the editions of Basiret translated for reading. Even these details are an indication that Bismarck followed the developments

interests.[40] This situation had consequences for the benefit of the Ottoman Empire as well. The salaries of civil servants could not be paid for more than two months in the Ottoman Empire, whose economy was devastated by the Russo-Turkish War (1877–1878), the Balkan Wars. On the other hand France, under pressure from Russia, refused to give loans due to political reasons[41] or requested preconditions and concessions to give credit to the Ottoman Empire.[42] The financing that the government could find usually came from German banks. The Ottoman Empire started to import capital and products from Germany, as well as exported grain and raw materials to Germany. In fact, these exports made the conditions so difficult in certain periods that in 1891, the prices of bread and cereals in the country increased due to the fact that the grain exported by the Ottoman Empire to Germany, England and France forced the food supply limits.[43]

Although there was a proportional increase in the volume of economic relations between the Ottoman Empire and Germany until 1889, when Kaiser Wilhelm II first visited the Ottoman capital, there was no significant volumetric increase. Although the total trade with Germany increased by 54 % from 1878 to 1889 in terms of value, its share in the total trade of the Ottoman Empire rose from 0.18 % to only 0.22 %.[44] One of the main reasons for this was that the sea transportation chain had not been established between Germany and the Ottoman Empire until the 1890s. The high cost of German goods transported by British, French, Dutch and Austro-Hungarian ships to the Ottoman Empire had weakened the competitiveness of German products in the Ottoman market. This situation changed with the granting of the construction concession of the Anatolian Railways to Deutsche Bank on October 4, 1888, because the

---

in the Ottoman Empire and valued the views in the Ottoman Empire. See, Ingeborg Böer et al., *Berlin'den Türkler Geçti 1871–1945,* trans. Can Uralcan (İstanbul: İleri Yayınları, 2012), 38. These examples can be multiplied. It should not be overlooked that Bismarck was a balance policy expert, he preferred actions that would provide rational benefits, and therefore his views could change according to his interests.

40 Gencer, *Jöntürk Modernizmi ve Alman Ruhu*, 273.

41 NARA, Decimal File 867.00, Internal Affairs Of States, Turkey, Political Affairs, January 31, 1913–October 12, 1914, 86700/490, 21 February 1913.

42 Cemal Paşa, *Anılarım (1913–1922)*, 92–93.

43 BOA – Y..PRK.ŞH, 3–71, H-13-09-1308.

44 In the same period, the share of the British decreased from 46,60 % to 41,36 % and the share of the French decreased from 20,4 % to 18.81 %. See Önsoy, *Türk-Alman İktisadi Münasebetleri (1871–1914)*, 24.

transportation of the materials necessary for the construction of the railway was seen as an investment that would be sufficient and affordable for the establishment of a sea line between Germany and the Ottoman Empire. With the establishment of Deutsche Levante Linie (German Levante Line) on September 6, 1889, a group of businessmen from Hamburg, who took this development as an opportunity, regular maritime voyages started between Germany and the Ottoman Empire. Thus, transportation costs decreased considerably, competitive rates were achieved in the entry prices of German products into the country. Accordingly, between 1889 and 1898, there was an increase of 1523 % in exports from Hamburg to the Ottoman Empire, and an increase of 140 % in imports. This increase had a very important contribution to Levante Linie, as well. Deutsche Levante Linie, which started to work with 4 ships in 1890, became a large company with 15 steamships and 61 voyages per year in 1898.[45]

Between 1889 and 1898, German trade increased by 788.6 % in terms of total value. Although Germany was not the leader in the Ottoman market, it was the country with the fastest increase at that period.[46]

The spread of German banking in the Ottoman Empire also had a positive effect. Deutsche Bank had a branch in Istanbul since 1888. The German Palestine Bank (Deutsche Palastinabank), the first German bank established in Ottoman lands in 1899, opened its branches in Jerusalem and Jaffa in the year of its establishment. It also opened branches in Haifa in 1904, Beirut in 1907, Tripoli and Damascus in 1910. Branches of the Deutsche Orientbank, which was established in 1905, were opened in Bursa in 1906, Adana in 1909, and Aleppo in 1911.[47] These banks were effective in increasing the trade in their regions with their financial policies.

Despite all these developments, Britain still held the flag of leadership with its commercial volume in the Ottoman Empire. There were also shares of France, Austria-Hungary and Italy, which started to gain a commercial share in the Ottoman Empire. Therefore, Germany's having a direct sea line did not put itself in a more advantageous position than countries such as England, which already had them. Even in 1918, while the share of German ships in Ottoman ports was 1,6 %, the share of England was 34.1 %, Austria-Hungary 15.7 %, France 8.7 %.[48]

45 Önsoy, *Türk-Alman İktisadi Münasebetleri (1871–1914)*, 25–28.

46 In the same period, trade with Italians increased by 73 %, trade with Austria-Hungary increased by 18 %, trade with the French decreased by 0,4 %, and trade with the British decreased by 0,6 %. See Önsoy, *Türk-Alman İktisadi Münasebetleri (1871–1914)*, 30–31.

47 Gencer, *Jöntürk Modernizmi ve Alman Ruhu*, 288.

48 Önsoy, *Türk-Alman İktisadi Münasebetleri (1871–1914)*, 29.

Since this date, Germany integrated its economic developments with its positive political influence and differentiated from other countries with its unique policy.

Although Germany had a self-sufficient economy in general just before the First World War, Germany was completely dependent on foreign markets for substances such as oil and rubber. In terms of agriculture, it was not able to meet its own needs in terms of agricultural products other than barley, potatoes and sugar beet.[49] This improved the raw material-product relationship between Germany and the Ottoman Empire, and the mutual trade volume increased year by year. While the share of Germany in the annual export of the Ottoman Empire was 6 % in 1887, this rate increased to 21 % in 1910.[50] While the Ottoman Empire offered agricultural products such as cotton, wool, grains and rich raw materials such as chromium necessary for Germany, it also became a potential market for German industrial products. The fact that Germany's imports from the Ottoman Empire increased from 1,910,000 to 25,900,000 between the years 1880–1896, and that the Ottoman imports from Germany increased from 6,710,000 to 28,000,000 in the same period, is an indication of mutual benefit.[51] While the rate of German goods overtaking British goods increased day by day, Germans' deferred sales in the Ottoman market also created a separate buying appetite. While the Americans made their sales in cash, the British offered their competitive advantage goods for sale either in cash or on a short-term basis. Their general attitude was 3.75 % discount on cash sales, 6 months maturity. Germans, on the other hand, were able to make sales in an average of 8 months of maturity, while discounting 5 % in cash sales.[52] Of course, these payment facilities were a situation that caused the Ottomans to increase their trade with Germany. Mutual economic gains were one of the reasons that formed the basis of political rapprochement. One of the most important developments caused by these economic rapprochement was undoubtedly the Baghdad Railway concession, which had important underground riches on the line it passed through.

---

49 Önsoy, *Türk-Alman İktisadi Münasebetleri (1871–1914)*, 48.

50 Jäckh, *Balkan Harbinden Sonra Şarkta Almanya*, 28.

51 In 1912, exports from Ottoman Empire to Germany would be 77,600,000 and the imports of Ottoman Empire from Germany would be 112,800,000 marks. See Naci Yorulmaz, *Arming the Sultan*, 63, 147.

52 Önsoy, *Türk-Alman İktisadi Münasebetleri (1871–1914)*, 88.

3.3.1. Railway Concessions

The riches underlying the Ottoman lands remained untouched for a long time, even while the industry was developing in the world. The main reason for this was that the Ottoman Empire did not have the technology, infrastructure and knowledge to process its own underground riches, and it did not want to hand over its own wealth to foreigners. The Ottoman Empire tried to do its own mining for a certain period, but almost every time, the effort and expenditure was more than the value of the obtained mine.

There were technological and financial reasons for the Ottoman Empire's inability to process the underground riches itself. However, one of the main reasons was the lack of railway lines for transportation. Of course, it was not sustainable to try to transport minerals such as copper and silver on the back of animals on hundreds of kilometers of mountain roads.[53] It was experienced in Germany that the construction of the railway was an investment that provided multiple benefits both in military and commercial terms. Also, the developments in the countries that owned the railways did not go unnoticed by the Ottoman Empire. The potential of the railways to enable the soldiers to quickly move to the region in case of a revolt or attack, to be an economical solution in the import and export of products, and to provide a sustainable speed and volume in both domestic and foreign trade were also factors considered by the Ottoman Empire.[54]

Although the sustainability of product supply was a very important state policy in the Ottoman Empire, this policy was not always implemented at the desired level. One of the reasons for this was the absence of a railway. Even during the reign of Sultan Abdulhamid, when the Haydarpaşa – İzmir railway could not reach Anatolia, potatoes were imported from the coasts of France facing the Atlantic Ocean, since potatoes could not be brought from Adapazarı to Istanbul.[55] Even this example alone clearly reveals the transportation problems experienced in the absence of the railway. The fact that shipping wheat from

---

53 James L. Barton, "The Ottoman Empire and the War", *The Journal of Race Development*, vol. 9, no. 1 (1918), 5.

54 One of the most concrete examples of this situation is that Sultan Abdulhamid II made the Baghdad Railway Company agree to erect telegraph poles at 65 m intervals along the entire route and to build military facilities along the line by spending 4,000,000 francs. It is obvious that the Sultan's thought here was to increase the mobility of the army with railways in case of need. See McMeekin, *Berlin – Bağdat Demiryolu*, 66.

55 Geyikdağı, *Osmanlı Devleti'nde Yabancı Sermaye 1854–1914*, 92–93.

Central Anatolia, the center of grain, to Istanbul in the 1870s was 75 % more expensive than importing wheat from New York,[56] is an illuminating and shocking example of how the Ottoman Empire could not benefit from their own resources in the absence of the railway. For these reasons, the idea of building a railway to Mesopotamian lands had been an issue that occupied the agenda of the Ottomans since the middle of the 19th century. Sultan Abdülmecid kept some pictures of the Liverpool – Manchester train[57] in his room and informed those around him that he wanted such trains in his country. Sultan Abdulaziz, on the other hand, not only allowed the railway line to pass through the garden of the palace, but also said, "Let a railway be built in my country, if it wants, it can pass over my back. I agree".[58]

The Ottoman Empire took the issue of railway construction more seriously from the second half of the 19th century. A number of concessions were granted from 1856 and some railway lines were built by the concessionaires. In the following years, the Ottoman Empire started to follow the West in order to take more responsibility for the construction of its own railways. For example, in 1878, information was received about the establishment dates and status of railways in Sweden and Switzerland.[59] However, despite all this interest, the Ottoman Empire could not take action because it had neither the infrastructure nor the capital to project its own railways at that time. Due to these shortcomings, the concession of the railway lines to be built had to be given to foreign companies. European states also viewed the railway projects to be built in the Ottoman Empire positively, as the railways were seen as a positive direct investment since they would facilitate the raw material import of the European countries. Among them, there were also very important projects such as the Rumeli Railways. However, the Baghdad Railway was strategically different from the others in terms of its size, passing through the routes with underground resources and connecting many lines.

---

56 Korkut Boratav, *Türkiye İktisat Tarihi: 1908–2009* (Ankara: İmge Kitabevi Yayınlar, 22nd Ed., 2016), 28

57 The Liverpool-Manchester Railway, with its success and profitability, was a line that railway advocates in Germany set as an example in the 1830s, and was followed closely by every country interested in the railways. See King, "The Ideology Behind a Business Activity: The Case of the Nuremburg-Fürth Railway", 165.

58 Engin, *Rumeli Demiryolları*, 37–38, 70.

59 BOA, Y..PRK.HR, 3–14, H-10-07-1295.

There were many countries willing to take the Baghdad Railway concessionIt was known that the Britain had given importance to this project for a long time.[60] Because this railway line was a way for Britain to reach its colonies in India and the only way to reach the Persian Gulf by rail. Knowing that it would be more convenient and economical to reach India by sea, Britain gave importance to the Baghdad Railway project, but did not accept it as a vital necessity. Due to its geographical conditions, Germany could not get a share from the trade by sea routes, and Germany, whose lands were covered with railways, had to be content with only land and railway alternatives in order to export its industrial products. Therefore, Germany had always understood what the Baghdad Railway concession meant. On the other hand, the fact that the Germans were getting more concessions in Anatolia day by day and the possibility that railway lines could be built from Istanbul to the Persian Gulf aroused great excitement in Germany. According to the Germans, this project could have also been a transport network scenario that could connect Berlin to India.[61]

The construction of the Baghdad Railway was not only in the interests of Britain or Germany. Goltz Pasha quoted Sultan Abdulhamid's words about a railway linking Istanbul and Persian Gulf. He mentioned in his report that Sultan Abdulhamid considered the Baghdad Railway as a vehicle to utilizate his armed forces from the Asian provinces, against an enemy that may come from

60 Britain's interest in railway lines in the Middle East was for strategic reasons in the middle of the 19th century. In the following years, this interest was for both strategic reasons and underground resources. The first railway line built in the Ottoman lands came to life as a result of the contract between the governor of Sudan and Egypt, Abbas Hilmi Pasha I, with the British engineer Robert Stephenson, and the first phase of the line from Alexandria to Kafr el-Zayat started to work in 1854. Within two years, this line extended to Cairo, and in 1858, the line was extended to Suez, creating the first modern transportation line connecting the Mediterranean Sea and the Indian Ocean. There was significant support and control of Britain in these constructions. So much so that in 1856 a British general, Francis Rawdon Chesney was sent for the strategic and economic analysis of the railway lines to be built around the Euphrates river. Chesney produced an analysis report of the construction of a line of approximately 1600 km from Iskenderun to Basra in 1857. See Peter Christensen, *Germany and the Ottoman Railways – Art, Empire, and Infrastructure* (Singapore: Yale University Press, 2017), 11.

61 In order for this to occur, the necessity of constructing a railway that had to cross the Bosphorus was foreseen and was described as an engineering problem that could be overcome under the conditions of the period. See Barton, "The Ottoman Empire and the War", 6.

whichever direction. He also mentoined that Sultan considered the railways as a vehicle that would increase the welfare of the country since it would be an alternative way for the commerce of India.[62]

Both of Sultan Abdulhamid's predictions were based on very solid foundations. If the Baghdad line had reached Aleppo during the Balkan Wars and had been united with the Syrian and Hejaz railways, the regiments to be brought from Damascus would have crossed the Amanos and Taurus mountain ranges in three days, not three weeks, with great difficulty and fatigue.[63]

It was also a well-founded prediction that the Baghdad Railway project would be a reason for preference on the Europe-India trade route and create a significant trade volume within its own structure The fact that the Baghdad Railway would reduce the Berlin-Baghdad distance to six days and the British, who went to India by sea in three weeks, would land in Bombay in just over a week, was a reasonable reason for the European-Indian trade to shift to the Berlin-Baghdad line.[64]

In the 19th century, there were certain countries that had industries at a level that could realize railway construction, and the Ottoman Empire naturally took certain criteria into consideration when choosing among these countries. Sultan Abdulhamid, who predicted that critical regions in the Middle East would get mixed up as a result of Britain's possession of the Mesopotamian railway concession, which tried to destroy the weakening dominance of the Ottomans in the Middle East with bilateral agreements with the Arabs, decided not to give the strategic railway construction concessions to Britain and France for similar reasons. For this reason, Germany, which had recently undergone a transportation revolution in its own country, was in a more advantageous position. Already before the concession of the Baghdad Railway was in question, the first major steps were taken with the Germans in the construction of the railway. One of these major steps was the granting of the construction and operation concession of the Anatolian Railways project to a German named Alfred Kaulla, on the occasion of a will on September 24, 1888. Since Kaulla could not finance this concession himself, he met with Deutsche Bank's general manager, Dr Georg von Siemens,[65] and started railway construction activities

62 Naci Yorulmaz, *Arming the Sultan*, 151.

63 Ernst Jäckh, *Balkan Harbinden Sonra Şarkta Almanya* (İstanbul: Yeditepe Yayınları, 2021), 58.

64 Jäckh, *Balkan Harbinden Sonra Şarkta Almanya*, 22–23.

65 The American historian Sean McMeekin claims that Dr Georg von Siemens was instrumental in securing an emergency loan of 30 million marks allocated to Sultan Abdulhamid by Deutsche Bank in 1888, and therefore this loan may have had an

with the financial power of Deutsche Bank.[66] On October 4, the operating rights of the Haydarpaşa – İzmit railway line were indirectly given to a consortium led by Deutsche Bank. On October 6, 1888, Deutsche Bank was granted expanded rights on the Anatolian Railways project.[67] The most important feature of this concession was that the company had the right to take priority in case it could be extended to Baghdad in the future, and it was promised that this company would be given priority regarding all kinds of mining rights on this line.[68]

By 1888, almost all of the existing railway lines in Anatolia were in the hands of British capitalists. Now the granting of these concessions to Germany was indicative of a political shift in foreign policy. The fact that the Germans bought the Anatolian Railways shares from the British also meant the Germanization of the Anatolian Railways. This situation created the expected excitement on the part of Kaiser Wilhelm II, and Kaiser Wilhelm II conveyed his satisfaction to Abdulhamid II that the Baghdad Railway concession was given to the Anatolian Railway Company.[69]

Sultan Abdulhamid was also pleased with the developments and wanted to put the idea of combining Haydarpaşa and Ankara with iron networks completely into the hands of the Germans. After Abdulhamid II gave the German group the right to buy the Haydarpaşa-İzmit railway line, he gave the concession to lay a railway network between İzmit and Ankara in October 1888, in return, he offered a guarantee of 15,000 francs per kilometer per year.[70] This railway line was finished in a short period of three years. This progress made the

---

impact on the granting of railway concessions. See McMeekin, *Berlin – Bağdat Demiryolu*, 57.

66 Ortaylı, *Osmanlı İmparatorluğu'nda Alman Nüfuzu*, 135–139.

67 As a result of this authorization, almost all of the locomotives and wagons to be used in the Ottoman railways were supplied from German companies, and the transportation of these products was also made by German companies. On this occasion, the railway projects received from the Ottoman Empire contributed significantly to the growth of many German companies. For example, Deutsche Levante Linie, which was founded in 1889 and started the transportation of locomotives and wagons to be used in Ottoman railways with 4 ships it owned in 1890, grew enough to have the finance and business volume to increase the number of its ships to 15 in 1898. The year 1888 was therefore a breaking point in the growth of the volume of imports from Germany. See Naci Yorulmaz, *Arming the Sultan*, 62.

68 Hikmet Uluğbay, *İmparatorluktan Cumhuriyete Petropolitik* (Ankara: Turkish Daily News Yayınları, 1995), 26.

69 BOA, Y..PRK.NMH, 8 – 11, H-26-07-1317.

70 Yorulmaz, *Arming the Sultan*, 59–60.

Sultan happy and was a positive reference for granting new concessions to the Germans. Until 1898, the Germans laid a total of 1020 km of lines, including Haydarpaşa – Izmit (91 km), Izmit-Ankara (485 km) and Eskişehir-Konya (444 km) lines. Thereupon, Abdulhamid II voluntarily gave the Germans the concession necessary for the extension of the Eskişehir – Konya line to Dinar via Afyon on December 4, 1897.[71] Although the guarantees given to these lines were financed by Ottoman bonds, income such as land tax was kept as a guarantee just in case.[72] The Anatolian Railways Company also actively operated in the Ottoman lands, It opened İzmit – Arifiye line (110 km) in 1890. It also opened Arifiye – Eskişehir line (223 km) in 1892, Eskişehir – Ankara line (197 km) in 1892, Eskişehir-Alayyurt-Kütahya line (134 km) in 1894, Alayyurt – Afyon line (202 km) in 1895 and Afyon-Konya line (274 km) in 1896. In total, Anatolian Railways Company opened 931 km of railway lines in the Ottoman lands between the years 1890–1896.[73]

From a relatively early date, like 1891, the Ottoman Empire was negotiating with the German ambassadors about the extension of the Anatolian Railway to Baghdad.[74] The Germans, too, continued to receive more and more concessions, and despite the severe pressures of Britain and the objections of the French,[75] they succeeded in creating a positive agenda as a result of Germany's meetings with both the Sultan and the Minister of War.[76] A will was issued by Sultan Abdulhamid on January 16, 1902 for the Baghdad Railway concession, and the concession was given to the Baghdad Railway Company, an Ottoman-German joint venture established on March 5, 1903.[77] However, this concession was

71 During the Ottoman-Greek War, the French did not provide convenience to the Ottoman army in the military transports on the railway lines they controlled. On the other hand, the Germans provided favorable conditions for the Ottoman army. This was also an important factor. See Ortaylı, *Osmanlı İmparatorluğu'nda Alman Nüfuzu*, 141–142.

72 Yorulmaz, *Arming the Sultan*, 60.

73 Yorulmaz, *Arming the Sultan*, 61.

74 BOA, Y.PRK.BŞK, 23 – 102, H-14-03-1309.

75 BOA, Y.EE, 82–1, H-28-06-1310.

76 BOA, Y.PRK.TŞF, 5/94, H-20-07-1317.

77 The contract for the line that would extend to Baghdad had been signed on December 23, 1899 between Zihni Pasha, the Ottoman Minister of Trade and Public Works, and Georg von Siemens, representing Deutsche Bank and the Anatolian Railway Company. However, due to the financial situation of the Ottoman Empire, the obligation to put a mortgage on the state revenues in the name of the usual interest and depreciation of the loans required for the construction of the railway could not be

not easily accepted for either Britain, France or Russia. The Baghdad Railway was seen as a political and military threat to Britain's ambitions in Egypt and the Persian Gulf, France's in Syria, and Russia's in Iran and Eastern Anatolia. Therefore, an unceasing fight began over the region. Of course, these were not the only reasons behind the objections of these countries. Building railways in Ottoman lands had different advantages. Railroad construction was an element that brought with it many economic and political dependencies. For a railway line to be built in the Ottoman lands, rails, stations, institutions, and various construction activities were needed.[78] Many engineers had built the Baghdad line in various parts,[79] and almost all of these parts were imported. Necessary calculations were made by German engineering firms, construction were made with German materials, expenses were financed by the loans given by German banks.[80]

Another advantage was a unique privilege for the Baghdad Railway. The fact that the Germans wanted to obtain oil exploration concessions near the construction line of the Baghdad Railway was a separate and very important factor that angered the competition between the countries according to the route of the railway to be built. The Germans were also aware of the resources in Mesopotamia, and therefore, as a result of their pressure, they had a special clause included in the concession agreement in July 1904. With this special article, the Germans would be able to get a concession for 40 years if oil was found during the explorations that would continue for one year in Mosul and Baghdad.[81] As a result of the acceleration of Germany's industrial development activities, the increase in the need for oil from 70 million tons to 926 million tons per year, increasing more than 13 times between 1870 and 1900, caused the Germans to increase their appetite for Mosul oil. However, the Germans, who could not

---

met. Therefore, the Baghdad Railway Company could only be established on March 21, 1903. See Gencer, *Jöntürk Modernizmi ve Alman Ruhu*, 291; McMeekin, *Berlin – Bağdat Demiryolu*, 62.

78 During the realization of the projects given to Germany by the Ottoman Empire, many industrial products were imported from Germany. An example of this situation was experienced in Rumeli railways. As expected, the Rumeli railways operator company had electrical equipment and machinery imported from German factories. See BOA, İ.RSM, 16 – 18-2, H-07-05-1320.

79 M. Larcher, *Büyük Harpte Türk Harbi*, vol 1, trans. and ed. Mehmet Nihad (İstanbul: Ötüken Neşriyat, 2018), 81.

80 Christensen, *Germany and the Ottoman Railways*, 1.

81 BOA, Y..MTV., 296 / 69, H-11-02-1325.

create the necessary budget for drilling activities and did not want to wake up the European states by noticing the existence of oil and announcing it, were slow to send the reports they obtained as a result of oil exploration. On January 27, 1907, the German oil exploration concession agreement was terminated unilaterally by the Ottoman Empire when the Germans requested additional time for drilling and exploration.[82] This development was an inevitable opportunity for the European states to get the concession that was wasted. In this period, even the United States, whose oriental policy had not yet become clear, gathered comprehensive intelligence about the Baghdad Railway, and a very detailed report was prepared by the American consulate in Baghdad on January 17, 1913. As it can be understood from the report, America was interested in the demographic structure of the region, the political tendencies of the people of the region, and the possible commercial contribution and profitability of the Baghdad Railway and sought answers for these. In the reply from the consulate, it was stated that under the administration of a strong government, this railway line would clearly contribute to the economic and commercial development of the society.[83] It was confirmed even from across the ocean that the effort for the Baghdad Railway would have a reward. Britain was the most insistent in making this effort. Britain, which made secret agreements with the Arab sheikhdoms under the auspices of the Ottoman Empire since the end of the 19th century, became a strong oil consumer due to the increasing role of oil in both industry and transportation. Since Britain wanted to dominate the road to India, it declared the Middle East a national issue. This was one of the main reasons why Britain entered into a tight bargain with Germany for the concession granted granted after the oil on Mesopotamian soil was proved. Companies from France, Russia, the Netherlands and America also accompanied this competition process, but the most intense competition was between Britain, which had taken over the dominance of the Ottomans up to the level of customs tax, and Germany, which declared that it assumed the protectorate of Pan-Islamism.[84] As a matter of fact, the Ottomans did not want to confront either Birtain or Germany regarding the oil exploration concession. In particular, thanks to Hakkı Pasha's attempts to establish a policy

---

82 Hikmet Uluğbay, *İmparatorluktan Cumhuriyete Petropolitik* (Ankara: Turkish Daily News Yayınları, 1995), 38–42.

83 NARA, Internal Affairs Of States, Turkey, Political Affairs. January 31, 1913–October 12, 1914, 867.00/493; NARA, Decimal File 867.501, Internal Affairs Of States, Economic Matters., Turkey, Statistics, General., July 29, 1914–May 20, 1929.

84 For the oil struggles of the Western states in the Ottoman Empire See. Volkan Ş. Ediger, *Osmanlı'da Neft ve Petrol* (Ankara: ODTÜ Yayıncılık, 3rd Ed., 2007).

of balance and with the mediation efforts of Kalust Gülbenkiyan (known as Mr Five Percent), the concession was given to Türk Petrol AŞ, which was established in 1912 by the German, British and Dutch oil companies.

The economic development in geographies with railways was undeniable. The annual income of the people in the surrounding settlements of the line, of which 1000 miles were completed by 1911, increased 15 times compared to 20 years ago. The agricultural activities of the Anatolian and Baghdad Railway companies in the regions where the lines passed were also worth mentioningAn "Agriculture Unit" was established with the aim of increasing the agricultural productivity of the Anatolian people. As a result of the activities of this unit, the German consultants sent to Anatolia brought modern agricultural tools, equipment and machinery to Anatolian farmers, gave training on the use of these, planting seedlings, obtaining first-class grain, and also carried out projects for the irrigation of unproductive barren lands. In the places on the route of the Anatolian Railway line, the crop tripled compared to the period before the line was built. The shipping rate fell by three quarters, and the state's revenue increased accordingly. It was aimed to increase the annual wheat production from 2,000 wagons to 20,000 wagons by increasing 10 times, by the irrigation of Konya plain with the water taken from Beyşehir lake alone.[85] This was also an indicator of development.

While the railway was a model of economic influence for the Germans, it was a response to both economic and military needs for the Ottomans. Of course, the political effect it would create was inevitable because the factor that contributed to these mutual interests was a railway line that would pass through Mesopotamia.

The Baghdad Railway concession was synthesized as the seal of the Turkish-German alliance on a global scale.[86] The nickname Berlin-Bosfor-Baghdad (BBB for short) began to settle in the political language of the British.[87]

Railway relations with Germany continued in the period of the Committee of Union and Progress. In 1910, control of the tram system in Istanbul, which

85 Gencer, *Jöntürk Modernizmi ve Alman Ruhu,* 293, 296,297.

86 The construction of the Baghdad Railways continued during the First World War. In this way, it was possible to establish a direct line from Istanbul to Nusaybin, and important support was provided to the Ottoman armies fighting in Palestine and Mesopotamia. At the end of the war, the railway constructions in Baghdad fell into the hands of the Allies, and the ones in Anatolia became the property of Turkey after nationalization. See Barton, *The Ottoman Empire and the War*, 7.

87 Larcher, *Büyük Harpte Türk Harbi*, Cilt 1, 82.

was in the hands of the Belgians and was in a very damaged condition and having difficulty in operating, was given to a German group supported by Deutsche Bank in 1910. And a first-class tram system was built in place of these trams. Even this was an indication that the German dominance of the railways continued independently of the change of administration in Ottoman Empire.[88] This dominance of the Germans on the railways continued until the end of the First World War.

3.4. Military Reasons for Turkish-German Rapprochement

The German victory as a result of the Franco-Prussian war had proven the German military power to the whole world. Sultan Abdulhamid II, who followed this process closely, made attempts to cooperate with Germany, which he saw as an expert in military matters, from the last quarter of the 19th century in order to make the necessary military and administrative reforms in the Ottoman Empire and to get away from the pressure of international diplomacy.

With the effect of industrialization, it became obvious that the Ottoman Empire needed military reforms. After the great losses in the Russo- Turkish War (1877–1878), the improvement of the army gained even more importance and began to occupy the top of the agenda. Thereupon, there was a significant increase in the number of delegations requested from Germany, and under the leadership of these delegations, German militarism began to penetrate the Ottoman army. Germany's warm attitude towards the development of military relations with the Ottoman Empire for some reasons, which will be discussed in detail below, facilitated the penetration of the German military school into the Ottoman army. During the reign of Abdulhamid II, 140 officers were sent to Germany, and the officers sent to Germany in groups were specialized in Germany and were assigned to the army[89] during the training process.[90] Even

88 NARA, Decimal File 867.78, Internal Affairs Of States, Turkey, Street Railway, August 31, 1910, GALE|SC5111509406.

89 Salih Kış, *Osmanlı Ordusunda Alman Ekolü Von der Goltz Paşa (1883–1895)* (Konya: Palet Yayınları, 2017), 144–145.

90 Soldiers were not the only ones sent to Germany for training. For example, until the First World War, 26 Turkish technicians were sent for internship in German factories. Of course, this was not limited only in technical terms. There were also students who were sent to Germany to studyAmong these students, there were those who studied philosophy and those who studied history. On November 13, 1916, von Loslow in Istanbul informed that Turkey had sent 2000 young people to Germany to receive education in German schools and German enterprises until then. In particular, the

this situation can be perceived as an indication that Germany wanted to support the military reform planned to be realized in the Ottoman army. These officers later traveled from city to city in the Ottoman Empire to both give theoretical training and give military training in the field and to convey what they had learnt in Germany.[91]

At that time, the fact that Britain and France did not want to give loans to the Ottoman Empire,[92] but Deutsche Bank provided the loans needed by the Ottoman Empire, also facilitated the German military influence in the Ottoman army. After all, the Ottoman Empire was arming its critical regions with these financings and was buying these weapons from Germany.[93] As a result of this capital flow, the arms order given to Germany was 5.9 million marks in 1889, became 13.1 million marks in 1893, reached 6 million marks in 1894, and rose to 12.2 million marks in 1895.[94]

The rapprochement born out of necessity had evolved into coexistence with the tools to be discussed in detail below, and close relations of nearly 25 years laid the foundations of an important alliance.

3.4.1. German Military Delegations in the Ottoman Army

Rumors about the first date when the Ottoman Empire demanded a military delegation from Prussia date back to the period of Sultan Mustafa III (1757–1774), who wanted to modernize his army. It is a fact that the Ottoman Empire followed the Prussian army closely even in the 18th century. The diplomatic report sent by the Berlin ambassador of the Ottoman Empire in 1764, praising the Prussian military system and victories, is an indication of this. In the report, the ambassador gave details about the military situation of the Prussian army, which attracted more attention after the Seven Years' War, to the Ottoman Empire.[95] The first known concrete activities were the Prussian Colonel von

---

activities of the German-Turkish Association on this issue were very active. Even in the summer of 1918, there were 1500 Turkish youth studying in Germany. See Gencer, *Jöntürk Modernizmi ve Alman ruhu*, 305, 307, 318.

91 Mehmet Cebeci, "II. Abdülhamid Döneminde Almanya'ya Gönderilen Askeri Öğrenciler", Altunkaya et al. (ed.). *Türk-Alman İlişkilerine Farklı Disiplinlerden Bakış* (Konya: Palet Yayınları, 2019), 77–79.

92 Ortaylı, *Osmanlı İmparatorluğu'nda Alman Nüfuzu*, 120.

93 The cannons placed in unsufficiently defended Sofia, which was critical for the Ottoman Empire, had been purchased from German factories in 1886. Bkz: BOA, Y..PRK.TNF, 1-61, H-24-10-1303.

94 Ortaylı, *Osmanlı İmparatorluğu'nda Alman Nüfuzu*, 119.

95 Grüßhaber, *The 'German Spirit' in the Ottoman and Turkish Army, 1908–1938*, 9.

Goetze's supervision of the Turkish ground troops at the request of Sultan Selim III in 1798, the presence of experienced Prussian officers beside the Turks in the wars against the Russians, and the activities of the Moltke delegation.[96]

Moltke delegation came to the Ottoman army in 1837 upon the invitation of Sultan Mahmud II,[97] after the decision to abolish the janissary corps, also known as Vaka-i Hayriye, and establish a modern army. Moltke's letters shed light on the situation of the Ottoman army at the time of the delegation's arrival. According to Moltke, the condition of the Ottoman army at the time of his arrival was very bad, the soldiers were quite uneducated and they avoided training. Health was deplorable. There was no doctor or medicine. In a war situation, soldiers were killed not by bullets, but by diseases. Nutritional conditions were very poor. The weapons were quite old and inaccurate. The equipment of the troops was very poor, the soldiers did not have all the necessary clothes and shoes. The hierarchical structure served the individual, not the army.. Since the army did not have high-ranking soldiers capable of carrying out reforms within its body, every foreign expert was listened to and a military confusion emerged that adopted different principles of more than one state. Members of an army, in which French manuals, Hungarian saddles, Belgian rifles, British swords and Russian jackets were used, wore Turkish fez over all of them. The soldier was unwilling to join the army, as there was no general draft scheme, most of the soldiers were drafted forcibly by the army.[98]

In such a period, Moltke's coming to the Ottoman Empire was a great chance that was not taken advantage of. Moltke was a very important name engraved in history with golden letters[99] and a visionary soldier who had seen the coming of the First World War 20-odd years before it happened.[100] Moltke's path passed

96 Jehuda L. Wallach, *Bir Askeri Yardımın Anatomisi – Türkiye'de Prusya-Alman Askeri Heyetleri 1835–1919*, trans. Em. Tuğgeneral Fahri Çeliker (Ankara: Gnkur. Askeri Tarih ve Stratejik Etüt Bşk. Yayınları, 1985), 7–10.

97 Christensen, *Germany and the Ottoman Railways*, 10.

98 Wallach, *Bir Askeri Yardımın Anatomisi – Türkiye'de Prusya-Alman Askeri Heyetleri 1835–1919*, 12–16.

99 Moltke, who served in the Ottoman army, later became the Chief of General Staff in Prussia and went down in history as one of the most important names in the Unification of Germany. See Annika Mombauer. "A Reluctant Military Leader? Helmuth von Moltke and the July Crisis of 1914", *War in History*, vol. 6, no. 4 (1999), 417–446.

100 In his memoirs, Ludendorff quotes Moltke's words in 1890 as follows: "If the war that has been hanging over our heads like Damocles' sword for 10 years becomes real, it is not possible to predict how long it will last and what the result will be. The great European states will engage in this war with their enormous armies equipped with

through the Ottoman army in an important position, but Moltke could not be useful in a way that he could reveal his true potential, as the Ottoman army at that time was not very enthusiastic about allowing German delegations to make direct decisions. The fact that the Battle of Nezib was fought against Moltke's proposal was a breaking point for Moltke's career in the Ottoman Empire. On the eve of this defeat, the application of the Sublime Porte to Friedrich Wilhelm III to send new military delegations from Prussia was considered, and while a group of officers was prepared for this, the decision to send new officers was withdrawn after the Nezib defeat, and Moltke and his delegation were urgently recalled.[101] Despite this, Sultan Abdulhamid II did not give up on his insistence on German delegations and considered it appropriate to invite a new German delegation to modernize the army again.[102] Sultan Abdulhamid was thoroughly convinced that the Ottoman Empire had no friends in Europe other than Germany. The Ottoman Empire wanted to both get rid of the loneliness it faced against Europe by making a friend in Europe and to benefit from the military abilities of Germany, which was victorious in the war against France. Thus, on May 14, 1880, through the German Ambassador von Hatzfeld, civil and military advisors were requested from Germany. However, Bismarck met this request with some suspicion and distance. Bismarck, who did not want to be a party in the oriental issues in the first place, did not want to confront Russia, which was tense because of the Berlin

---

unprecedented equipment. They will be willing to admit defeat in one or two blows and be compelled to sign peace under harsh conditions, and none of them will be able to pull themselves together to re-enter the battle. This war may be another Seven Years' or Thirty Years' War…" See Ludendorff, *Birinci Dünya Savaşı'nda Gördüklerim ve Yaşadıklarım*, 253.

101 Wallach, *Bir Askeri Yardımın Anatomisi – Türkiye'de Prusya-Alman Askeri Heyetleri 1835–1919*, 18–19.

102 Although Sultan Abdulhamid wanted to modernize the army with modern equipments, on the one hand, he was afraid of the development in the administrative structure of the army and paid great attention to the army to stay away from politics. The failure of the German delegations to implement the reform proposals in the administrative structure was an indicator of this. Since Sultan Abdulhamid knew that some rulers before him were dethroned by the sheikh al-Islam fatwa, he chose the people in administrative positions from those he knew and trusted, and always kept the places of those who occupied these positions intact. As an example, Serasker Mehmet Rıza Pasha served for 17 years, Minister of War Ahmed Şefik Pasha served for 14 years, Armed Forces Supervisor Mustafa Zeki Pasha served for 18 years, and Minister of Interior Mehmed Faik Memduh Pasha served for 15 years. See Vahdettin Engin, *Asayiş – Sultan II. Abdülhamid'in İç Güvenlik Politikası* (İstanbul: Yeditepe Yayınevi, 2013), 43.

Conference. This reason, of course, was only one side of the scale. Bismarck also considered that the Ottoman Empire, which was isolated against Britain, would have to get closer to Russia, and beyond that, he undoubtedly took into account that Germany would want to benefit from an Ottoman military power in a possible France-Russia alliance.[103] In the light of these thoughts, Bismarck started to look at the Ottoman request more positively, but he still did not act in a hurry to give a positive answer. At that time, Bismarck contacted Vienna to get the opinion of Austria and asked whether Austria would like to see Prussian officers in the Ottoman Empire rather than the officers of other Western countries and he received a positive answer. Austria would have liked to see Prussian officers instead of other Western officers. This reply increased Bismarck's inclination towards the Orient issue. On June 1, 1880, Bismarck informed the King in writing that the delegation request from the Ottoman Empire should have been accepted positively,[104] but still no approval had been formed yet.

In December 1881, Sultan Abdulhamid sent a delegation to Berlin to express his insistence and to speed up the process. In the reports in which Ali Nizami Pasha and Reşit Bey stated the details of their meetings, it was stated that Bismarck especially emphasized the minority issue and stated that no concessions should be made to minorities and non-Muslim subjects.[105] The reason behind Bismarck's attitude could clearly have been to further strain the Ottoman-British relations.

Reşit Bey included Bismarck's recommendations in his report. Bismarck gave advice to Reşit Bey such as raising the level of education, increasing the productivity in agriculture, increasing the trade volume, giving importance to mining, expanding the railways, getting rid of the past disasters with a few righteous and loyal people.[106] These recommendations of Bismarck support the view that Bismarck supported the development of the Ottoman Empire and that he thought this process would be beneficial for German companies. Also, Ali Nizami Bey included Bismarck's views on some critical subjects. According to the report, Bismarck reacted to the dissolution of the Parliament as a "right

103 In November 1883, Sultan Abdulhamid's statement to the German Ambassador Radowitz that the Ottoman Empire would provide military support to Germany in the event that France and Russia would attack Germany, in return for a German guarantee that Britain would not attack the Ottoman Empire, was a sign of mutual expectations. See Yasamee, *Abdülhamid'in Dış Politikası*, 122

104 Wallach, *Bir Askeri Yardımın Anatomisi – Türkiye'de Prusya-Alman Askeri Heyetleri 1835–1919*, 25.

105 BOA, Y.EE. 7/5 (02.02.1299/24.12.1881); BOA, Y.EE. 7/6 (02.02.1299/24.12.1881).

106 BOA, Y.EE. 7/6 (02.02.1299/24.12.1881).

step", contrary to the severe reaction of Britain, and stated that the parliament should be from a single nation and that the multinational parliament would only harm the state.[107] These views of Bismarck can be perceived as a sincere comment considering his policies in Germany. Ali Nizami Bey also stated in his own report that the Ottoman Empire was left alone and that the state that the Ottomans had to lean their back against should be Germany, which had been giving moral support from the past.[108] These comments of Ali Nizami Bey point to the positive views of the Ottoman delegation of establishing positive relations with Germany.

Despite all this positive dialogue, Germany still had not given a definite approval on the military delegations. Probably Bismarck, who gave importance to the functionality of the League of the Three Emperors,[109] did not want to confront Russia after the treaty, which was still young.

One event radically changed Bismarck's stance on delegations. In February 1882, Mikhail Dmitrievich Skobelev, a young general and known for his anti-German thoughts, said in Paris that "a war between Russia and Germany is inevitable".[110] This statement made Bismarck, who had differences of opinion since the Berlin Conference, adopted the prediction that Russia's long-term policies were unreliable. Thus, he decided no to take Russia's into consideration and in March 1882,[111] two years after the first attempt, he accepted to send a German military delegation to Ottoman Empire. Bismarck wanted the officers

---

107 BOA, Y.EE. 7/5 (02.02.1299/24.12.1881).

108 BOA, Y.EE. 7/5 (02.02.1299/24.12.1881).

109 In the Treaty of Berlin, especially due to Austria's interests in the Balkans and Brtain's attitude that did not allow Russia to connect to the warm seas, Russia's gains in Treaty of San Stefano were rasped. Some critical areas in the Balkans were returned to the Ottoman Empire. Subsequently, the First League of the Three Emperors was dissolved. It was re-signed in a more formal framework on June 18, 1881, and it was also terminated in 1887 due to the problems in the Balkans. The Triple Alliance, which was established in May 1882 with the rapprochement of Italy and Germany, lasted until 1912. See W. N. Medlicott, "Bismarck and the Three Emperors' Alliance, 1881–87", *Transactions of the Royal Historical Society*, vol. 27 (1945), 61,62.

110 After this speech, Skobelev was condemned by Alexandr III and was found dead in the Angleterre Hotel in Moscow on June 25, 1882. All Moscow argued that this death occurred as a result of poisoning Skobelev's wine on Bismarck's order, and they claimed that an agent had passed from Moscow to St Petersburg by an express train at the time of Skobelev's death. See Lev Aranov et al., "Toward the Prehistory of the Protokols", *The Global Impact of the Protocols of the Elders of Zion: A Century-Old Myth,* ed. Esther Webman (Abingdon: Routledge, 2011), 35.

111 Yasamee, *Abdülhamid'in Dış Politikası*, 121.

in the delegation to come under the patronage of the Sultan and cut off their relations with the German government. Hopkirk argues that Bismarck put this condition in order to throw the responsibility off Germany in a possible bad scenario.[112] Considering Bismarck's political behavior, there may be some realism in Hopkirk's prediction.

The acceptance of the sending of the German military delegation to the Ottoman Empire could be considered as the beginning of a period that would radically change the Ottoman-German relations. Within the delegation that reached Istanbul in May, four military advisors were sent despite the Ottoman's request for eight military advisors. These people were high-ranking staff officer and head of the delegation Colonel Otto Kähler, who was the Commander of the Silesian 2nd Hassa Regiment, infantry officer Captain Kamphövner from the no.79 3rd Hanover Infantry Regiment, artillery officer Captain Ristow from the 2nd Pomeranian Field Artillery Regiment, and cavalry officer Captain Von Hobe, who was the Third Division Adjutant Captain of the 1st Silesian Dragon Regiment No.4. Kähler was a highly referenced colonel. The other three captains were also introduced as distinguished officers of the German army. Just before they left Germany they had been promoted to the rank of major and their term of office had been extended.[113] As each of them entered service in the Ottoman army, they were promoted to higher ranks as promised before, and they were brought to very important positions during their service in the Ottoman army. Otto Kähler entered the Ottoman army service with the rank of brigadier general on June 14, 1882, and after Wilhelm I promoted him to the rank of major general 15 days later, he became a lieutenant general and the sultan's aide-de-camp in the Ottoman army, and he died as a field marshal in 1885. Ristow, Von Hobe and Kamphoevener entered the service of the Ottoman army as colonels, Kamphövener was promoted to the rank of marshal in 1895, after his long service. The salaries of all of them were not only higher than the soldiers in the same rank in the Ottoman army, but even higher than the soldiers in the same ranks in their own countries. A monthly salary of 30,000 Francs (1316 Ottoman Liras) was paid to Kähler, and a monthly salary of 23,000 Francs (1010 Ottoman Liras) was paid to the other three military advisers, their rent was covered from the Sultan's disguised allowance and they received a food aid. Considering that an Ottoman major general received 480 Ottoman Liras and

112 Peter Hopkirk, *On Secret Service East of Constantinople* (Oxford: Oxford University Press, 1995), 13–14.

113 Wallach, *Bir Askeri Yardımın Anatomisi – Türkiye'de Prusya-Alman Askeri Heyetleri 1835–1919*, 32.

an Ottoman Colonel 240 Ottoman Liras in the same period, the high salaries of German military advisers can be revealed.[114] In addition, due to the agreement made, Kähler was awarded the second degree Ottoman order and the other three delegation members were awarded the third degree Ottoman order.[115]

The influence of the Kähler-led delegation is questionable. In the letter Kähler sent during his duty in Istanbul, he stated that he had been reading Moltke's letters, which Moltke had been sending during his duty in Ottoman army, with greater interest. Moreover, he added that the conditions at that time were exactly the same as those of Moltke's time. This statement is a sign of Kähler's failure to make reformist changes in the army.[116] Kähler's inability to realize the changes he wanted to make in the Ottoman army also had an effect on this view. For example, Kähler prepared a 400-page memorandum for the modernization of the Ottoman army, as requested from him. This memorandum was reviewed and accepted by the commission appointed by the sultan, and the sultan approved the commission report on 11 December 1882. However, none of the reccomendations in the memorandum was taken into consideration until January 1884.[117] This indifference was a reason for Kähler to give up.

The activities of Goltz Pasha, the head of the delegation that came after Kähler, were quite active, clearly and generally accepted. The arrival of von der Goltz in the Ottoman army took place when the Ottomans requested an officer from Germany in 1883 with the aim of regulating the education system in military schools. Goltz came to the Ottoman Empire on 18 June 1883 and took office. When Kähler Pasha died on November 3, 1885, Goltz became the head of the delegation as colonel. A year later he was promoted to general. He remained in the service of the Ottoman army until he returned to Germany in 1895.[118]

---

114 Three military advisers serving with the rank of major in Germany were paid more than four times the salary of a colonel in the Ottoman Empire and more than eight times the salary of a major. Yorulmaz, *Arming the Sultan*, 78–79.

115 Wallach, *Bir Askeri Yardımın Anatomisi – Türkiye'de Prusya-Alman Askeri Heyetleri 1835–1919*, 33.

116 Wallach, *Bir Askeri Yardımın Anatomisi – Türkiye'de Prusya-Alman Askeri Heyetleri 1835–1919*, 12–16.

117 Wallach, *Bir Askeri Yardımın Anatomisi – Türkiye'de Prusya-Alman Askeri Heyetleri 1835–1919*, 41.

118 Even though Goltz Pasha returned to Germany in 1895, the Ottoman army could not cut off his relations or communication with Goltz Pasha after 1895. Goltz Pasha was both a very good soldier and a very good diplomat. For this reason, Goltz Pasha was loved by both Germans and Turks. He died on April 19, 1916 in Baghdad, where he served as the commander of the 6th Army. His coffin was carried on the shoulders of the Ottoman officers. He was buried in the garden of the German embassy building

Following the Serbian-Bulgarian war of 1886, Sultan Abdulhamid II appointed von der Goltz to the position of Kähler Pasha on the general staff. Goltz was appointed to Kähler's position as the president's authorized representative, not as the second president like Kähler. Goltz's main task was to improve the military education system. Goltz focused on removing unnecessary theory courses and introducing practical courses. He stipulated the abolition of the punishment of beating in the military when he started his duty. He also organized nutrition programs.

During his time in office,[119] Goltz Pasha published more than 4,000 Ottoman lithographed textbooks.[120]

---

in Istanbul on June 24, 1916. See Wallach, *Bir Askeri Yardımın Anatomisi – Türkiye'de Prusya-Alman Askeri Heyetleri 1835–1919*, 169.

119 Even Goltz Pasha, who resisted all negativities, wanted to return to Germany without extending his contract due to the obstruction of reform efforts in the Ottoman army, However, Sultan Abdulhamid directly communicated with the Kaiser Wilhelm I on this issue, and Kaiser asked Goltz to stay, through the Head of the Military Cabinet. For this reason, Goltz Pasha had to extend his contract on July 26, 1886. These repeated extensions continued until 1 November 1895, when Lieutenant General von der Goltz left Ottoman army service to rejoin the German army. The Committee of Union and Progress, which took over the administration after Abdulhamid II was dethroned in 1908, thought that reorganizing the army was impossible without Goltz Pasha, who was a full general in Germany at that time. There were also many former students of Goltz Pasha under the Committee of Union and Progress administration. Goltz Pasha, who resisted the insistence of Abdulhamid II and managed not to re-enter the Ottoman army service, could not resist the pressure of the German and Austrian governments. Austria had to ask for a strong Ottoman army, because it could foresee what the regional tension was about. Germany, on the other hand, could not find someone like Goltz who could establish a diplomatic and commercial bond between Germany and the Ottoman army after von der Goltz. Moreover, the fact that the Committee of Union and Progress was questioning the high salaries of existing German officers was in a way that could disrupt the German influence in the Ottoman army. For this reason, the Germans and Austrians wanted Goltz Pasha to be in the Ottoman Empire. However, Goltz Pasha found it more appropriate to visit and report periodically instead of entering the Ottoman service directly, and this was also accepted by the Kaiser. Goltz Pasha remained in the service of the Ottoman Empire from October 1909 to January 1910 as an adviser and made many arrangements and maneuvers. Until the First World War broke out, he did not physically return to the Ottoman Empire and continued his consultancy from afar through letters. See Wallach, *Bir Askeri Yardımın Anatomisi – Türkiye'de Prusya-Alman Askeri Heyetleri 1835–1919*, 51.

120 Wallach, *Bir Askeri Yardımın Anatomisi – Türkiye'de Prusya-Alman Askeri Heyetleri 1835–1919, 54.*

Goltz Pasha's greatest contribution to Germany during his duty in the Ottoman army was that he worked as a diplomat. Goltz Pasha gave great importance to equipping the Ottoman army with German defense industry equipment, and warned the Germans directly in case of a contrary development. In 1891, when the Ottoman Empire was going to buy weapons from the French, Goltz Pasha informed the manager of the Krupp company and put pressure on him. He complained about the German ambassador Radowitz's passive and ineffective stance and he insisted on the importance of the issue and indirectly ensured the direct involvement of the Kaiser.[121] This insistence is an indication of the seriousness and influence that Goltz Pasha gave to the subject.

The fact that Goltz Pasha was the head of the Military Reform Commission also enabled him to communicate directly with the Sultan and brought Goltz Pasha to an even more important position. In this way, he was able to persuade the Sultan to accept the military reforms he had reported. As a result, important reforms and recruitment arrangements were made in the Ottoman army.

In order to increase the mobility of the Ottoman army in a possible war, modernizing and arranging the railways for military use was another issue that Goltz Pasha gave importance. The project of reducing military expenses and increasing the redif organization was also one of the contributions of Goltz Pasha. Of course, this situation also worked for German companies. Although the fixed expenses in the army decreased, the total number of soldiers increased with both the new recruitment law and the increased capacity of the redif organization. The demand for military equipment also increased accordingly. The money to meet this additional demand was also provided from the financing to be obtained due to the reduction in fixed expenses. Goltz Pasha's regular supply of intelligence to Germany is another indicator of his skills in the process of German defense industry equipment penetrating the Ottoman army. For example, in 1885–86, he had a great influence on the purchase of Krupp cannons for the straits. He was also the one who suggested the establishment of a torpedo fleet for the defense of the straits and who recommended Schichau Shipyard for the torpedoes to be built. He also ensured that 500,000 Mauser rifles and 50,000 carbines were purchased for the modernization of the Ottoman army.[122]

The "recruitment law" and "reorganization of the troops" projects completed by Goltz Pasha in March 1886 were also an important development. Goltz Pasha reorganized the Ottoman army into divisions, brigades, regiments and battalions

---

121 Naci Yorulmaz, *Arming the Sultan*, 85.
122 Yorulmaz, *Arming the Sultan*, 95.

and increased the number of soldiers in total. As supply increased, demand increased in direct proportion.

Delegations had a great importance in the establishment of German militarism in the Ottoman army. However, it should be noted that the activities of the delegations were also supoorted by Bismarck and Kaiser Wilhelm II. Kaiser Wilhelm II made his first Ottoman visit between 2 and 6 November in 1889, one year after his accession to the throne. During this visit he made with his wife, he visited Sultan Abdulhamid and toured Istanbul with Kaiserin.[123] After this visit, Kazyer's oriental policy was further shaped. The Kaiser was also very well received during this visit. One of the most beautiful mansions in Tarabya was gifted to him, The construction permit of the first German Evangelical Church *(Erlöserkirche)* to be built in Jerusalem was extended, He was presented with the Order of Osmaniye on November 4, 1889. Moreover, due to his contributions to the trade with Krupp, he was given the title of Grand Master Honorary Ottoman Artillery (*Grand Maître Honoraire Artillerie Ottomane*).[124]

After Bismarck's resignation in 1890, Kaiser Wilhelm became the only practical authority on foreign policy.[125] Although names such as Leo von Caprivi, Prince of Hohenlohe-Schillingsfürst Chlodwig Karl Viktor, Bernhard von Bülow and Theobald von Bethmann Hollveg took office as chancellors in the post-Bismarck period, none of them could reach Bismarck's influence. Since Bismarck was a self-interested politician, he was able to change his attitude from time to time, especially in the early 1880s, when rational interests came into play, However, Kaiser Wilhelm's approach to the Ottomans was different from Bismarck's. Instead of implementing a flexible policy according to the conditions of the day, the Kaiser displayed a policy that proceeded without stretching in line with the target he set. This policy was mostly brought good relations with the Ottoman Empire.

Kaiser Wilhelm's visit in 1898, also called the Second Orient visit, was a very important event that had a repulsive effect on German-Ottoman trade relations.

---

123 The fact that Sultan Abdulhamid sent a telegram inviting Kaiser Wilhelm II to Istanbul on September 4, 1889 was also effective for this visit. See BOA, Y.PRK. NMH.4/42 – 08.01.1307/04.09.1889.

124 Yorulmaz, *Arming the Sultan*, 58.

125 In addition to the personal contributions of Kaiser Wilhelm, in Germany's relations with the Ottoman Empire, Baron Marschall von Bieberstein, who was appointed as the ambassador to Istanbul in 1897 and was a firm supporter of Wilhelm's policies, also had an impact. See W. O. Henderson, "German Economic Penetration in the Middle East, 1870–1914", *The Economic History Review*, vol. 18, no. 1/2 (1948), 58.

The data of the following period also support the effectiveness of this visit. As a result of the Kaiser's second visit to the East, which started in Istanbul on October 18, 1898, many agreements were signed.

The Kaiser's Second Orient visit also had several important consequences. The concession for the construction of Haydarpaşa Station was given to the Anatolian Railways Company. The concession to operate the ferryboat on the Haydarpaşa-Sirkeci line and the concessions to lay the Constanta-Istanbul telegraph line were again given to the Germans, but the most important was undoubtedly the Baghdad Railway concession. This railway was both a project that Sultan Abdulhamid had desired for many years and that Kaiser Wilhelm desired in order to boost Germany's export potential with live consumption markets. Before 1889, when the Kaiser made his first visit, all of the railway projects were under French and British domination. The fact that the tender for the Anatolian Railway was given to the Germans in 1889, and then the concession of the Baghdad Railways was given to the Germans, can reveal how the British and French plans were turned upside down within 10 years.

The fact that the Committee of Union and Progress took over the administration after Sultan Abdulhamid was dethroned and exiled to Thessaloniki did not lead to a radical change in Turkish-German military relations. This was due to the desire of German companies not to want to lose their target market with a rational approach and the continuation of communication within the military. On the other hand, Goltz Pasha had many students in the Committee of Union and Progress. Mahmut Şevket Pasha even asked for a new military delegation from Germany after a short time. The name requested by Mahmut Şevket Pasha was Goltz Pasha, as would be expected. Kaiser Wilhelm, who predicted that the German delegations would be the most effective solution to restructure relations with the new government, sent Goltz Pasha to Istanbul immediately. Goltz Pasha, who came to Istanbul on 12 July 1909, was appointed as the vice president of the Important Military Affairs Council, which was established on 14 August 1909. Weapon purchases continued again from German companies.

In the report dated March 28, 1910, which was sent to Washington by the American consulate in Istanbul, it was mentioned that foreign officers in the Ottoman army and navy greatly influenced not only the commercial orientation of the Ottoman Empire, but also its foreign policy. In the report, which also included data on the arms trade, it was stated that the most important name affecting the tendencies of the Ottoman defense industry and foreign policy was von der Goltz Pasha, and that most of the equipment in the Ottoman army was German-made.[126] The West, which thought that its military attitude in the Ottoman Empire could change with the Committee of Union and Progress's takeover, had to openly accept the German influence in the Ottoman Empire.

The last delegation from Germany to the Ottoman army was the delegation headed by Liman von Sanders, who came to Istanbul on December 14, 1913, on the eve of the First World War.[127] This delegation continued its activities during the First World War.

3.4.2. Arms Trade

Technological developments that did not have a negative impact on employment in Germany were always welcomed with enthusiasm, because technology was also used by German rulers to expand their authority. It can be said that from Frederick the Great to Wilhelm II, technology contributed positively to the influence of the central authority.[128] Therefore, the government was not against technological developments. As of the 19th century, the development of defense industry technologies had a similar effect both in domestic and foreign policy and came to the fore as a priority area.

The rapid and efficient progress of industrialization, and especially of the iron and steel industry, had increased the arms production capacity. This increase in capacity became more evident in the middle of the 19th century, and companies that would become giants in the Ottoman market such as Krupp and Mauser began to show themselves in this period, especially in the 1880s, when German delegations began to exert influence in the Ottoman army. The reason why Krupp and Mauser are frequently emphasized is that these companies have achieved a sustainable trade volume with the Ottoman Empire. Otherwise, there were other German companies that received orders from the Ottoman Ministry of War and caught a limited trade volume, albeit at a relatively low level. For example, Gaganau company in Karlsruhe did business with Ottoman Empire on automobile orders, Bromberg canned goods factory on canned meat orders, Simson arms factory on weapons orders, optics factory in Wetzlar on various military optical material orders, Berlin chemical factory on various chemical

126 NARA, 867.00, 10044/287, January 24th, 1910–February 27, 1913.

127 Liman von Sanders, *Türkiye'de Beş Yıl*, trans. Eşref Bengi Özbilen (İstanbul, Türkiye İş Bankası Kültür Yayınları, 4th Ed., 2016), 9.

128 Thorstein Veblen, *Imperial Germany and the Industrial Revolution* (London: Macmillan & Co Ltd, 1915), 75.

products orders. They all received and delivered orders from the Ottoman Ministry of War, particularly during the Balkan Wars.[129]

It is an expected process for industrializing countries to realize the excess supply they can obtain due to the increase in their arms production capacity and to start looking for target markets for themselves. This was also the case in Germany. For Germany, these target markets were countries that wanted to strengthen their army but did not have enough defense industry to do so on their own, and at this point the Ottoman Empire stood out. Although the arms trade between Germany and the Ottoman Empire started to accelerate with the Otto Kähler delegation that came in 1882, German arms companies had taken initiatives before this date, considering the Ottoman Empire as a target market. The fact that the rifle samples manufactured in the factories of the city of Summarde, Germany, were presented to Sultan Abdulhamid in 1881 and it was stated that they could be sent to the sultan if he liked it,[130] is an indication that German gun manufacturers were following this rapprochement. The Ottoman Empire started to pay more attention to armament, especially after the 1877 Ottoman-Russian war. However, it was obvious that it could not provide sufficient armament with its own defense industry capacity. While the Ottoman Empire was able to manufacture 397.228 light weapons in its own factories between 1864 and 1883, it imported 1.227.666 light weapons. The fact that some articles could not be produced at all in the domestic industry also created foreign dependency.[131]

At the time when the German military delegation came to Istanbul in 1882, the weapon production capacity of the Ottoman Empire was quite limited. There were five main facilities managed by the Ministry of Imperial Ordnance (Ministry of Tophane-i Amire) and these were; *Tophane-i Amire* (Imperial Cannon Foundry), *Tüfekhane-i Amire* (Imperial Light Arms Factory), *Baruthane-i Amire* (Imperial Gunpowder Factory), *Kırkağaç Fişekhanesi* (Kırkağaç Cartridge Facory) and *Zeytinburnu Fabrika-yı Hümayun* (Imperial Foundry). The productivity of these limited production plants also showed a downward trend from year to year. In 1881, between May 31 and June 7, 306 Springfield rifles with bayonets (with Snider system), 181 Enfield with bayonets (with Snider system), 200 Martini-Henry rifles with bayonets, and 50 Winchester rifles could be produced in a

129 Mustafa Gencer, *Jöntürk Modernizmi ve Alman Ruhu – 1908–1918 Dönemi Türk-Alman İlişkileri ve Eğitim* (İstanbul: İletişim Yayınları (3rd Ed., 2015)), 55–56.

130 BOA, Y. PRK. AZJ, 1 – 75, H-07-08-1294.

131 Zengin, *Osmanlı Devleti'nde Harp Sanayii*, 71.

weekly cycle.[132] Apart from these, there were also factories producing military cloth and shoes, a carpentry shop, a printing house and production facilities where by-products were produced such as cranes.[133] However, as can be understood from Moltke's memoirs, the production capacity was quite low and insufficient even for the existing soldiers. The level of weapon production was sufficient neither for the developing technology nor the Ottoman army, which was aiming to grow.[134]

The Ottoman Empire tried to meet its arms need with imports from Britain, the USA[135] and France. So much so that at the end of 1869, the Ottoman Empire bought 239,000 Enfields and Springfields from the USA.[136] However, this habit began to change as a result of the Franco-Prussian War in 1870 and the deterioration of the Ottoman economy with the Russo-Turkish War (1877–1878). The fact that Prussia defeated France and paved the way for the proclamation of the German Empire proved the superiority of German weapons against the French and drew the attention of the Ottomans to German weapons, as well as the whole world. On the other hand, the fact that the Ottoman Empire could not make payments to US arms manufacturers such as Winchester was another factor that shifted the Ottoman Empire to German companies.[137]

---

132 Yorulmaz, *Arming the Sultan*, 97–99.

133 Zengin, *Osmanlı Devleti'nde Harp Sanayii*, 94–139.

134 The Ottoman Empire encouraged and made plans for domestic weapons production in certain periods, but the actual output was always far below the target. For example, the production amounts in Zeytinburnu Cartridge Factory are a striking example of this situation. While the targeted daily production amount between 1890–99 was 100–150 thousand, the actual daily amount was 1200–1500. In 1906–1908, while the target was 100–200 thousand per day, the production was 20–30 thousand per day. See Tetik, *Sultan'ın Silahları*, 267.

135 In particular, the USA started an aggressive weapon sales policy in this period in order to melt the stocks left in the hands of the arms manufacturers after the 1861–1865 American Civil War. Until the end of 1869, the USA sold 114.000 Enfiled rifles at 0,91 Ottoman liras each and 125.000 Springfield rifles at 1,60 Ottoman liras each to the Ottoman Empire. Although these sales were made for used weapons in the first place, new weapons started to be purchased from the factory as of 1869. While arms and ammunition sales accounted for 97 % of US exports to the Ottoman Empire in 1877, it decreased to 3 % in 1883 with German weapons dominating the market. See. Önsoy, *Türk – Alman İktisadi Münasebetleri (1871–1914)*, 95; Metin Ünver, "Teknolojik Gelişmeler Işığında Osmanlı-Amerikan Silah Ticaretinin İlk Dönemi", *Tarih Araştırmaları Dergisi* 32/54 (2013), 210.

136 Ali Serdar Mete, *Türk Mavzeri* (İstanbul: Doğu Kütüphanesi, 2022), 69.

137 Mete, *Türk Mavzeri*, 69.

The Germans had an effective method in the arms trade, which was unique to them and called the "German-style arms trade". The fact that the state gave importance to the arms industry and therefore supported the arms manufacturers enabled the arms manufacturers to grow easily and to create a market for themselves by using politics. Through the delegations the German government sent, they both marketed their own products and were able to provide loans through banks when necessary so that these products could be purchased by the Ottoman Empire. For example, the 21 million marks (1,335,000 lira) loan that the Ottoman Empire received from Deutsche Bank in 1888 had two important consequences. The first was that the monopoly of the French-dominated Banque Ottoman in loans given to the Ottoman Empire was disrupted and German financing was introduced into the Ottoman Empire. The second was that these loans were used for German weapons and the money from Germany returned to Germany.[138] For example, out of the loan of 1,135,000 liras, with 299,664.42 liras Mauser rifles were purchased, with 213,236.75 liras Krupp cannons were purchase, and with 100,000 liras the necessary war materials for the navy were purchased from the Germania Shipyard.[139] All in all, with the 54 % of the loan the German arms were purchased, with the 21 % of the loan the receivables of military officials were paid, and with the 25 % of the loan weekly wages of military officials were paid and other military expenditures were made.[140] This mutual relationship produced more concrete results in the following years. Between 1888 and 1893, Germany's exports to the Ottoman Empire increased by 350 %[141] and a large part of this increase was provided by the arms industry. In particular, between 1885 and 1887, Ottoman orders to German arms companies were at an interesting level. The Krupp firm received orders for 20.74 million marks, while the Schichau and Germania shipyards received orders for 10 torpedo boats worth

138 This cycle was repeated many times. For example, the cannons purchased from the Krupp company for the protection of the castles in 1873 were also purchased with a bank loan. See BOA, A. MKT.MHM, 460–18, H-06-06-1290.

139 The Germania shipyard was originally established in 1882 to manufacture warships and merchant ships in accordance with Germany's Weltpolitik doctrine. The Germania shipyard was a strategic enterprise that also handled the iron casting operations. It was acquired by Krupp in 1896. See Epkenhans, "Military—Industrial Relations in Imperial Germany, 1870–1914",5.
Yorulmaz, *Arming the Sultan*, 39–40.

140 Yorulmaz, *Arming the Sultan*, 39–40.

141 Gregor Schöllgen, *Imperialismus und Gleichgewicht: Deutschland, England und die orientalische Frage 1871–1914* (Munich: Oldenbourg, 1984), 49.

2.455 million marks, but the largest share was Mauser's, who received orders for rifles and ammunition worth 45.75 million marks.[142]

Although there were private companies among the players of this cycle, it was the duty of the government not to disturb the order of the cycle. So much so that, when appropriate, Bismarck, and even the German Kaiser, were able to directly intervene in matters related to the arms trade and attempt to persuade the Sultan directly.[143] The order of 500,000 rifles and 50,000 carbines received from the Ottoman Empire on February 9, 1887,[144] which enabled the rapid growth of Mauser, was also received as a result of the joint efforts of Bismarck, Goltz Pasha and Paul Mauser. The fact that the German delegations were also in decision-making positions at that time and that both military and political recommendations were overlapping ensured that these interventions were extraordinarily effective. There is no doubt that Mauser's superior technique and superiority over others in spare parts production also had a great effect on this high trade volume.[145] The Ottoman Empire also inspected the quality of these products by itself. In order to ensure the quality of Mauser, he established an Inspection Commission after his first order in 1887 and had both the commission members and the military officials in Germany inspected the quality of the orders given to Mauser in Obendorf.[146] Beyond mutual relations, both the satisfaction with quality and the successful order management of the Huber Brothers who hold the Istanbul representative of Krupp and Mauser,[147] were the most important factors in the continuity of the arms orders given to German companies from the Ottoman Empire.

The commitment of German arms companies to the state was also notable. Krupp's experience in the steel industry, its successful team, its quality, its

---

142 Epkenhans, "Military—Industrial Relations in Imperial Germany, 1870–1914", 14–15.

143 For the letter of recommendation sent to Sultan Abdulhamid, in which Bismarck stated the necessity of using Rottweiler gunpowder in Mauser rifles, See BOA, Y.PRK. ESA 6/61 (H. 25.07.1304) (M. 10.04.1887). Similarly, when the agreement between Bab-ı Ali and the British Martini-Henry for 400,000 rifles was about to be signed, Bismarck wrote to Sultan Abdülhamid and recommended Mauser rifles. Thus, Sultan Abdulhamid ordered 300,000 rifles from Mauser. For details See Yorulmaz, *Arming the Sultan*, 34. After this process, with the influence of the German advisers in the Ottoman Empire, Mauser began to take over the rifle monopoly in the Ottoman Empire.

144 Türk, *Türkiye ile Almanya Arasındaki Silah Ticareti 1871–1914*, 202.

145 Fatih Tetik, *Sultan'ın Silahları* (İstanbul: Dergah Yayınları, 2018), 183.

146 Mete, *Türk Mavzeri*, 76–77.

147 Mete, *Türk Mavzeri*, 78.

production capacity and its innovative products had made Krupp the number one business partner of the German state. However, there was another very important reason that should not be ignored in the Krupp choise of the German state. Krupp did not hesitate to act as if it were a public institution serving the German state. Krupp did not give importance to profit when it came to strategic orders. Krupp took the strategic navy orders that other companies did not take because it did not even cover the cost. When the time came, upon the request of the German army, Krupp did not hesitate to invest a budget of 5 million marks in weapons R&D activities in order to get ahead of its British and French rivals.[148]

For all these reasons that differentiated Krupp, Germany, until the 1890s, actually did not give any job to Krupp's rivals. The fact that 30 % of Germany's exports to the Ottoman Empire were made by the Krupp in 1906[149] is a phenomenon that reveals the macroeconomic importance of Krupp.

In this section, it is revealed once again that the Turkish-German rapprochement was born out of necessity. While industrializing Germany needed a target market, the Ottoman Empire, which was dealing with many problems around and within itself, needed the support of a strong and industrialized state that would approach it friendly, not hostile. It is seen that most of the actions that caused Turkish-German rapprochement occurred as a result of demands of the Ottoman Empire. One of the notaworhy points of German Industrialization is the commitment of the leading arms companies to German state and the financing of these companies by German banks. This cycle sheds light on the "German-style arms trade". It surely constituted one of the most important foundations of the Turkish-German rapprochment in the second half of 19th century.

148 For example; Between 1905 and 1908, Krupp's investment of 28 million marks and increased capacity in order to meet the demands of the expanded navy program of the German state indicates the advantage of the existence of strong companies affiliated with them for the German state. See Epkenhans, "Military—Industrial Relations in Imperial Germany, 1870–1914",12, 17.

149 Epkenhans, "Military—Industrial Relations in Imperial Germany, 1870–1914", 16.

Chapter 4 Turkish-German Military and Poltical Relations after the First World War from Industrial Perspective (1914–1929)

Germany in the First World War and Germany after the First World War were very different from each other due to both internal factors and external sanctions. Therefore, Turkish-German relations in the First World War and Turkish-German relations after the First World War were also different from each other.

It would be a correct and meaningful approach to examine separately the effects of German Industrialization on the path to the First World War, its role in the First World War and its rebirth after the First World War.

4.1. Turkish-German Relations on the Eve of the First World War

Germany in 1914 differed from Germany in 1871 in many respects. Germany's population, which was approximately 40 million in 1871, increased to approximately 65 million by 1914, and 3/4 of this population lived in big cities and became a part of industrial and commercial enterprises.[1] In 1914, Germany created capital accumulation with its industry and succeeded in being a self-sufficient economy in many respects. In 1914, Germany was the second country in terms of volume in world trade, and the development that took place before 1914 was remarkable. While the Reich's imports and exports were 6,500 million marks in 1888, it increased to 20,000 million marks in 1913. The most important part of this development was that more than 70 % of imports were covered by goods such as raw materials, food, beverages and tobacco, the rest were semi-finished and finished products. About 75 % of exports were semi-finished or finished products. Processing the raw material and selling it as a final product provided Germany with added value gains, which significantly moved the German economy forward.[2]

Giving an example of the income obtained by processing raw materials and adding value will shed light on the economic importance of industrialization. In

---

1 Marie von Eschen "The Commercial Expansion of Germany 1871–1914", *Social Science*, vol. 2, no. 3 (1927), 225.

2 Henderson, *The Industrial Revolution on the Continent*, 72.

Germany in 1913, 100 kg of impure iron was 3 marks. If this iron was purified, the price of pure iron would be 6 marks per 100 kg. If this iron was made into steel, its price would be 11 marks per 100 kg. If it was made into tins, the price would be 16 marks per 100 kg. If it was made into a knife iron, its price would rise to between 1,500 marks and 2,100 marks per 100 kg. If it was made into a clock spring, the price would be 40 million marks for 100 kg. In the period when 100 kg of gold was 280,000 marks, the way to earn 40 million marks from 100 kg of imported iron was to add value by industrialization.[3]

On the eve of the First World War, Germany's production of coal, iron and steel exceeded the combined output of all its competitors on the European continent, and Germany's population increased significantly. Germany had become a country where highly educated workers produced qualified products. From machine building to the chemical industry, from electrical engineering to metallurgy, a wide range of German products and companies took the lead. Germany, which is not an island country and most of its borders are covered by the continents of other countries, even reached the capacity to build the world's largest navy in 1914.[4] Between 1871 and 1914, Germany's industrial output increased sixfold, while Britain's industrial output in the same period could only double.[5] By 1914 German Industry had surpassed Britain in the steel, machine tools, textiles, dyestuffs and many other chemical products sectors.[6]

Britain, which had struggled for centuries in order to preserve the balances on the European continent and to prevent a superpower from appearing on the continent, started to fail to get what it wanted from the end of the 19th century, and Germany began to stand out as a potential superpower in the European continent. The industrialization of a powerful new competitor, Germany, brought to light the threat that the usual gains from Britain would not be regained. Industrialized Britain was accustomed to obtaining its own economic prosperity with a global order that worked for it. Except for the Napoleonic era, Britain had significantly increased its level of economic prosperity in the nearly 100-year period from the middle of the 18th century to the middle of the 19th century, with the advantage of early industrialization and the sanctions supported by its political power. In accordance with the Maritime Laws, which remained in

---

3 Jäckh, *Balkan Harbinden Sonra Şarkta Almanya*, 26.

4 Steinberg, *Bismarck*, 376.

5 Braun, *The German Economy in the Twentieth Century*, 19.

6 Timothy W. Guinnane, "Delegated Monitors, Large and Small: The Development of Germany's Banking System, 1800–1914", *Center Discussion Paper, no. 835* (2001), 6.

effect until the middle of the 19th century, even colonial goods such as tea and coffee had to pass through Britain before going to Europe and also they had to be transported to Europe by British ships.[7] From the middle of the 19th century, wooden and sailing ships were replaced by iron and steam powered ships in the transport of commercial goods in Britain. This change not only brought down the freight prices, but also caused an explosion in ship production as the demand for commercial ships increased.[8] With the advantage of the advanced shipbuilding industry, no state throughout history has dominated the open waters more than the 19th century Britain did.[9] In 1860, the British navy, which had a strength of 40,000 men and 240 ships, had about one-third of the world's trade tonnage,[10] but as of the beginning of the 20th century, this balance began to change. While 6,500 workers were working in the shipyards serving the German navy in 1888, this number increased to 15,500 in 1900 and to 21,500 in 1912. Successful shipyards began to deliver important orders.[11] The ship Imperator, which was launched on June 11, 1913, succeeded in gaining the title of the world's largest passenger ship with a weight of 52,000 gross tons, and the existence of ships such as SS Vaterland and SS Bismarck, which were her other two sisters, were an indicator of the progress made by the Hamburg shipyards.[12] From 1885 to the First World War, German shipyards grew at an annual rate of 9 % in terms of final product output. Thanks to giant shipbuilding companies such as Blohm + Voss, Germany increased its share of shipbuilding in the world from 7.3 % to

---

7 Breuilly, *Avusturya, Prusya ve Almanya'nın Oluşumu 1806–1871*, 54.

8 Another factor in this increase in demand was the decrease in shipbuilding prices in Britain. with the developing technology and the decrease in iron prices. From the late 1860s to the early 1890s, the prices of British ironships dropped by about 40 %. See Charles K. Harley, "British Shipbuilding and Merchant Shipping: 1850–1890." *The Journal of Economic History*, vol. 30, no. 1 (1970), 262.

9 Britain started investing in naval forces quite early. Even in the 1650s, at least 90 % of public expenditure went to the land and navy, which is an enormous proportion. However, even this rate was not enough, the salaries of the newly established army and navy could not be paid on time, and Foreign Minister Thurloe complained about the obstacles created by the lack of money in a period like 1658. See Geoffrey Parker, *Askeri Devrim – Batı'nın Yükselişinde Askeri Yenilikler 1500–1800*, trans. Tuncay Zorlu (İstanbul: Küre Yayınları, 2018), 131.

10 Niall Ferguson, *İmparatorluk-Britanya'nın Modern Dünyayı Biçimlendirişi*, trans. Nurettin Elhüseyni (İstanbul: Yapı Kredi Yayınları, 2019), 169.

11 Epkenhans, "Military—Industrial Relations in Imperial Germany, 1870–1914", 3.

12 Niall Ferguson, *Paper and Iron* (Cambridge: Cambridge University Press, 2002), 31.

14 % between 1892 and 1913. These developments were an important cause of uneasiness for Britain.[13]

4.1.1. Trade

Germany underwent a major structural transformation in the 19th century. While the population in Germany (within the borders of 1871) was 23.5 million and the labor force was 10 million in 1816, the population increased to 35 million and the labor force to 15 million in 1850. In 1913, the population was 67 million, the active labor force was 27 million.[14] Germany increased its labor force 2.7 times in the 100 years period untill 1913. The increase in the workforce in this period should not be evaluated only as a regular change. The shift of the workforce from agriculture to industry, work experience based on technical education and the master-apprentice system, technological developments came with industrialization, greatly increased the productivity of the worker. In other words, the worker's opportunity to practice led to a tremendous educational integration in the light of theoretical knowledge, while ongoing technological developments reduced the burden per worker and increased productivity. As a result, both a high-quality worker class was formed in Germany and the productivity of the workers increased. This situation had very positive reflections on trade, as expected. Germany's export capacity increased, and the gained share of the existing market was generally those of Britain and France. Particularly on this subject, the second half of the 19th century, when the effects of industrialization in Germany began to be seen concretely, is quite interesting. German foreign trade grew unusually at an annual rate of over 4 % during this period.[15] Labor force, raw materials, industrial products, ready-made products and capital could enter and leave Germany quickly.

While the world trade volume increased in ready-made products, not every country could benefit from this increase at the same rate. The increase in Germany's exports, especially in ready-made products, worried Britain and France, because while Germany was increasing its exports in this area, it had determined its target market as the markets of Britain and France. As Germany's share rose, it lowered theirs. While the Germany's share in World exports of manufactured goods was 19.3 % in 1880, its share increased to 26.6 % in 1913.

---

13 The number of workers that Blohm + Voss employed in July 1914 was 10.853. See Ferguson, *Paper and Iron*, 42.

14 Tilly – Pierenkemper, *The German Economy During the Nineteenth Century*, 103.

15 Tilly – Pierenkemper, *The German Economy During the Nineteenth Century*, 145.

At the sime time period share of Britain decreased from 41.4 % to 30.2 % and the share of France decreased from 22.2 % to 12.1 %.[16]

Competition and early industrialization had effects in the decline of Britain's share. The private sector in Britain was not so eager to make new investments continuously to the new technologies and this led to a decrease in their productivity and competitiveness. On the other hand, the decrease in the share of France was due to both the decrease in population growth after the 1870s and the dependence on agriculture. Of course, these reasons alone would not be enough to explain the share Germany gained. The tendency of Germany's exports also played a role in this success. Considering that British and French exports were mainly focused on textiles, and Germany's was focused on steel, chemistry and machinery, it could be understood why Germany increased its trade volume faster, because towards the end of the 19th century, many countries had become self-sufficient in textiles. Germany, on the other hand, created its workforce from qualified personnel, both with the advantage of cheap labor given by its late industrialization and firstly with theoretical and then practical training, and directed this qualified workforce to areas with ever-increasing demand. By making good use of its modern equipment, cheap and qualified workforce and sufficient raw materials, Germany managed to capture a significant part of the trade volume in Europe quite quickly until the First World War.

Germany's geopolitical position also had a significant impact on the rapid increase in trade volume. Germany was surrounded by many neighbors, and furthermore, it had a gateway to the vast eastern lands. When Germany turned its geographical position into an advantage with its wide railway networks, it was able to export to Italy on the one hand and Russia on the other hand, with relatively low transportation costs. While Britain's exports to Europe accounted for 35 % of all exports, Germany's exports to Europe accounted for 75 % of all exports.[17] This criterion is an indication of how actively Germany traded with its neighbor, contrary to the colonial policy of Britain, in particular.

Considering the situation of the four countries, that influenced the world trade volume, in 1913, it can be better observed how Germany, which was once seen as closer to the east and whose development was questioned, made a progress in the 19th century. In 1880 Britain controlled 22.4 % of world trade, while Germany's share was 10,3 %. In 1913, Britain's share fell to 14.2 %, Germany's share rose to 12.3 %. Between 1895 and 1913, Germany's industrial production increased by

---

16 Tilly – Pierenkemper, The German Economy During the Nineteenth Century, 147.

17 Tilly – Pierenkemper, *The German Economy During the Nineteenth Century*, 149.

150 %, metal production by 300 %, and coal production by 200 %. In 1913, the German economy produced and consumed 20 % more electricity than Britain, France and Italy combined.[18]

In 1912, Germany's exports rose to $405,000,000, surpassing Britain's exports by $15,000,000. In the same year, Germany's exports to Britain were $119,000,000 more than five years ago, while Britain's exports to Germany were only $16.5 million more than five years ago.[19] By 1913, it was impossible to ignore Germany's significant development in world trade.

4.1.2. Population

Germany's population more than doubled in 1914 compared to a 100 years ago. In 1914, the population of Germany was more than one and a half times that of France and Italy, and about 20 million more than the United Kingdom.[20] Adding to all these, life expectancy, which more than doubled between 1700 and 1933 in Germany, and the associated fall in mortality, the reason for the population increase becomes more apparent.

The times when immigration turned negative were the times when economic prosperity and confidence increased in Germany.

Germany had periods of three major immigration waves. The first of these was the period of 1846–1857, when political unrest was experienced due to the Revolutions of 1848. The second wave was a period of wars that would end with the procolamation of the German Empire. Due to this period, there was a wave of immigration between 1864 and 1873. The third wave was experienced due to the economic collapse between 1880 and 1893.

In 1900s the emigration rates were no longer high in Germany. However, at the sime time Germany did not want to accept immigrants. Due to the shortage of agricultural workers, especially in the East Elbe, Germany took in large numbers of seasonal workers, as mentioned above. In 1906, 71.5 % of the non-German agricultural workers in Prussia were Poles. Considering that Russian Poland was divided between Russia, Austria-Hungary and Prussia and ruled under the auspices of the Russians, it can be predicted that Germany looked at the possibility of the colonization of Poles in its own territory as a political problem; therefore, Germany tried to prevent the spread of Polish nationalism in its territory by pursuing a policy of Germanization of all Polish speakers. In

18 Clark, *Uyurgezerler*, 160.
19 Von Eschen, "The Commercial Expansion of Germany 1871–1914", 230.
20 Naci Yorulmaz, *Arming the Sultan*, 49.

Germany, even more stringent restrictions were placed on Polish employees from Russian occupied territories, allowing all of them to leave Germany on 20 December each year and only be able to re-enter Germany from 1 February next year.[21] Germany did not want foreigners in its own territory, on the contrary, it began to seek a place to live for its own citizens, because the concentration of the existing population surplus in certain cities made the population increase even more evident. Population increases in some cities are given in the table below.

Table 4.1. Population Growth in Some Selected German Cities

City	1800	1850	1910
Munich	40,000	110,000	596,000
Frankfurt	48,000	65,000	415,000
Essen	4,000	9,000	443,000
Kiel	7,000	44,000	206,000
Dusseldorf	10,000	29,000	410,000

Source: Data from Jean Maillet, *18. Yüzyıldan Bugüne İktisadi Olayların Evrimi*, Remzi Kitabevi, İstanbul: 1983, 88.

The radical increase in the population of cities such as Essen between 1800 and 1910 sheds light on the impact of industrialization on urbanization. All this general population growth led the German Kaiser to the *Lebensraum*[22] All this general population growth led the German Kaiser to the *Lebensraum*.

4.1.3. Foreign Policy

Bismarck, who focused on domestic politics after the unification of Germany, determined Germany's foreign policy generally focused on defense and tried to establish close relations with Austria in order to protect its borders. Thus, Bismarck formalized the close relations between Germany and Austria by establishing a Bilateral Alliance with Austria in 1879. Three years later, with the inclusion of Italy in this alliance, the Triple Alliance was born, and in 1887, a

21 Tilly – Pierenkemper, *The German Economy During the Nineteenth Century*, 100.

22 The *Lebensraum* doctrine was defended by highly influential people in Germany of the period. People like Friedrich Naumann, Paul de Legarde, Ernst Hasse, who had a very important place in society, had texts or discourses that argued that the geographical expansion of Germany was a socially deserved need. For some of these statements, See James L. Barton, "The Ottoman Empire and the War", *The Journal of Race Development*, vol. 9, no. 1 (1918), 3.

reassurance agreement was signed with Russia.[23] Bismarck always preferred to keep Russia on its side rather than against it, with the aim of creating a safe zone around Germany; therefore, Germany's foreign policy alliances started relatively early.[24]

Population growth caused economic and social problems for Germany in some certain areas, so the *Lebensraum* doctrine, which was also advocated by Kaiser Wilhelm II, was adopted more strongly. Kaiser Wilhelm II thought that the solution was in Germany's own territory as well as in territories outside Germany, and began to pursue an expansionist policy. Expansionist policies are war-fed by their nature, and Germany was also aware that a great war was waiting for them eventually, although the time was not certain. This prediction can also be understood by looking at Germany's military expenditures, as Germany's military expenditures increased from 348,6 million marks to 1771,2 million marks between 1874 and 1913. This indicates that although there was an increasing inflation and increasing other state expenditures the share of military expenditures in the total state budget increased one and a half times in the related period.[25] This increase was a significant increase for Germany, which in 1874 was now a significant military power.

The actions of Kaiser Wilhelm II, who decided to personally manage the foreign policy after Bismarck, were carried out in accordance with the *Weltpolitik*[26] doctrine. It is quite understandable that Germany felt insecure at a time when global balances were constantly changing and counter alliances were being made. With the Balkan Union, Germany was literally surrounded by an iron circle. This loneliness was one of the reasons that pushed the Germans to new solution efforts in the east. In the east, it was not Iran or China, but the Ottoman Empire, which welcomed Germany in a friendly way and gave messages of sustainability in bilateral relations. For these reasons, Turkish-German relations, which developed in the light of industrialization, were strengthened not in Bismarck era, but in Kaiser Wilhelm II era.

---

23 Fulbrook, *Almanya'nın Kısa Tarihi*, 135.

24 The Triple Entente did not develop at the same pace. While the agreement between France and Russia was in 1891, Britain's agreement with France was in 1904, and its agreement with Russia was in 1907.

25 Epkenhans, "Military—Industrial Relations in Imperial Germany, 1870–1914", 11.

26 In short, it can be expressed as world politics politics, which envisages that Germany has a say not only in politics within its own borders, but also in geographies outside its borders.

The Turkish-German rapprochement was a process that attracted the attention and reaction of Britain, France and Russia. Because these countries, whose targets were outside their own lands and which followed an expansionist policy, had plans regarding the Ottoman lands. According to them, the most decisive threat were the Anatolian and Baghdad Railway constructions and their routes. Mesopotamia and Basra for Britain, Syria for France were the regions where they saw Germany as a threat. Russia, on the other hand, chose to settle its plans regarding Istanbul, the Straits and the Caucasus with France and Britain, not with Germany, even though it confronted Germany on the issue of Iran.

Against the tension that had been going on and increasing for decades, Germany chose to increase its influence in the region as of 1910, not by opposing Britain, France and Russia, but by reconciling with these countries.

First of all, Kaiser Wilhelm II and Tsar Nicholas II held a meeting in Potsdam in November 1910. In this meeting the Russians agreed not to object to the Baghdad Railway, Germans on the other hand accepted to recognize the Russian interests in Iran.[27]

A similar agreement was made between Germany and France on February 15, 1914. In return for France's acceptance of the Anatolian and Baghdad Railways, the control of the railways in Syria and North Anatolia was left to France.[28] Moreover, it was decided to combine the railway built by Germany and the railway built by France in Aleppo. This agreement was also accepted by the Ottoman Empire.[29]

As a result of the negotiations held between Britain and Germany since 1913, an agreement was signed in London on 18 June 1914. According to this agreement, Germany made Britain accept that the Baghdad Railways would extend from Konya to Basra, ports would be built in Basra and irrigation works would be carried out in Konya. In return, Britain made Germany accept that it would carry out irrigation activities in Mesopotamia. Also, Germany accepted the British presence in the Persian Gulf, and British oil production around Mosul. Moreover, it was agreed that the Liman von Sanders delegation and the British naval delegation under the auspices of Admiral Limpus should work in cooperation.[30]

---

27 H. Bayram Soy, "Birinci Dünya Savaşı Osmanlı Devleti'ni Parçalamak İçin mi Yapıldı? Savaşın Çıkış Sebeplerine Osmanlı Devleti Bağlamında Yeniden Bir Bakış", *100. Yılında Birinci Dünya Savaşı ve Mirası,* ed. Halil Çetin et al. (Çanakkale: Çanakkale Valiliği, 2015), 1/32.

28 Soy, "Birinci Dünya Savaşı Osmanlı Devleti'ni Parçalamak İçin mi Yapıldı?", 1/32.

29 Jäckh, *Yükselen Hilal*, 142.

30 Ernst Jäckh, *Yükselen Hilal* (İstanbul: Temel Yayınları, 1999), 141.

After these developments, Lloyd George stated in his speech in the House of Commons in June 1914 that the relations between Britain and Germany were now very good compared to previous periods and that a significant reduction could be made in the British military budget for this reason.[31] However, after the assassination of Archduke Franz Ferdinand in Sarajevo, all the balances changed and the agreement between Britain and Germany was shelved before it could be ratified in the parliament.

4.2. German Industrialization and Turkish - German Allience

Germany's economic influence in the Ottoman Empire and its recent strong rapprochement with Austria were perceived as an important threat by Britain. As a result of the possibility of Austria to establish dominance in the Balkans, the borders of such an alliance could extend from the North Sea to the Persian Gulf. This was a difficult scenario for Britain to accept. Such an alliance was quite likely to gain easy access to Egypt and to pose a threat to Britain's strategic interests on the routes to his colonies.[32] On the other hand, it was also possible that this scenario would pose a great threat to the continuity of the oil resources of the British oil companies in the Middle East. Indeed, Britain's uneasiness was not in vain. Upon the realization of such an alliance, some negotiations had already begun. For example, one of these meetings was held in 1882 when the embassy delegation in Vienna met with the emperor. In this meeting, it was emphasized that the Ottoman Empire should have gotten along well with Austria and that the railways should have been combined.[33]

Britain, which was a close follower of these developments and wanted to take urgent action to disrupt further steps such as the unification of railways, saw the solution as disrupting the lines of alliance. With this goal, Britain targeted the Balkans, the region where nationalism was most alive and most susceptible to

---

31 Jäckh, *Yükselen Hilal*, 141.

32 From the end of the 19th century, Britain sought more profitable markets, both because of its inability to compete with the aggressive progress of the USA and Germany in free markets, and because of its decreased profitability. For this reason, Britain focused on trade with its colonies and tried not to bring any competition to these countries. For this purpose, Britain, which gave various incentives and indirect supports to British companies trading with its colonies, succeeded in bringing the trade with its colonies to 1/3 of its total exports in 1902. At the beginning of the 20th century, protecting their colonies was equivalent to protecting the British economy for Britain. See Önsoy, *Türk-Alman İktisadi Münasebetleri (1871–1914)*, 85.

33 BOA, Y.PRK.HR, 6-6-2, H-11-02-1299.

being mixed with a little influence. The Balkans had a very fractional structure. Bulgaria and Romania stood close to the German-Austrian alliance. The threat posed by the formation of an uninterrupted line from Berlin to Baghdad could only be prevented by the buffer zones in the Balkans. This fractional structure enabled Britain and Russia to deepen the conflicts in the Balkans. Moreover Serbia, which was under the influence of panslavism, was used as a leading actor here. One of the first actions as a result of these provocations was Serbia's attack on Novi Pazar. This attack was a sign that the great powers were behind Serbia. Otherwise, it would not be wise for Serbia to provoke Austria into a war.[34] The Balkan Union and the Balkan Wars were the facts that showed the success of this project. The ineffectiveness and silence of Austria and Germany in the Balkan Wars also ensured that the scenario planned by Britain and Russia proceeded without interruption. Eventually, a geographically uninterrupted alliance, which would consist nearly 150 million people, between Ottoman Empire, Austria and Germany was prevented with Romania and Serbia. Britain also aimed to change the existing geographical balances by turning the turmoil in the Balkans into a bigger crisis. The fact that Britain had attempted to wage war many times since the beginning of the 20th century was another indication of this. Britain's confrontation of the Serbs with Austria in 1909 created an expectation of war, but Russia's silence ruined Britain's plans and war did not break out. The Italo-Turkish War took place in 1911, the Italians attacked the lands of the Ottoman Empire in Libya, and the Serbs, who took advantage of this, declared war on the Ottoman Empire in the Balkans. Britain wanted to further confuse Austria through Italy and to draw Austria into the Balkan mess at the same time. However, Italy did not interfere with Serbia as a result of Austrian threats and war did not break out. In 1912, alliances were made in the Balkans, Serbia persistently provoked Austria into the Balkan Wars. But Austria was not involved in the war. During these time, the gathering of the British fleet in the North Sea, France's preparation of its ships for war in the Mediterranean, Russia's mobilization of its army for a month, showed how the great powers under the leadership of Britain were confident that a war would break out in 1912.[35] At the beginning of the

34 Austria thought that the only way to go south in the relevant period was via the Novi Pazar -Thessaloniki road. For this reason, there were many newspapers that wrote about these possibilities. They argued that if the Serbs attacked Novi Pazar, such an attempt would bring Austria and Russia against each other and a world war might break out. See Salim Aydın, *Balkanların Acı Tarihi* (İstanbul: Yeditepe Yayınevi, 2013), 345–346.

35 Winterstetten, *Berlin Bağdat – Alman Yayılmacılığı ve Osmanlı Politikaları*, 50–51.

20th century, everyone was waiting for war. Russia did not increase the number of corps from 38 to 41 for no reason and likewise, France did not increase its compulsory military service to three years for no reason.[36] However, the great powers gave up the war every time because they did not feel militarily ready, and the war did not break out.

In such a period when the cauldrons were boiling in Europe, the Ottoman Empire began to feel the uneasiness of its loneliness even more. It was obvious that Russia's eyes were on Istanbul. The alliance of France and Britain with Russia led to the conclusion that the only country that could make an alliance with the Ottoman Empire was Germany. Anticipating that a world war was approaching, the Ottoman Empire made alliance offers to both Britain and France, but received no positive response from any of them.[37] Grand Vizier Said Halim Pasha, who was going to sign an alliance treaty with Germany, interpreted this situation as an indication of the efforts of those countries to destroy the Ottoman Empire. According to Said Halim Pasha, while the Allied Powers made many concessions to attract Italy and Romania, they did not give any positive reaction to the demands of the Ottoman Empire and tried to keep the Ottoman Empire away from them. Russia's desire to seize Istanbul,[38] France's Syria, and the British's desire to seize Iraq had been obvious for years.[39] The only logical option that the

---

36 Winterstetten, *Berlin Bağdat – Alman Yayılmacılığı ve Osmanlı Politikaları*, 74.

37 Cemal Paşa, *Anılarım (1913–1922)*,152.

38 Said Halim Pasha, making a big claim, attributes Russia's rush to enter the First World War and its immediate involvement in the desire to take Istanbul. See Paşa, *Osmanlı İmparatorluğu ve Dünya Savaşı*, 29. It was a known fact that the issue of the straits was quite vital for the Russians. The Straits were vital not only for the military strategic ambitions of the Russians, but also for their economy. Between 1903 and 1912, 37 % of Russian exports passed through the straits. This ratio increased to around 75–80 % in the export of wheat and rye, with which Russia provided the capital accumulation for industrialization. The closure of the straits in the Balkan Wars dealt a great blow to Russian exportersAs a result of giving Liman von Sanders the responsibility for the defense of the Straits and Istanbul in 1913, the Russians, who interpreted this situation as giving the Germans the initiative to close the Straits to the Russians, even took the risk of war. See Clark, *Uyurgezerler*, 328–331. There were even rumors in the French newspapers that Russia would occupy some places on the eastern border of the Ottoman Empire in order to respond to this decision. See Özgür Yılmaz – Eyyub Şimşek, "Fransızlara Göre Türk-Alman Askeri Yakınlaşması ve İttifakı", ed. Necmettin Alkan et al., *Savaşanların Gözüyle Türk – Alman İttifakı* (İstanbul: Kronik Kitap, 2018), 123.

39 British interest in Basra and Baghdad turned into concrete actions in the 19th century. These actions were replaced by projects of establishing a strategic long-term order

Ottoman Empire could make an alliance with was Germany. In his memoirs, Cemal Pasha made the following defense against those who accused him of not making an alliance with Britain and France.

> *"How can an alliance be possible with a state that does not want us? How can we ally with it? They say it would be better to keep our neutrality. On the condition that the passage of ships in the straits is allowed, right? In that case, Russia would emerge from this general war with such a great victory that it would not even wait for the outcome of the war and would have the opportunity to occupy Istanbul and Eastern Anatolia."*[40]

Many military alliances in the world were established in line with economic interests.[41] Therefore, the possibility that Germany, which increased its trade volume by 732 % in the Ottoman Empire between 1898 and 1913,[42] could form an alliance with the Ottoman Empire when the war bells began to ring, was not surprising for other states. Germany, on the other hand, was not very enthusiastic about an alliance with the Ottoman Empire at first. The reports of both Liman von Sanders, the German ambassador Wangenheim, and Moltke stated that an alliance with the Ottoman Empire would create more burden than benefit, and these reports were obviously also effective. The attitude of Austria-Hungary towards the Ottoman alliance was more insistent. Because Austria-Hungary was considerably afraid of the danger that would arise in the Balkans, especially with the influence of Russia, in the event that the Ottoman Empire sided with the Allied Powers. Austria clearly stated that it needed Germany's help to pull the Ottomans to their side. Eventually, Berlin agreed to act together with Austria-Hungary on the Balkans issue.[43] However, Berlin did not show the same attitude with Austria on the Ottoman issue. While Austria was making war calculations after the assassination of Franz Ferdinand, it emphasized that if the Ottoman Empire joined the war on the side of the Allies, Bulgaria would be threatened from every corner and that Bulgaria was the only country that could open a second front against Serbia. With those thoughts on mind, on 14 July 1914, Austria made a call to the German Foreign Minister Jagow for a joint action on the integration of the Ottoman Empire to the Central Powers.

---

during the years of occupation. For the plans and analyzes of the British in those regions during the years of occupation, See Ali Satan, *Irak'ta İngiliz İşgal Yönetimi 1914–1918 – İngiltere Devlet Arşivi Raporu* (İstanbul: Tarihçi Kitabevi Yayınları, 2016).

40 Cemal Paşa, *Anılarım (1913–1922)*,152.

41 Önsoy, *Türk-Alman İktisadi Münasebetleri (1871–1914)*, 83.

42 Önsoy, *Türk-Alman İktisadi Münasebetleri (1871–1914)*, 82.

43 Bilge Karbi, *Gölgedeki İttifak: Harb-i Umumi'de Osmanlı-Habsburg İktisadi İlişkileri* (İstanbul: Libra Yayınları, 2021), 69.

However, Jagow stated that the Ottoman Empire did not have a military power that could take an aggressive attitude towards Russia and that the alliance with the Ottoman Empire would create a military burden for Germany on the Eastern Front. The head of the German delegation in the Ottoman Empire, Liman von Sanders, and the German Ambassador Wangenheim also conveyed their reports of similar thoughts. Upon these views, Jagow rejected the offer of alliance with the Ottoman Empire from Austria.[44] However, as of mid-July, the situation changed as a result of both Said Halim Pasha's and Enver Pasha's renewing their alliance demands,[45] Austria's pressure and the Kaiser's warm attitude towards the alliance. Kaiser II. Wilhelm had always favored an alliance with the Ottomans. Even in 1910, he took a note, "Let's hope things get here," on rumors that an alliance would form between Germany, Austria and the Ottoman Empire, which appeared in the Ottoman newspapers.[46] After the assassination of the Archduke, the Kaiser's views became clearer. On July 22, Wangenheim sent a telegram to the Kaiser, in which Enver Pasha's statements demanding an alliance were quoted and Wangenheim's negative opinion against the alliance was conveyed. Kaiser, on the other hand, took a note beside the telegram stating that a Turkish-Bulgarian and Austrian alliance should have been formed to support Austria's attempt against the Slavs in the Balkans, and he argued that this was a policy of opportunity.[47] Germany, with the influence of Kaiser Wilhelm II, had focused on the benefits of the alliance with the Ottoman Empire, particularly considering the geographical and Islamic influence advantages of the Ottoman Empire.[48] Thus, on August 2, 1914, a secret Turkish-German alliance agreement was signed between the Grand Vizier Said Halim Pasha and the German ambassador

---

44 Mustafa Aksakal, *Harb-i Umumi Eşiğinde – Osmanlı Devleti Son Savaşına Nasıl Girdi?* (İstanbul: İstanbul Bilgi Üniversitesi Yayınları, 2018), 108.

45 Aksakal, *Harb-i Umumi Eşiğinde – Osmanlı Devleti Son Savaşına Nasıl Girdi?*, 109–111.

46 Aksakal, *Harb-i Umumi Eşiğinde – Osmanlı Devleti Son Savaşına Nasıl Girdi?*,78.

47 Mustafa Çolak, *Komitenin Kahramanı: Enver Paşa* (İstanbul: Yeditepe Yayınevi, 2019), 44.

48 According to the calculations of the German General Staff, the military strength of Germany could reach up to 2.15 million soldiers. and the combined military strength of Russia, Britain, France, Belgium and Serbia was 64 % more than the military strength of Germany and Austria-Hungary alone. It should have been taken into account that a part of this 64 % difference could be closed with the Turkish army. See Ferguson, *Paper and Iron*, 96.

Baron Wangenheim.[49] This alliance agreement was followed by the secret annex to the agreement signed on 6 August, as a result of the pressures on Said Halim Pasha, due to the reaction of the Turkish side's lack of interests and especially the inability to benefit from the capitulations. However, there were those who were not entirely satisfied with this treaty. Some thought that the Turkish side could gain little from the treaty. According to these people, there was no benefit in caputulations.[50] Said Halim Pasha, who was put under serious pressure, put pressure on the German side and a secret annex was included in the treaty on 6 August. According to some articles in this appendix, Germany would assist the Ottoman Empire in the abolition of the capitulations, and Germany would not sign peace unless the enemy troops left the Ottoman lands. Moreover, if Greece entered the war and was defeated, Germany would help Turkey take the archipelago lost in the Balkan Wars. In addition, Germany would assist Turkey in putting its northern border in order so that Turkey could establish direct contact with the Muslim elements in Russia.[51]

The Ottoman Empire tried to resist pressures such as being involved in the war and declaring war on Russia, which started to come from Germany with the signing of the treaty, and wanted to preserve its independence until it completed its mobilization. However, Enver Pasha's permission of two German warships (Goeben and Breslau) chased by the British navy on the evening of 10 August to pass through the Dardanelles, enabled the Allied Powers to exert a strong pressure on the Ottoman Empire. The Allies demanded that Goeben and Breslau be promptly removed from the Dardanelles or disarmed and demilitarized.[52] Talat Pasha, in his memoirs, states that Grand Vizier Said Halim Pasha and some ministers were in favor of fulfilling the request of the Allied Powers. According to Talat Pasha's memoirs, this offer was conveyed to the German ambassador

---

49 Said Halim Paşa, *Osmanlı İmparatorluğu ve Dünya Savaşı*, trans. Fatih Yücel (İstanbul: Kronik Kitap, 2nd Ed., 2019), 16.

50 Council of Ministers took its first official decision to abolish the capitulations on 29 August 1914 to be reconsidered, and on 8 September 1914 the commission made a recommendation on the abolition of the capitulations totaly. Thereupon, a sultan's will was issued on the same day, and this decision was officially published on 9 September with a decree and was reported to all embassies. As proclaimed in the decree, on 1 October 1914 capitulations and all special privileges based on capitulations were abolished. See Stanford J. Shaw, *Birinci Dünya Savaşı'nda Osmanlı İmparatorluğu – Savaşa Giriş* (Ankara: Türk Tarih Kurumu, 2014), 226.

51 Gencer, *Jöntürk Modernizmi ve Alman Ruhu*, 69–70.

52 Cemal Paşa, *Anılarım (1913–1922)*,150.

Wangenheim, but Wangengeim was very angry at this offer and at that time Halil Bey had the idea of purchasing the ships.[53] The answer given to the Allies that the ships were bought was not an excuse but a fact. However, this statement did not convince the Allied Powers, and the fact that the ships were not disarmed was enough to make the Ottoman Empire a potential target to the Allied Powers. Britain was told that these ships were substitutes for the fully paid ships that were not delivered to the Ottoman Empire by them with the beginning of the First World War, and that they had been purchased months in advance.[54] But the British did not pay much attention to this. The fact that the ship's crew, consisting of Germans, was not sent back despite their demands, created an awareness in the British to target every Ottoman flagged ship.[55]

On July 30, the password of the Minister of Internal Affairs, Talat Pasha, was communicated to the Sixth Corps Command. As it is understood from this

53 Talat Paşa, *Talat Paşa'nın Hatıraları*, ed. Hüseyin Cahit Yalçın (İstanbul: Cumhuriyet Gazetesi Yayınları, 1998), 27–28.

54 This detail was very effective in the Ottoman Empire's taking Goeben and Breslau into its territorial waters. The Ottoman Empire had ordered two dreadnoughts before the war. The first dreadnought, named Reşadiye, was ordered in 1911, and the other dreadnought, named Sultan Osman, was ordered in 1913. Both of these dreadnoughts were originally built for the Brazilian government and were bought by the Ottoman Empire for 3.680.650 pounds. This money had been collected through public donations. The motivation behind the people's donation of this money was to ensure the Ottoman navy's superiority over Greece in the Aegean and Eastern Mediterranean and to secure the taking back of the Aegean islands. However, unexpected developments took place. On 28 July, before the Ottoman Empire signed an alliance with Germany, First Lord of the Admirality Winston Churchill ordered the seizure of the already paid ships. The process did not end there, either. An Ottoman crew led by Rauf Orbay had set out on 15 August (before Churchill's decision to seize the ships) to take Sultan Osman, and on 29 July, one day after the seizure order, they came to London with the last installment payments of the both dreadnoughts. As soon as they learned of the decision, they were instructed to take both Sultan Osman and Reşadiye, which was expected to be completed at the end of August, and to come. The British naval forces played a game here, although they knew the decision, they accepted the final installment payments for both ships, and then they declared that they could not deliver the ships. When the Ottoman Empire demanded the return of the money, they declared that they would not return the ships or the money until the war was over. This attitude of the British was a factor in the acceptance of Goeben and Breslau by the Ottoman Empire into its territorial waters. See Shaw, *Birinci Dünya Savaşı'nda Osmanlı İmparatorluğu*, 545–548.

55 Said Halim Paşa, *Osmanlı İmparatorluğu ve Dünya Savaşı*, 21–26.

communiqué, the British and French ships that came in front of the Dardanelles stated that they would open fire on the ships taken from Germany even if they had the Ottoman flag on them.[56] This statement shows that the Allied Powers did not accept the explanation of Ottoman Empire very much. All this tension and uncertainty left its place to a transparent clarity when two German ships, now named Yavuz and Midilli, sank a Russian minelayer belonging to the Russian fleet that followed them. Yavuz and Midilli, after capturing 72 soldiers and 3 officers, capturing a coal ship and severely damaging a torpedo boat, chased the remaining ships of the fleet to the port of Sevastopol and bombarded various ports for a while.[57] The Ottoman Empire actually entered the war on October 29, 1914. This entereance became official with Russia, Britain and France declaring war on the Ottoman Empire first, and then with the Ottoman Empire declaring war on the Allied Powers on 11 November.[58]

The Ottoman Empire's support for Germany as an ally was substantial. The Ottoman Empire mobilized approximately 2,900,000 people from its estimated population of 22–23 million during the First World War.[59] This military force achieved important successes. As the Speaker of the Parliament, Halil Menteşe[60] mentioned in his speech of thanks, the Ottoman army divided the Balkan forces with its dominance in the straits, prevented the Balkan armies from attacking to Austria-Hungary as a whole and the loss of Vienna and Pest to the Russians when the Russians were in the Carpathians. In addition, if the defense of the Dardanelles had not been possible or had failed, the Russian Empire could have

---

56 BOA - TŞR.HL, 1 - 96, R-17-07-1330.

57 Sanders, *Türkiye'de Beş Yıl*, 51.

58 Ahmet Hurşit Tolon, *Birinci Dünya Savaşı Sırasında Taksim Anlaşmaları ve Sevr'e Giden Yol* (Ankara: Atatürk Araştırma Merkezi, 2004), 34–35.

59 Mehmet Beşikçi, "On Yıllık Harp ve Topyekün Seferberlik", *Osmanlı Askeri Tarihi - Kara, Deniz ve Hava Kuvvetleri 1792–1914*, ed. Gültekin Yıldız (İstanbul: Timaş Yayınları, 2013), 219.

60 Halil Menteşe was sent to Berlin in 1915 in order to provide the weapon aid needed by the Turkish army faster. In his memoirs, he stated the advice given to him by the German Emperor at the dinner he was invited to. Two advices given by the German Emperor sheds light on Germany's perspective on the Ottoman Empire in the first years of the First World War. One of the advices was that the honor of the officers should have been kept high and that the officers should have been paid enough to protect their honor. The second was that importance should have been given on village cooperatives. These two advices are an indication that the Germans saw the Ottoman Empire as an ally. See Ingeborg Böer et al., *Berlin'den Türkler Geçti 1871–1945*, 156–157

suppressed the Bolshevik revolt and continued the war, advancing to Istanbul. This is also a remarkable scenario.[61] In such a case, as Halil Menteşe stated, Russian civilization could not have been prevented from dominating Europe.[62] German General Ludendorff, who is called the architect of Germany's military strategy in the First World War, makes a similar inference. Ludendorff states in his memoirs that if the straits had been captured by the Allies, Russia would have had the war materials it needed, the battles in the east would have been fraught, the Allied Powers would have been in a position to fully benefit from the wheat warehouses that in Southern Russia and Romania, and that the only way supplying Russia's war material would have come out of the Central Powers' control. According to Ludendorff, the straits increased the importance of the alliance with Ottoman Empire.[63]

Similarly, regarding the benefit of the Turks' resistance to the British on the Eastern Front, Ludendorff said in his memoirs: "As long as Turkey continued to resist, the British were compelled to use a lot of force. In this way, the value of the Turkish army gained great importance for us. When the Turks heroically defended Palestine and Iraq and pulled the British troops there to reach their targets, our burden on the Western Front was lightened as well."[64] Ludendorff

---

61 It is useful to mention the pre-war situation of the Russians, to shed light on the importance of the straits for the Russians. The late industrialization of the Russians made the Russian Empire dependent on imports, especially in the areas such as chemistry and machinery. Some of the final products, such as machinery and chemical products, came from Germany. With the outbreak of the First World War, when the existing economic relations with Germany were interrupted, it was very important for Russia that substitute products and other import articles on which Russia was dependent could be delivered to Russia by the Entente States or independent countries. The Baltic sea was closed. The Arctic line was generally covered with ice. Rail links were just being built and were still inadequate. The only way for these compulsory imortt articles to come was the Turkish Straits. Some articles could arrive via Sweden. However, Sweden's refusal to allow the shipment of weapons and ammunition deprived the Russians of firepower, which was one of their basic needs. The closure and defense of the straits left the Russian Empire helpless. The closure of the straits played a vital role in world history, as it made the Russian Empire unable to resist the Bolshevik revolts and caused the early withdrawal of the Russians from the First World War. See Kurtbek, *Harp ve Ekonomi*, 23.

62 Ali Satan, *100 Soruda Milli Mücadele* (İstanbul: Timaş Yayınları, 2018), 25.

63 Erich Ludendorff, *Birinci Dünya Savaşı'nda Gördüklerim ve Yaşadıklarım* (İstanbul: Dün Bugün Yarın Yayınları, 2014), 186- 187.

64 Ludendorff, *Birinci Dünya Savaşı'nda Gördüklerim ve Yaşadıklarım*, 265.

was not the only German to share this thought. After the victories of Gallipoli Campaign and Siege of Kut, it is a fact that the perspectives of the German press, the German people and the German parliaments towards the Ottoman army changed.[65]

The Germans' expectations from the Ottoman Empire were not just military support. The effect of a declaration of jihad by the caliph of all Muslims had created a great expectation in the eyes of both the Germans and the Turks. Jihad was declared in November 1914. The declaration of jihad invited the Muslim communities in Egypt and India under the auspices of the British, in North Africa and the Levant under the protection of France, in the Caucasus and Central Asia under the protection of Russia,[66] to war against the infidels. Pamphlets were prepared to keep Germany apart from the jihad declaration read in all mosques of the Ottoman Empire, and the call for jihad was limited to all infidels in Islamic lands except those who ally with Muslims.[67] Muslims had no difficulty in accepting this detail, because there was a sympathy towards the Germans in the Muslim geographies under Ottoman rule. For example, in 1914, the Christian population in Mosul prayed for France, while the Muslim population prayed for Germany.[68] Moreover, the military censorship detected that many of the newspapers in Beirut were publishing in favor of France and against Germany in 1914, and this situation was notified to the Ottoman Empire. This is another example of how the Ottoman Empire preserved the German perception in the Middle East.[69] Despite all this, at the end of the day, British gold outweighed and the result was not what Germany and the Ottomans expected. Britain and France fed the local tribes with gold-based Money. On the other hand, Ottomans could not scatter gold to every tribe like the British. In the end the Muslim subjects did not revolt against the British and French.[70] Therefore, the declaration of jihad was not effective.

Despite the failure of the Jihad declaration, the Turkish-German alliance established a significant force in military, commercial and strategic contexts.

65 Ingeborg Böer et al., *Berlin'den Türkler Geçti 1871–1945*, 151.
66 Mustafa Aksakal, "'Holy War Made in Germany'? Ottoman Origins of the 1914 Jihad", *War in History*, vol. 18, no. 2 (2011), 185.
67 Hopkirk, *On Secret Service East of Constantinople*, 60–61.
68 BOA – DH.EUM.2.Şb, 1 – 25, H-27-09-1332.
69 BOA – DH.EUM.5.Şb, 1 – 32, H-14-10-1332.
70 Orhan Koloğlu, *Prusya'dan Enverland'a ve Günümüze Türk-Alman Tarihi* (İstanbul: Tariçi Kitabevi, 2018), 167–168.

In this period, both industrial and military relations took place with an intense volume.

4.2.1. The Secret Treaties that Envisaged the Sharing of the Ottoman Empire

During the First World War, the Allied Powers made four secret agreements related to sharing the Ottoman lands. The first of these was the Constantinople Agreement, which included the guarantee that Istanbul and the straits would be left to Russia after the war.

4.2.1.1. Constantinople Agreement

For Russia, the First World War in general was about turning the Ottoman Empire, which they described as a "sick man", into a "dead man" and sharing the Ottoman heritage. Russian Foreign Minister Sasanov stated that the main target of Russia was Istanbul, with the following words: "Istanbul is our true goal. Capturing Lemberg and Warsaw, as well as gaining many things for Russia, will be possible by getting Istanbul."[71]

It had been known for a long time by Britain and France that the Russians had an eye on the Straits and Istanbul. Even, in November 1914, British Foreign Minister Sir Edward Gray told the Russian Ambassador Benckendorff that the fate of Istanbul and the Straits would be determined according to the will of Russia.[72]

Knowing that they could not keep the Russians, whose main aim was the Straits and Istanbul, in war otherwise, Britain and France had been giving verbal guarantees of acceptance of Russian demands focused on Istanbul and the Straits since 1914. As a result of the negotiations between March 4, 1915 and April 10, 1915, they concluded the Russian demands focused on Istanbul and the Straits with a note exchange and completed the process leading to the Istanbul Treaty. The Straits and Istanbul were to be ceded to Russia after the war in response to France's demand for Palestine to be left to its concession zone and Britain's demand for uncompetitive dominance in the Arabian peninsula. These conditions were guaranteed to Russia by Great Britain and France with the Constantinople Agreement.[73]

---

71 Jäckh, *Yüselen Hilal*, 151.

72 İsmail Köse, "I. Dünya Savaşı'nın İlk Gizli Anlaşması: İstanbul ve Boğazlar'ın Rus Çarlığı'na Bırakılması (March-April 1915)" *Bilig – Türk Dünyası Sosyal Bilimler Dergisi*, no. 89 (2019), 6.

73 Köse, "I. Dünya Savaşı'nın İlk Gizli Anlaşması", 20.

4.2.1.2. Treaty of London

The second secret agreement of the Allied Powers on the sharing of Ottoman lands was the London Agreement, which included the concessions they made to attract Italy to their side.

The Treaty of London, signed on April 26, 1915, consisted of 16 articles. In these articles, promises were made to Italy, such as leaving most of Slovenia and the north of the Dalmatian border. The parts of the treaty related to the Ottoman lands included leaving the Dodecanese Islands, Antalya and its surroundings and the privileges that still belong to the Ottoman Sultan in the Benghazi and Derne regions to Italy.[74] As a result of this treaty, Italy, which had bargained with both the Allied Powers and the Central Powers for a long time, predicted that it could gain even more from the Allied Powers and became a party by declaring war against Austria-Hungary on 23 May.[75]

4.2.1.3. Sykes-Picot Agreement

The third secret agreement of the Allied Powers, which included the sharing of Ottoman lands, was the Sykes-Picot Agreement.

The Sykes-Picot Agreement, like the Istanbul Agreement, was not a text prepared in a single meeting, but a process. It started in March 1916 between British, French and Russians and continued for several months with the exchange of notes and lettersA draft agreement was signed on January 4, 1916 between Lieutenant Colonel Sir Mark Sykes of the British War Office and French diplomat François Georges-Picot. This draft treaty was accepted by the Nicolson Committee on February 4, and after Sazanov's signature in March, the Sykes-Picot Agreement was ratified on May 16, 1916 between Great Britain and France.[76]

Sir Mark Sykes was a diplomat who visited the region in 1915 and developed relations with Arab leaders who could raise a rebellion when necessary, as well as being an expert on the Syrian and Arabian regions. Georges Picot was the former French political representative of Beirut. In this memorandum, prepared jointly by Sykes and Picot and submitted to Russia's approval, issues such as the establishment of an independent Arab State under the auspices of England and France and the separation of this state into French and British protectorates were

---

74 Tolon, *Birinci Dünya Savaşı Sırasında Taksim Anlaşmaları ve Sevr'e Giden Yol*, 54.

75 Soy, "Birinci Dünya Savaşı Osmanlı Devleti'ni Parçalamak İçin mi Yapıldı?", 36.

76 Ediger, *Osmanlı'da Neft ve Petrol*, 330–331.

included. This memorandum also included issues such as the establishment of an international administration in Palestine, giving the ports of Haifa and Akka to Britain, Haifa Port being considered a free port for the commercial goods of France and its colonies, the Iskenderun Port being considered a free port for British commercial goods, and giving the islands east of the Red Sea to the independent state of Arabia.[77]

Sykes-Picot was an agreement that underlined the importance of the Gallipoli Campaign on the sharing of Ottoman lands. Because, according to the Sykes-Picot Agreement, a small area under the name of Turkish Sultanate would be left to the Turks in Anatolia and the lands in Turkey's Asia would be left to Russia, France, Britain and the planned independent Arab state.[78] However, this agreement, which also formed the basis of the post-war disagreements, did not realized as planned due to the effects of the Turkish victory in Gallipoli Campaign and the Bolshevik Revolution.

4.2.1.4. Agreement of St. Jean De Mairune

The fourth secret agreement of the Allied Powers including the sharing of Ottoman lands was St. Jean de Maurienne.

The reason for the emergence of the Agreement of St. Jean De Mairune was the Sykes-Picot Agreement. Sykes-Picot Agreement was a secret treaty made without informing Italy. Italy became aware of this treaty by being suspicious of British Prime Minister M. Asquith's speech at a banquet given to the members of the Duma Assembly. At the banquet, British Prime Minister M. Asquith stated that one of the happiest results of their alliances was the full agreement between the Russian and British governments on eastern problems. Suspicious of this statement, the Italian Ambassador asked for an explanation about the existence of such an agreement and put pressure on the Britain. As a result of these pressures, the Italian Ambassador Imperiali recived the reply that Italy should have immediately determined its side and declare war on Germany in order to learn everything that was going on between the allies. Thus, Italy declared war on Germany on 28 August 1916. Upon this, Italy, which increased its pressure even more, made separate demands to both the Russians, the British and the French, and the British Foreign Minister Edward Gray gave Italy the texts of the secret treaties made in 1916 without the knowledge of Italy. Examining the treaties, Italy gave a memorandum to Russia, France and Britain on November 4, 1916.

77 Tolon, *Birinci Dünya Savaşı Sırasında Taksim Anlaşmaları ve Sevr'e Giden Yol*, 63.
78 Tolon, *Birinci Dünya Savaşı Sırasında Taksim Anlaşmaları ve Sevr'e Giden Yol*, 68–70.

With this memorandum, Italy demanded that Adana, Konya, İzmir and Aydın be given to it, apart from what was promised to it in 1915. Moreover, it stipulated that the right of free passage through the Straits, the establishment of a free port in Istanbul, and the granting of the rights and privileges enjoyed by the other allies in Istanbul to Italy. And under these conditions, Italy declared that it would accept the demands of the Russians regarding the Straits and Istanbul.[79]

Upon the discussion of these demands, a conference was held in London on January 29, 1917. However, due to Italy's refusal to give up on its demands and Russia and France's opposition to Italy's demands, the London Conference could not yield any results. Despite the fact that the provisional government established in Russia after the Revolution in March 1917, stated that it would abide by the old agreements, a mistrust arose against Russia and Britain became ready to make concessions to Italy in order to win Italy. This attitude of British also affected the French and it was decided to hold a new conference in Saint-Jaint de Maurienne on April 10. As a result of this conference, which was held between 10 and 21 April 1917, privileges were also granted to Italy in Turkish Asia, and the treaty was ratified by correspondence between 18 August and 2 September 1917.[80]

As it can be seen, all of the Allied Powers, who did not want to see the Ottomans by their side, had an expectation about the Ottoman lands and they put their expectations in writing during the war. However, all these plans about the Ottoman lands were invalidated first with the Gallipoli Victory and then with the Turkish War of Independence. The promises outside the Ottoman lands had to be changed as a result of the USA's involvement in the war and the effective diplomacy of US President Wilson after the war.

The most striking point in these treaties was that they all reveal that Britain, France, Russia and Italy had their eyes on the Ottoman lands for a long time. Moreover, it shows that each country had already determined its target region before the war, and that they were ready to make a written agreement on geographical gains from a date like 1915. Cemal Pasha also referred to this subject in his memoirs. Cemal Pasha referred to the louder support of French and British to the harsh reactions of Russia when the Liman von Sanders delegation was given the task of defending the Straits, and he asked in his memoires that "Since the French and the British almost did not refrain from making more fuss

79 Tolon, *Birinci Dünya Savaşı Sırasında Taksim Anlaşmaları ve Sevr'e Giden Yol*, 76–77.
80 Tolon, *Birinci Dünya Savaşı Sırasında Taksim Anlaşmaları ve Sevr'e Giden Yol*, 82–86.

than the Russians, shouldn't it be necessary to have concluded that the triple entente had already promised Istanbul to the Russians?"[81]

When these secret treaties are examined, there are answers to the question why Ottoman Empire could not make ally with any other country than Germany. And it becomes meaningful why Allied Powers rejected Ottomans when the Ottomans wanted to make an alliance.

4.2.2. Turkish-German Industrial Relations during the First World War

The Ottoman Empire could not become an industrial country even though it had raw materials due to reasons such as the fact that domestic industrialization moves were prevented by capitulations over the years, lack of capital in the private sector and insufficient level of technical education.[82] So much so that even in 1916, copper was sent to Germany from the Ottoman Empire during the war in order to manufacture the copper pipes necessary for the Hejaz railways.[83] Moreover, in 1916, 170 tons of copper scrap was sent from Ottoman Empire to Germany to be used in the manufacture of locomotives to be imported from Germany.[84] Similarly, in 1917, 150 tons of copper scrap was sent from Ottoman Empire to Germany for the manufacture of locomotive spare parts and machinery to be imported from Germany.[85] These amounts were just some of the copper sent upon use in products to be imported. During the war, copper exports were

81 Cemal Paşa, *Anılarım (1913–1922),* ed. Fahri Parin (İstanbul: Paraf Yayınları, 2010), 85–86.

82 The Ottoman Empire had taken some steps towards industrialization. For example, in 1873, the state granted customs and tax exemptions to industrial facilities to be established. In 1888 this exemption was extended to include the raw materials needed to build factories. In 1897, this exemption was extended again with the decision not to collect taxes from newly established industrial establishments for a period of ten years. However, although these incentives were a tool for industrialization, they could not be a driving force in an environment where there was no capital, market, technical education or banking, on the contrary, there were capitulations which continued to exist in a threatening manner. See Önsoy, *Türk-Alman İktisadi Münasebetleri (1871–1914),* 50.

83 BOA- MV, 204 – 24, H-29-01-1335.

84 BOA – DH.İ.UM.EK, 18 – 109, H-28-10-1334.

85 BOA- MV, 205 – 109, H-30-03-1335.

repeated many times.[86] Similarly, 300 kilos of bronze were sent to Germany in 1918 for the manufacture of the products needed by the navy.[87] These examples are an indication that there were raw materials in the Ottoman Empire, but there was no industry to turn raw materials into industrial products.

Even in 1915, 28.6 % of the main industrial establishments in the Ottoman Empire was in the food industry.[88] This shows that even in 1915, the Ottoman Empire was a state dependent on the agricultural economy. Considering these, it is an expected result that the Ottoman Empire imported the industrial products it needed. During the First World War, Germany was the main country that met the industrial product needs of the Ottoman Empire. A Turkish purchasing commission was established in Berlin in order to fulfill the demands of the Ottoman Empire. The money necessary to meet these purchases was provided by German loans. During the First World War, Germany continued some construction activities in the Ottoman lands, especially the railway, which started before the First World War and was planned during the First World War.[89] The Ottoman Empire, on the other hand, either bartered the materials or demanded its money from Germany in advance.[90]

The fact that the Ottoman Empire, that also experienced a loss of workforce during the war, increased its need for industrial products even more. In 1915, 48 % of the workers working in the industry, whose number had decreased by 17 % compared to two years ago,[91] were working in the weaving sector and 27.8 % in the food industry, while the total of all workers in other industries was only 24.2 %. This situation was not unique to the war. In 1913, the share of the weaving sector in industrial employment was 45.8 %.[92] Depending on this workforce, 68.6 % of industrial production in the Ottoman Empire in 1913 and 70.3 % in 1915 belonged to the food industry.[93] Therefore, it is not possible to talk about

---

86 A few more examples of these exports can be found in these archival documents: BOA-MV, 210 – 99, H-28-02-1336; MV, 207 – 97, H-12-06-1335; DH.İ.UM.EK, 19 – 55, H-07-11-1334; DH.İ.UM, 20 – 8, H-19-07-1336.

87 BOA – DH.İ.UM, 20 – 2, H-07-01-1337.

88 *Osmanlı Sanayii 1913–1915 Yılları Sanayi İstatistiki*, 14.

89 BCA, 30-18-1-1/ Kararlar Daire Başkanlığı, 5 – 16 – 10, 10.05.1922.

90 Zengin, *Osmanlı Devleti'nde Harp Sanayii,* 268.

91 *Osmanlı Sanayii 1913–1915 Yılları Sanayi İstatistiki*, 20.

92 Despite this employment, weaving was not very effective. According to the 1913–1915 industry census, the total number of spindles in the Ottoman Empire was 68,000, while in 1910 the number of spindles in Germany was 5.279.595. See *Osmanlı Sanayii 1913–1915 Yılları Sanayi İstatistiki*, 115.

93 *Osmanlı Sanayii 1913–1915 Yılları Sanayi İstatistiki*, 22,27.

the industrialization of the Ottoman Empire before and during the war. Of the mills that accounted for 44 % of all food manufacturing, British machines were seen in the older ones, while most of the newer mills used German machinery and German internal combustion and electric motors.[94] This situation sheds light on two points. The first of these points was that the Ottoman Empire had to import machinery even in the food industry. Secondly, by the First World War, England had lost certain markets for industrial products to Germany. The same was true in printing and the manufacture of other printing products. In this area, almost all of the machines in the newly established factories were German made.[95] The majority of the machines used in the manufacture of candy and sugar products, tahini and biscuits, canned food were made in Germany. Moreover, in other wood production, wool yarn manufacturing, wool weaving, other weaving manufacturing, dyeing stage, box manufacturing, printing and printing products manufacturing German machines were used.[96] Even the paper money of the Ottoman Empire was printed in Germany. With the abolition of the capitulations, the Ottoman Bank's monopoly on printing paper money was also abolished, and paper money indexed to gold was printed and stored in Berlin banks upon the recommendations of the German financiers. Until the end of the war, paper money worth 159 million lira was printed in Germany.[97]

Thirty-four percent of imports related to porcelain,[98] tile, soil and stone products, 9.1 % of imports related to shoe manufacturing, 23.6 % of imports related to wool products, 17 % of imports related to other weaving manufacturing, %20 of paper imports, 35.1 % of the imports related to the production of acorn pulp, the majority of the imports related to the cement production and the majority of the imports related to the other chemical production were made from Germany.[99] On the other hand, 19 % of tobacco exports[100] and a significant amount of critical minerals such as sulfur and cerium,[101] which were not included in the 1913–1915

94 *Osmanlı Sanayii 1913–1915 Yılları Sanayi İstatistiki*, 41.
95 *Osmanlı Sanayii 1913–1915 Yılları Sanayi İstatistiki*, 156.
96 *Osmanlı Sanayii 1913–1915 Yılları Sanayi İstatistiki*, 53,59, 108, 109, 125, 140, 156.
97 Çağlar Keyder, *Dünya Ekonomisi İçinde Türkiye (1923–1929)* (Ankara: Yurt Yayınevi, 1982), 143.
98 Porcelain products were also among the products imported from Germany to the Ottoman Empire for many years. While Ansbach alone exported 48.000 coffee cups to the Ottoman Empire in 1799, this amount reached 1 million in the 1830s. See Önsoy, *Türk-Alman İktisadi Münasebetleri (1871–1914)*, 8.
99 *Osmanlı Sanayii 1913–1915 Yılları Sanayi İstatistiki*, 79, 83, 90, 125, 141, 145, 173, 176.
100 *Osmanlı Sanayii 1913–1915 Yılları Sanayi İstatistiki*, 66
101 Zengin, *Osmanlı Devleti'nde Harp Sanayii*, 266.

census, were also exported to Germany. Important raw materials such as cotton were also products exported to Germany even during wartime.[102]

Although there were some disagreements during the war due to the conflicting interests of Germany and the Ottoman Empire in the Caucasus, as in the case of the Baku offensive, the Turkish-German alliance continued relatively smoothly. German officers and soldiers actually fought together with Ottoman soldiers in Gallipoli, Iraq, Syria and Palestine fronts, as it is also mentioned in the memoirs of the British officers, and they were actively present in the central headquarters in Istanbul.[103] Engineers, doctors, technicians and workers came from Germany, roads were built, and they inflicted significant casualties on the British, especially with cannons and machine guns.[104] During the First World War, the need for weapons and ammunition was generally met by the German industry. Moreover, the Germans continued to invest for the post-war period of the Ottoman Empire. These attempts of the Germans are also striking in the reports prepared by the Austrian diplomats during the war. One of them is a work prepared by Consul Buchberger in 1916. In this study, it is stated that Germany tried to modernize production techniques, establish factories and increase production and carry the education system to advanced levels by carrying out cultural reforms in the Ottoman Empire both before the war and during the war period.[105] The fact that the existence of the Mauser Cartridge Factory, which was established in the Ottoman lands in 1901, and the Zeytinburnu Cartridge Factory's supply of materials from the Karlsruhe Cartridge Factory, and the fact that the machinery tenders in the defense industry were taken by German companies, are indications that Germans did not hesitate to transfer their defense industry technology to the Ottoman Empire. As a matter of fact, both the 7.65 diameter Mauser cartridge and the Mauser rifle parts were manufactured at the Zeytinburnu Factory.[106] This

---

102 BOA – MV- 202 – 19, H-18-07-1334; MV- 208 – 28, H-28-07-1335.

103 In 1918, towards the end of the war, the number of German officers serving in the Ottoman Empire was around 1500, and the number of German military and technical personnel fighting on the side of the Ottoman Empire was around 13.000–14.000. See Mustafa Çolak, "Alman Subaylarının Bakışına Göre Ermeni Techiri", ed. Necmettin Alkan et al., *Savaşanların Gözüyle Türk – Alman İttifakı* (İstanbul: Kronik Kitap, 2018), 192.

104 Mehmet Alaaddin Yalçınkaya, "İngiliz Subaylarının Anlatımıyla Osmanlı Cephelerindeki Alman Subayları", ed. Necmettin Alkan et al., *Savaşanların Gözüyle Türk – Alman İttifakı* (İstanbul: Kronik Kitap, 2018), 90.

105 Karbi, *Gölgedeki İttifak: Harb-i Umumi'de Osmanlı-Habsburg İktisadi İlişkileri*, 195–197.

106 Zengin, *Osmanlı Devleti'nde Harp Sanayii,162–163.*

process continued even during the war. The 9-item military alliance agreement signed between the Ottoman Empire and Germany on October 18, 1917 is one of the most important indicators of this. With this treaty, it was decided to equip, train and manage the Ottoman army at the same standards as the German army. On November 27, 1917, another treaty was signed, the peace treaty to be signed after the end of the war was discussed, and it was agreed to share the post-war spoils together, not to accept the capitulations and to refuse any restrictions on the imperial lands together.[107] These treaties not only reveal the state of Turkish-German relations during the war, but also shed light on their vision of joint action, development and mutual benefit after the war, and reveals Germans' perspectives on Turkey after the war.

During the First World War, some of Germany's food and industrial raw material needs were met by the Ottoman Empire. Only in May and July 1916, 50 wagons of ore, 280 tons of wheat, tons of butter, olive oil and dried fish were sent from the Ottoman Empire to Germany.[108]

The volume of shipments also had to vary throughout the war years, as Germany and the Ottoman Empire did not have a direct border connection. Like many of the countries that participated in the First World War, the Germans did not think that the war would last four years. Foreseeing that the war would be short, the Germans had made their stocks to a certain extent. In the worst case scenario, they predicted that food could be provided from the places planned to be occupied during the war.[109] In the first years of the war, the Germans managed to maintain their subsistence despite the British and French blockade. The German Navy's deployment at critical points in the North Sea and Baltic Sea, posing a threat to the British and Russians, had a significant impact on the supply stability in the early years. On the other hand, it was also a factor that the Germans kept good relations with independent states and provided regular supplies to their

107 Ali Satan, *100 Soruda I. Dünya Savaşı* (İstanbul: Yazıgen Yayınevi, 2017), 88.

108 Celalettin Yavuz, *Atatürk ve Almanya* (Ankara: Berikan Yayınevi, 2010), 164.

109 For example, the occupation of Romania was a result of this idea. Romania was very rich in agricultural products and had a productive geography in animal husbandry. After 1916, Romania played a significant role in the Germans' ability to maintain their agricultural subsistence, even to some extent. The presence of oil brought Romania to a completely different level of importance. However, these oil stocks became unusable after the drilling installations in the oil wells in Romania, which Germany took control of, were skillfully destroyed by the British colonel Thomsen. It took a long time for the oil wells to become productive again. See Ludendorff, *Birinci Dünya Savaşı'nda Gördüklerim ve Yaşadıklarım*, 360–361.

own lands by purchasing through these states or through the ports of Rotterdam, Copenhagen and Bergen. For example, Sweden imported five times more cotton and four times more tea than it needed in 1915, and sold some of these with overprices to Germany, and earned significant income. Similarly, Denmark and the Netherlands sold their agricultural and animal products, Norway sold its fish, Sweden sold its iron to Germany in the first years of the war. Even British products came to Germany through independent countries during the war. However, this situation started to change after 1916, especially as a result of the pressures of British on independent countries. When independent states such as Sweden, Norway, Denmark, Switzerland and the Netherlands agreed to control the exported products under the pressure of the British and not to deliver them to Germany, sustainability problems began to arise in Germany's supply.[110]

When the supply decreased in Germany, the quality of the products acquired decreased and their prices increased in accordance with the *Ersatz* (substitution) policy. Among children, malnutrition and related diseases such as rickets increased rapidly. In the winter of 1916–1917, when a large part of the potato harvest was frosted early, most of the population had to be fed only with turnips, and this period was called the Turnip Winter. The situation of Germany's ally Austria-Hungary became even more deplorable. Between 7 % and 11 % of civilian deaths in Vienna in 1918 were due to starvation, and people were condemned to starve to death in their homes or on the streets.[111] As the war progressed, Austria's food shortages reached such a point that in June 1918 Austria seized the wheat that was destined to leave Romania and be sent to Germany via Austria. Upon this incident, the Austrian general said, "I know this is banditry, but there was no other way out. Now the Viennese have food for at least 15 days".[112] In such an environment, there was a radical decline in the performance of the Central Powers, who were in trouble for their own lives, to send additional aid to the Ottoman Empire.

Another reason for the decrease in German support after 1916 was the increase in transportation difficulties. Coal and war materials, one of the most important raw materials of the First World War, regularly came from Germany. In fact, 20 trains were sent to Istanbul per week by the railway, which was repaired again in 1916 and made transfers between Berlin and Istanbul, and 2/3 of these 20

110 Kurtbek, *Harp ve Ekonomi*, 24–27.

111 Colin Storer, *Weimar Cumhuriyeti'nin Kısa Tarihi*, trans. Sedef Özge (İstanbul: İletişim Yayınları, 2015), 45.

112 Kurtbek, *Harp ve Ekonomi*, 30–31.

trains carried coal.[113] The fact that the Russian ships in the Black Sea prevented the transportation of coal from Zonguldak[114] and that the destruction of the war hindered production[115] also made it impossible for the Ottoman Empire to meet its coal needs with its own resources. Coal from Germany had to come from Upper Silesia to Turkey via Sofia, and coal kept these train cars constantly busy. The work of hundreds of German locomotives and tens of thousands of German wagons for Austria-Hungary[116] made shipments difficult from time to time, causing the war materials needed by the Ottoman Empire to not arrive in sufficient quantities. Especially to places where transportation was limited, such as Palestine, the Caucasus and Iraq, shipments were very limited.[117] Although the railway constructions in the Ottoman lands continued in order to overcome these problems during the First World War, significant results could not be achieved in a short time.

Since the Ottoman Empire was a state dependent on imports in many articles and had met a significant part of these imports from countries such as England and France before the war, it was heavily dependent on the support of Germany during the war period. Germany also significantly increased the production efficiency in the war industry during the war. The production of 7.5 bullets, which was calculated as 13,600 before the war, increased to 200,000 per day in 1916.[118] Both the Turkish side and the German side were able to provide mutual assistance at a relatively sufficient level in the first years of the war. Only between May-July 1916, 280 wagons of grain, agricultural products such as wool, 50 wagons of raw materials such as iron, copper mines, 13,000 tons of oil, sesame, meat, fish, and furry leather were sent to Germany by the Ottoman Empire.[119] On the other hand, insufficient financing, war industry and various industrial products came to the Ottoman Empire from Germany.

In the later years of the war, with the effect of the blockades, Germany began to worry about trying to be self-sufficient and could not send as much support to the Ottoman Empire as before. Germany's support in this period was realized with transfering final products through Romania, Dobruca and Ukraine, and

113 Larcher, *Büyük Harpte Türk Harbi*, vol. 1, 218.
114 Zengin, *Osmanlı Devleti'nde Harp Sanayii*, 267.
115 For example, the port of Zonguldak, which was the only route, was bombarded by the Russian fleet. See. Larcher, *Büyük Harpte Türk Harbi*, vol 1, 220.
116 Ludendorff, *Birinci Dünya Savaşı'nda Gördüklerim ve Yaşadıklarım*, 347.
117 Ludendorff, *Birinci Dünya Savaşı'nda Gördüklerim ve Yaşadıklarım*, 256, 266–267.
118 Kurtbek, *Harp ve Ekonomi*, 53.
119 Larcher, *Büyük Harpte Türk Harbi*, vol 1, 220.

with the technical support in the Ottoman lands in order to increase agricultural productivity, which did not pay off much. The Ottoman Empire had to provide its own food after a while, and towards the end of the war, hunger started to show itself both in the army and in the civilian life. The decrease in the production of agricultural products of the Ottoman Empire between 1913 and 1918 is as in the table below.

Table 4.2. Decrease in Agricultural Product Manufacturing of the Ottoman Empire (1913–1918)

Agricultural Product	**Decrease**
Wheat	%48
Tobacco	%60
Raisins	%70
Nuts	%75
Cotton	%90
Olive Oil	%90

Source: Data from Orhan Koloğlu, *Prusya'dan Enverland'a ve Günümüze Türk-Alman Tarihi* (İstanbul: Tariçi Kitabevi, 2018), 167.

These decreases are of the kind that reveal the subsistence problem of the Ottoman Empire at the end of the First World War.[120] While bread was rationed in cities, the assignment of soldiers was reduced to 250 grams of black bread per day. Only in Syria, 60,000 people died of hunger, and the dead began to be robbed for clothes.[121] In some parts of the Eastern Front, only the meat of one sheep were given to 400 soldiers.[122]

While Enver, Halil and Şükrü Pashas always supported continuing the war under the leadership of Germany, other cabinet members such as Talat, Cavit, Ahmed Nesimi defended the independence of the Ottoman Empire from Germany. However, despite this polarization, the Turkish-German alliance and coordination continued. The Americans attributed this situation to the financial

120 In addition to the 80 % decrease in the purchasing power of the Ottoman lira, the fact that the inflation in food was above 100 % also created another purchasing difficulty for the public. See Koloğlu, *Prusya'dan Enverland'a ve Günümüze Türk-Alman Tarihi*, 167.

121 Kurtbek, *Harp ve Ekonomi*, 41–43.

122 Larcher, *Büyük Harpte Türk Harbi*, vol 1, 220.

situation of the Ottoman Empire as well as the Ottoman Empire's belief in Germany. According to the Americans, the only country from which the Ottoman Empire could receive financial support after the war was Germany. Since it was not possible to return to the old relations with British and Frech, the Ottoman Empire had to take its relations with Germans to the end.[123] Germany gave a loan of 142,000,000 lira to the Ottoman Empire until August 1916, and an additional loan of 56,500,000 lira in September 1917. According to the information that the Americans claim they received from Cavit Bey, Germans promised to give another 75,000,000 liras to Ottoman Empire after the war. These were the factors that financially tied the Ottoman Empire to Germany.[124]

4.3. Turkish-German Relations after the First World War

After the First World War, wartime alliances were replaced by wars of interest, the defeated did not want to accept the liabilities, and the victors wanted more. In addition to the establishment of new governments and states, the Bolshevik threat made it necessary to take new measures apart from the ones taken during the war. The interlocutors during the war and those after the war differed. Each state began to pursue its own interests.[125] In such turmoil, two ruthless treaties such as Sevres and Versailles emerged.

In order to get rid of the Sevres conviction, Turkey started a formidable war of independence and confronted the victorious states. However, devastated Germany, dealing with its own internal turmoil, could not escape the Versailles conviction. In Germany, the administration was first handed over to the social democrats, then a republic was proclaimed on November 9, 1918 to stop the Spartacists, and the Treaty of Versailles was signed on June 28, 1919.[126] Germany's debt, which had been 5 billion marks before the war, increased to 210 billion marks after the war.[127]

Adding the pressure of the compensation payments caused by Versailles to the financial blood loss during the war, Germany found the solution by printing free money and buying gold. These unrequited money issued by the

---

123 NARA, 867.00/7950, September 26, 1914–November 6, 1917. September 26, 1914–November 6, 1917, 5 June 1917.

124 NARA, 867.50, June 2, 1910–December 17, 1929.

125 M. Larcher, *Büyük Harpte Türk Harbi*, vol 3, trans. and ed. Mehmet Nihad (İstanbul: Ötüken Neşriyat, 2018), 155.

126 Storer, *Weimar Cumhuriyeti'nin Kısa Tarihi*, 53.

127 Kurtbek, *Harp ve Ekonomi*, 47.

Reichsbank paved the way for devastating hyperinflation.[128] In June 1922, Germany requested a moratorium on compensation payments, but this request was denied. Moreover, the assassination of Foreign Minister Walther Rathenau in the same month was also the factor that ignited the fuse. The value of the mark dropped so much that 400 marks were only worth 1 dollar. Things got worse in January 1923, when the French occupied the Ruhr alongside with Belgium. With the decrease in production by half, the mark-dollar parity decreased to 7,000 to 1.[129] 1923 was a year in which hyperinflation could not be controlled in general. The wages of the workers depreciated from morning to evening. A wheelbarrow full of paper money could only buy a piece of bread. On November 23, 1923, 4.2 trillion marks was worth only $1.[130] Germany was able to stop hyperinflation only by issuing a new temporary currency called the *Rentenmark*, backed by agricultural and industrial property. 1 *Rentenmark* was valued at 1 trillion old marks. Accordingly, 1 US dollar was worth 4.2 *Rentenmarks*.[131] However, since Germany knew that this was not a long-term solution, it expected an immediate regulation regarding war reparations payments. This regulation initiative came from British and Americans.

In particular, the occupation of the Ruhr meant the rupture of one of the lifebloods of the German economy. This situation was not well received by the U.S.A. The U.S.A., which became a creditor from Britain, France and Italy during the First World War,[132] was in favor of a balanced Europe both in order to collect its receivables and to export to Europe. It was obvious that a Germany with a bad and weak economy would not be able to continue importing from America, could not pay war reparations, would seek solutions within itself, and if this crisis went further, it would shift to the side of the Bolsheviks. This was the last

---

128 James, "Monetary and Fiscal Unification in Nineteenth Century Germany: What can Kohl Learn from Bismarck?", 2.

129 P. Michael, et al. "The German Hyperinflation and the Demand for Money Revisited", *International Economic Review*, vol. 35, no. 1 (1994), 3–4.

130 Robert Weidenhammer, *The American Economic Review*, vol. 22, no. 1 (1932), 146.

131 The Rentenmark was replaced by the gold-indexed currency Reichsmark in 1924. See O. C. Kiep, "The Basis of German Credit." *Proceedings of the Academy of Political Science*, vol. 15, no. 1 (1932), 86–87.

132 At the 1932 Lausanne Conference, it was discussed that the US should have given up its receivables in return for the write-off of Germany's debts. On December 15, 1932, America had $91,950,000 in receivables from Great Britain, $30,000,000 from France, and $7,395,520 from Italy. See "The Result of the Lausanne Conference." *World Affairs*, vol. 95, no. 2 (1932), 76.

scenario America would wantAs a matter of fact, as of 1923, American exports of cotton, copper and food products to Germany also dropped radically. On the other hand, the disproportionate strengthening of France in heavy industry with the occupation of the Ruhr was also a problem for the United States. The occupation of the coal-rich Ruhr by France, which took back the iron-rich Lorraine after the war, made France a country rich in raw materials. France could have monopolized enough to throw America out of the game in Europe. Foreseeing all these, America exposed France, which realized its post-war recovery with an uncontrolled expenditure, to economic pressure and a policy of political isolation, with the support of Britain. France was also compelled to accept a business committee to discuss post-war reparations payments. The head of the committee was Chicago banker Charles G. Dawes. Other key figures on the committee were Owen D. Young, chairman of General Electric and the Radio Corporation of America, and Henry M. Robinson, a Los Angeles banker.[133] Having the support of the American state, these people came together at the London Conference and made France accept the plan known as the Dawes Plan. As a result of the Dawes Plan adopted on August 16, 1924, it was decided to end the occupation of the Ruhr by France and to support Germnay with 800 million marks for ecomomic recovery. The structure of the Reichsbank was re-planned and made independent, foreign representatives were appointed to the general assembly to prevent the Reichsbank from issuing money outside the legal limits, and it was decided that the Reichsbank would have the necessary gold reserves. Apart from that, the state railways were transferred to a private company and paying with railway revenues became possible. Moreover, it was decided that the war compensation payments, which were determined as 132 billion gold marks after Versailles, would start as 1 billion marks in the first year and be paid as 2.5 billion marks annually within five years.[134]

The German economy only reached a sustainable level after the Dawes Plan, but this was not a long-term solution, as well. After the Dawes Plan, the Young Plan, which was adopted in 1929 and implemented in 1930, came into effect. Germany's total war reparations debt was reduced and it was decided to be paid in 58 years. Germany was again supported by loans. But this was not a long-term

---

133 Frank Costigliola, "The United States and the Reconstruction of Germany in the 1920s." *The Business History Review*, vol. 50, no. 4 (1976), 482–485.

134 Thomas W. Lamont, "The Dawes Plan and European Peace", *Academy of Political Science*, vol. 11, no. 2 (1925), 181 and See S. Parker Gilbert, "The Meaning of the 'Dawes Plan.'" *Foreign Affairs*, vol. 4, no. 3 (1926), 6–10.

solution either.[135] The German economy worsened with the effect of the 1929 World Economic Depression, and the Germans began to seek radical solutions.[136]

On the victors' side, the situation was quite different. Until America entered the war, it increased the gold reserves in its banks from $2,930,000,000 to $4,148,000,000 with the war industry products it sold to the warring parties. This amount was equivalent to half of the world's gold stock at that time.[137] On the other hand, America began to enter the European market. The Republic of Poland, which was established as an independent state after the First World War, bought 4000 rail cars from America in 1920.[138] This alone was an indication that the American industry was beginning to grab a share from the European market.

On the Turkish side, the situation was not very encouraging. Turkey's debt, which was 143 million in 1914,[139] had increased to 457 million Turkish liras during the war, of which 296 million were non-reciprocal war debts. When war taxes, demolitions, the purchase of Goeben and Breslau and similar expenses were added to this, a debt of approximately 500 million lira[140]

---

135 Carl Bergmann, "Germany and the Young Plan." *Foreign Affairs*, vol. 8, no. 4 (1930), 58.

136 At the Lausanne Conference in 1932, European states agreed to renounce their war reparations from Germany, whose economy had collapsed, in return for a single payment of approximately 3 billion marks. See "The Result of the Lausanne Conference.", 75. However, these proposals were not approved or implemented. The wrong policies that had been going on since 1918, dragged Europe into a new warIn 1932, the German people, whose economic situation was very bad, found the solution in radical policies, the National Socialist party, which came to power in 1933, rejected all obligations arising from Versailles, quickly armed Germany and prepared for a more destructive war.

137 Kurtbek, *Harp ve Ekonomi*, 51.

138 *ADAP*, Serie A: 1918–1925, Band IV (1 Oktober 1920 bis 30 April 1921), Göttingen, 1986 "Gesandtschaftsrat von Dirksen (Warschau) an das Auswärtige Amt" Nr. 74, 8.12.1920 (K 1809/K 456 623–27)

139 According to a document in the American archives, Turkey's pre-war debt was 151,000,000 liras and the annual interest on this debt was 7,000,000 liras. In September 1917, this debt increased to 380,000,000 liras. See NARA, 867.50, June 2, 1910–December 17,1929.

140 As a result of the Treaty of Lausanne, it was decided to share the debts of the Ottoman Empire by the countries that gained independence on the Ottoman lands, and Turkey's share was 105,559,623 gold liras. However, with the effect of the 1929 depression, the planned payments could not be made. As a result of a series of negotiations with the Council of Debts from 1930 to 1932, the issue was agreed upon and with the agreement signed on April 24, 1933, Turkey's debt of 107,528,461

emerged.[141] The fact that 26 % of the financing used by the Ottoman Empire in the First World War consisted of advances given by Germany and Austria also created an economic dependence on the Ottoman Empire.[142] This rate was 10 % for the Turkish War of Independence.[143] While considering the economic conditions in the period of Turkish War of Independence, it is necessary to consider the volume of financial opportunities that a war-weary nation and a movement that does not have external links like a state. This is another indication that the Turkish War of Independence was carried out with a very limited economy. On the other hand, the lack of agricultural and industrial power required for the payment of this debt was also an important factor. The population, which was 16,3 million in 1914, fell to 13,6 million in 1927. A significant portion of the male population died in war or became a veteran. Moreover, there was a loss of manpower due to the fact that the workforce was under arms.[144] During the war years, wheat production decreased by 47 %, tobacco production by 51 %, raisins by 54 %, hazelnut by 65 %, fresh cocoon by 69 %, the number of sheep decreased by 45 % and the number of goats by 33 %.[145] These rates shed light on the difficulty and necessity of development in post-war Turkey.

Germany and Turkey, which were allied during the war, talked about sharing the spoils of war in November 1917,[146] and as of 1918, they became fateful partners against the Entente Powers. The Entente Powers were determined

gold liras was reduced to 8,578,343 gold liras. See Hasan Aslan Akpınar, *Türkiye'de Milli Sanayinin Mimarlarından Nurullah Esat Sumer* (İstanbul, Türkiye İş Bankası Yayınları, 2020), 38.

141 Larcher, *Büyük Harpte Türk Harbi*, Cilt 3, 191.

142 Germany and Turkey held several meetings on the pre-war debts to German industry and Germany, and the issue remained controversial for years. See *ADAP*, "Aufzeichnung ohne Unterschrift" Nr. 241, 03.12.1926, (4578/E174 801–02) ve bkz: *ADAP*, Serie B: 1925–1933,Band XIV, (1 Januar bis 30 April 1930), Göttingen, 1980, *ADAP*, "Auzeichnung des Ministerialdirektors de Haas " Nr. 189, 8.3.1924, (2980/D 584 137–41).

143 These aids were generally Soviet aid and donations. See Boratav, *Türkiye İktisat Tarihi: 1908–2009*, 32.

144 Yahya Tezel, *Cumhuriyet Tarihinin İktisadi Tarihi (1923–1950)* (İstanbul: Türkiye İş Bankası Yayınları, 2015), 114.

145 Boratav, *Türkiye İktisat Tarihi: 1908–2009*, 34.

146 On 27 November 1917, a secret agreement was made between Germany and the Ottoman Empire. With this treaty, both countries agreed on sharing the spoils of war, rejecting the restriction of the sovereignty rights on the imperial lands together, and rejecting the caputulations. See. Satan, *100 Soruda I. Dünya Savaşı*, 88.

not to allow Turkish-German rapprochement for any reason. The relations between the Ottoman Empire and Germany were terminated in accordance with the 23rd article of the Armistice of Mudros signed on 30 October 1918 between the Ottoman Empire and the Allied Powers. Similarly, the purpose of paragraph 4 of the Article 22, and articles 155, 258, 261, 434 of the Treaty of Versailles, which was signed by Germany, was to cut off the relations between the Ottoman Empire and Germany and prevent their re-establishment.[147] These attempts of the Allied Powers were indeed successful. During the Turkish War of Independence, diplomatic relations between Germany and Turkey were reduced to a minimum, and there were no relations even at the level of ambassadors.[148] The limited communication available was only possible through the Swedish embassy in Istanbul. In the first place, Turkey turned to the Bolsheviks for the urgent help it needed.[149]

It was the Treaty of Lausanne that abolished these prohibitions. With the Treaty of Lausanne signed on July 24, 1923, previous treaties and/or articles that restricted the establishment of diplomatic relations with Germany were invalidated. On this occasion, a period of controlled diplomatic rapprochement began between Turkey and Germany. With Turkey-Germany Friendship Treaty signed on March 3, 1924, the foundation of diplomatic relations to be re-established between the Republic of Turkey and the State of Germany was laid. Relations were further strengthened with a series of treaties that lasted until the 1930s.[150]

147 Cemil Koçak, *Türk-Alman İlişkileri (1923–1939)* (Ankara: Türk Tarih Kurumu Yayınları, 2nd ed., 2013), 1.

148 Koçak, *Türk-Alman İlişkileri (1923–1939)*, 6.

149 Larcher, *Büyük Harpte Türk Harbi*, Cilt 3, 157.

150 The Turkey-Germany Friendship Treaty was approved by the Grand National Assembly of Turkey on 13 April and by Germany in April, and entered into force on 16 May after the change of approval documents on 1 May. See Koçak, *Türk-Alman İlişkileri (1923–1939)*, 9, 36–39.

Table 4.3. Some Agreements between Germany and Turkey (1927–1932)[151]

Name of the Agreement	**Effective Date**	**Period of Validity**
Turkish-German Trade Agreement	12 January 1927	-
Contract of Residence	27 July 1927	2 Years
Turkish-German Conciliation, Judicial Resolution and Arbitration Agreement	1 September 1930	-
Turkish-German Consular Agreement	18 November 1931	5 Years
Consular Agreement between the Republic of Turkey and Germany and its Annex	18 September 1931	-
Extradition Agreement Between the Republic of Turkey and Germany	19 June 1932	-

Source: Data from Koçak, *Türk-Alman İlişkileri (1923–1939)*, 36–38.

The most important indicator of the establishment of diplomatic relations was undoubtedly the mutual ambassador appointments of Germany and Turkey. Before the Treaty of Lausanne was officially ratified, especially by United Kingdom and France, many states chose to appoint an informal representative instead of appointing ambassadors to Turkey. Among them were very active and effective names such as the French Colonel Mougin. However, Mustafa Kemal Atatürk, who was disturbed by the fact that only representatives were sent, brought this issue to the parliamentary speeches and conveyed to the Western powers that a regular ambassador was expected, not official representatives.[152] This attitude of Atatürk made the Western powers feel the seriousness of Turkey regarding the ambassadors. During the period when Lausanne was not officially signed and ratified by the king of the UK, Germany preferred to be cautious and always expected the first step from the UK. Germany tried to take its steps in this period of time by informing the British and minimizing possible reactions. Due to Versailles, Germany remained dependent on the British on many issues such as colonies, taxes, Rhineland policy, and negotiated and made demands on these

151 Koçak, *Türk-Alman İlişkileri (1923–1939)*, 36–38.

152 *ADAP*, Serie A: 1918–1925,Band IX, (16 November bis 6 April 1924), Göttingen, 1991, *ADAP*, "Der Gesandte in Bukarest Freytag (z. Z. Konstantinopel) an das Auswärtige Amt" Nr. 192, 8.3.1924, (4578/E 174 618–22). Also See *ADAP*, Serie A: 1918–1925,Band IX, "Aufzeichnung des Ministeraldirektors von Schubert", Nr. 209, 15.03.1924, (4578/E 174 632–33).

issues for years.[153] The British also did not want to let any steps to be taken in Turkey without their knowledge.[154] Even when they learned of Deutsche Bank's intention to open a branch in Istanbul, they sought information from Germany on the subject and sought to prevent any action that would harm their interests. While the British were planning to open a branch of Lloyd Bank in Istanbul, even hearing that Deutsche Bank was planning such an initiative was enough to make the British uneasy.[155] As the Treaty of Lausanne was ratified by the British government with the signature of the King, Germany began to act more effectively in its initiatives with Turkey. Rudolf Nadolny was appointed as the ambassador to Turkey after Turkey gave an aggregation for Rudolf Nadolny[156] on May 8, 1924. Nadolny's presentation of his letter of credence to Mustafa Kemal Atatürk[157] on 16 June 1924 and Kemalettin Sami Gökçen's[158] appointment as the

153 *ADAP*, Serie A: 1918–1925, Band XIV, "Der Staatssekretär des Auswärtigen Amts Freiherr von Maltzan an die Botschatt in London", Nr. 248, 6.4.1924, (3088/D 625 480–81).

154 *ADAP*, Serie A: 1918–1925, Band XIV, "Aufzeichnung des Ministerialdirektors von Schubert", Nr. 203, 13.04.1924, (4578/E 174 663–64).

155 *ADAP*, Serie A: 1918–1925, Band XIV "Aufzeichnung des Ministerialdirektors von Schubert", Nr. 173, 28.02.1924, (4578/E 174 668–69).

156 Rudolf Nadolny was born in 1873 in East Prussia. After his education, he started his professional career as a trainee judge in 1896 and continued at the Königsberg Court of First Instance. He applied to the German Foreign Ministry in 1901 and started working for the German Foreign Ministry in 1902. After serving in Russia, the USA, Iran and Sweden, he was appointed to Turkey in 1924, becoming the first ambassador of Germany to the Republic of Turkey and remained in this position until 1933. Nadolny died in Dusseldorf in 1953. See Koçak, *Türk-Alman İlişkileri (1923–1939)*, 10–11.

157 It is also available in the reports of the British that Mustafa Kemal Atatürk had a different attitude than Enver Pasha in relations with Germany and was more cautious towards the Germans. See Ali Satan, *İngiliz Yıllık Raporlarında Türkiye – 1920* (İstanbul: Tarihçi Kitabevi, 2010), 158. Mustafa Kemal Pasha did not look at Germany from the perspective of Enver Pasha, and advocated rapprochement without feeling any commitment or obligation. The new German government also took into account the reaction of the British more than the political steps of Turkey. This was one of the factors that ensured that political relations were not as interdependent as they used to be, and that they were slowly recovering. There is a remarkable point here. Although political figures and regimes changed, it is interesting that commercial relations progressed independently of all these developments and recovered quickly. The influence of German Industrialization clearly shows itself here.

158 Kemalettin Sami Pasha, who was born in Sinop in 1884, was appointed as a Staff Captain to the 4th Army after graduating from the Erkan-ı Harbiye Mektebi

Berlin ambassador in the same year and his presentation of letter of credence in Berlin on 8 October 1924 ensured the start of uninterrupted diplomatic relations. Thereupon, Nadolny was officially appointed to the embassy and presented his credentials officily as German ambassador on March 30, 1925.[159]

It had been frequently stated by the German economic circles that it would be in the interest of the German economy for Germany to revive trade with Turkey as soon as possible.[160] As a result of these pressures and mutual requests, the Chamber of Commerce was established in April 1924.[161] Relying on the German industry, the Turkish Republic made some demands from the Germans. Among these, there were demands such as the expansion of Mersin and Samsun ports, the reorganization of agriculture in the presence of German experts to be sent, the increasing agricultural productivity by taking over the renovation works by the Germans, the creation of an export organization and takeover of tobacco exports by the Germans, the support in working together to establish a state bank and stabilizing the Turkish lira, the arrival of experts in the academic field and the creation of exchange programs.[162] Thanks to these demands, economic relations began to come to life again, and Turkish-German relations began to flourish again in many areas. After all, it should not be ignored that German culture was still in Turkey. German experts who stayed in Turkey and tens of thousands of Turkish youth who were admitted to Germany at the request of the Ottoman government during the First World War and received technical and vocational training[163] continued to be the bridge between Germany and Turkey. Even in the Turkish army, the German influence continued to be seen. German manuals remained in force, and German military literature remained the main

---

(military school) in 1908. Kemalettin Sami Pasha, who received vocational training in Germany in 1912, took part in the Balkan Wars, the First World War and the Turkish War of Independence. He was promoted to brigadier general due to his success in the Great Offensive. Kemalettin Sami Pasha, who was appointed to the Berlin Embassy in 1924, died in 1934 after gastric surgery in Berlin. See Halil Bal, "Kemalettin Sami Paşa (1884–1934)", *Ataturkansiklopedisi* (Accessed: 15.12.2021)

159 Koçak, *Türk-Alman İlişkileri (1923–1939)*, 10, 12,15.

160 *ADAP*, Serie A: 1918–1925, Band XIV, "Der Reichsminister des Auswärtigen Stresemann and den Gesandten in Bukarest Freytag" Nr. 88, 10.01.1924, (L101/L 016 287–91).

161 Keyder, *Dünya Ekonomisi İçinde Türkiye (1923–1929)*, 110.

162 *ADAP*, Serie B: 1918–1925, Band VII (1 Oktober bis 31 Dezember 1927), Göttingen, 1974 "Aufzeichnung des Vortragenden Legationstrats Freiherr von Richtofen" Nr. 35, 10.01.1924, (L101/L 016 484–86).

163 Akpınar, *Türkiye'de Milli Sanayinin Mimarlarından Nurullah Esat Sumer*, 8.

source in the Turkish army. After 1925, German officers took charge in Turkey again and they also worked as instructors.[164]

4.3.1. Quick Recovery of German Industries: The Case of Ruhrlade

German industry has an important tradition. It is the discipline of ensuring rapid restructuring and coordination between cartels, as German industrial giants have knowledge transferred from generation to generation through education and culture. *Ruhrlade* is a prime example of this.

The conditions that started in the First World War and continued for a certain period after the war allowed some German industrial companies to grow even more. Those from the private sector who had access to the limited raw materials available monopolized the iron-steel shortage that occurred during the war, and in this way, they were able to dominate the market as they wished. In the same period, companies holding stocks were able to take advantage of the high inflation that lasted until the mid-1920s,[165] and they started to sell their stocked products, which they had produced with reasonable purchase prices, at very profitable prices due to the increasing inflation. They were almost able to paid off their debts by only the help of inflation.

In this period, some oligarchic unions were established in order to keep the sectors alive against the existing problems and they were quite effective. Some of these were trade associations such as the "VDMA" (Verein Deutscher Maschinenbauanstalten) in the machine building industry, the "VDESI" (Verein Deutscher Eisen und Stahlindustrieller) which was formed by northwestern iron and steel manufacturers, or the "*Ruhrlade*", which aimed to dominate the entire Rhine-Westphalia region in heavy industry industries. Ruhrlade's first meeting was held on January 9, 1928, at Villa Hügel, the palace of the Krupp family in the suburbs of Essen, with the participation of 12 men in tuxedos.[166] In particular, the ban on bringing guests in the *Ruhrlade* meetings, which was limited to 12

---

164 Gencer Özkan, "Türkiye'de Cumhuriyet Dönemi Ordusunda Prusya Etkisi" *Türkiye'de Ordu, Devlet ve Güvenlik Siyaseti* ed. Evren Balta Paker et al. (İstanbul: İstanbul Bilgi Üniversitesi Yayınları, 2010), 197.

165 Gerald D. Feldman - Ulrich Nocken, "Trade Associations and Economic Power: Interest Group Development in the German Iron and Steel and Machine Building Industries, 1900–1933", *The Business History Review*, vol. 49, no. 4 (1975), 424.

166 Henry Ashby Turner, "The Ruhrlade, Secret Cabinet of Heavy Industry in the Weimar Republic", *Central European History*, vol. 3, no. 3 (1970), 195.

members and was held each first Monday of every month, reveals the seriousness of the union.[167] The *Ruhrlade* was quite successful in a short time.

Especially after the occupation of the Ruhr in 1923, the balance in the region was lost and uncertainty prevailed. In such an environment, radical decisions brought about by irregularity also caused a multi-headed disorder in the sector. In order to prevent this, Paul Reusch, who had tried to establish similar unions in Essen and Magdeburg before, and who had been the general manager of the coal, steel and production cartel *Gutehoffnungshütte* since 1908, pioneered the establishment of *Ruhrlade* this time. *Ruhrlade,* with its member names, was the most serious and most effective of these trials.

The names in *Ruhrlade* were names that had placed their companies among the leading companies of the sectors before the First World War and had known each other since this process. These names were as the following. Gustav Krupp von Bohlen from *Krupp*. Fritz Thyssen, chairman of the board of *Vereinigte Stahlverke*, Germany's largest steel company at that time. Erich Fickler, managing director of the Dortmund coal mining firm *Harpener Bergbau A.G.* Karl Haniel, chairman of the board of *Gutehoffnungshütte.* Peter Klöckner, founding chairman of the coal and steel cartel *Klöckner-Werke A.G.* Arthur Klotzbach, director of *Fried Krupp A.G.* Ernst Poensgen, former managing director of *Phönix A.G.* and current director of *Stahlverein*, which *Phönix* was a part of. Paul Silverberg, chairman of the board of *Rheinische A.G. für Braunkohlenbergbau und Brikettenfabrikation*, Germany's largest lignet mining firm. Fritz Springorum, managing director of *Eisen und Stahlwerk Hoesch A.G.* Albert Vögler, chairman of the board of directors of *Stahlverein. Fritz Winkhaus,* managing director of *Köln-Neussener Bergwerksverein*, the coal mining subsidiary of *Hoesch.*[168]

The most authoritative names of these giant companies were able to solve the problems among themselves in the sector, and developed sectoral strategies for re-development after the closure period in 1928. They worked onoligarchic regulations such as production quota and pricing. They discussed the issues such as workers' salaries in the sector.[169]

---

167 Another example was the necessity of obtaining a majority of at least 3/4 in order to take decisions. See Turner, "The Ruhrlade, Secret Cabinet of Heavy Industry in the Weimar Republic", 197–198.

168 Turner, "The Ruhrlade, Secret Cabinet of Heavy Industry in the Weimar Republic", 196.

169 Turner. "The Ruhrlade, Secret Cabinet of Heavy Industry in the Weimar Republic", 198.

Undoubtedly, the positions of these names in different companies or unions and their connections with the government provided the opportunity to directly convey their sectoral needs to the government. This union, which was constantly opposed to the devastating conditions of Versailles and Germany's compensation payments, soon sought to gain a place in politics and even in the parliamentfor this reason. Therefore, they financially supported parties such as DNVP (Deutschnationale Volkspartei), DVP (Deutsche Volkspartei).

In a structure where industry was included in the administration, the way for cartelization had been reopened. One of the reasons behind the rapid re-establishment of industrial relations with Turkey was this rapid recovery. There were certain sectors and sub-sectors that pioneered the re-establishment of these relations. One of the main ones was the railways, which was the pioneer of German Industrialization.

4.3.2. Railways

Even shortly after Lausanne, as in 1926, administrations such as Yenice-Nusaybin Railways imported coal from Germany.[170] As early as 1927, authorized people for the designation of wagon and locomotive types to be used for narrow gauge lines were sent from Turkey to Germany.[171] In 1928, Germany held 90 % of the market in Turkey in the steam engine trade.[172] The State Railways continued to import a number of tools from Germany to be used in the construction of railways in the early 1930s.[173] In short, the railways, which were the pioneers of German Industrialization, continued to be a part of Turkish-German relations. Turkey also put its determination to bring railways to every part of the country more and more into action. The railway lines and their lengths in Turkey as of 31 December 1927 can be seen in the table below. The lines built here in the early years of the young republic are also noteworthy.

170 BCA, 30-18-1-1 / Kararlar Daire Başkanlığı, 22-74-15, 12.12.1926.

171 BCA, 30-18-1-1/ Kararlar Daire Başkanlığı, 23-7-15, 13.02.1927.

172 Keyder, *Dünya Ekonomisi İçinde Türkiye (1923–1929)*, 110.

173 BCA, 30-18-1-2 / Kararlar Daire Başkanlığı, 17 – 3 – 12; BCA, 30-18-1-2 / Kararlar Daire Başkanlığı, 17 – 1 – 12, 07.01.1931.

Table 4.4. Railway Lines and Railway Lengths in the Republic of Turkey, 31 December 1927[174]

Name of Line	Date of Construction	Operated by	Lenght (Km)
Anatolian – Bagdad	1871–1903	State	1,378
Angora – Cesarea – Eregli	1923	State	361
Samsoun – Sivas	1925	State	133
Erzroum – Frontier	1916	State	356
Yenidje – Nirsibine (Extension)	1922	Company	632.5
Smyrna – Cababa (Extension)	1864	Company	703.2
Aidin	1856	Company	610.3
Oriental	1870	Company	337.1
Mudania – Brousa	1892	Company	42
Ilidja – Palamoutlouk	1924	Company	28.4
Samsoun – Tsharshauba	1926	Company	37

Source: NARA, 867.501, July 29, 1914–May 20, 1929.

An example of the trust in German railways can be seen in Mustafa Kemal Atatürk's private wagon, where he made his domestic journeys, and in the White Train, which was identified with the republican period. Atatürk, who usually traveled by rail, wanted to order a wagon to be connected to the end of the passenger train, and he gave this order to the German company Wegmann & CO in Kassel. This German company delivered the wagon that Atatürk would use in his domestic travels in 1927. The wagon with a hall, meeting room, bedroom, compartment, toilet and bathroom, was frequently used by Atatürk. When a special train was wanted to be built to replace this wagon, which was not sufficient after a certain time due to its five-person capacity, this order was also given to a German company. In the first half of the 1930s, a train was ordered to the German LHV Linke Hofmann-Werke factory in Breslau and this special train with nine wagons arrived in Haydarpaşa on 19 July 1935. Although this special train, called the White Train, was used in a limited number by Atatürk, it was identified with the republican period.[175]

174 NARA, 867.501, July 29, 1914–May 20, 1929.

175 The White Train was also used after Atatürk. İsmet İnönü made his domestic travels with the White Train, and made his famous meeting with Churchill in 1943 on the White Train at Adana-Yenice station. See Eminalp Malkoç, "Beyaz Tren", *Ataturkansiklopedisi* (Accesed: 12.04.2022)

Atatürk's yacht Savarona, which was the largest non-royal and the fourth largest yacht in the world at the time of its construction, was built at the Blohm & Woss shipyard in Hamburg, Germany. Savarona, which was started to be built on 29 July 1930 and launched on 28 March 1931, is an indication that Germany, which was crushed under the Versailles obligations, had an industry that could build one of the best yachts in the world even in 1930.[176]

4.3.3. Defence Industry

One of the most obvious goals of Versailles was not to bring the German army to a level that would pose a threat to Europe again. For this purpose, with Versailles, the number of military personnel of Germany was limited to 100.000 in the army and 15.000 in the navy.[177] A sembolic military force was left to Germany only to maintain internal security and control its borders. The Inter-Allied Military Commission of Control was sent to Germany to the execute the military restrictions and to remove the existing military elements in Germany. However, both these measures and restrictions were functional up to a certain point. German companies carried out their production outside of Germany, especially in Russia. Paramilitary organizations continued to operate against the restrictions and controls.[178] After the departure of the Inter-Allied Military Commission of Control from Germany in January-February 1927, Germany tried to strengthen its defense industry by going beyond the restrictions in its

176 The Savarona had been ordered by Emily Roebling Cadwallader, the granddaughter of John Roebling, the American engineer who built the Brooklyn Bridge. When the construction of the ship was completed, the USA wanted a customs tax almost equal to the cost of the yacht to bring the yacht into the country, so the yacht could not be brought to the USA and was put up for sale. Although the Germans wanted to acquire this yacht cheaply by placing a lien on Savarona, the US President Roosevelt stepped in and announced that if the lien on this yacht belonging to his own citizen was not lifted, a German transatlantic in New York at that time would be foreclosed. Thereupon, the German government did not insist on lifting the lien and the Savarona was sold. Savarona was purchased by the Turkish government in 1938 for 1 million dollars, much below the cost of construction, and brought to Turkey. See Cemal Avcı, "Savarona Yatı", *Ataturkansiklopedisi* (Accessed: 12.04.2022)

177 Max Hantke- Mark Spoerer, "The Imposed Gift of Versailles: The Fiscal Effects of Restricting the Size of Germany's Armed Forces, 1924–9." *The Economic History Review*, vol. 63, no. 4 (2010), 849–850.

178 Berenice A. Carroll, "Germany Disarmed and Rearming, 1925–1935." *Journal of Peace Research*, vol. 3, no. 2 (1966), 114–115.

own territory.[179] The German defense industry was already at an advanced level before the First World War, it developed further during the First World War. Therefore, Turkish-German industrial relations continued in defense industry even after the Treaty of Lausanne. Turkey had prepared a plan to establish an independent and domestic defense industry since 1925. For this purpose, Presidential Secretary General Tevfik Bey[180] held talks with both the German Ministry of Foreign Affairs and German industrialists regarding the Turkish defense industry program and possible imports of defense industry products. He stressed that Turkey would establish its own defense industry and demanded the support of Germany on this subject. Tevfik Bey questioned whether the Locarno Treaties[181] had secret articles preventing German industry from making defense industry investments in Turkey and requested expert support from the German government in evaluating the offers made by German companies to the Turkish government.[182] Upon the positive responses of Germany, mutual defense industry relations started.

One of the experts who came to Turkey in this process was Gustaw Wesemann, who was sent as an expert to supervise and regulate the economic operation of the Defence Industry Factory (İmalat-ı Harbiye) in Ankara. Wesemann was a representation of the trust in the German defense industry and in the German business discipline in the Republic of Turkey.[183]

Although the Weimar Republic[184] was proclaimed in the last days of the First World War and the monarchists were replaced by social democrats, public discipline in Germany remained. This situation provided confidence in the German defense industry for Turkey, which wanted both a rapid recovery and independence of the defense industry. For example, in 1926, the cabinet in

179 Carroll, "Germany Disarmed and Rearming, 1925–1935.", 114.

180 Tevfik Bıyıklıoğlu (1891 – 1961)

181 A set of agreements signed in 1925, aiming to establish border balances in Europe, emphasizing that Germany's western border would not change. With Locarno Treaties Germany, France, Belgium, the U.K. and Italy gave mutual guarantees of non-aggression and military assistance. For furher information about the Locarno Treaties See W. R. Bisschop, "The Locarno Pact. October 15–December 1, 1925." *Transactions of the Grotius Society*, vol. 11 (1925).

182 *ADAP*, Serie B: 1925–1933, Band III, (Dezember 1925 bis Dezember 1926), Göttingen, 1968, *ADAP*, "Undatierte Aufzeichnung ohne Untershcrift – Aufzeichnung Über die Türkischen Rütungspläne" Nr. 14, (4580/E 174 990–5 004).

183 Özkan, "Türkiye'de Cumhuriyet Dönemi Ordusunda Prusya Etkisi", 198.

184 9 Kasım 1918 – 30 Ocak 1933.

Germany approved a 175-mark export credit guarantee fund in order to support exports and made it available to railway companies that would also build Turkish railways.[185] This was an example of how Germany, crushed under the articles of Versailles and unable to pay its own installments, continued its tradition of public support under all circumstances.

This determination in Germany and Turkey's appetite to invest in the defense industry resulted in the development of Turkish-German defense industry relations. During this process, Turkey imported defense industry products from different German companies. For example, in 1930, an agreement for the purchase of motor land vehicles worth 1 million marks was signed between the Ministry of National Defense and the Büssing company.[186] In 1925, Kırıkkale Artillery Ammunition Factory was awarded to the German company Nielsen Winther with a tender and production started in 1929. In 1926, the Ankara Fisek Factory, which had not been producing cartridges since 1828, started to produce cartridges with the workbenches purchased from the German Fritz Werner company. Kırıkkale Steel Casting and Rolling Mill started proction in 1933 with the investments of the German Gutehoffnungshütte – Demag group of companies.[187]

Although Turkey continued to trust German companies, it continued to develop its commercial relations with different countries in order to become completely independent in the defense industry. Attempts to hand over the construction project of the domestic bullet production factory to the Danes[188] was another attempt by Turkey to nationalize the defence industry and to make it independent. On the other hand, Turkey's attempts to make the defense industry independent did not go unnoticed by the Germans. After Turkey considered the proposal of a consortium of 14 French workshops for the repair of Goeben, German Ambassador Nadolny conveyed this development in a telegram he sent

185 *ADAP*, Serie B: 1925–1933, Band III, (Dezember 1925 bis Dezember 1926), Göttingen, 1968, *ADAP*, "Aufzeichnung ohne Unterschrift" Nr. 241, 03.12.1926, (4578/E174 801–02).

186 Koçak, *Türk-Alman İlişkileri (1923–1939)*, 68.

187 Yavuz, *Atatürk ve Almanya*, 269.

188 *ADAP*, Serie A: 1918–1925, Band XIV, "Der Staatssekretär des Auswärtigen Amts von Schubert an die Gesandschaft in Konstantinopel" Nr. 70, 20.9.1925, (K 152/K 016 952–53).

to the German Foreign Ministry. He emphasized in his telegram that Turkey did not feel dependent on Germany in defence industry.[189]

Nevertheless, German companies were generally preferred due to Turkey's trust in German industry. One of the most important examples of this is seen in the French, Italian and German competition that occurred when Turkey decided to establish its national air defense industry. Although more attractive offers came from the French and Italians at some points,[190] Turkey preferred to cooperate with the German company Junkers. Thus, the Kayseri Aircraft Factory project, one of the most important initiatives of the period, was born.

4.3.3.1. Turkish Government and Junkers

On August 15, 1925, a contract was signed between the Turkish government and the German Junkers company, which included the establishment of an aircraft and aircraft engine factory in Kayseri. As a result of the completion of the first phase of the project, which was transferred to the Turkish-German joint venture Tayyare ve Motor Türk Anonim Şirketi (TOMTAŞ), the first phase of the Kayseri Aircraft Factory was opened on 6 October 1926.[191] Some details in the contract signed between Junkers company and the government of the Republic of Turkey are remarkable and are indicative of Turkey's investments in the future. Pursuant to article 14 of the contract, Junkers committed to train engineers, foremen, plumbers, workers and pilots assigned by the Turkish government to serve in the Turkish war and commercial air fleet. Junkers committed to employing only Turkish workers, engineers, pilots, mechanics and other personnel, with the exception of senior specialists required for production in the opinion of the supervisory board, six years later.[192] This article put by the Turkish government emphasizes the Turkey's determination for the independent air defense industry.

In the contract signed between Junkers and the government of the Republic of Turkey, the capital of the company was determined as 3,36 million liras. According to the contract, within two years following the establishment of

189 *ADAP*, Serie B: 1925–1933, Band III, (Dezember 1925 bis Dezember 1926), Göttingen, 1968, *ADAP*, "Der Botschafter in Konstantinopel Nadolny an das Auswärtige Amt" Nr. 215, (K152/K017 071–72).

190 *ADAP*, Serie A: 1925–1933, Band XIII, (April 1925 bis August 1925), Göttingen, 1968, *ADAP*, *"Der Gesandte in Konstantinopel Botschafter Nadolny an das Auswärtige Amt "* Nr. 52, 14.05.1925, (9297/H 256 130).

191 Koçak, *Türk-Alman İlişkileri (1923–1939)*, 71.

192 *ADAP*, Serie A: 1918–1925, Band XIV, "Der Gesandte in Konstantinopel Boschafter Nadolny an das Auswärtige Amt" Nr. 31, 25.8.1925, (K 150/K 015 981–84).

the venture, which would establish aircraft and aircraft engines factories, the factory would have the capacity to produce 250 aircraft per year, and the start up capital would be paid equally by the parties. In fact, as stated in Article 11 of the contract, the Turkish government agreed to make critical raw materials for the air defense industry such as aluminum, iron and oil available to Junkers and to operate them together with Junkers.[193] Beyond all of this, the preliminary contract made shows the traces of the further steps Turkey wanted to take with Junkers. In the preliminary contract with Junkers, it was also planned to establish an airline company and a similar company that would produce toxic gas, with the same capital participation.[194] Turkey gave great importance to R&D of toxic gases in order to strengthen its defense industry and to take measures against all kinds of attacks.[195] However, the German government in particular showed a very cautious approach to the production of toxic gas. They thought that Junkers' deal with the toxic gas plant would be devastating to foreign policy, and that this initiative, which would surely come to light in the long run, would be a source of discredit that could hinder Junkers' future ventures. In particular, they considered the effect of the Geneva Protocol[196] signed in Geneva on 17 June 1925 in order to prevent chemical and biological wars.[197]

Another striking point in the Kayseri Aircraft Factory process was that Germany's public intervention discipline frequently showed itself here as well.

Although The German Ministry of Defense did not have a direct interest in Turkey's armament, it accepted to develop the Turkish air defense industry due

---

193 *ADAP*, Serie A: 1918–1925, Band XIV, "Der Gesandte in Konstantinopel Boschafter Nadolny an das Auswärtige Amt" Nr. 31, 25.8.1925, (K 150/K 015 981–84).

194 *ADAP*, Serie A: 1925–1933, Band XIII, (April 1925 bis August 1925), Göttingen, 1968, *ADAP*, "Der Gesandte in Konstantinopel Botschafter Nadolny an das Auswärtige Amt " Nr. 52, 14.05.1925, (9297/H 256 130).

195 Turkey maintained its stance on toxic gas even though it did not cooperate with Junkers. At the beginning of 1929, an instruction was given to the Ministry of Education to urgently establish an institute to conduct toxic gas research within the Darülfünun. See BCA, 30-10-0-0 / Muamelat Genel Müdürlüğü, 45 – 292 – 19, 13.02.1929

196 The Geneva Protocol was prepared at a conference held in Geneva between 4 May and 17 June 1925 under the leadership of the League of Nations and signed on 17 June 1925. It entered into force on February 8, 1928. See United Nations (UN), "1925 Geneva Protocol" (Accessed: 11.04.2022)

197 *ADAP*, Serie A: 1918–1925, Band XIV, "Der Staatssekretär des Auswärtigen Amts von Schubert an die Gesandtschaft in Konstantinopel" Nr. 70, 20.9.1925, (K 152/K 016 952–53).

to the necessity of the German industry to practice in the production of defense industry technologies.[198] This situation indicates the importance given to the industrialists by the state in Germany. On the other hand, concrete interventions came from the German government in the process.

The financial problems that Junkers experienced during the construction of the Kayseri Aircraft Factory prevented it from meeting its own financing, and in order to obtain this financing, the Junkers firm demanded a lump-sum license payment of 1.8 million lira from the Turkish government.[199] The Turkish government, on the other hand, rejected this proposal and demanded that the one-off volume license payment be divided into five years with 5 % payments to be made over the turnover of the factory. Junkers, which urgently needed the money, wanted to get a loan from Germany in return for these installments, based on the Turkish government's offer.[200] Thinking that Junkers would not be able to complete the factory due to financial difficulties and that this situation would shake Turkey's trust in German companies, the German government stepped in. Two million marks of the average amount of four and a half million marks that the Junkers firm had committed in order for the contract to be valid was given as a loan from one of the secret funds of the German Ministry of Foreign Affairs in Orient Bank.[201]

At a time when the Junkers company was experiencing financial problems, the German Finance Minister von Schlieben requested from the German Foreign Minister Stresemann to examine the management of the company in depth in order to analyze the Junkers company's capacity to implement the contract it made with Turkey. This was another example of the Germany's public intervention in strategic issues.[202]

---

198 *ADAP*, Serie B: 1925–1933, Band III, (Dezember 1925 bis Dezember 1926), Göttingen, 1968, *ADAP*, "Aufzeichnung über die Türkischen Rüstungspläne" Nr. 14, (4580/E 174 990–5 004).

199 *ADAP*, Serie A: 1925–1933, Band XIII, (April 1925 bis August 1925), Göttingen, 1968, *ADAP*, *"Der Gesandte in Konstantinopel Botschafter Nadolny an das Auswärtige Amt "* Nr. 52, 14.05.1925, (9297/H 256 130).

200 *ADAP*, Serie A: 1925–1933, Band XIII, (April 1925 bis August 1925), Göttingen, 1968, *ADAP*, *"Aufzeichnung des Geheimen Legationstrats de Haas"* Nr. 217, 20.07.1925, (K 150/K015 941–42)

201 *ADAP*, Serie A: 1918–1925, Band XIV, (14 August bis 30 November 1924), Göttingen, 1995, *ADAP*, "Aufzeichnung des Konsuls Ziemke" Nr. 258, 23.11.1925, (K 150/K 016 079–80).

202 *ADAP*, Serie A: 1918–1925, Band XIV, "Der Reichsminister der Finanzen von Schlieben an den Reichsminister des Auswärtigen Stresemann", Nr. 182, 24.10.1925, (K 150/K 016 071–72).

During the period when Junkers continued to experience financial difficulties, telegrams were sent to the German Foreign Ministry from the embassy in Istanbul many times. In these telegrams, it was stated that the distrust that would occur on the Turkish side as a result of the bankruptcy of Junkers would affect the orders of the Turkish Ministry of Defense to German companies, and this situation might cause a pause in the German industry. Therefore, embassy in Istanbul asked from the government to prevent the bankruptcy of the Junkers company in order to prevent the decrease in the export capacity of the German industry and Germany's economic activities abroad. In telegrams they even asked for a loan to be given to Junkers.[203] Even when the bankruptcy of Junkers was finalized, the Ministry of Transportation tried again to take the necessary measures to prevent the bankruptcy. An assurance was requested from the Ministry of Foreign Affairs about the fulfillment of the obligations of the Junkers company in Turkey and the completion of the construction of the aircraft factory, no matter what.[204]

It had been planned to establish an aircraft and aircraft engine factory, which would produce 250 aircraft per year, an airline company and a chemical gas factory in Kayseri.[205] However, some obstacles such as financial difficulties for Junkers and wage differences between German and Turkish employees, could not be overcome and the the project did not go as planned. On May 3, 1928, TOMTAŞ, Turkey's first aircraft factory, ceased to operate. As a result of the protocol signed with Junkers, the shares were transferred to the Turkish Aircraft Society for 520.000 liras.

Turkey continued its initiatives in the air defense industry in the following period and first signed a contract with the American The Curtiss Aeroplane and Motor Company Inc. in 1932 and continued to produce at the Kayseri Aircraft Factory. The factory was completely transferred to the Ministry of National

---

203 *ADAP*, Serie B: 1925–1933, Band III, (Dezember 1925 bis Dezember 1926), Göttingen, 1968, *ADAP*, "Der Botschafter in Konstantinopel an das Auswärtige Amt" Nr. 136, 21.05.1926 (K150/K 06 166–67), Also See *ADAP*, Serie B: 1925–1933, Band III, (Dezember 1925 bis Dezember 1926), Göttingen, 1968, *ADAP*, "Der Botschafter in Konstantinopel Nadolny an das Auswärtige Amt" Nr. 194, 18.09.1926, (K150/K 016 466–68).

204 *ADAP*, Serie B: 1925–1933, Band III, (Dezember 1925 bis Dezember 1926), Göttingen, 1968, *ADAP*, "Undatierte Aufzeichnung des Vortragenden Legationsrats Freiherr von Richthofen" Nr. 244, (K150/K016 585–86).

205 *ADAP*, Serie A: 1918–1925, Band XIV, "Der Gesandte in Konstantinopel Boschafter Nadolny an das Auswärtige Amt" Nr. 31, 25.8.1925, (K 150/K 015 981–84).

Defense in 1933, and in 1935, a total of 50 gliders of 3 different types, named Türkkuşu, were produced. In the following period, license agreements were signed with the German company Gothaer Waggon Fabrik A.G, the Polish company PanstwoweZakladyLotnicze, and the British company Philips And Powis Aircraft Ltd. 134 aircraft of 5 different types were produced at the Kayseri Aircraft Factory, namely Fledling, Türkkuşu, Gotha 145, PZL-24A-24C and Magister. With the aircraft aid coming as a result of Marshall Plan surpassing the domestic industry, Kayseri Aircraft Factory completely ended its aircraft production activities.[206]

4.3.4. Banking

The fact that an expert was brought from Germany to protect and increase the value of the Turkish lira and to organize the state bank during the 1929 World Economic Depression[207] is an indication of the confidence in German economic knowledge even in 1929, when the economy in the Weimar Republic was quite bad. Deputy Minister of Finance Şükrü Saracoğlu invited Reichsbank President Hjalmar Schact to Turkey at the beginning of 1929 with the aim of establishing a Central Circulation Bank. However, upon Schact's inability to come to Turkey, Schact's colleague Karl Müller came to Turkey with his own suggestion in April 1929.[208] The Republic of Turkey needed this support, because with the increase in exchange rate fluctuations, the Turkish lira lost 2,5 times its value against the dollar in 10 years, and with this development, imports and paying foreign debts became more difficult. Most of this increase took place before the proclamation of the Republic of Turkey and points to the heavy economic burden that the Republic of Turkey inherited. On the other hand, 1929 was a critical year in terms of being the year when the first installments of foreign debts would be paid. The war debt of the Ottoman Empire had been divided between the Republic of Turkey and the other states that shared the Ottoman Empire's lands, leaving the Republic of Turkey with a debt of approximately 85 million, which was two-thirds of the total debt. Although it was decided to postpone the first installment of these debts to 1929, 1929 was an important year in which the first installment of 15 million liras would be paid. Moreover, it was a critical year when there was a great depression in the world. The export amounts in Turkey had decreased

---

206 İhsan Tayhani, "Kayseri Uçak Fabrikası", *Ataturkansiklopedisi* (Accessed: 09.12.2021)
207 BCA, 30-18-1-2 / Kararlar Daire Başkanlığı, 2 – 17 – 28 / 243–39, 06.03.1929.
208 Koçak, *Türk-Alman İlişkileri (1923–1939),* 83.

by 10 % compared to the previous year.[209] The table below sheds light on the depreciation of Turkey's currency.

Table 4.5. Ratio of US Dollar to Kuruş by Years[210]

Year	US Dollar	Kuruş (Year Average)
1919	1	79
1920	1	116
1921	1	153
1922	1	162
1923	1	167,83
1924	1	188,24
1925*	1	187
1926	1	193
1927	1	196
1928	1	197
1929	1	208

Source: NARA, 867.501., July 29, 1914–May 20, 1929; Yahya Tezel, Cumhuriyet Tarihinin İktisadi Tarihi (1923–1950), (İstanbul: Türkiye İş Bankası Yayınları, 1. Edition, 2015), 203.

*The data up to 1924 were taken from NARA, and from 1925, the table prepared by Yahya Tezel taking into account the Central Bank data.

Similarly, the cost of living continued to rise. In 1923, the cost of living had increased by 1098 % compared to 1914. This data is a sign of the heavy economic burden that the Republic of Turkey took over. In such a period, the young Republic of Turkey preferred to receive expert support from Germany.

4.3.5. Agriculture

In the Republican period, the importation of German machinery continued in agricultural activities. An example of this is the purchase of the necessary materials for the seed sieve machine stations in the wheat exporting areas of Eskişehir, Ankara, Konya and Adana in 1925 from Germany.[211]

209 Boratav, *Türkiye İktisat Tarihi: 1908–2009*, 44, 49.

210 NARA, 867.501,, July 29, 1914–May 20, 1929; Yahya Tezel, *Cumhuriyet Tarihinin İktisadi Tarihi (1923–1950)* (İstanbul: Türkiye İş Bankası Yayınları, 1st Ed., 2015), 203.

211 BCA, 30-18-1-1 / Kararlar Daire Başkanlığı (1920–1928), 14 – 48 – 15/214–32, 05.08.1925.

Since the early 1900s, companies such as *Anatolische Industrie und Handelsgesellschaft m.b.H*[212] opened branches in many cities in order to mechanize agriculture, provide farmers with loans and agricultural machinery. They even opened courses for farmers to learn how to use these machines and to practice modern agriculture. They encouraged the development of agriculture by printing brochures in Turkish. These were domestic industry incentives that would not be overlooked. These incentives paid off and both production and trade volume increased in Turkey.[213] While only 4 % of the land was made suitable for agriculture in the pre-war periods,[214] the area covered by the agricultural lands cultivated with cereals increased to 39,093,220 decares, vegetable planted areas to 1,740,403 decares, and industrial agriculture to 2,804,104 decares in 1927.[215]

Although Turkey was an agricultural country, an expert was asked from Germany in 1932 to show and teach the methods of exporting vegetables without losing their freshness.[216] This situation pointed out that technology, R&D and education are values that are at the foundation of a nation regardless of wars and instant developments. After a short time, the requests for experts gave way to the demands of the delegations and delegation requests started to come from Turkey. In order to carry out the task of establishing and organizing the Higher Agricultural Institute in Ankara, the expert German Agricultural Committee consisting of 14 members came to Turkey in the spring of 1928 and laid the foundations of the Higher Agricultural School to be opened in 1930.[217]

4.3.6. Industry and Mining

The number of industrial enterprises also increased in the young Turkish Republic. The number of industrial enterprises in Turkey increased to 65,245, the number of workers in the industry increased to 265,855, and the total horsepower used in the industry increased to 163,548.[218] Mining developments were also evident. Some of the mine outputs of 1926 are as shown in the table below.

212 It was founded in 1911 by Deutsche Bank, Deutsch-Levantinische Baumwollgeselschaff and Baumwoll-Dampfpresse – Gesselschaft. See Önsoy, *Türk-Alman İktisadi Münasebetleri,* 56.

213 Önsoy, *Türk-Alman İktisadi Münasebetleri,* 56.

214 NARA, 867.50, June 2, 1910–December 17,1929.

215 NARA, 867.501, July 29, 1914–May 20, 1929.

216 BCA, 30-18-1-2 / Kararlar Daire Başkanlığı, 28 – 37 – 2, 14.05.1932.

217 Koçak, *Türk-Alman İlişkileri (1923–1939),* 40–41.

218 NARA, 867.501, July 29, 1914–May 20, 1929.

Table 4.6. Mining Outputs in Turkey in 1926[219]

Product	**Amount**
Coal	1,222,367 tons
Lignite	12,207 tons
Copper	7,534 tons
Emery	6,060 tons
Lead	17,673 tons
Antimony	600 tons
Chrome	6,415 tons
Magnesia	38 tons
Boracite	18,360 tons
Mercury	161 bottles
Argil (clay)	57,650 tons

Source: NARA, 867.501, July 29, 1914–May 20, 1929.

Although the development rate of the industry reached a significant rate of 10.2 % in the 1923–1929 period, its share in the gross national product was only 11 % as the period average.[220] The striking point in the Republic of Turkey was the concrete actions aimed at providing the import articles with domestic production. For example, while the looms and machines required for military factories were imported,[221] the companies producing these products were asked to give internships to Turkish workers in their factories and commitments to train Turkish personnel were taken.[222] This attitude is a concrete indicator of the efforts of the young Turkish Republic to become independent even in its military factories.

219 NARA, 867.501, July 29, 1914–May 20, 1929.

220 Boratav, *Türkiye İktisat Tarihi: 1908–2009*, 51.

221 Turkey's exports to Germany also continued. For example, in 1926, Germany was Turkey's second largest dried fruit importer. See NARA, 867.50, June 2, 1910–December 17,1929.

Between 1924 and 1929, Turkey's most important export points, Italy, the USA, Germany and France, had a combined share of 60 % in Turkey's exports. Trade rates were relatively evenly split compared to the prewar period. During this period, Italy came to the fore with the efficiency of the port of Trieste. Both Italian traders and Greek traders who used to live in Turkey and settled in Italy used the port of Trieste as a transit center opening to Europe. See Yahya Tezel, *Cumhuriyet Tarihinin İktisadi Tarihi (1923–1950)*, 196.

222 BCA, 30-18-1-2 / Kararlar Daire Başkanlığı, 12–47 – 5 / 60–52, 05.07.1930.

In this section, it has been seen that the German industry was the main support of the Central Powers in the First World War. However, more importantly, it has been seen that Turkey was eager to cooperate with Germany in certain fields after the First World War. The willingness of the two allies to start their commercial activities immediately after a world war, reflects both the competence of German Industrialization in rapid recovery and Turkey's trust in German industry. The German industry, which quickly recovered after the First World War, shows that industrialization is a memory, and even if the state administrations change, if the necessary tools are there, the only thing required to be a pioneer in the global markets is organizational skill.

Epilogue

German Industrialization is not a subject that has been written about much or studied thoroughly. Unfortunately it almost does not exist in Turkish literature.

Trying to create a holistic approach to German Industrialization means embarking on a very challenging journey for the researcher. There are many components in German Industrialization that do not repeat the experiences of Britain and France (especially in banking). It will not be enough to shed light on German industrialization entirely when any of the headings or subheadings in this study is taken alone, and therefore it is necessary to examine each factor separately, both historically and geographically, and to create a common meaning from the data obtained. With this study, it has been tried to put forward a permanent answer with the aforementioned holistic approach, and it has been concluded that there are many sub-topics in the field of German Industrialization that needs be researched in detail.

As a result of our study, it has been revealed that German Industrialization cannot be attributed to a single cause. Contrary to what economic historians generally argue, the inadequacy and inaccuracy of the general view that only protectionist customs tariffs, cartelization or railway constructions caused German industrialization is one of the conclusions reached with this study. There were also some other countries with higher protective tariffs than Germany in the relevant period. When cartelization is considered, it can be seen that there were no cartelization in every sector, and there was no sector, other than three or four sectors, in which more than three-quarters of the product output was owned by the cartels. When railways are considered, there were countries that made important railway constructions such as Belgium and Russia. Therefore, it cannot be said that neither cartelization nor protective tariffs nor railway constructions alone caused German industrialization. As a conclusion of our study, it has been seen that German industrialization is an organizational process as a whole, and with this study, German industrialization, which has a very limited and fragmented place in the literature, has been revealed in an integrated way.

There is a general view that German Industrialization imitated British Industrialization. When the German and British Industrializations are compared, it is one of the conclusions reached with this study that this view, which has spread to the world with the widely translated works of names such as Karl Marx and Thorstein Veblen, especially defended by anti-capitalist and Marxist circles, is a shallow and generally wrong view. The effects of German education, original German banking models, German cartels, innovative fields such as chemistry, and Bismarck's original policies, which were examined in detail in our study, are the factors that directly separate German Industrialization from British Industrialization.

As a result of the data in our study, it was concluded that as Germany industrialized, it created a surplus and gradually increased its share in the world trade volume with its innovative products. It has been observed that one of these sectors is chemistry. Innovative products, particularly in the field of dyestuff, created new markets for Germany, offered the late industrialized Germany the chance to obtain uncompetitive markets. It is one of the results of our study that Germany, under the leadership of its innovative sectors, managed to capture a significant part of the trade volume in Europe quite quickly until the eve of the First World War, by making good use of its modern equipment, cheap and qualified workforce and sufficient raw materials. The Turkish-German rapprochement took place in such a period. In such a period where political alliances are constantly changing and every state in Europe feels insecure, military relations have undoubtedly been one of the most important relations.

In the light of the arms trade data in our study, it has been seen that the influence of the German school and the products of the German defense industry in the Ottoman Empire was realized through military relations. According to our findings, the most important factor in the entry of the German defense industry into the Ottoman army was the German military delegations and Kaiser Wilhelm II's individual influence. Within our study, it has been seen that with the effects of both the delegations and the Kaiser Wilhelm II, the Ottoman army was equipped with German defense industry equipment in a short time. With the support of German Empire, Krupp and Mauser companies achieved a large volume of trade in the Ottoman market.

In Turkish-German relations, it was seen that military relations became a tool for economic developments in a short time, and these relations began to form into an alliance in a short time with the effects of railway concessions, exports of defense industry products and active actions of military advisors. As a result of this study, it was concluded that the Turkish-German relations before the First World War developed based on mutual needs, not within the framework of domination by any side.

It is necessary to mention the existence of different views and different theories about the reasons for the rapidly developing Turkish-German relations. The view advocated by writers such as Rosa Luxemburg and Lothar Rathmann, that the German Empire established its relations with the Ottoman Empire with the aim of colonizing the Ottoman Empire, has been ingrained in Turkish literature in general. However, it has been seen in our study that Turkish-German relations were not directed only by German Empire in the period from the arrival of the German military delegations to the alliance in the First World War, the demands were mostly created by the Ottoman Empire's own will. Within the scope of our study, it was concluded that the Ottoman Empire followed a strategic balance policy behind each demand. Similarly, the common view that Germany dragged the Ottoman Empire into the First World War seems to be wrong. Because, within our study, it was seen that the Ottoman Empire made offers to both British Empire and France Empire to make alliances. However these proposals were not accepted. Moreover, the proposals presented to the German Empire were rejected at the first stage too. It is one of the conclusions of this study that both the view that German Empire dragged the Ottoman Empire into the First World War and the view that German Empire saw the Ottoman Empire as a future colony are not true.

Another question sought to be answered within our study is whether the German Empire saw the Ottoman Empire only as a target market or a geography to be colonized, or as a future ally. When the Ottoman Empire's declaration of jihad in the First World War, Enver Pasha's Caucasus and Cemal Pasha's Egypt invasions are taken into consideration, it is concluded that German Empire wanted to play a chess game in the East. Moreover, when the German Empire's support for Indian rebels taken into consideration too, it can be concluded that the German Empire needed a strong ally who could weaken Britain with the problems in India and in Egypt. For this reason, in our opinion, German Empire's need for a strong Ottoman Empire is more realistic than the claim that German Empire only saw the Ottoman Empire as a target market. In fact, German Empire did not prevent the Ottoman Empire from producing its own weapons even before the First World War. Ottoman soldiers were trained in the German Empire, a Mauser rifle factory was established in the Ottoman lands, Mauser rifle parts and cartridges were manufactured in the Ottoman Empire. One can say that the German Empire was a supporter. With this study, it has been proven that the German-Ottoman alliance is far beyond an industrial country – target market relations.

This alliance continued along a similar line during the First World War and became a strategic alliance. In our study, it has been seen that Turkish-German relations were based on mutual support in the first years of the war. While raw materials were shipped from the Ottoman Empire to the German Empire, weapons, ammunition, military personnel and money came to the Ottoman Empire from the German Empire. However, the regular support in the first years was disrupted in the following years due to the fact that the war lasted longer than expected by both the German Empire and the Ottoman Empire, and with the increase in blockades, both empires became lonely and had difficulty even providing their own needs. However, one of the results of the 1917 secret alliance renewal agreements mentioned in our study is that both sides were willing to extend the alliances and act jointly after the war, even if the conditions deteriorated. With the secret alliance renewal agreements in 1917, it was signed that the Turkish soldiers would receive the same training as the German soldiers and that the soldiers of both empires should have the same equipment. All these show that the Turkish-German alliance was a strategic alliance between equal states. The renewal agreements, which include benefiting from the victory together, are a separate indicator of this and a detail emphasized in our study. On the other hand, in the arguments that Germany viewed the Ottoman Empire as a country to be colonized, the words of German persons with a certain status are always referenced. It is one of the results of our study that Germany did not make any serious attempts or demands to settle its citizens in the Ottoman lands.

Although the Central Powers were the losing side, the possibility of the reccuring Turkish-German alliance after the war was also seen as a threat by the Allies. The purpose in the certain articles of the Armistice of Mudros, Treaty of Versailles and Treaty of Sèvres was to cut the relations between Germany and the Ottoman Empire. One of the reasons why the Allies gave importance to this issue was undoubtedly the fact that the German-Turkish alliance would become more strategic with the development of technology and transportation. Another was the fact that the Turkish-German alliance could be revived at the slightest contact, especially through entrenched military relations. The fact that, after the war, retired German officers were teaching in Turkish military academies, German engineers were employed in Turkey, German experts were invited to provide benefits in many areas that Turkey needed were also indicators of this. Although administrative structures changed after the First World War, ingrained basic structures such as the military did not change at the same pace. As a result of our study, it has been seen that Turkish-German relations developed rapidly again with the contact established after the Treaty of Lausanne. The underlying reason for this was the desire to develop the relations established with the German Industrialization, as well as the penetration of the German school into Turkey. The process of Kayseri Aircraft Factory described in detail in our study, is a very valuable indicator of the importance that both states attached to Turkish-German relations.

In our opinion, despite the unsuccesful alliance in the First World War, the continuation of the trust in German technology and industry after the war is an indicator of Turkey's trust in the basic components of German Industrialization. With this study, there is also an answer to how Germany rapidly re-industrialized after the First World War. In our study, it has been seen that German industrialization was built on important norms such as education, discipline, organizational skills, innovation based on research and development, and experience of cartelization. Even though the political administrations changed, this perception in the industry remained, and that after the war, the factories only needed demands and obligations related to the agreements to start production. In our study, the details of these norms were given, and the rapid industrialization of Germany in the post-war period was conveyed to the reader with examples such as Ruhrlade and the commercial volume data of the postwar period. One of the factors making this study unique is that it reveals that the German industrialization, which is thought to have taken place all of a sudden, was a long process and had a memory. That memory was also one of the main reasons for the rapid development after the Second World War.

Within the results of our study; It is possible to say that German industrialization changed the existing political and commercial balance in Europe, pushed European states to seek new balances, and this process brought Germany and the Ottoman Empire closer together. However, with our study, contrary to the existing literature, it has been seen that Germany was not the party that disrupted the status quo. It has been seen that Britain and France, which saw German industrialization as a threat, ignored the problems between them and formed a bloc against Germany and the Ottoman Empire, they even made alliances with Russia. This new order formed at the beginning of the 20th century brought Germany and the Ottoman Empire closer together politically. However, this time, Britain and France accepted this rapprochement as an even greater threat. The scenarios of the merger of German industry and Ottoman oil, the blending of German locomotives and the strategic Ottoman geography created a new power focus that had to be destroyed by the Allies. These political blocs were one of the main causes of World War I. On the other hand, for the Ottoman Empire, who hadn't been making alliances with Western states since the Crimean War and whose territories were invaded frequently by the Western states, German – Ottoman alliance was a strong support. It has been seen with the secret agreements made during the war that the development of the whole Ottoman geography was aimed after the war. It is possible to say that the new world order aimed by both Germany and the Ottoman Empire was Ottoman-German centered.

Bibliography

Archive Documents

1. German Archive Documents

Akten zur Deuscthen Auswärtigen Politik 1918–1945 (ADAP)

Serie A: 1918–1925, Band IV, (1 Oktober 1920 bis 30 April 1921), Göttingen, 1986.

ADAP, "Gesandtschaftsrat von Dirksen (Warschau) an das Auswärtige Amt" Nr. 74, 8.12.1920, (K 1809/K 456 623–27).

Serie A: 1918–1925, Band IX, (16 November bis 6 April 1924), Göttingen, 1991.

ADAP, "Der Gesandte in Bukarest Freytag (z. Z. Konstantinopel) an das Auswärtige Amt" Nr. 192, 8.3.1924, (4578/E 174 618–22).

ADAP, "Aufzeichnung des Ministeraldirektors von Schubert", Nr. 209, 15.03.1924, (4578/E 174 632–33).

ADAP, "Aufzeichnung des Ministerialdirektors von Schubert" Nr. 203, 13.04.1924, (4578/E 174 663–64).

ADAP, "Aufzeichnung des Ministerialdirektors von Schubert", Nr. 173, 28.02.1924, (4578/E 174 668–69).

ADAP, "Der Reichsminister des Auswärtigen Stresemann and den Gesandten in Bukarest Freytag" Nr. 88, 10.01.1924, (L101/L 016 287–91).

ADAP, "Der Staatssekretär des Auswärtigen Amts Freiherr von Maltzan an die Botschatt in London" Nr. 248, 6.4.1924, (3088/D 625 480–81).

Serie A: 1918–1925, Band XIII, (27 April bis 13 August 1925), Göttingen, 1995.

ADAP, "Der Gesandte in Konstantinopel Botschafter Nadolny an das Auswärtige Amt " Nr. 52, 14.95.1925, (9297/H 256 130).

ADAP, "Aufzeichnung des Geheimen Legationstrats de Haas" Nr. 217, 20.07.1925, (K 150/K015 941–42)

Serie A: 1918–1925, Band XIV, (14 August bis 30 November 1925), Göttingen, 1995.

ADAP, "Aufzeichnung des Konsuls Ziemke" Nr. 258, 23.11.1925, (K 150/K 016 079–80).

ADAP,"Der Reichsminister der Finanzen von Schlieben an den Reichsminister des Auswärtigen Stresemann", Nr. 182, 24.10.1925, (K 150/K 016 071–72).

ADAP, "Der Gesandte in Konstantinopel Boschafter Nadolny an das Auswärtige Amt" Nr. 31, 25.8.1925, (K 150/K 015 981–84).

ADAP, "Der Staatssekretär des Auswärtigen Amts von Schubert an die Gesandschaft in Konstantinopel" Nr. 70, 20.9.1925, (K 152/K 016 952–53).

Serie B: 1925–1933, Band III, (Dezember 1925 bis Dezember 1926), Göttingen, 1968.

ADAP, "Aufzeichnung über die Türkischen Rüstungspläne" Nr. 14, (4580/E 174 990–5 004).

ADAP, "Der Botschafter in Konstantinopel an das Auswärtige Amt" Nr. 136, 21.05.1926, (K150/K 06 166–67).

ADAP, "Der Botschafter in Konstantinopel Nadolny an das Auswärtige Amt" Nr. 194, 18.09.1926, (K150/K 016 466–68).

ADAP, "Undatierte Aufzeichnung des Vortragenden Legationsrats Freiherr von Richthofen" Nr. 244, (K150/K016 585–86).

ADAP, "Aufzeichnung ohne Unterschrift" Nr. 241, 03.12.1926, (4578/E174 801–02).

ADAP, "Undatierte Aufzeichnung ohne Untershcrift – Aufzeichnung Über die Türkischen Rütungspläne" Nr. 14, (4580/E 174 990–5 004).

ADAP, "Der Botschafter in Konstantinopel Nadolny an das Auswärtige Amt" Nr. 215, (K152/K017 071–72).

Serie B: 1925–1933, Band VII, (1 Oktober 1927 bis 31 Dezember 1927), Göttingen, 1974.

ADAP, "Aufzeichnung des Vortragenden Legationstrats Freiherr von Richtofen" Nr. 35, 10.01.1924, (L101/L 016 484–86).

Serie B: 1925–1933, Band XIV, (1 Januar 1930 bis 30 April 1930), Göttingen, 1980.

ADAP, "Auzeichnung des Ministerialdirektors de Haas " Nr. 189, 8.3.1924, (2980/D 584 137–41).

2. American Archive Documents

National Archives and Records Administration (NARA)

NARA, Decimal File 867.00, Internal Affairs Of States, Turkey, Political Affairs., January 24th, 1910–February 27, 1913, 10044/287, Gale Document No: GALE|SC5111491762.

NARA, Decimal File 867.501, Internal Affairs Of States, Economic Matters., Turkey, Statistics, General., July 29, 1914–May 20, 1929, Gale Document No: GALE|SC5111526563.

NARA, Decimal File 867.501, Internal Affairs Of States, Economic Matters., Turkey, Statistics, General., July 29, 1914–May 20, 1929, Gale Document NO: GALE|SC5111526563.

NARA, Internal Affairs Of States, Turkey, Political Affairs., January 31, 1913–October 12, 1914, 867.00/493, Gale Document No: GALE|SC5111497457.

NARA, Decimal File 867.78, Internal Affairs Of States, Turkey, Street Railway, August 31, 1910, 867.784/80, Gale Document No: GALE|SC5111509406.

NARA, Decimal File 867.00, Internal Affairs Of States, Turkey, Political Affairs., January 31, 1913–October 12, 1914, 86700/490, 21 February 1913.

NARA, Internal Affairs Of States, Turkey, Political Affairs., September 26, 1914–November 6, 1917. September 26, 1914–November 6, 1917, 867.00/7950, 5 June 1917.

NARA, Decimal File 867.501, Internal Affairs Of States, Economic Matters., Turkey, Statistics, General., July 29, 1914–May 20, 1929, Gale Document Number: GALE|SC5111526563.

NARA, Central File: Decimal File 867.50, Internal Affairs Of States, Turkey, Economic Matters., June 2, 1910–December 17,1929, Gale Document Number: GALE|SC5111519615.

NARA, Central File: Decimal File 867.501, Internal Affairs Of States, Economic Matters., Turkey, Statistics, General., July 29, 1914–May 20, 1929 Gale Document Number: GALE|SC5111526563.

NARA, Central File: Decimal File 867.50, Internal Affairs Of States, Turkey, Economic Matters., June 2, 1910–December 17,1929, Gale Document Number: GALE|SC5111519615.

3. Turkish Archive Documents

The Directorate of Ottoman Archives (BOA)

A.MKT.MHM, 460/18, H-06-06-1290.

DH.EUM.2.Şb, 1 – 25, H-27-09-1332.

DH.EUM.5.Şb, 1 – 32, H-14-10-1332.

DH.İ.UM.EK, 18 – 109, H-28-10-1334.

DH.İ.UM.EK, 19 – 55, H-07-11-1334.

DH.İ.UM, 20 – 2, H-07-01-1337.

DH.İ.UM, 20 – 8, H-19-07-1336.

İrade Mabeyn-i Hümayun, 2-19 H-28-04-1328.

İ.RSM, 16 – 18-2, H-07-05-1320.

MV- 202 – 19, H-18-07-1334.

MV, 204 – 24, H-29-01-1335.

MV, 205 – 109, H-30-03-1335.

MV- 208 – 28, H-28-07-1335.
MV, 210 – 99, H-28-02-1336.
MV, 207 – 97, H-12-06-1335.
TŞR.HL, 1 – 96, R-17-07-1330.
Y.EE, 82-1, H-28-06-1310.
Y..MTV., 296–69, H-11-02-1325.
Y.PRK.HR., 3-14-1, H-10-07-1295.
Y.PRK. TŞF, 5-94, H-20-07-1317.
Y. PRK. HR, 6-6-2, H-11-02-1299.
Y. PRK. BŞK, 23 – 102, H-14-03-1309.
Y.PRK. TNF, 1-61, H-24-10-1303.
Y.PRK. AZJ, 1-75, H-07-08-1294.
Y.PRK.MM, 1 – 89, H-05-01-1316.
Y..PRK.NMH, 8 – 11, H-26-07-1317.
Y.PRK.ŞH, 3-71, H-13-09-1308.
Y.EE., 7/5, H-02.02.1299.
Y.EE., 7/6, H-02.02.1299.
Y.PRK.ESA, 6/61, H-25.07.1304.
Y.PRK.NMH, 4/42, H-08.01.1307.

The Directorate of Republican Archives (BCA)

30-18-1-1/ Kararlar Daire Başkanlığı, 5 – 16 – 10, 10.05.1922.
30-18-1-2 / Kararlar Daire Başkanlığı, 17 – 3 – 12.
30-18-1-2 / Kararlar Daire Başkanlığı, 17 – 1 – 12, 07.01.1931.
30-18-1-1 / Kararlar Daire Başkanlığı, 22-74-15, 12.12.1926.
30-18-1-1/ Kararlar Daire Başkanlığı, 23-7-15, 13.02.1927.
30-18-1-2 / Kararlar Daire Başkanlığı, 2 – 17 – 28 / 243–39, 06.03.1929.
30-18-1-1 / Kararlar Daire Başkanlığı (1920–1928), 14 – 48 – 15/214–32, 05.08.1925.
30-18-1-2 / Kararlar Daire Başkanlığı, 28 – 37 – 2, 14.05.1932.
30-18-1-2 / Kararlar Daire Başkanlığı (1928-), 12 – 47 – 5 / 60–52, 05.07.1930.

Books

Abrams, Lynn. *Bismarck and the German Empire 1871–1918*. New York: Routledge, 2nd Ed., 2006 .

Akpınar, Hasan Aslan. *Türkiye'de Milli Sanayinin Mimarlarından Nurullah Esat Sumer*. İstanbul: Türkiye İş Bankası Yayınları, 2nd Ed., 2020.

Aksakal, Mustafa. *Harb-i Umumi Eşiğinde - Osmanlı Devleti Son Savaşına Nasıl Girdi?*. İstanbul: İstanbul Bilgi Üniversitesi Yayınları, 2nd Ed., 2018.

Aksoy, Suat. *Kapitalizmin Lokomotifi Demiryolları*. İstanbul: Sav Sosyal Araştırmalar Vakfı, 2016.

Akyıldız, Ali. *Sürgün Sefir Sadullah Paşa*. İstanbul: Türkiye İş Bankası Kültür Yayınları, 2011.

Alkan, Necmettin et al. (ed.). *Savaşanların Gözüyle Türk-Alman İttifakı (1914–1918)*. İstanbul: Kronik Kitap, 2018.

Aranov, Lev et al. "Toward the Prehistory of the Protokols". *The Global Impact of the Protocols of the Elders of Zion: A Century-Old Myth*. ed. Esther Webman. 27–43. Abingdon: Routledge, 2011.

Aydın, Salim. *Balkanların Acı Tarihi*. İstanbul: Yeditepe Yayınevi, 2013.

Beiser, Frederick C. *Enlıghtenment, Revolutıon, and Romantıcısm the Genesis of Modern German Political Thought, 1790–1800*. London: Harvard University Press, 3rd Ed., 1992.

Belge, Murat. *Militarist Modernleşme - Almanya, Japonya ve Türkiye*. İstanbul: İletişim Yayınları, 2014.

Beşikçi, Mehmet. "On Yıllık Harp ve Topyekün Seferberlik". *Osmanlı Askeri Tarihi - Kara, Deniz ve Hava Kuvvetleri 1792–1914*. ed. Gültekin Yıldız. İstanbul: Timaş Yayınları, 2013.

Bonner, Thomas Neville. *Becoming A Physician: Medical Education in Britain, France, Germany, and the United States, 1750–1945*. New York: Oxford University Press, 1995.

Boratav, Korkut. *Türkiye İktisat Tarihi 1908–2009*. Ankara: İmge Kitabevi, 22nd Ed., 2016.

Borchardt, Knut. *The Fontana Economic History of Europe – The Industrial Revolution in Germany 1700–1914*. ed. Carlo M. Cippola, trans. George Hammersley. London and Glasgow: Collins Clear-Type Press, 1972.

Böer, Ingeborg et al. *Berlin'den Türkler Geçti 1871–1945*. trans. Can Uralcan. İstanbul: İleri Yayınları, 2012.

Braun, H. J. *The German Economy in the Twentieth Century*. London: Routledge, 1990.

Breuilly, John. *Avusturya, Prusya ve Almanya'nın Oluşumu 1806–1871*. trans. Ali Selman. İstanbul: İletişim Yayınları, 2nd Ed., 2020.

Cebeci, Mehmet. "II. Abdülhamid Döneminde Almanya'ya Gönderilen Askeri Öğrenciler". ed. Altunkaya et al. *Türk-Alman İlişkilerine Farklı Disiplinlerden Bakış*. Konya: Palet Yayınları, 2019.

Cemal Paşa. *Anılarım (1913–1922)*. ed. Fahri Parin. İstanbul: Paraf Yayınları, 1st Ed., 2010.

Chandler, David G. *The Campaigns of Napoleon*. New York City: The MacMillan Company, 1966.

Christensen, Peter. *Germany and the Ottoman Railways – Art, Empire, and Infrastructure*. Singapore: Yale University Press, 2017.

Claphamm, J. H. *The Economic Development of France and Germany 1815–1914*. London: Cambridge at the University Press, 1921.

Clark, Christopher. *Iron Kingdom – The Rise and Downfall of Prussia 1600–1947*. London: Penguin Books, 2007.

Clark, Christopher. *Uyurgezerler*. trans. Cem Demirkan. İstanbul: Pegasus Yayınları, 2017.

Çolak, Mustafa. "Alman Subaylarının Bakışına Göre Ermeni Techiri". ed. Necmettin Alkan et al. *Savaşanların Gözüyle Türk – Alman İttifakı*. İstanbul: Kronik Kitap, 2018.

Çolak, Mustafa. *Komitenin Kahramanı - Enver Paşa*. İstanbul: Yeditepe Yayınevi, 3rd Ed., 2019.

Dietmar, Petzina. *Die deutsche Wirtschaft in der Zwischenkriegszeit*. Stuttgart: Steiner, 1977.

Dipper, Christoph. *Die Bauernbefreiuna in Deutschland. 1790–1850*. Stuttgart: Kohlhammer, 1980.

Ediger, Volkan Ş. *Osmanlı'da Neft ve Petrol*. Ankara: ODTÜ Yayıncılık, 3rd Ed., 2007.

Eley, Geoff. "Bismarckian Germany". *Modern Germany Reconsidered 1870–1945*. ed. Gordon Martel. 1–33, London: Routledge, 1992.

Engels, Friedrich. *Almanya'da Devrim ve Karşı Devrim*. trans. Kenan Somer. Ankara: Sol Yayınları, 1975.

Engin, Vahdettin. *Rumeli Demiryolları*. İstanbul: Eren Yayıncılık, 1993.

Engin, Vahdettin. *Asayiş – Sultan II. Abdülhamid'in İç Güvenlik Politikası*. İstanbul: Yeditepe Yayınevi, 2013.

Engin, Vahdettin. *II. Abdülhamid ve Dış Politika*. İstanbul: Yeditepe Yayınevi, 6th Ed., 2017.

Falkus, M. E. *Rusya'nın Endüstrileşmesi 1700–1914*. trans. Alaeddin Şenel. Ankara: V Yayınları, 1986.

Fenske, Hans. (ed.). *Quellen zur Deutschen Revolution 1848–49*. Darmstadt: Wissenschaftliche Buchgesellschaft, 1996.

Ferguson, Niall. *Paranın Yükselişi – Dünyanın Finansal Tarihi*. trans. Barış Pala. İstanbul: Yapı Kredi Yayınları, 6th Ed., 2018.

Ferguson, Niall. *İmparatorluk-Britanya'nın Modern Dünyayı Biçimlendirişi*. trans. Nurettin Elhüseyni. İstanbul: Yapı Kredi Yayınları, 5th Ed., 2019.

Ferguson, Niall. *Paper and Iron*. Cambridge: Cambridge University Press, 2002.

Field, A. J. " The Relative Stability of German and American Industrial Growth, 1880–1913: A Comparative Analysis". In W. H. Schröder, & R. Spree (Eds.), *Historische Konjunktivforschung*, 208–233. Stuttgart: Klett-Cotta, 1980. https://nbn-resolving.org/urn:nbn:de:0168-ssoar-340214. Accessed: 19.01.2021.

Frambach, Hans A. "Great Nations at Peril – Rise and fall of Prussia". *Great Nations at Peril*. ed. Jürgen Backhaus, 21–37. Switzerland: Springer International Publishing, 2015.

Fröhlich, Michael. *Imperialismus. Deustsche Kolonial und Weltpolitik 1880–1914*. München: Deutscher Taschenbuch Verlag, Originalausg Edition, 1994.

Fulbrook, Mary. *Almanya'nın Kısa Tarihi*. trans. Sabri Gürses. İstanbul: Boğaziçi Üniversitesi Yayınları, 3rd Ed., 2017.

Gencer, Mustafa. *Jöntürk Modernizmi ve Alman Ruhu*. İstanbul: İletişim Yayınları, 3rd Ed., 2015.

Genç, Mehmet. *Devlet ve Ekonomi*. İstanbul: Ötüken Neşriyat A.Ş, 14th Ed., 2017.

Gerschenkron, Alexander. *Bread and Democracy in Germany*. Berkeley: University of California Press, 1943.

Gerschenkron, Alexander. *Economic Backwardness in Historical Perspective – A Book of Essays*. Cambridge, Massachussets: The Belknap Press of Harvard University Press, 1962.

Geyikdağı, Necla V. *Osmanlı Devleti'nde Yabancı Sermaye 1854–1914*. İstanbul: Hil Yayın, 2008.

Grüßhaber, Gerhard. *The 'German Spirit' in the Ottoman and Turkish Army, 1908–1938*. Oldenbourg: de Gruyter, 2018.

Gunlicks, Arthur B. *The Länder and German federalism*. Manchester: Manchester University Press, 2003.

Gülboy, Burak Samih. "İngiltere ile Almanya Arasındaki Donanma Rekabeti ve Büyük Güç Olma Paradoksu". *100. Yılında Birinci Dünya Savaşı ve Mirası*, ed. Halil Çetin vd. 1/27–42. Çanakkale: Çanakkale Valiliği, 2015.

Hardach, Karl W. *Die Bedeutung wirtschaftlicher Faktören bei der Weidereinführung der Eisen und Getreidezölle in Deustchland 1879*. Berlin: Duncker & Humblot, 1967.

Henderson, William Otto. *The Industrial Revolution on the Continent – Germany, France, Russia 1800–1914*. London: Frank Cass & Co. Ltd., Sec. Ed.,1967.

Henderson, William Otto. *Zollverein*. New York: Routledge, 2018.

Higonnet, Patrice L. R. vd. *Favorites of Fortune: Technology, Growth, and Economic Development Since the Industrial Revolution*. Cambridge: Harvard University Press, 1991.

Hobsbawm, E. J. *Sanayi ve İmparatorluk*. trans. Abdullah Ersoy. Ankara: Dost Kitabevi Yayınları, 2013.

Hobsbawm, Eric. *Devrim Çağı 1789–1848*. trans. Bahadır Sina Şener. Ankara: Dost Kitabevi, 8th Ed., 2016.

Hoffmann, W. G. *The Growth of Industrial Economies*. Manchaster: Manchester University Press, 1958.

Hopkirk, Peter. *On Secret Service East of Constantinople*. Oxford: Oxford University Press, 1995.

Huber, E. R. (ed.). *Dokumente zur deutschen Verfassungsgeschichte 1803–1850*. 1 Cilt. Stuttgart: Kohlhammer, 3rd Ed., 1978.

Iggers, G. Georg. *The German Conception of History*. Connecticut: Wesleyan University Press, 1983.

Jäckh, Ernst. *Balkan Harbinden Sonra Şarkta Almanya*. İstanbul: Yeditepe Yayınları, 2021.

Jäckh, Ernst. *Yükselen Hilal*. İstanbul: Temel Yayınları, 1999.

John Röhl C. G. John. *From Bismarck to Hitler*. London: Longman Publishing Group, 1970.

Johnson, A. Jeffrey. "The academic-industrial symbiosis in German chemical research,1905–1939". *The German Chemical Industry in the 20th Century, Chemist and Chemistry Series*. ed. John E. Lesch, vol. 18, 15–57. Dordrecht: Springer-Science+Business Media, B.V, 2000.

Karabekir, Kazım. *Tarihte ve Abdülhamid Döneminde Türk-Alman İlişkileri*. İstanbul: Truva Yayınları, 2021.

Karaca, Taha Niyazi. *Büyük Oyun – İngiltere Başbakanı Gladstone'un Osmanlı'yı Yıkma Planı*. İstanbul: Timaş Yayınları, 4th Ed., 2018.

Karbi, Bilge. *Gölgedeki İttifak: Harb-i Umumi'de Osmanlı-Habsburg İktisadi İlişkileri*. İstanbul: Libra Yayınları, 2021.

Karl-Heinz Manegold. *Universitaet, Technische Hochschule und Industrie. Bin Beitrag zur Emanzipation der Technik im 19. Jahrhundert*. Berlin: Duncker and Humblot, 1969.

Keyder, Çağlar. *Dünya Ekonomisi İçinde Türkiye (1923–1929)*. Ankara: Yurt Yayınevi, 1982.

Keynes, John Maynard. *The Economic Consequences of the Peace*. San Diego: Brace and Howe, 1920.

Kıray, Emine. *Osmanlı'da Ekonomik Yapı ve Dış Borçlar*. İstanbul: İletişim Yayınları, 5th Ed., 2015.

Kış, Salih. *Osmanlı Ordusunda Alman Ekolü Von der Goltz Paşa (1883–1895)*. Konya: Palet Yayınları, 2017.

Kiaulehn, Walther. *Demir Melekler*. İstanbul: Remzi Kitabevi, 1971.

Kirkaldy, Adam Willis. *The History and Economics of Transport*. London: Sir I. Pitman & Sons, 1920.

Koçak, Cemil. *Türk-Alman İlişkileri (1923–1939)*. Ankara: Türk Tarih Kurumu Yayınları, 2nd Ed., 2013.

Koloğlu, Orhan. *Prusya'dan Enverland'a ve Günümüze Türk-Alman Tarihi*. İstanbul: Tarihçi Yayınevi, 2018.

Kula, Onur Bilge. *Alman Kültüründe Türk İmgesi I*. Ankara: Gündoğan Yayınları, 1992.

Kurmuş, Orhan. *Emperyalizmin Türkiye'ye Girişi*. İstanbul: Yordam Kitap, 2007.

Kurtbek, Seyfi. *Harp ve Ekonomi*. İstanbul: İnsel Kitabevi, 1942.

Landes, David S. *The Unbound Prometheus*. Cambridge: Cambridge University Press, 1969.

Larcher, M.. *Büyük Harpte Türk Harbi*. Vol 1-2-3. trans. and ed. Mehmet Nihad. İstanbul: Ötüken Neşriyat, 2018.

Lehmann, Hartmut – Lehmann, Silke. *Das Nationalitätenproblem in Österreich: 1848–1918*. Göttingen: Vandenhoeck & Ruprecht, 1973.

Liefmann, Robert. *Kartelle und Trusts und die Weiterbildung der volkswirtschaftlichen Organisation*. Stutgart: Moritz, 1922.

Ludendorff, Erich. *Birinci Dünya Savaşı'nda Gördüklerim ve Yaşadıklarım*. ed. Asiye Yıldırım. İstanbul: Dün Bugün Yarın Yayınları, 2014.

Lutz, Heinrich. *Zwischen Habsburg und Preussen. Deutschland 1815–1866*. Berlin: Im Siedler Verlag, 1985.

Luxemburg, Rosa. *Die Krise der Sozial Demokratie*. Grafrath: Boer Verlag, 2019.

MacGregor, Neil. *Germany-Memories of a Nation*. Great Britain: Penguin Books, 2016.

Maillet, Jean. *18. Yüzyıldan Bugüne İktisadi Olayların Evrimi*. İstanbul: Remzi Kitabevi, 1983.

Marx, Karl – Engels, Friedrich. *The German Ideology*. New York: Prometheus Books, 1998.

Marx, Karl. *Das Kapital - Kritik der politischen Oekonomie*. Hamburg: Verlag von Otto Meissner, 1867.

McMeekin, Sean. *Berlin – Bağdat Demiryolu*. trans. Azize F. Çakır. İstanbul: Picus Yayınları, 1st Ed., 2012.

Menand, Louis (ed.) vd. *The Rise of the Research University*. Chicago: University of Chicago Press, 2017.

Mete, Ali Serdar. *Türk Mavzeri*. İstanbul: Doğu Kütüphanesi, 2022.

Milward, Alan S. – S. B. Saul. *The Economic Development of Continental Europe 1780–1870*. London: George Allen & Unwin, 1973.

Moore, Barrington. *Injustice*. London: The Macmıllan Press, 1978.

Naszádos, Zsófia. "The Involvement of the State in the German Economy". *Seeking the Best Master*. ed. Miklós Szanyi. pp.79–100, Budapest: Central European University Press, 2010.

Nipperdey, Thomas. *Deutsche Geschichte 1800–1866: Bürgerwelt und starker Staat*. Münih: C.H.Beck, 1983.

Ortaylı, İlber. *Osmanlı İmparatorluğu'nda Alman Nüfuzu*. İstanbul: İletişim Yayınları, 6th Ed., 2004.

Osmanlı Sanayii 1913–1915 Yılları Sanayi İstatistiki. Tarihi İstatistikler Dizisi vol. 4 (ed. A. Gündüz Ökçün), Ankara: TC. Başbakanlık Devlet İstatistik Enstitüsü, 1997.

Önsoy, Rifat. *Türk-Alman İktisadi Münasebetleri (1871–1914)*. İstanbul: Enderun Yayınları, 1982.

Östling, Johan. *Humboldt and the Modern German University – An Intellectual History*. trans. Lena Olsson. Lund: Lund University Press, 2018.

Özkan, Gencer. "Türkiye'de Cumhuriyet Dönemi Ordusunda Prusya Etkisi". *Türkiye'de Ordu, Devlet ve Güvenlik Siyaseti*. ed. Evren Balta Paker et al., 175–222. İstanbul: İstanbul Bilgi Üniversitesi Yayınları, 2010.

Pamuk, Şevket. *Osmanlı Ekonomisinde Bağımlılık ve Büyüme, 1820–1913*. İstanbul: Türkiye İş Bankası Kültür Yayınları, 2nd Ed., 2020.

Pamuk, Şevket. *Osmanlı-Türkiye İktisadi Tarihi 1500–1914*. İstanbul: İletişim Yayınları, 11th Ed., 2017.

Parker, Geoffrey. *Askeri Devrim – Batı'nın Yükselişinde Askeri Yenilikler 1500–1800*. trans. Tuncay Zorlu. İstanbul: Küre Yayınları, 2nd Ed., 2018.

Parker, Geoffrey. *Cambridge Savaş Tarihi*. trans. Füsun Tayanç; Tunç Tayanç. İstanbul: Türkiye İş Bankası Kültür Yayınları, 2nd Ed., 2014.

Parvus Efendi. *Cihan Harbine Doğru Türkiye*. İstanbul: Ayrıntı Yayınları, 2013.

Parvus Efendi. *Türkiye'nin Mali Tutsaklığı*. İstanbul: May Yayınları, 1977.

Piketty, Thomas. *Yirmi Birinci Yüzyılda Kapital.* trans. Handa Koçak. İstanbul: Türkiye İş Bankası Kültür Yayınları, 2014.

Rathmann, Lothar. *Alman Emperyalizminin Türkiye'ye Girişi.* trans. Ragıp Zaralı. İstanbul: Gözlem Yayınları, Türkiye, 1976.

Reddy Prassada. "The Evolving Role of Universities in Economic Development: The Case of University-Industry Linkages" *Universites in Transition*, ed. Bo Göransson-Claes Brundenius, 25–49. Ottawa: Springer, 2011.

Resmi Ahmed. *Ahmed Resmi Efendi'nin Viyana ve Berlin Sefaretnameleri.* İstanbul: Tercüman 1001 Eser, 1980.

Riesser, J. *The German Great Banks and Their Concentration in connection with The Economic Development of Germany.* Washington: Government Printing Office, 1911.

Ritter, Gerhard A. *Das Deutsche Kaiserreich 1871–1914: Ein historisches Lesebuch.* Göttingen: Vadenhoeck & Ruprecht, 1992.

Rohrbach, Paul. *Der deutsche Gedanke in der Welt.* Leipzig: Karl Robert Langewiesche, 1912.

Rosenberg, Hans. *Grosse Depression und Bismarckzeit: Wirtschaftsablauf: Gesellschaft und Politik in Mitteleuropa.* Berlin: Walter de Gruyter & Co, 1967.

Royal Historical Society. *British Envoys to Germany 1816–1866: Volume 1, 1816–1829.* ed. Sabine Freitag - Peter Wende. London: Cambridge University Press, 2000.

Said Halim Paşa. *Osmanlı İmparatorluğu ve Dünya Savaşı.* trans. Fatih Yücel. İstanbul: Kronik Kitap, 2nd Ed., 2019.

Sanders, Liman von. *Türkiye'de Beş Yıl.* trans. Eşref Bengi Özbilen. İstanbul, Türkiye İş Bankası Kültür Yayınları, 4th Ed., 2016.

Satan, Ali, *100 Soruda I. Dünya Savaşı.* İstanbul: Yazıgen Yayınevi, 2017.

Satan, Ali. *100 Soruda Milli Mücadele.* İstanbul: Timaş Yayınları, 2018.

Satan, Ali. *Irak'ta İngiliz İşgal Yönetimi 1914–1918 - İngiltere Devlet Arşivi Raporu.* İstanbul: Tarihçi Kitabevi Yayınları, 2016.

Satan, Ali. *İngiliz Yıllık Raporları'nda Türkiye 1920.* İstanbul: Tarihçi Kitabevi Yayınları, 2010.

Schmoch, Ulrich. "Germany: The role of Universities in the Learning Economy". *Universites in Transition.* ed. Bo Göransson-Claes Brundenius, 25–49. Ottawa: Springer, 2011.

Schmoller, Guftav von. *Zur Geſchichte der deutſchen Kleingewerbe im 19. Jahrhundert. Statiſtiſche und nationalökonomiſche Unterſuchungen.* Halle: Verlag der Buchhandlung des Waiſenhauſes, 1870.

Schöllgen, Gregor. *Imperialismus und Gleichgewicht: Deutschland, England und die orientalische Frage 1871–1914.* Münih: Oldenbourg, 1984.

Seshadri, B. *Industrialisation and Regional Development*. New Delhi: Concept Publishing Company, 1991.

Shaw, Stanford J. *Birinci Dünya Savaşı'nda Osmanlı İmparatorluğu - Savaşa Giriş*. Ankara: Türk Tarih Kurumu, 2014.

Soy, H. Bayram. "Birinci Dünya Savaşı Osmanlı Devleti'ni Parçalamak İçin mi Yapıldı? Savaşın Çıkış Sebeplerine Osmanlı Devleti Bağlamında Yeniden Bir Bakış". *100. Yılında Birinci Dünya Savaşı ve Mirası*, ed. Halil Çetin et al. 1/ 27–42. Çanakkale: Çanakkale Valiliği, 2015.

Steinberg, Jonathan. *Bismarck - A Life*. New York: Oxford University Press, 2011.

Steinberg, Jonathan. *Bismarck*. trans. Hakan Abacı. İstanbul: Türkiye İş Bankası Kültür Yayınları, 2015.

Storer, Colin. *Weimar Cumhuriyeti'nin Kısa Tarihi*. çev. Sedef Özge. İstanbul: İletişim Yayınları, 2015.

Talat, Paşa. *Talat Paşa'nın Hatıraları*, ed. Hüseyin Cahit Yalçın. İstanbul: Cumhuriyet Gazetesi Yayınları, 1998.

Taylor, A. J. P. *The Course of German History - A survey of the development of German history since 1815*. London: Routledge, 2001.

Tekeli, İlhan. *Sanayi Toplumu İçin Sanayi Yazıları*. İstanbul: Tarih Vakfı Yurt Yayınları, 2009.

Tetik, Fatih. *Sultanın Silahları - II. Abdülhamid Dönemi Savunma Sanayii ve Silah Teknolojisi*. İstanbul: Dergah Yayınları, 2018.

Tezel, Yahya. *Cumhuriyet Tarihinin İktisadi Tarihi (1923–1950)*. İstanbul: Türkiye İş Bankası Yayınları, 1st Ed., 2015.

The Reichsbank 1876–1900. National Monetary Commisionon, 61st Congress \ 2d Session. Document No: 48. Washington: Washington Post Office, 1910.

Tilly, Richard - Pierenkemper, Tony. *The German Economy During the Nineteenth Century*. Oxford: Berghahn Books, 2004.

Tolon, Ahmet Hurşit. *Birinci Dünya Savaşı Sırasında Taksim Anlaşmaları ve Sevr'e Giden Yol*. Ankara: Atatürk Araştırma Merkezi, 2004.

Trebilcock, Clive. *The Industrialisation of the Continental Powers 1780–1914*. London: Routledge, 2014.

Türk, Fahri. *Türkiye ile Almanya Arasındaki Silah Ticareti 1871–1914*. İstanbul: IQ Kültür Sanat Yayıncılık, 2012.

Uluğbay, Hikmet. *İmparatorluktan Cumhuriyete Petropolitik*. Ankara: Turkish Daily News Yayınları, 1995.

Veblen, Thorstein. *Imperial Germany and the Industrial Revolution*. London: The Macmilan Company, 1915.

Von der Goltz, Golmar. *Millet-i Müselleha*. ed. İsmet Sarıbal. İstanbul: Otorite Yayınları, 2nd Ed., 2016.

Wallach, Jehuda L. *Bir Askeri Yardımın Anatomisi - Türkiye'de Prusya-Alman Askeri Heyetleri 1835–1919*. trans. Em. Tuğgeneral Fahri Çeliker. Ankara: Gnkur. Askeri Tarih ve Stratejik Etüt Bşk. Yayınları, 2nd Ed., 1985.

Winterstetten, Karl von. *Berlin Bağdat - Alman Yayılmacılığı ve Osmanlı Politikaları*. ed. Faruk Yılmaz. İstanbul: İz Yayıncılık, 2011.

Wolfgang Neugebauer (ed.). *Handbuch der preußischen Geschichte. Band 2: Das 19. Jahrhundert und große Themen der Geschichte Preußens*. Berlin: Verlag De Gruyter, 1992.

Yalçınkaya, Mehmet Alaaddin. "İngiliz Subaylarının Anlatımıyla Osmanlı Cephelerindeki Alman Subayları". ed. Necmettin Alkan et al., *Savaşanların Gözüyle Türk - Alman İttifakı*. İstanbul: Kronik Kitap, 2018.

Yasame, Feroze A. K. *Abdülhamid'in Dış Politikası*. trans. Yusuf Selman İnanç. İstanbul: Kronik Kitap, 1996.

Yavuz, Celalettin. *Atatürk ve Almanya*. Ankara: Berikan Yayınevi, 2010.

Yerasimos, Stefanos. *Azgelişmişlik Sürecinde Türkiye - Tanzimattan I. Dünya Savaşı'na*. İstanbul: Gözlem Yayınları, 1975.

Yılmaz, Özgür et al. "Fransızlara Göre Türk-Alman Askeri Yakınlaşması ve İttifakı". ed. Necmettin Alkan et al. *Savaşanların Gözüyle Türk - Alman İttifakı*. İstanbul: Kronik Kitap, 2018.

Yorulmaz, Naci. *Arming the Sultan*. New York: I.B.Tauris &Co. Ltd, 2014.

Zengin, Ersoy. *Osmanlı Devleti'nde Harp Sanayii (1861–1923)*. İstanbul: Kitabevi Yayınları, 2020.

Articles, Journals and Periodicals

"German Bank Act of the 30th January, 1875." *Journal of the Statistical Society of London*, vol. 38, no. 2, 1875, pp. 267–282. JSTOR, www.jstor.org/stable/2338666

"The Result of the Lausanne Conference." World Affairs, vol. 95, no. 2, 1932, pp. 75–77, http://www.jstor.org/stable/20662122. Accessed 21 Apr. 2022.

Aaslestad, Katherine – Hagemann, Karen. "1806 And Its Aftermath: Revisiting the Period of the Napoleonic Wars in German Central European Historiography." *Central European History*, vol. 39, no. 4, 2006, pp. 547–579. JSTOR, www.jstor.org/stable/20457177

Aksakal, Mustafa. "'Holy War Made in Germany'? Ottoman Origins of the 1914 Jihad." *War in History*, vol. 18, no. 2, 2011, pp. 184–199. JSTOR, www.jstor.org/stable/26098597

Arslan, Ozan. "I. Dünya Savaşı Başında Kapitülasyonların İttihad Ve Terakki Yönetimi Tarafından Kaldırılması Ve Bu Gelişme Karşısında Büyük Güçlerin Tepkileri" *Sakarya Üniversitesi Fen-Edebiyat Fakültesi Dergisi*, vol. 10, no. 1, 2018, pp. 261–278.

Barton, James L. "The Ottoman Empire and the War." *The Journal of Race Development*, vol. 9, no. 1, 1918, pp. 1–15. JSTOR, www.jstor.org/stable/29738266

Bergmann, Carl. "Germany and the Young Plan." *Foreign Affairs*, vol. 8, no. 4, 1930, pp. 583–97, https://doi.org/10.2307/20030309. Accessed 21 Apr. 2022.

Bisschop, W. R. "The Locarno Pact. October 15-December 1, 1925." *Transactions of the Grotius Society*, vol. 11, 1925, pp. 79–115, http://www.jstor.org/stable/742835. Accessed 21 Apr. 2022.

Bogart, Dan. "Nationalizations and the Development of Transport Systems: Cross-Country Evidence from Railroad Networks, 1860–1912." *The Journal of Economic History*, vol. 69, no. 1, 2009, pp. 202–237. JSTOR, www.jstor.org/stable/40263925.

Böhme, Helmut. "Big-Business Pressure Groups and Bismarck's Turn to Protectionism, 1873–79." *The Historical Journal*, vol. 10, no. 2, 1967, pp. 218–236. www.jstor.org/stable/2637863.

Bradford, Ernest S. "Prussian Railway Administration." *The Annals of the American Academy of Political and Social Science*, vol. 29, 1907, pp. 66–78. JSTOR, www.jstor.org/stable/1010852.

Brandt, Karl. "The German Back-to-the-Land Movement." *The Journal of Land & Public Utility Economics*, vol. 11, no. 2, 1935, pp. 123–32. JSTOR, https://doi.org/10.2307/3158656. Accessed 7 Dec. 2022.

Breitman, Richard. "Education and Class Cleavage in Late 19th Century Germany." *International Labor and Working-Class History*, no. 12, 1977, pp. 19–23. JSTOR, www.jstor.org/stable/27671219.

Burhop, Carsten, and Thorsten Lübbers. "Cartels, Managerial Incentives, and Productive Efficiency in German Coal Mining, 1881–1913." *The Journal of Economic History*, vol. 69, no. 2, 2009, pp. 500–527. JSTOR, www.jstor.org/sta ble/40263965.

Burhop, Carsten. "Did banks cause the German industrialization?" *Explorations in Economic History*, Elsevier, vol. 43, no. 1, 2006, pp. 39–63.

Cameron, Rondo. "A New View of European Industrialization." *The Economic History Review*, vol. 38, no. 1, 1985, pp. 1–23. JSTOR, www.jstor.org/stable/2596641

Carroll, Berenice A. "Germany Disarmed and Rearming, 1925–1935." *Journal of Peace Research*, vol. 3, no. 2, 1966, pp. 114–24, http://www.jstor.org/stable/422650. Accessed 21 Apr. 2022.

Cohn, Gustav. "On the Nationalisation of Railways." *The Economic Journal*, vol. 18, no. 72, Dec. 1908, pp. 520–531, JSTOR, https://www.jstor.org/stable/2220620, https://doi.org/10.2307/2220620

Costigliola, Frank. "The United States and the Reconstruction of Germany in the 1920s." *The Business History Review*, vol. 50, no. 4, 1976, pp. 477–502, https://doi.org/10.2307/3113137. Accessed 21 Apr. 2022.

Da Rin, Marco – Hellmann, Thomas. "Banks as Catalysts for Industrialization" *William Davidson Working Paper*, no. 443, October 2001, https://deepblue.lib.umich.edu/bitstream/handle/2027.42/39827/wp443.pdf;jsessionid=255123A7D53AD3A817674578DA05ADB7?sequence=3.

Dovring, Folke. "Eighteenth-Century Changes in Eropean Agriculture: A Comment." *Agricultural History*, vol. 43, no. 1, 1969, pp. 181–86. JSTOR, http://www.jstor.org/stable/4617640. Accessed 27 Nov. 2022.

Edwards, Jeremy – Ogilvie, Sheilagh. "Universal Banks and German Industrialization: A Reappraisal." *The Economic History Review*, vol. 49, no. 3, 1996, pp. 427–446. JSTOR, www.jstor.org/stable/2597758.

Epkenhans, Michael. "Military—Industrial Relations in Imperial Germany, 1870–1914." *War in History*, vol. 10, no. 1, 2003, pp. 1–26. www.jstor.org/stable/26061939

Eröz, Mehmet. "Parvus'un Türkiye Hakkındaki Yazıları." *İstanbul Üniversitesi İktisat Fakültesi Mecmuası*, vol. 43, 1917, pp. 347–356.

Fay, Sidney B. "State Ownership In Germany." *Current History*, vol. 18, no. 103, 1950, pp. 129–33. JSTOR, http://www.jstor.org/stable/45307704. Accessed 19 Dec. 2022.

Feldman, Gerald D. – Nocken, Ulrich. "Trade Associations and Economic Power: Interest Group Development in the German Iron and Steel and Machine Building Industries, 1900–1933." *The Business History Review*, vol. 49, no. 4, 1975, pp. 413–445.

Ford, Guy Stanton. "The Prussian Peasantry Before 1807." *The American Historical Review*, vol. 24, no. 3, 1919, pp. 358–78. JSTOR, https://doi.org/10.2307/1835774. Accessed 9 Dec. 2022.

Fremdling, Rainer. "Railroads and German Economic Growth: A Leading Sector Analysis with a Comparison to the United States and Great Britain." *The*

Journal of Economic History, vol. 37, no. 3, 1977, pp. 583–604. JSTOR, www.jstor.org/stable/2119597

Gilbert, S. Parker. "The Meaning of the 'Dawes Plan.'" *Foreign Affairs*, vol. 4, no. 3, 1926, pp. i–xii, https://doi.org/10.2307/20028477. Accessed 21 Apr. 2022.

Green, Abigail. "Representing Germany? The Zollverein at the World Exhibitions, 1851–1862." *The Journal of Modern History*, vol. 75, no. 4, 2003, pp. 836–863. JSTOR, www.jstor.org/stable/10.1086/383355

Guinnane, Timothy W. "Delegated Monitors, Large and Small: The Development of Germany's Banking System, 1800–1914." *Center Discussion Paper*, No. 835. New Haven, CT: Yale University, Economic Growth Center, 2001.

Günther, Karl H. "Profiles of Educators: Wilhelm von Humboldt (1767–1835)". *Prospects*, vol. 18, 1988, pp. 127–136, https://doi.org/10.1007/BF02192965

Hahn, Hans-Werner. "Zwischen Deutscher Handelsfreiheit Und Sicherung Landständischer Rechte. Der Liberalismus Und Die Gründung Des Deutschen Zollvereins." *Geschichte Und Gesellschaft. Sonderheft*, vol. 9, Vandenhoeck & Ruprecht (GmbH & Co. KG), 1983, pp. 239–71, http://www.jstor.org/stable/40186167

Hantke, Max – Spoerer, Mark. "The Imposed Gift of Versailles: The Fiscal Effects of Restricting the Size of Germany's Armed Forces, 1924–9." *The Economic History Review*, vol. 63, no. 4, 2010, pp. 849–64, http://www.jstor.org/stable/40929862. Accessed 21 Apr. 2022.

Harold, James. "Monetary and Fiscal Unification in Nineteenth Century Germany: What can Kohl Learn from Bismarck?." *Essays in International Finance*, No:202, Deparment of Economics. Princeton: Princeton University, March 1997.

Hebeler, Bernard. "Statistics of Prussia." *Journal of the Statistical Society of London*, vol. 10, no. 2, [Royal Statistical Society, Wiley], 1847, pp. 154–86, https://doi.org/10.2307/2337688

Henderson, W. O. "German Economic Penetration in the Middle East, 1870–1914." *The Economic History Review*, vol. 18, no. 1/2, (Economic History Society, Wiley), 1948, pp. 54–64, https://doi.org/10.2307/2590262

Henderson, W. O. "The German Zollverein and the European Economic Community." *Zeitschrift Für Die Gesamte Staatswissenschaft / Journal of Institutional and Theoretical Economics*, vol. 137, no. 3, 1981, pp. 491–507. JSTOR, www.jstor.org/stable/40750372

Henderson, W. O. "The Rise of German Industry." *The Economic History Review*, vol. 5, no. 2, 1935, pp. 120–124. JSTOR, www.jstor.org/stable/2599206

Hirsch, Felix E. "Frankfurt, 1848 and 1948: The Problems of German Liberty and Unity." Current History, vol. 14, no. 81, University of California Press, 1948, pp. 283–88, http://www.jstor.org/stable/45307345.

Hochstadt, Steve. "Migration and Industrialization in Germany, 1815–1977." *Social Science History*, vol. 5, no. 4, 1981, pp. 445–468. JSTOR, www.jstor.org/stable/1170824.

Hornung, Erik. "Railroads and Growth In Prussia." Journal of the European Economic Association, vol. 13, no. 4, 2015, pp. 699–736. JSTOR, http://www.jstor.org/stable/24539267. Accessed 7 Dec. 2022.

Keller, Wolfgang – Carol H. Shiue. "Endogenous Formation of Free Trade Agreements: Evidence from the Zollverein's Impact on Market Integration." *The Journal of Economic History*, vol. 74, no. 4, [Economic History Association, Cambridge University Press], 2014, pp. 1168–204, http://www.jstor.org/stable/24550697

Khoudour-Castéras, David. "Welfare State and Labor Mobility: The Impact of Bismarck's Social Legislation on German Emigration before World War I." *The Journal of Economic History*, vol. 68, no. 1, 2008, pp. 211–243. JSTOR, www.jstor.org/stable/40056781

Kiep, O. C. "The Basis of German Credit." *Proceedings of the Academy of Political Science,* vol. 15, no. 1, 1932, pp. 84–93, https://doi.org/10.2307/1172745. Accessed 21 Apr. 2022.

King, David J. S. "The Ideology Behind a Business Activity: The Case of the Nuremburg-Fürth Railway." Business and Economic History, vol. 20, 1991, pp. 162–70. JSTOR, http://www.jstor.org/stable/23702813. Accessed 6 Dec. 2022.

Kissinger, Henry A. "The Congress of Vienna: A Reappraisal." *World Politics*, vol. 8, no. 2, 1956, pp. 264–280. JSTOR, www.jstor.org/stable/2008974

Klemann, Hein A. M., – Joep Schenk. "Competition in the Rhine Delta: Waterways, Railways and Ports, 1870–1913." *The Economic History Review*, vol. 66, no. 3, 2013, pp. 826–47. JSTOR, http://www.jstor.org/stable/42922024. Accessed 5 Dec. 2022.

Klíma, Arnošt. "The Role of Rural Domestic Industry in Bohemia in the Eighteenth Century." *The Economic History Review*, vol. 27, no. 1, 1974, pp. 48–56. JSTOR, https://doi.org/10.2307/2594203. Accessed 11 Dec. 2022.

Kocka, Jurgen. "Capitalism and Bureaucracy in German Industrialization before 1914." *The Economic History Review*, vol. 34, no. 3, 1981, pp. 453–468. JSTOR, www.jstor.org/stable/2595883

Kopsidis, Michael – Daniel W. Bromley. "The French Revolution and German Industrialization: The New Institutional Economics Rewrites History" *Discussion Paper*, No. 149, 2014, Leibniz Institute of Agricultural Development in Transition Economies (IAMO), Halle (Saale), http://nbn-resolving.de/urn:nbn:de:gbv:3:2-29260

Kopsidis, Michael – Nikolaus Wolf. "Agricultural Productivity across Prussia during the Industrial Revolution: A Thünen Perspective." *The Journal of Economic History*, vol. 72, no. 3, 2012, pp. 634–670, www.jstor.org/stable/23254939

Köse, İsmail. "I. Dünya Savaşı'nın İlk Gizli Anlaşması: İstanbul ve Boğazlar'ın Rus Çarlığı'na Bırakılması (Mart-Nisan 1915)." *Bilig - Türk Dünyası Sosyal Bilimler Dergisi*, no. 89, 2019, pp. 1–27.

Kuczynski, Jurgen. "Productivity and Exploitation under German Capitalism." Science & Society, vol. 9, no. 1, 1945, pp. 55–66. JSTOR, http://www.jstor.org/stable/40399667. Accessed 11 Dec. 2022.

Kyte, George W. "Frederick the Great and the Development of the Prussian Army." *The Historian*, vol. 5, no. 1, Wiley, 1942, pp. 24–32, http://www.jstor.org/stable/24442204

Lago, Armando M. "The Hoffmann Industrial Growth Development Path: An International Comparison." *Weltwirtschaftliches Archiv*, vol. 103, 1969, pp. 41–57. JSTOR, www.jstor.org/stable/40437181

Lamont, Thomas W. "The Dawes Plan and European Peace." *Academy of Political Science*, vol. 11, no. 2, 1925, pp. 177–184. https://www.jstor.org/stable/1180443

Lehmann – Hasemeyer, Sibylle H., and Wahl, Fabian. "Savings Banks and the Industrial Revolution in Prussia: Supporting Regional Development with Public Financial Institutions." *Hohenheim Discussion Papers in Business, Economics and Social Sciences*, no.18, 2017. Stuttgart: Universität Hohenheim, Fakultät Wirtschafts- und Sozialwissenschaften, Accessed: 12 December 2020, http://nbn-resolving.de/urn:nbn:de:bsz:100-opus-13885

Lenoir, Timothy. "Revolution from above: The Role of the State in Creating the German Research System, 1810–1910." *The American Economic Review*, vol. 88, no. 2, 1998, pp. 22–27. JSTOR, www.jstor.org/stable/116886

Light, Donald W. "Values and Structure in the German Health Care Systems." *The Milbank Memorial Fund Quarterly. Health and Society*, vol. 63, no. 4, 1985, pp. 615–47. JSTOR, https://doi.org/10.2307/3349852. Accessed 21 Dec. 2022.

Locke, Robert R. "Business Education in Germany: Past Systems and Current Practice." *The Business History Review*, vol. 59, no. 2, 1985, pp. 232–253. JSTOR, www.jstor.org/stable/3114931

Lotz, Walther. "The Commercial Policy of Germany." *Journal of Political Economy*, vol. 15, no. 5, 1907, pp. 257–83. JSTOR, http://www.jstor.org/stable/1819398. Accessed 21 Dec. 2022.

McDonald, H. Brooke – Rosecrance, Richard. "Alliance and Structural Balance in the International System: A Reinterpretation." *The Journal of Conflict*

Resolution, vol. 29, no. 1, Sage Publications, Inc., 1985, pp. 57–82, http://www.jstor.org/stable/174039

Medlicott, W. N. "Bismarck and the Three Emperors' Alliance, 1881–87." *Transactions of the Royal Historical Society*, vol. 27 (Cambridge University Press, Royal Historical Society), 1945, pp. 61–83, https://doi.org/10.2307/3678575

Medlicott, W. N. "The Gladstone Government and the Cyprus Convention, 1880–85." *The Journal of Modern History*, vol. 12, no. 2, 1940, pp. 186–208. JSTOR, www.jstor.org/stable/1874896

Meyer-Thurow, Georg. "The Industrialization of Invention: A Case Study from the German Chemical Industry." *Isis*, vol. 73, no. 3, 1982, pp. 363–381. JSTOR, www.jstor.org/stable/231441

Michael, P., et al. "The German Hyperinflation and the Demand for Money Revisited." *International Economic Review*, vol. 35, no. 1, 1994, pp. 1–22. JSTOR, www.jstor.org/stable/2527088

Mombauer, Annika. "A Reluctant Military Leader? Helmuth von Moltke and the July Crisis of 1914." *War in History*, vol. 6, no. 4, Sage Publications, Ltd., 1999, pp. 417–46, http://www.jstor.org/stable/26013968

Murphy, David T. "Prussian Aims for the Zollverein, 1828–1833." *The Historian*, vol. 53, no. 2, 1991, pp. 285–302. JSTOR, www.jstor.org/stable/24447861

Neuberger, Hugh – Houston H. Stokes. "German Banks and German Growth, 1883–1913: An Empirical View." *The Journal of Economic History*, vol. 34, no. 3, 1974, pp. 710–731. JSTOR, www.jstor.org/stable/2116759

Neuberger, Hugh. "The Industrial Politics of the Kreditbanken, 1880–1914." The *Business History Review*, vol. 51, no. 2 [President and Fellows of Harvard College, Cambridge University Press], 1977, pp. 190–207, https://doi.org/10.2307/3113479

Nipperdey, Thomas. "Mass Education and Modernization: The Case of Germany 1780–1850: The Prothero Lecture." *Transactions of the Royal Historical Society*, vol. 27, 1977, pp. 155–172. JSTOR, www.jstor.org/stable/3679192

O'Boyle, Lenore. "Learning for Its Own Sake: The German University as Nineteenth-Century Model." *Comparative Studies in Society and History*, vol. 25, no. 1, 1983, pp. 3–25. JSTOR, www.jstor.org/stable/178570

Ohno, Eiji. "The Hıstorıcal Stage of German Capıtalısm—An Analysis of the Bismarck Regime." *Kyoto University Economic Review*, vol. 40, no. 2 (89), 1970, pp. 18–43. JSTOR, http://www.jstor.org/stable/43217180. Accessed 12 Dec. 2022

Papayoanou, Paul A. "Interdependence, Institutions, and the Balance of Power: Britain, Germany, and World War I." *International Security*, vol. 20, no. 4, 1996, pp. 42–76. JSTOR, www.jstor.org/stable/2539042

Pfister, Ulrich, Agricultural development during early industrialization in alow-wage economy: Saxony, c. 1790–1830, *Ehes Workıng Papers In Economıc Hıstory*, No. 39, June 2013, Accessed: 21 July 2020, http://www.ehes.org/EHES_No39.pdf

Pollard, Sidney. "Industrialization and the European Economy." *The Economic History Review*, vol. 26, no. 4, 1973, pp. 636–648. JSTOR, www.jstor.org/stable/2593702

Randeraad, Nico. "The International Statistical Congress (1853–1876): Knowledge Transfers and their Limits." *European History Quarterly*, vol. 41, no. 1, February 2011, pp. 50–65. DOI: 10.1177/0265691410385759

Reuleke, Jürgen. "Population Growth and Urbanization in Germany in the 19th Century." *Urbanism Past & Present*, no. 4, 1977, pp. 21–32. JSTOR, www.jstor.org/stable/44403540

Ringer, Fritz K. "Higher Education in Germany in the Nineteenth Century." *Journal of Contemporary History*, vol. 2, no. 3, 1967, pp. 123–138. JSTOR, www.jstor.org/stable/259810

Ritschl, Albrecht. "How and when did Germany catch up to Great Britain and the US? Results from the official statistics, 1901–1960." *London School of Economics and Political Science*, Accessed: 18 May 2020, https://personal.lse.ac.uk/ritschl/pdf_files/KETCHUP.pdf

Roderick, G. W. – M. D. Stephens. "Scientific Education in England and Germany in the Second Half of the Nineteenth Century." *The Irish Journal of Education / Iris Eireannach an Oideachais*, vol. 16, no. 1, 1982, pp. 62–83. JSTOR, www.jstor.org/stable/30077299

Rosenberg, Hans. "The Struggle for a German-Austrian Customs Union (1815–1931)." *The Slavonic and East European Review*, vol. 14, no. 41, 1936, pp. 332–342. JSTOR, www.jstor.org/stable/4203123

Rostow, W. W. "The Stages of Economic Growth." *The Economic History Review*, vol. 12, no. 1, 1959, pp. 1–16. JSTOR, www.jstor.org/stable/2591077

Roussakis, Emmanuel N. "The Common Market and the Zollverein: Experiences in Integration." *Recherches Économiques De Louvain / Louvain Economic Review*, vol. 35, no. 3, 1969, pp. 201–208. JSTOR, www.jstor.org/stable/40723212

Rowe, Michael. "France, Prussia, or Germany? The Napoleonic Wars and Shifting Allegiances in the Rhineland." *Central European History*, vol. 39, no. 4, 2006, pp. 611–640. JSTOR, www.jstor.org/stable/20457179

Schleunes, Karl A. "Enlightenment, Reform, Reaction: The Schooling Revolution in Prussia." *Central European History*, vol. 12, no. 4, 1979, pp. 315–342. JSTOR, www.jstor.org/stable/4545874

Sorkin, David. "Wilhelm Von Humboldt: The Theory and Practice of Self-Formation (Bildung), 1791–1810." *Journal of the History of Ideas*, vol. 44, no. 1, 1983, pp. 55–73. JSTOR, www.jstor.org/stable/2709304

Temizer, Abidin. "The Independence Process of Bulgaria and the First Ambassador of the Ottoman Empire to Sofia, Mustafa Asım Bey." *Belleten*, vol. 85, no. 304, 2021, pp. 1073–1104.

Tilly, Richard H. "Banking Institutions in Historical and Comparative Perspective: Germany, Great Britain and the United States in the Nineteenth and Early Twentieth Century." *Journal of Institutional and Theoretical Economics (JITE) / Zeitschrift Für Die Gesamte Staatswissenschaft*, vol. 145, no. 1, 1989, pp. 189–209. JSTOR, www.jstor.org/stable/40751183

Tipton, Frank B. "Government Policy and Economic Development in Germany and Japan: A Skeptical Reevaluation." *The Journal of Economic History*, vol. 41, no. 1, 1981, pp. 139–150. JSTOR, www.jstor.org/stable/2120909

Torp, Cornelius. "The Coalition of 'Rye and Iron' under the Pressure of Globalization: A Reinterpretation of Germany's Political Economy before 1914." *Central European History*, vol. 43, no. 3, 2010, pp. 401–427. JSTOR, www.jstor.org/stable/27856214

Turner, Henry Ashby. "The Ruhrlade, Secret Cabinet of Heavy Industry in the Weimar Republic." *Central European History*, vol. 3, no. 3, 1970, pp. 195–228. https://www.jstor.org/stable/4545572

Ünver, Metin. "Teknolojik gelişmeler ışığında Osmanlı-Amerikan silah ticaretinin ilk dönemi". *Tarih Araştırmaları Dergisi,* vol. 32, no. 54, 2013, pp. 195–220, https://doi.org/10.1501/Tarar_0000000560

Von Eschen, Marie. "The Commercial Expansion of Germany 1871–1914." *Social Science,* vol. 2, no. 3, 1927, pp. 223–235. JSTOR, www.jstor.org/stable/23902678

Webb, Steven B. "Agricultural Protection in Wilhelminian Germany: Forging an Empire with Pork and Rye." *The Journal of Economic History*, vol. 42, no. 2, 1982, pp. 309–326. JSTOR, www.jstor.org/stable/2120130

Webb, Steven B. "Cartels and Business Cycles in Germany, 1880 to 1914." *Zeitschrift Für Die Gesamte Staatswissenschaft / Journal of Institutional and Theoretical Economics*, vol. 138, no. 2, 1982, pp. 205–224. JSTOR, www.jstor.org/stable/40750491

Webb, Steven B. “Tariffs, Cartels, Technology, and Growth in the German Steel Industry, 1879 to 1914.” *The Journal of Economic History*, vol. 40, no. 2, 1980, pp. 309–330. JSTOR, www.jstor.org/stable/2120181

Weidenhammer, Robert. *The American Economic Review*, vol. 22, no. 1, 1932, pp. 146–149. JSTOR, www.jstor.org/stable/1807287

Wolf, Nikolaus. “Agricultural Productivity across Prussia During the Industrial Revolution: A Thünen Perspective.” *Ehes Workıng Papers In Economıc Hıstory*, No. 13 (January 2012), Accessed: 20 Haziran 2020, http://www.ehes.org/EHES_No13.pdf

Unpublished Works

Aktaş, Hayati. *Türk-Alman Askeri İlişkileri (1913–1918).* Konya: Selçuk Üniversitesi, Institute of Social Sciences, Doctoral Thesis, 1994.

Finlay, Mark Russel. *Science, Practice and Politics: German Agricultural Experiment Stations in the Nineteenth Century*. Iowa: Iowa State University, History of Technology and Science, Doctoral Thesis, 1992.

Okumuş, Ali. *Gülbenkiyan.* İstanbul: Marmara Üniversitesi, Institute of Turkic Studies, Master’s Thesis, 2014.

Internet Sources

Avcı, Cemal. “Savarona Yatı”. *Ataturkansiklopedisi.* Accessed: 12.04.2022. https://ataturkansiklopedisi.gov.tr/bilgi/savarona-yati/

Bal, Halil. “Kemalettin Sami Paşa (1884–1934)”. *Ataturkansiklopedisi.* Accessed: 15.12.2021. https://ataturkansiklopedisi.gov.tr/bilgi/kemalettin-sami-pasa-1884-1934/

Encyclopaedia Britannica. “Battle of Leipzig”. Accessed: 18 July 2020. https://www.britannica.com/event/Battle-of-Leipzig

Encyclopaedia Britannica. “Frederick I”. Accessed: 2 October 2022. https://www.britannica.com/biography/Frederick-I-king-of-Prussia

Encyclopædia Britannica. “Humboldt University of Berlin”. Accessed: 05 December 2020. https://www.britannica.com/topic/Humboldt-University-of-Berlin

Encyclopædia Britannica. “International Postal Reform: The Universal Postal Union”. Accessed: 03 December 2022. https://www.britannica.com/topic/postal-system/History#ref367093

Encyclopædia Britannica. “Punctation of Olmütz”. Accessed: 14 October 2020. https://www.britannica.com/event/Punctation-of-Olmutz

Fiano, Andrea. "World's 50 Bıggest Banks 2012". *Global Finance.* Accessed: 12 December 2020. https://www.gfmag.com/awards-rankings/best-banks-and-financial-rankings/worlds-50-biggest-banks-2012

Hirth, Lion. "State, Cartels and Growth: The German Chemical Industry". *Grin.* Accessed: 09 December 2020. https://www.grin.com/document/78269

Malkoç, Eminalp. "Beyaz Tren". *Ataturkansiklopedisi.* Accessed: 12 April 2022. https://ataturkansiklopedisi.gov.tr/bilgi/beyaz-tren/

Ortaylı, İlber. "200. Yılına Doğru Viyana Kongresi". *Milliyet.* Accessed: 22 May 2020. https://www.milliyet.com.tr/yazarlar/ilber-ortayli/200-yilina-dogru-viyana-kongresi-1763688

Tayhani, İhsan. "Kayseri Uçak Fabrikası". *Ataturkansiklopedisi.* Accessed: 09 December 2012. https://ataturkansiklopedisi.gov.tr/bilgi/kayseri-ucak-fabrikasi/

UN, United Nations. "1925 Geneva Protocol". Accessed: 11 April 2022. https://www.un.org/disarmament/wmd/bio/1925-geneva-protocol/

The World Bank. "Listed Domestic Companies, Total". Accessed: 12 December 2020. https://data.worldbank.org/indicator/CM.MKT.LDOM.NO

www.ingramcontent.com/pod-product-compliance
Ingram Content Group UK Ltd.
Pitfield, Milton Keynes, MK11 3LW, UK
UKHW041834100926
8556IPUK00018B/955

9 783631 891322